Mastering Python 3 Programming

*Ultimate guide to learn Python coding
fundamentals and real-world applications*

Subburaj Ramasamy

www.bpbonline.com

First Edition 2024

Copyright © BPB Publications, India

ISBN: 978-93-55517-128

LIMITS OF LIABILITY AND DISCLAIMER OF WARRANTY

To View Complete
BPB Publications Catalogue
Scan the QR Code:

Dedicated to

*My better half **Chandra** and my sons **Prabhu and Kumar***

About the Author

Dr. Subburaj Ramasamy, currently an independent research professor, specializes in machine learning for artificial intelligence, programming languages, secure coding and software reliability engineering. He is an Udemy instructor and has published courses on machine learning, Python and C++. He served as a professor and consultant in the Department of Information Technology, SRM Institute of Science and Technology, Kattankulathur, for 17 semesters. Earlier, he was a Scientist "G"/ Senior Director in the Ministry of Electronics and Information Technology, Government of India. He obtained his PhD degree from the University of Madras. He holds a Masters degree from Indian Institute of Technology, Delhi and Bachelors degree from Alagappa Chettiar College of Engineering and Technology. He guided four research scholars till award of the Ph.D. degree, having published about 90 research papers in international journals and conferences with 500 citations. He was teaching and providing project guidance to B.Tech and M.Tech students at the School of Computing in SRMIST. Dr. Subburaj is an esteemed member of various associations, such as the Computer Society of India and IETE. He received the 17th IETE Lal C Verman Award in 2003. He is the author of several books on topics such as Total Quality Management, Software Reliability Engineering, Programming in Python, Programming in C, and Object Oriented Programming with C++. He was an authorized trainer of Carnegie Mellon University/SEI, USA, for software CMM and certified by Stanford University/ Course era on Machine Learning.

About the Reviewer

Peyush Kumar is an experienced IT professional, with a distinguished career that spans over 25 years. Graduating with a B.Tech in Computer Science from Punjabi University, his journey has been marked by impactful contributions from major tech players, including Zensar, Wipro, and HCLTech. This includes employment in global settings while residing for an extended period in the USA. Beyond showcasing his prowess as a skilled programmer, Peyush has proved himself as a proficient manager, steering software development teams towards success.

Peyush's enthusiasm extends beyond coding; he is also a passionate educator. His teaching legacy is witnessed in the diverse array of students, spanning from high school enthusiasts to seasoned graduates, who have benefited from his insightful guidance. Residing in Noida with his family, Peyush balances his love for technology with an unwavering commitment to family values.

Acknowledgement

I would like to express my sincere gratitude to all those who contributed to the successful completion of this book.

First and foremost, I extend my appreciation to my family and friends for their unwavering support and encouragement throughout this journey.

I am immensely grateful to BPB Publications for their guidance and expertise in bringing this book to fruition. I would like to especially appreciate the alert, sharp and knowledgeable technical reviwer for reviewing the manuscript thoroughly. I also thank the editors and administrators of BPB for their support and assistance, which were invaluable in navigating the complexities of the publishing process.

Last but not least, I want to express my gratitude to the readers who have shown interest in my book.

Thank you to everyone who has played a part in making this book a reality.

Preface

Mastering Python 3 Programming is a must for every literate. Irrespective of whether you are a seasoned programmer looking to expand your skill set or an absolute beginner taking baby steps into the world of programming, this book is designed to be your companion and comprehensive guidebook to mastering Python.

Python has emerged as one of the most sought-after programming languages due to its agility. Its simplicity, readability, and versatility make it a preferred language for a wide range of applications, from web development and data analysis to artificial intelligence and machine learning.

In this book, we have described everything you need to know to become proficient in Python 3. We will start with the fundamentals, including basic syntax, data types, and control structures, before moving on to more advanced topics such as built-in containers like lists and dictionaries, object-oriented programming, functional programming, and advanced file and exception handling.

Throughout the book, you will find bountiful hands-on examples and exercises to help reinforce your learning. Whether you prefer to follow along with the code examples or dive in and start coding on your own, you will have abundant opportunities to practice and experiment with Python.

One of the fascinating things about Python is its thriving ecosystem of batteries included - libraries and frameworks. In the later chapters, we will explore some of the most popular Python libraries for tasks such as data structures and data visualization, giving you the tools you need to start building your own projects right away.

Whether your goal is to grab a job as a Python developer, advance in your current career, or simply explore the exciting world of programming, this book will provide you with the knowledge and skills you need to succeed. So, without further ado, let us dive in and start exploring the wonderful world of Python 3 programming!

The contents of the book are given chapter-wise below:

Chapter 1: Introduction to Python 3 - Discusses the motivation to learn Python and how to install the Python development environment. We will be discussing programming in the interactive mode and script mode and give examples of both using the above. We will be using IDLE, throughout the book owing to its merits. We will learn that the Python frozen binaries bundle together the byte code of our program files, along with the Python Virtual Machine interpreter and any Python support files our program needs, into a single package, a single binary executable program like .exe file on Windows. By the end of the chapter, students would have experimented with the interactive mode as well as create frozen binaries in the script mode.

Chapter 2: Algorithmic Problem Solving - In this chapter, the student will learn to design computer based solutions to problems using algorithms and flow charts. At the end of the chapter, we describe some of the popular algorithms in Python. This chapter aims to prepare freshers for programming with algorithmic thinking. Furthermore, the algorithms discussed here are used in the rest of the book.

Chapter 3: Numeric Computations and Console Input - An overview of the major tokens of the Python language, such as identifiers, keywords, constants or literals, and operators, is given in this chapter. We will also discuss expressions, operator precedence, and type conversion. In this chapter, we also introduce console input using input and eval functions. We will discuss operations on the bits using bitwise operators.

Chapter 4: Unicode, Strings and Console Output - In this chapter, we will discuss character coding, strings, and slicing. String methods and methods to modify strings will also be discussed. Then, the chapter teaches converting ASCII characters to numbers and vice versa using ord () and chr () functions. We will then move on to discuss console output. Several methods of formatted printing are also discussed in the chapter. Then we discuss the bytes () function, which returns an immutable bytes object. It can convert strings into bytes objects.

Chapter 5: Selection and Loops - In this chapter, we will discuss relational operators and logical operators. Then we will describe the selection constructs of if, elif, and else and give programs to illustrate their use. Next, we will give examples of nested selection constructs and the use of a ternary operator. Then we will move on to discuss iterations using *while* and then *for* and give examples. We will demonstrate the use of break and continue keywords in programs.

Chapter 6: Functions and Recursion - In this chapter, after discussing the features and benefits of structured programming, we will give examples of calling a function multiple times and calling more than one function in a program. We will also discuss void functions. Then we discuss fruitful functions, return values, runtime stack, and Boolean functions. Then, we will discuss the local and global scope of function parameters. This is followed by positional arguments and default arguments.

Chapter 7: Lists - In this chapter, we carry out an in-depth analysis of the Python container list. Then we will discuss list concatenation, slicing, and nesting. Then we will highlight the differences between functions and methods in Python and give examples of methods and functions using lists. List comprehension, aliasing list, and cloning lists are also discussed. This chapter also includes several case studies.

Chapter 8: Tuples, Sets, and Dictionaries - In this chapter, we will discuss 3 more containers – tuples, sets, and dictionaries. We will discuss the methods and functions used with all three containers. We will carry out mathematical operations using sets and set comprehension. The chapter gives some examples of dictionaries and iterations over dictionaries, dictionary comprehension, and nested dictionaries.

Chapter 9: Introduction to Object-Oriented Programming - In this chapter, we give an overview of the characteristics of **Object-Oriented Programming (OOP)**. Class as a blueprint for objects, access control, initializer, and destruction of objects are discussed in this chapter. After carrying out operations on objects, the distinction between class variables and instance variables is brought out. The overloading functions supported in Python are illustrated with examples addressing overloading binary operators - minus operator and the equality operator. At the end of the chapter, we discuss documentation strings.

Chapter 10: Inheritance and Polymorphism - In this chapter, we discuss single inheritance, multi-level inheritance, and multiple inheritance. We will give a comparison between containership and inheritance, and implement various types of inheritances. Then we will discuss the *object* class and diamond problem. It is followed by method overriding, polymorphism, and abstract class. This chapter ends with a discussion on iterators. iterable and generators.

Chapter 11: File Handling - This is a comprehensive and important chapter in the book in the context of Machine Learning and big data analytics. We will discuss reading from and writing to text and binary files. Implicit reading is an important addition. It has an interesting case study on counting the occurrence of each word and each alphabet in a text file. **Java Script Object Notation (JSON)** and the pickle solution are interesting and useful in many applications. The CSV Files and Command line arguments are also illustrated in this chapter.

Chapter 12: Exception Handling - We begin the chapter with a listing of exception classes provided by the Python standard library. The chapter describes all the five keywords provided by Python for exception handling. The chapter has two case studies, building an exception class and knowingw the cause of the error in the custom exception class

Chapter 13: Gems of Python - This is one of the power-packed chapters in the book, addressing various special features of Python 3 such as lambda functions, modules, date and time, functional programming, first class functions, decorator function, namespaces and packages.

Chapter 14: Data Structures and Algorithms using Python - This chapter gives several case studies after explaining stack, queue, and exception handling. The chapter briefly explains algorithm analysis - space complexity, time complexity, and Big Oh notation. We discuss four popular sorting algorithms in this chapter, such as bubble sort, selection sort, insertion sort and merge sort.

Chapter 15:Data Visualization - In this chapter, we will use Python libraries - pandas, Matplotlib and Seaborn to plot various graphs, charts and diagrams using two datasets publicly available on the Internet. The reader will be given URLs to download the data and steps to install libraries.

Chapter 16 : Python Applications and Libraries - In this chapter, we give an overview of applications of Python, including libraries used therein as a ready reckoner to help students to select their future areas of learning. This chapter covers areas such as web development, data science and machine learning, **Natural Language Processing (NLP)**, GUI applications, game development, scripting and automation, web scraping, database applications, **Internet of Things (IoT)** and education.

Code Bundle and Coloured Images

Please follow the link to download the
Code Bundle and the *Coloured Images* of the book:

https://rebrand.ly/syyxw8e

The code bundle for the book is also hosted on GitHub at
https://github.com/bpbpublications/Mastering-Python-3-Programming.
In case there's an update to the code, it will be updated on the existing GitHub repository.

We have code bundles from our rich catalogue of books and videos available at
https://github.com/bpbpublications. Check them out!

Errata

We take immense pride in our work at BPB Publications and follow best practices to ensure the accuracy of our content to provide with an indulging reading experience to our subscribers. Our readers are our mirrors, and we use their inputs to reflect and improve upon human errors, if any, that may have occurred during the publishing processes involved. To let us maintain the quality and help us reach out to any readers who might be having difficulties due to any unforeseen errors, please write to us at :

errata@bpbonline.com

Your support, suggestions and feedbacks are highly appreciated by the BPB Publications' Family.

Did you know that BPB offers eBook versions of every book published, with PDF and ePub files available? You can upgrade to the eBook version at www.bpbonline.com and as a print book customer, you are entitled to a discount on the eBook copy. Get in touch with us at :

business@bpbonline.com for more details.

At **www.bpbonline.com**, you can also read a collection of free technical articles, sign up for a range of free newsletters, and receive exclusive discounts and offers on BPB books and eBooks.

Piracy

If you come across any illegal copies of our works in any form on the internet, we would be grateful if you would provide us with the location address or website name. Please contact us at **business@bpbonline.com** with a link to the material.

If you are interested in becoming an author

If there is a topic that you have expertise in, and you are interested in either writing or contributing to a book, please visit **www.bpbonline.com**. We have worked with thousands of developers and tech professionals, just like you, to help them share their insights with the global tech community. You can make a general application, apply for a specific hot topic that we are recruiting an author for, or submit your own idea.

Reviews

Please leave a review. Once you have read and used this book, why not leave a review on the site that you purchased it from? Potential readers can then see and use your unbiased opinion to make purchase decisions. We at BPB can understand what you think about our products, and our authors can see your feedback on their book. Thank you!

For more information about BPB, please visit **www.bpbonline.com**.

Join our book's Discord space

Join the book's Discord Workspace for Latest updates, Offers, Tech happenings around the world, New Release and Sessions with the Authors:

https://discord.bpbonline.com

Table of Contents

CHAPTER 1
Introduction to Python 3

Introduction

Python is one of the popular and widely used high-level programming languages. It is both a procedure-oriented and object-oriented programming language like C++. It is also a web-scripting language like Javascript. The Python Virtual machine, like Java virtual machine, is the key element of Python, which facilitates the portability of Python programs across platforms. Python's **batteries included** philosophy is a boon to the programmers to write compact and error-free code.

In this chapter, we will be learning the history of Python, its features, applications, and advantages. The Python 3 language system matching the operating system in our computer system can be downloaded from **www.python.org**. After installation, if our computer runs under Windows operating system, we will get the Python command line interpreter and **Integrated Development Environment (IDLE)** under the *start* menu in Windows in the system. We use the statement prompts in the above, in the interactive mode, to confirm our understanding of the Python language syntax. The IDLE, in addition, can be used for writing and executing the programs in script mode. We get a glimpse of the use of mathematical and other functions received along with the Python language system. We will also write simple Python programs in this chapter.

Structure

The chapter covers the following topics:

- History of Python
- Major users
- Features of the language
- Applications of Python 3
- Advantages of Python 3
- Interpreters and compilers
- Python Virtual Machine
- Interpretation process
- Versions of Python
- Python implementations
- Installing Python
- Interactive mode
- Integrated Development Environment
- Execution of Python programs
- Dynamically typed vs. statically typed language
- Memory administration in Python
- Python calculator
- Special characters
- Batteries included philosophy
- Mathematical functions in Python
- Other built-in functions
- Frozen binaries executables
- Types of errors in programs

Objectives

After studying this chapter, you will understand how to invoke the Python command line interpreter, carry out a few calculations, and display a few messages. You would have invoked IDLE, created a new file, typed a program, saved it in a directory, and executed the program. You would be able to use mathematical and other functions and execute programs in IDLE.

History of Python

Python is a high-level procedure-oriented programming language like BASIC, COBOL, FORTRAN, and C. It is also an object-oriented programming language like C++, C sharp, and Java. It can thus be used for procedure-oriented programming as well as object-oriented programming. Python was released for use in the year 1991 by *Guido Van Rossum* (b 1956) in Netherlands. Python was named after the popular British comedy troupe, Monty Python's Flying Circus. It is freeware and not a proprietary product. We can say that it is community owned. It is an open-source programming language, and software professionals all over the world contribute to the development of the language. Python is managed officially by Python Software Foundation, a not-for-profit organization with its headquarters in Delaware, United States.

Major users

Many world-class organizations, such as those listed below, use Python for the development of software products in their organizations:

- Google

- Facebook

- Instagram

- YouTube

- Spotify

- Quora

- Netflix

- Dropbox

The **National Aeronautics and Space Administration (NASA)**, an independent agency of the U.S. Federal Government responsible for the civilian space program, as well as aeronautics and space research, uses Python to develop their professional applications. It is a meritorious programming language, and hence such big names are using it extensively, and the user base is growing continually, besides also being used by tens of thousands of small/mid to large enterprises.

Python 3 is a popular and high-level computer programming language known for its simplicity, readability, learnability, and versatility. We will briefly peruse the features, applications, and advantages of Python 3 language.

Features of Python 3

Python 3 has many special features, some of them are unique. The special features of Python are listed below:

- **Simple and readable syntax:** Python emphasizes code readability and uses a clean and straightforward syntax, which makes it easy for developers to write and understand code.

- **Interpreted language:** Python is an interpreted language, which means code is executed line by line, making it easy to test and debug.

- **High-level language:** Python abstracts many low-level details, allowing developers to focus on solving problems rather than managing memory and other system-level concerns.

- **Dynamically typed:** Python is dynamically typed, which means variable types are determined at runtime, providing flexibility but requiring careful attention to data types.

- **Multi-paradigm:** Python supports multiple programming paradigms, including procedural, object-oriented, and functional programming.

- **Rich standard library:** Python has a rich standard library that provides modules and packages for a wide range of tasks, reducing the need for reinventing the wheel.

- **Cross-platform:** Python is available on multiple platforms, making it a portable choice for software development.

- **Community and ecosystem:** Python has a large and active community of developers, which means a wealth of third- party libraries, frameworks, and tools are available.

Python 3 is a versatile language with a strong community and ecosystem, making it a valuable choice for various programming tasks and industries.

Applications of Python 3

Python is widely used in a variety of applications, both scientific and commercial. Some applications of Python are listed below:

- **Web development:** Python is used for web development with frameworks like Django and Flask, making it easy to build web applications and APIs.

- **Data analysis and visualization:** Python, along with libraries like NumPy, pandas, and Matplotlib, is widely used for data analysis, scientific computing, and data visualization.

- **Machine learning and AI:** Python has become the de facto language for machine learning and artificial intelligence with libraries such as TensorFlow, PyTorch, and scikit-learn.

- **Scientific computing:** Scientists and researchers use Python for numerical and scientific computing tasks due to its rich ecosystem of scientific libraries.

- **Automation and scripting:** Python is often used for automating repetitive tasks and writing system scripts.

- **Game development:** Python has libraries like Pygame for game development.

- **Desktop applications:** Python can be used to build desktop applications using frameworks like PyQt and Tkinter.

- **Networking and cybersecurity:** Python is used for network programming, penetration testing, and cybersecurity tasks.

- **Education:** Python is a popular choice for teaching programming due to its simplicity and readability.

Advantages of Python 3

The advantages of Python as a programming language are plentiful. Some advantages are highlighted here:

- **Ease of learning:** Python's simple and readable syntax makes it an ideal language for beginners and experienced developers alike.

- **Productivity:** Python's high-level abstractions and rich standard library allow developers to write code quickly and efficiently.

- **Large community:** The large and active Python community means extensive documentation, support, and a wealth of third-party libraries.

- **Cross-platform compatibility:** Python code can run on various platforms with minimal modifications, making it highly portable. Availability of interpreters for a host of operating systems such as Windows, Linux, Ubuntu and Apple's Mac OS.

- **Versatility:** Python is suitable for a wide range of applications, from web development to data science and artificial intelligence.

- **Open source:** Python is open source, which means it is freely available and can be used and modified without cost.

- **Interoperability:** Python can easily integrate with other languages like C/C++ and Java, making it suitable for extending existing software.

- **Community-driven updates:** Python's development is community-driven, with regular updates and improvements.

- Produces compact, portable, and readable code.

- Needs little memory space for installation and use.

- Structured coding to reduce errors.

- **Dynamic typing**: No need to declare the data types of variables.

- Interpreter based language, which finds errors in statements as soon as they are typed. When we make a mistake while typing, we hear a beep.

- It is both a programming language and a web scripting language. Since it is interpreted like PHP, it can perform support functions on the Internet, such as taking input from HTML and transferring it to the web server. It can translate source code to machine code when the program is being executed.

- There are no perceptible compiling, linking, and loading steps before program execution. We simply type and run the program without these time-consuming steps visible to the programmer.

- Interactive mode is useful for prototyping of the program before actual coding.

- Support for reusability.

- No pointers as in language C/C++.

- Automatic allocation of memory and garbage collection.

- It has four powerful containers as given below:
    - o Lists
    - o Tuples
    - o Dictionaries
    - o Sets

- Can interact with popular frameworks such as .com, .net.

- Supports **JavsScript Object Notation (JSON)** for data exchange with files and websites.

- Libraries available for game development, database access, scripting websites and Operating system interfacing.

- Built-in Graphics

- Due to the availability of a rich collection of third-party libraries used for building a host of applications ranging from websites to scientific tools.

These are some of the power-packed features of the Python language, and the reader will discover more advantages of Python as they learn and start using the language for solving problems in the real world.

Interpreters and compilers

Interpreters and compilers are designed to translate programs written in high-level languages (source code understandable by human beings) into machine code (understandable by computing machines). They have a similar purpose, that is, they both convert source code to machine code. They also have differences. A compiler in general, translates the entire source code into machine code, which can, in turn, be executed (run) directly by the operating system as an executable program. Interpreters execute the code directly. They bypass the compilation process, or the compilation process is carried out in the background and not visible to the user, as is the case with Python. Python is popularly known as an interpreted language. The term interpreted means that the code is translated into machine-readable form and executed by the interpreter one statement at a time. Common interpreters include BASIC, Perl, Python, and Ruby interpreters.

Python Virtual Machine

The programs we write in Python using its syntax or rules are stored with **.py** extension and are called source code. Python, like many interpreted languages, actually compiles source

code to a set of instructions for a virtual machine. The virtual machine is software that emulates physical computer hardware. Python code is translated into intermediate code by the Python compiler, which has to be executed by a virtual machine known as the **Python Virtual Machine (PVM)**. The concept is similar to Java. There is even a way of translating Python programs into Java bytecode for the **Java Virtual Machine (JVM)**. The Python virtual machine is a stack machine. It manipulates several stacks to perform its operations. This is in contrast with register machines, which write to and read from memory locations. The outcome of compilation is neither a source code nor machine code. It is an intermediate code called bytecode.

PVM is software/interpreter that converts the bytecode to machine code for the given platform - operating system and **Central Processing Unit (CPU)**. PVM is also called Python Interpreter, and this is the reason Python is called an interpreted language. The user cannot see the bytecode of the program because this happens internally in memory.

Before the interpreter takes over, Python performs three other steps, which are lexing, parsing, and compiling, not visible to the programmer. Together, these steps transform the programmer's source code from lines of text into structured code objects containing instructions that the interpreter can understand. The interpreter's job is to take these code objects and convert them to machine code matching the CPU and the platform used for executing the Python programs.

There is a relationship between the compiler and interpreter when it comes to the Python language. The compiler converts the Python code to bytecode. Bytecode is an intermediate representation of Python code, which expresses the source code that we write in a way the interpreter can understand.

The bytecode is interpreted by the interpreter. The Python interpreter is a bytecode interpreter. Its input is instruction sets called bytecode. When we write a Python program, the lexer, parser, and compiler generate code objects for the interpreter to operate on. Each code object contains a set of instructions to be executed. It is the bytecode and other information that the interpreter will need.

The Python compiler converts the file with **.py** extension, the source file into a **.pyc** bytecode for the Python virtual machine. The **.pyc** file contains bytecode, which is a compiled version of the Python file. Python automatically generates this file to improve performance. The **.pyc** file has a bytecode which is platform independent. It can be executed on any operating system that supports a **.pyc** format. An interpreter executes this bytecode on the virtual machine of the computer.

It may be a surprise to hear that compiling is a step in executing Python code at all. Python is often called an **interpreted** language like Ruby or Perl, as opposed to a **compiled** language like C or Java. However, this terminology is not as precise as it may seem. Most interpreted languages, including Python, do involve a compilation step. The reason Python is called interpreted is that the compilation step does relatively less work than in a compiled language and the interpreter does relatively more.

While interpreters offer several advantages for running small programs, interpreted languages also have some limitations. Programs written for an interpreter may not be able to use built-in system functions or access hardware resources like compiled programs. The interpreters are slower than compilers.

Interpretation process

When we write Python programs, the compiler converts source code written by the developer into an intermediate language which is again translated by the interpreter into machine language that is executed. The Python program we write is compiled into Python bytecode by the compiler, which creates a file with the extension **.pyc**. The bytecode compilation happens internally and is completely hidden from the programmer. Compilation is simply a translation step, and bytecode is a lower-level and platform-independent representation of the source code. Each of the source statements is translated into a group of bytecode instructions. This bytecode translation is performed to quicken the execution of source code statements.

The **.pyc** file, is created corresponding to each **.py** file in the compilation step. The **.pyc** files are typically generated automatically by the Python interpreter when you import or run a Python script (**.py** file). They are stored in a directory called **__pycache__**. The __ **pycache__** directory is located in the same directory as the corresponding Python source file. The .pyc is then executed by appropriate virtual machines. We can see the contents of

.**pyc** (Python Compiled) files, but they are not meant to be human-readable. They contain bytecode, which is a lower-level, platform-independent representation of the original Python code.

The Virtual Machine iterates through the bytecode instructions, one by one, to carry out their operations. The Virtual Machine is the runtime engine of Python, and it is always present as part of the Python system, and is the component that truly runs the Python scripts.

Versions of Python

There are 2 versions of Python:

- Python 2
- Python 3

Python 2 is the legacy version. We will learn the latest version, that is, Python 3, since Python 2 may eventually not exist. The applications/programs developed in Python 2 may cease to be used.

Python implementations

Python represents the specifications of the programming language. It is implemented with compilers and interpreters. They can be implemented in different ways. The various Python implementations are discussed below:

- **CPython:** This is the default and most widely used implementation of Python and is written in C. This is an interpreter and has a foreign function interface with languages like C. When we download Python from **www.python.org** we get this implementation.

- **PyPy:** written in a subset of Python language called RPython. The programs execute fast in PyPy since there is a **Just-In-Time (JIT)** compiler added to the PVM.

- **Jython:** It is written in Java language. It is designed to run Python in the Java platform. Jython compiler compiles Python programs, not as Python bytecode, but as Java bytecode. Obviously, Java bytecode can be executed in JVM and not PVM.

- **Iron Python:** It is written in C# (C sharp).

- **Anaconda Python:** It is meant for big data applications.

Installing Python

The following are the web resources for downloading the Python language system from Python Software Foundation:

- **www.python.org/** to download Python version 3.x.x.

- **www.python.org/doc** for downloading official tutorial and documentation.

We will be starting the Python learning journey along. You can download Python language software for free. While downloading, choose Python 3.x.x, matching the operating system on your computer. Follow the steps, and choose the default option for every question, and install Python for the chosen operating system. Python will be installed in your system.

Once Python is installed, we find new items under the Start menu in Windows platform. Python installer has given us two important tools, as given below:

- Command-line Python Interpreter

- A program called **Integrated Development Environment (IDLE)**

Python provides a Python Shell (also known as Python Interactive Shell) which is used to execute a single Python command and get the result. Once you have installed Python 3, for instance for Windows 11, search for Python in the command prompt in desktop, select it, and hit the *Enter* key. By hitting the *Enter* key we are executing Python. Immediately, we are presented with an interactive Python shell known as Python Command-line Interpreter or **Read Evaluate Print Loop (REPL)**. The REPL, as shown in the following figure will appear on your video monitor and will be waiting for our command to be typed:

Figure 1.1: A view of the Command Line Interpreter

Interactive mode

On top of the screenshot, represented by *Figure 1.1*, you can see that we have downloaded the latest Python version. On the third line, you can see the symbol >>>. This is called the

Python statement prompt. At this stage, we should understand console input and console output. Console input means receiving input from the keyboard and console output means displaying output to the monitor in your laptop.

Python is waiting for us to give our commands for execution. Now type the following in the console input, that is, the keyboard, after the statement prompt, and press the *Enter* key in your keyboard. You will see the output immediately following what you typed, in the console output that is, the video monitor:

```
>>> print('Hello World')
Hello World
```

Congrats! You now have experience of running a Python program.

The *print* is a built-in function of Python, and it is typed in lowercase. It is used to print or display a word or string on the console monitor. A string is one of the built-in datatypes containing Unicode characters. The collection of characters 'Hello World' is enclosed within single quotation marks and parentheses. The collection of characters is known as a string in the programming world. We have carried this out in the console. We received the input from the keyboard when we typed the statement: `print('Hello World')`. The statement we typed appears on the monitor, followed in the next line by the output of the program. It would be interesting to learn Python if the reader follows the author by typing and executing the programs.

The string can also be enclosed within double quotes, and you will get the same result. Let us repeat the same exercise with double quotes:

```
>>> print("Python is easy to learn")
Python is easy to learn
```

We will notice two things:

- Double quotes to enclose string works fine. So, strings can be enclosed either between single quotes or double quotes.

- The output of the program statement, if it is correctly entered, appears instantly. If not, we will get an error message and cannot proceed with the execution of the program.

The reader may be curious to know how Python gives an error message. An erroneous statement captured is shown in the following figure for you to observe:

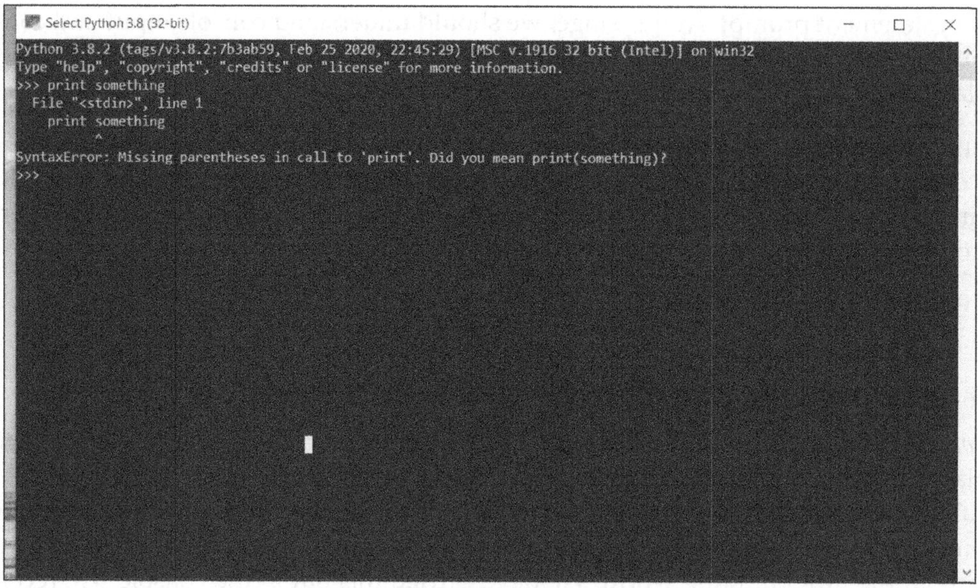

Figure 1.2: An instance of syntax error

What do you notice? It says syntax error and gives some ideas to correct the same. We will study syntax errors at the end of the chapter. Let us correct the error and run the program again. It is given in the following figure:

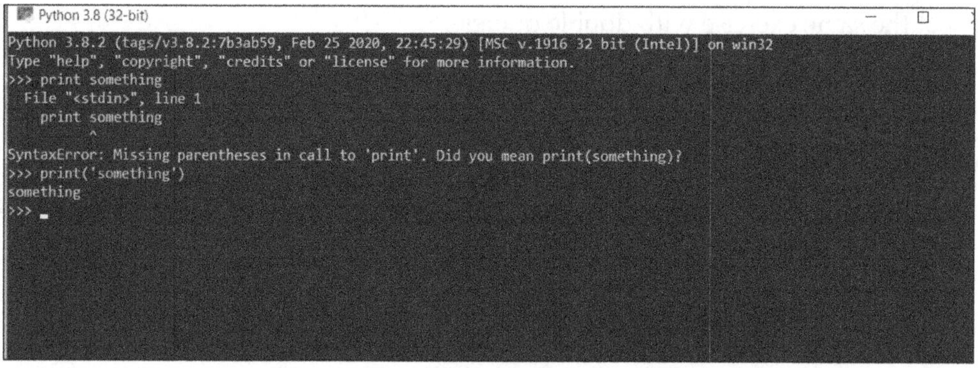

Figure 1.3: Display after the error was corrected

This type of program execution is called program execution in the interactive mode.

In this mode, we typed only one statement at a time. The prompt (three greater than signs: >>>) is also called the primary prompt. Sometimes, we may need to execute a multiline construct in the interactive mode. In such cases, the interpreter provides a secondary prompt which is 3 dots (…), as the following code illustrates:

```
>>> cond=True
>>> if cond==True:
```

```
...     print('condition is ', cond)
...
condition is True
```

When the program statement continues to the next line, the Python shell adds the three dots automatically, indicating that it is a continuation line.

We carried out the above experiments in Python interactive shell. It is also called Python Command-line Interpreter or Read Evaluate Print Loop or simply Python interpreter.

Integrated Development Environment

Running a program in the interactive mode in the Python interpreter is fine for prototyping or clearing our doubts. But, in practice, we must create fruitful programs in the file and not in the command line. What do we do then? We can use an integrated program development environment.

What is an Integrated Development Environment?

An **Integrated Development Environment** (**IDE**) includes not just the standard code editor for managing the code but also provides a comprehensive set of tools for its debugging, execution, and testing, which is an absolute must for software development. Some IDEs also come with built-in compilers and interpreters. Some of the popular IDEs for Python are given below:

- PyCharm
- Spyder
- Eclipse+Pydev
- Python's IDLE
- Wing IDE
- Cloud9 IDE
- Visual Studio Code
- Atom
- Jupyter Notebook

Python's Integrated DeveLopment Environment

We will use **Python's Integrated DeveLopment Environment** (**IDLE**) in this book, which is easy to use and comparable in performance to the IDEs listed above. Furthermore, IDLE is given to us by **www.python.org** along with the Python language system. When we download Python on the Windows platform, an Integrated Development Environment called IDLE will also be downloaded automatically with the interpreter. On Windows, IDLE is bundled with a Python interpreter. If you are using other operating systems, you need to install them separately.

We can launch IDLE by searching and selecting IDLE on the desktop. When we type IDLE and hit the Enter key, the following figure is displayed:

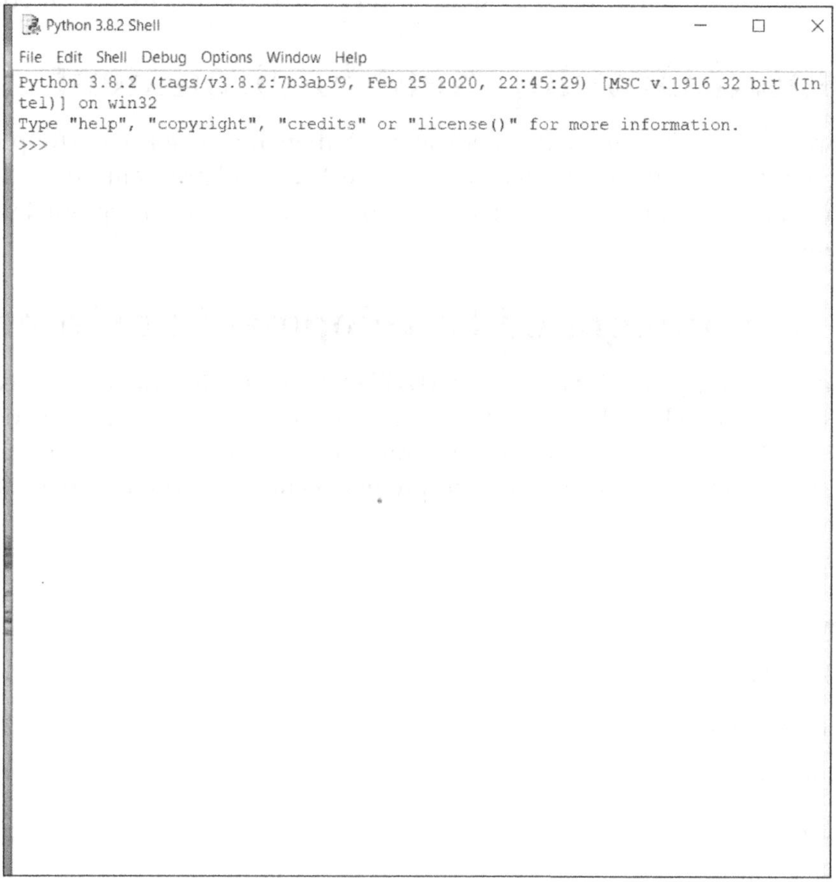

Figure 1.4: *A view of IDLE*

As you will see, it is a Python 3.8.2 Shell. IDLE comprises of a Python shell and Python editor. Note that we can also use the IDLE shell in the interactive mode as an interpreter to run or execute program statements as we had carried out with the command line interpreter. Type the following in the statement prompt in IDLE, and the output follows instantly:

```
>>> print('working with Python is simple')
working with Python is simple
```

Notice that IDLE also provides a statement prompt, and thus we get two sources for Python shell when we download Python for Windows. IDLE is an alternative to the command-line interpreter.

The Python editor in IDLE provides the following facilities:

- Create a new program file in the text editor of IDLE by selecting file new in the menu on top of IDLE.

- Open an existing file by selecting file open.

- Save the file by selecting file save as.

- Edit the file by selecting edit.

- Run the file by selecting file run.

Script mode programming

In IDLE, open a new file and type the following:

```
# python Ex1x1.py
print('Python is an interpreted language')
print('python is also a scripting language')
```

Now save the file as **Ex1x1.py**.

Now click **Run** in the task bar of IDLE or press the shortcut key *F5*, and you will get the following output:

```
=============================== RESTART: E:/Ex1x1.py
=============================
Python is an interpreted language
python is also a scripting language
```

The steps involved in creating a text file and executing in IDLE are as follows:

1. Open a new file in the IDLE text editor.

2. Type the program in the text editor.

3. Save it.

4. Select **Run** in the Run menu or press *F5*.

The first line in the above program starts with a #. It indicates that whatever is typed in that line following # is a comment, and it will not be executed. The other two statements following it are executable. The result indicates the same.

A text file can be created in the built-in text editor of IDLE or Notepad++.

Typing a statement in the statement prompt either in Python interpreter or IDLE and executing it is called running Python in interactive mode. Running a program from a script file is called running Python in script mode.

Colour coding by IDLE

IDLE is a multi-window text editor. It provides syntax highlighting and smart indenting. Indenting is a rule in Python and if indenting is not appropriate, the interpreter will throw a syntax error. A new Python programmer may have trouble with indenting. IDLE groups statements by proper indenting through its built-in smart indenting facility.

Notice that IDLE has its own color coding scheme to assist the user. When we executed the above statements on the computer, we would have noticed three different colors in the program statements. IDLE uses a color scheme as given below for the guidance of the programmer:

- Dark red: Comments
- Green: String
- Purple: Built-in functions such as print. User-defined functions will be coded in Blue.
- Light red: Error messages like Syntax Errors
- Blue: Program output and user defined functions
- Orange: Keywords/commands
- Black: Data and variables

We can type or write statements in any text editor, such as Notepad. Do not use Microsoft Word or other documents to write the code. When we open a new file in IDLE, we get a text editor automatically in which we can write the program. We can also open an existing file and modify it. The files we create in this manner are known by the following names:

- Source file
- Script file
- Module

Since Python files are stored with **.py** extension, they are called dot py files.

Execution of Python programs

Let us get a clear picture of how a Python program is executed:

1. We type the source code in Notepad and save it with **.py** extension. For example, **prog.py**.

2. Python compiler converts the above as a bytecode understandable by the interpreter in PVM. It is stored internally as **prog.pyc**. The size of each bytecode is 1 byte (or 8 bits), hence the name. The bytecode is computer hardware and platform independent. It can be executed in any PVM.

3. The PVM and the interpreter therein converts bytecode to executable code for the system and platform in which it will be executed.

4. The machine code is executed in the target machine or CPU.

Dynamically typed vs. statically typed language

Typing refers to type-checking in programming languages. The programming languages such as C, C++, Java, and Golang are statically typed languages, but Python is a dynamically typed language.

All programming languages classify objects into various types such as int, float, byte, double, etc. to manage storage space effectively. While programming in statically typed languages, the programmer must specify the type of objects before compilation; otherwise, it will lead to errors. Each identifier holds an object of a specific type, which cannot be altered later in statically typed languages. Correct usage of types will be checked at the time of compilation.

Python being a dynamically typed language, treats all variables and objects alike, and there is no need to specify their type in advance. It understands the types and handles them at the time of execution of the program dynamically without compromising the quality of the programs. Suppose var1 is assigned to a string. It can later be assigned to a list in the same program. Hence it is called a dynamically typed language. However, such reassignment will lead to errors in statically typed programming languages such as C, C++, and Java.

Statically typed programming languages like C, C++, Java, C#, FORTRAN, BASIC, etc. do type checking (that is, the process of verifying and enforcing the constraints of types) at compile-time as opposed to run-time. Dynamically typed programming languages such as Python do type checking at run-time instead of compile-time.

A language is dynamically typed if the type of a variable is checked during run-time. In dynamically typed languages, variables are bound to objects at run-time through assignment statements, and it is possible to bind the same variables to objects of different types during the execution of the program. Python is a dynamically typed language. It does not determine the variable type until the code is run. There is no type declaration in Python. What it does is to store that value at some memory location and then bind that variable name to that memory container. To summarize, type-checking is carried out in two ways as summarized below:

- **Static**: Data types are checked during compilation.

- **Dynamic**: Data types are checked during execution.

Python being an interpreted language, executes each statement line by line and thus type-checking is done on the fly, during execution. Hence, Python is a dynamically typed language.

Memory administration in Python

In any computer system, the **Central Processing Unit (CPU)** is the most important part to carry out various operations such as arithmetic and logical operations. It is supported by memory devices to store and retrieve values temporarily and permanently. Temporary storage is provided by the read and write memory, popularly called **Random Access Memory (RAM)** which is a fast memory device. Permanent storage is carried out in disc drives, compact discs, and flash. We also know that the keyboard is the standard input device, and the console monitor is the output device.

In Python, everything – various data types such as strings, containers, functions, and modules - is an object. They need to be allocated storage or memory space when the program is executing. When we execute Python programs, memory allocation, and deallocation are carried out automatically. Unlike some other languages like C, C++ and Java, users need not allocate the memory either statically or dynamically. The memory manager in PVM administers the memory management for the objects and programs. The memory manager in the PVM does this job efficiently. To take care of the storage or memory space, the computer system or the operating system, allocates memory space called heap to the programming environment. The size of heap may vary from machine to machine and depends on the size of the available RAM in the machine and other workload in the computer system at that time. The various objects are allocated memory space in the heap, which is not transparent to the programmer, but the job is done.

Python calculator

Python, in interactive mode, can be used like a pocket calculator. It is easy, as the following sections will indicate. We always wish to execute simple arithmetic operations to check whether we are doing it right. Therefore, we will carry out some common arithmetic operations in the Interactive mode.

Python interpreter acts as a calculator to carry out simple operations. Let us carry out the basic arithmetic operations using IDLE in the interactive mode. It can also be carried out in the command line interpreter.

Addition

Look at the following additions carried out in IDLE. When both the numbers are integers, we get an integer as output; otherwise, we get a floating-point number as output as the listing below indicates:

```
>>> 5+4
9
>>> 6+3.6
9.6
>>> 3.9+7.1
11.0
```

We have been adding two numbers at a time. We can add more numbers as the listing below indicates:

```
>>> 7+8+9
24
>>> 2.9+3+4+6
15.9
>>> 1+2+3.0+4+5
15.0
```

Note: When one of the numbers is a floating-point number as 3.0 in the above example, the result is displayed as a real number.

Subtraction

In Python, there is no need to specify the type of data. Moreover, the types can be mixed. The listing of a few subtractions carried out are shown below:

```
>>> 8-5
3
>>> 5-8
-3
>>> 10-7.5
2.5
>>> 7.5-10
-2.5
>>> 8.7-3.1
5.6
```

Multiplication

The addition and subtraction were carried out in interactive mode in IDLE. Let us carry out multiplication in the command-line interpreter. The output is listed below:

```
>>> 5*6
30
>>> 5.0*6
30.0
>>> 7.9*8.1
63.99
```

There is no difference in execution between Python command-line interpreter and IDLE as far as executing statements in the interactive mode. When the types are mixed such as integer and Floating-point number, Python recognizes it and deals with it correctly. Notice the comfort, which is absent in other statically typed languages.

Division

Python supports two types of divisions as written:

- Float division using operator /

- Integer division using operator //

Float division

Float division means, the division operation continues till the numbers after decimal point do not exceed the capacity of a float number. The result, which is the quotient, contains decimal part. When we carry out float division using /, we always get the result (quotient) as a real number, even when the number is evenly divisible by the divisor (that is, remainder =0) as the listing below indicates. To perform float division in Python, you can use the / operator:

```
8/4
2.0
>>> 8/12
0.6666666666666666
>>> 6.25/1.5
4.166666666666667
>>> 2.25/1.5
1.5
```

Integer division

Integer division means, the output of the division will be an integer. The decimal part is ignored. In other words, you would get only the quotient part. The integer division operation is performed with a double slash //. The following listing may be perused:

```
>>> 12//3
4
>>> 13//3
4
>>> 15//3
5
>>> 16.5//4
4.0
>>> 16.5//4.5
3.0
```

The remainder is ignored in integer division.

Modulus

The modulus (% operator) returns the remainder, irrespective of whether the numbers are integers or real numbers:

```
>>> 8%5
3
>>> 7%2
1
>>> 18%2
0
>>> 18.0%2
0.0
>>> 18.0%2.0
0.0
>>> 12.5%2
0.5
>>> 12.5%2.5
0.0
```

Exponentiation

The exponentiation operator is double *. Look at the examples below:

```
>>> 2**3
8
>>> 2**0.5
1.4142135623730951
>>> 2**2.0
4.0
>>> 2.0**3.0
8.0
```

The results give no surprises.

Special characters

We use a few special characters in Python, some of which are listed in *Table 1.1*:

Special character	Meaning
()	Hold parameters passed to a function. For example: print()
#	Precedes a comment line
" "	Enclosing a string
' '	Enclosing a string
''' '''	Enclosing paragraph comment, used when the comments exceed a line.

Table 1.1: Special characters

Batteries included philosophy

The Python language provides several built-in standard library functions, which we get automatically when we download Python. The Python source distribution has long maintained the philosophy of **batteries included** - having a rich and versatile standard library that is immediately available, without making the user download separate packages on a need basis. This gives the Python language a head start in many projects. The **Python Enhancement Proposal (PEP)** 206 describes the Python Advanced Library, a collection of high-quality and frequently used third-party extension modules. The batteries, that is, the libraries/frameworks, are available for the following domains:

- Web tasks

- Scientific programming

- Applications development

- Education: Game development

Mathematical functions in Python

The *math* module is a built-in module in Python, which provides mathematical functions for use in our programs. To use mathematical functions grouped under this module, we must import the module using import math. The list of important functions and constants defined in the math module is given in *Table 1.2*:

Function	Explanation
ceil(x)	Returns the smallest integer greater than or equal to x.
fabs(x)	Returns the absolute value of x.
factorial(x)	Returns the factorial of x.
floor(x)	Returns the largest integer less than or equal to x.
fmod(x, y)	Returns the remainder when x is divided by y.
frexp(x)	Returns the mantissa and exponent of x as the pair (m, e).
isfinite(x)	Returns True if x is neither an infinity nor a **Not a Number** (**NaN**).
isinf(x)	Returns True if x is a positive or negative infinity.
isnan(x)	Returns True if x is a NaN.
modf(x)	Returns the fractional and integer parts of x.
trunc(x)	Returns the truncated integer value of x.
exp(x)	Returns e**x.
log(x[, base])	Returns the logarithm of x to the base (defaults to e).
log2(x)	Returns the base-2 logarithm of x.
log10(x)	Returns the base-10 logarithm of x.
pow(x, y)	Returns x raised to the power y.
sqrt(x)	Returns the square root of x.
acos(x)	Returns the arc cosine of x.
asin(x)	Returns the arc sine of x.
atan(x)	Returns the arc tangent of x.
cos(x)	Returns the cosine of x.
hypot(x, y)	Returns the Euclidean norm, sqrt(x*x + y*y)
sin(x)	Returns the sine of x.
tan(x)	Returns the tangent of x.

Function	Explanation
degrees(x)	Converts angle x from radians to degrees.
radians(x)	converts angle x from degrees to radians
acosh(x)	Returns the inverse hyperbolic cosine of x
asinh(x)	Returns the inverse hyperbolic sine of x
atanh(x)	Returns the inverse hyperbolic tangent of x
cosh(x)	Returns the hyperbolic cosine of x
sinh(x)	Returns the hyperbolic cosine of x
tanh(x)	Returns the hyperbolic tangent of x
pi	Mathematical constant, the ratio of circumference of a circle to it's diameter (3.14159...)
e	mathematical constant e (2.71828...)

Table 1.2: Important mathematical functions and constants in Python

Sample program with built-in mathematical functions

Let us write a program to understand the following three mathematical functions:

- `math.ceil(x)`

- `math.fabs(x)`

- `math.factorial(x)`

To use mathematical functions, we must import math on top of the program. We must call the functions with **math** prefixes as given below:

```
# Program E1x2.py
# Mathematical Functions
Import math
x= -4.51
print(math.ceil(x)) # prints the smallest integer >= x
print(math.fabs(x)) # prints the absolute value of x
print(math.factorial(5))# prints the factorial of 5
```

The result of the program is given below:

```
========================= RESTART: E:/Py programs/E1x2.py
======================
-4
```

```
4.51
120
```

Note that the smallest integer greater than -4.51 is -4. The absolute value of -4.51 is 4.51 and factorial (5) is 120.

Other built-in functions

There are several other built-in functions in Python in addition to mathematical functions and the list of some built-in functions used often are given in Appendix 2. We do not have to import **math** to use them. A few such functions are given with their explanations in *Table 1.3*:

Function	Meaning
`abs(var)`	Absolute value of var
`min(x1, x2,…)`	Smallest element in the collection
`max(x1, x2,…)`	Largest element in the collection
`bin(var)`	Binary equivalent of var
`oct(var)`	Octal equivalent of var
`hex(var)`	Hexadecimal equivalent of var
`round(x[,d])`	x rounded to d digits after decimal point
`divmod(x,y)`	Returns a pair of (x//y, x%y)

Table 1.3: Other built-in functions in Python

We will use the built-in functions as needed. For the time being, realize that we can make use of the built-in functions when needed in our programs conveniently.

Let us understand the following three library functions:

- `bin(x)`
- `oct(x)`
- `hex(x)`

There is no need to import **math**. The program is given below:

```
# Program E1x3.py
# library Functions
x= 27
print(bin(x)) # prints the binary value of x
print(oct(x)) # prints the octal value of x
print(hex(x)) #prints the hex value of x
```

The result of the program is as follows:

```
===================== RESTART: E:/Py programs/E1x3.py =====================
0b11011
0o33
0x1b
```

We used the **bin(x)**, **oct(x)** and **hex(x)** library functions. Note the 0b prefix of binary numbers, 0o prefix of octal numbers and 0x prefix of hexadecimal numbers. There is no prefix for decimal numbers. This is an example of the clarity of Python.

Frozen binaries executables

Frozen binary executables are packages that combine a program's bytecode and the Python interpreter into a single executable program. With these, programs can be launched in the same way that we launch any other executable program. While this option works well for delivery of products, it is not really intended for use during program development. We normally freeze just before shipping the code after development is completed.

Types of errors in programs

Programming is a human activity and not a machine or robot performed activity so far. It is therefore to err is human, but the errors should not be repeated. The errors committed during programming can be classified into the following categories:

- Syntax errors
- Semantic errors

We will discuss them briefly now.

Syntax errors

We witnessed a syntax error in this chapter. The Python language has a set of pre-defined rules for constructing a program. For instance, the language requires that definition of every *class, method, if, elif, else, for, while,* etc. shall end with a colon. If any of the definitions does not end with a colon, then it is a syntax error. This is analogous to a grammatical error in simple English, where if a statement does not have a verb, we say that there is a grammatical error. We know that **does** is a valid verb. But it cannot be used with **we**. If we do so, we commit a grammatical error. Similarly, in Python, braces are a valid language construct for a **set**, and the square bracket is used to hold elements of a **list** in Python. But they cannot follow the **main** or any other method respectively, as given below:

```
def main{}:    # syntax error

def get_data[]:    # syntax error
```

The above are syntax errors. We should use () followed by a colon after the **main** and **get_data**. Thus, we commit syntax errors when we do not adhere to the rules governing the Python language. A program with syntax error will give errors when it is run. What is the secret of eliminating syntax errors? They are:

- Understand the concepts governing the language thoroughly.

- Enter the code carefully.

- Read the code, preferably with a checklist containing commonly committed syntax errors.

- Give the code to another person who is knowledgeable to check independently.

Only after we are satisfied that there are no syntax errors should we run the program. If any errors are left, the program will not run, and the run-time system will list the type of errors along with the statement number in the program. Sometimes, we may be able to fix the error quickly by knowing the statement number and the type of error, such as missing colon or missing parentheses. However, the interpreter may, at times, flag errors in the wrong place due to errors in the previous statements. Therefore, one must check the full program carefully again, find all errors, and correct them.

Semantic errors

These are other types of errors we find after programming. The interpreter will not catch these errors since the code does not violate the language's syntax. For instance, we want to square a variable called **var** and store it to **var1**. Therefore, we must write as given below:

```
var1 = var * var
```

Instead, we might have written as given below:

```
var1 = var + var
```

The computer does not know our true intention. Therefore, in the above case, it will assume that we want to double the value of **var**. Hence, it will not flag an error. Thus, the above is a logical error or semantic error. A semantic error is an error due to error in the meaning. This is like saying *I am going to school* when actually, the person is going to market. The above sentence is syntactically correct but semantically wrong. Then, how to find semantic errors? This can be found by testing the program. Suppose we want the program to square a number, then try with a number greater than 2. From the result obtained, we can conclude whether the program is semantically correct or not. Even before execution, the programmer can compute the actions taking place in each statement and the value of variables in each step. If we can manually capture the state of each variable in the program, then it might help to identify the semantic errors early. The ultimate verification is executing the program and comparing the actual result with the expected result.

Conclusion

In this chapter we looked at the history, users, features, applications, and advantages of Python 3 language. Python language system was downloaded from **www.python.org,** and the following were installed in our computer system:

- Command line Python Interpreter

- Python's Integrated Development Environment

We used both the above to execute python programs in interactive mode. IDLE was used to write and execute Python programs in the script mode. We use the "batteries included" – built-in functions in Python- Mathematical library and other Python libraries.

In the next chapter, we will study algorithmic problem solving and learn a dozen widely used algorithms.

Points to remember

- Python is a high-level programming language. It was created in the year 1991 by *Guido Van Rossum.*

- The Python interpreter is a virtual machine, meaning that it is a program that emulates physical computer hardware.

- Before the interpreter takes over, Python performs three other steps i.e. lexing, parsing, and compiling. The compiler converts the Python code to intermediate bytecode. The bytecode is interpreted by the interpreter.

- The Python interpreter is a bytecode interpreter.

- The *CPython* is the default and most widely-used implementation of Python and is written in C language.

- We will use the new version, Python 3, since Python 2 will cease to be used.

- Python installer gives us the following two tools as given below.

    o   Python command- line interpreter

    o   A tool called IDLE

- Notice that IDLE also provides a statement prompt.

- A Python program can be created in the built-in text editor of IDLE.

- Typing a statement in the statement prompt either in Python interpreter or IDLE and executing it is called running Python in Interactive mode. Running a program from a script file is called running Python in script mode.

- In Python, there is no need to specify the type of variables, which is known as dynamic typing.

- The Python language provides several built-in library functions, which we get automatically when we download Python. It is called batteries included philosophy.

- There are several other built-in functions in Python in addition to Mathematical functions, which are listed in Appendix 2.

- The executable code in Python can be frozen along with interpreter before delivery to customers, which is known as frozen binaries executables.

Questions

Choose the most appropriate answer.

1. **Python is:**

    a. High-level language

    b. Object-oriented language

    c. Freeware

    d. All the above

    e. None of the above

2. **IDLE:**

    a. Does not provide interactive mode

    b. Does not provide GUI

    c. Integrated Development Environment

    d. All the above

    e. None of the above.

3. **Python was created in the year:**

    a. 2001

    b. 1991

    c. 1956

    d. None of the above

4. **Major users of Python include:**

   a. Google

   b. Facebook

   c. NASA

   d. All the above

   e. None of the above

5. **Python has:**

   a. An interpreter

   b. Compiler

   c. Virtual Machine

   d. All the above

   e. None of the above

6. **A comment statement:**

   a. Starts with '''

   b. Ends with '''

   c. Ignored during execution

   d. All the above

   e. None of the above

7. **The output of the following program is:**

   ```
   print(math.floor(5.6))
   ```

   a. 5

   b. 6

   c. 5.6

   d. None of the above

8. **Print('largest number') has:**

   a. Semantic error

   b. Syntax error

   c. No error

   d. All the above

   e. None of the above

9. **Semantic error occurs when:**

    a. When run-time error occurs

    b. When the interpreter flags an error

    c. When it gives wrong result

    d. All the above

    e. None of the above

10. **Math is:**

    a. Library

    b. Method

    c. All the above

    d. None of the above

- Write short notes on the following:

    o History of Python

    o Frozen binaries

    o Why is Python popular?

    o Interpretation process in Python

    o Virtual Machine

    o Syntax and semantic error

    o Interactive mode

    o Executing code in script mode

    o Color coding in text editor

    o Batteries included

    o Mathematical functions

    o Other built-in functions

- Match the following:

A	B
REPL	1. Single line comment
fabs()	2. Interpreter
CPython	3. Mathematical function
#	4. Multiline comment
''' '''	5. Default

- Write programs for the following:

  o   Print div and modulus for 500/6.

  o   Find the smallest and largest number in a collection of numbers.

  o   Given 5 numbers, find their average.

  o   Given the length of a square, print its perimeter and area.

  o   Convert degree in degree Fahrenheit to degree Celsius.

  o   Find the remainder when 567 is divided by 2, 3, 5, and 7.

  o   Given 3 float numbers, add them.

  o   Calculate the volume of a sphere.

  o   To convert foot to meters.

  o   To convert time given in hours and minutes to seconds.

Join our book's Discord space

Join the book's Discord Workspace for Latest updates, Offers, Tech happenings around the world, New Release and Sessions with the Authors:

https://discord.bpbonline.com

CHAPTER 2

Algorithmic Problem Solving

Introduction

Computer programming is an engineering task that must be carried out systematically and using proper tools. In this chapter, we will look at a few sound and proven programming principles, techniques, and tools for program development, such as algorithms, namely, flowcharts and pseudocode.

Structure

The chapter covers the following topics:

- Computer program development
- Steps in computation
- Algorithm
- Testing algorithm
- Good programming practices
- Divide and conquer
- Program design

- Top-down and bottom-up design

- Data organization and data structures

- Construction of loops

- Writing programs

- Sample algorithms

Objectives

After completing the chapter, the reader will be equipped with the skills to develop algorithmic techniques for problem solving and program development. The sample algorithms will lay a strong foundation for solving complex problems and writing code in a step-by-step manner.

Computer program development

When human civilization was advancing, the Industrial Revolution began in Britain in the year 1760 AD. This led to reducing manual labor through inventing or developing appliances to reduce the drudgery of human beings in their day-to-day life. This fire of innovation continued endlessly, leading to the invention of computers later. Computers are designed to solve problems in various activities involving human beings. They increase efficiency, productivity, and quality of life wherever they are used. Algorithms are also developed side by side to solve problems more accurately without missing any details. Algorithms give solutions to the problems step by step. Although algorithms are used in many fields, they have become pervasive in computing. We will discuss algorithmic problem solving in this chapter to lay the foundation for writing Python programs of better quality consistently.

Programming is synonymous with computers. Computer programming is a widely sought after profession and a hobby that has attracted millions of young minds. Millions of programmers are engaged in program development all over the world, and billions of lines of program code have been developed and delivered for use by wide cross-sections of society. Computer programs, also known as software systems, have helped in breaking many technological barriers. Today, a fly-by-wired aircraft cannot even take off without its computer and corresponding software functioning perfectly. Satellite and space shuttle technology, weather forecasting, oil exploration, e-commerce, e-governance, Internet, Intranet, e-mail, data mining, business intelligence, cloud computing, etc. have been made possible by successful computer programs. People all over the world are convinced that computer programs (also known as software) have helped humankind to enhance the quality of life.

There are, however, darker sides to programming, as is the case with everything on earth. For instance, the failure of Apollo 13 due to programming errors, the loss of US $ 100 million in one year to an American airline company due to defects in the software system developed for determining excess flight bookings, etc. Such case studies of hardship caused by programming errors are many. Nevertheless, when we weigh the advantages and disadvantages of computers, the advantages overshadow the disadvantages clearly and unambiguously.

Many software development projects go haywire due to a poor understanding of customer requirements, programming concepts, and poor workmanship. The right understanding of requirements is, therefore, essential. The programmers should attempt to keep programs short, simple, and elegant. Program coding should be conducted with care. Program development must be conducted after program design and documentation of the algorithms.

Steps in computation

Those who live in the 21st century is fortunate since they are witness to the dramatic improvement of quality of life. The major contributors to the computer revolution are the availability of computers and telecommunication facilities at affordable costs. What is a computer? It is a manufactured device that is commercially available off-the-shelf now. A computer system comprises hardware and associated software. The hardware has a physical form whereas the latter is intangible. Computer hardware can be made to perform a wide variety and range of tasks by developing appropriate software systems. Software is nothing but a set of instructions to the computer to conduct specific tasks. The software is also known as a computer program. The task of developing software is known as programming, the person conducting the task of programming is known as a programmer. Programming is the task of developing a set of instructions for a computer to provide a solution to the chosen problem. It must be conducted systematically through the following steps:

1. Defining the problem.

2. Designing a solution to the problem.

3. Writing the program.

4. Executing the program in the computer system and testing that it works correctly.

Defining the problem

What is computer programming? It is a process of evolving a solution to real-life problems with the help of computers. The success of the computer program lies in the ability to define the problem clearly. The analyst must understand the problem, define it, and document it with full involvement of the customer. For instance, in the case of oil exploration, we write a program to determine whether oil exists in each location or not. This one-line statement is not enough to define the problem. The detailed requirements, including the expected outcomes, are to be documented.

Designing a solution to the problem

Software professionals develop algorithms to understand the problem and design a solution for the same. The computer must be instructed as to how to solve the problem. Then it will conduct the assigned tasks in a faithful manner. We must tell the computer what it has to do in the programming language it can understand. Programming languages such as Python, Java, C, C++, etc. are tools to communicate with computers. However, we cannot directly write the program code as we hear the requirements. We must understand the problem completely, and for this purpose, a problem is converted first into an algorithm.

Algorithm

An algorithm gives a step-by-step instruction that can be converted into statements in the programming language and fed to the computer. A simple definition of an algorithm is given below:

An algorithm is a computable set of steps to achieve the desired result.

Thus, an algorithm is a collection of steps. Each step can be converted into a program statement. The set of steps helps in solving the given problem. The definition of the algorithm as per IEEE Standard Glossary of Software Engineering Terminology -IEEE Std 610. 12-1990, is given below:

A finite set of well-defined rules for the solution of a problem in a finite number of steps.

Thus, an algorithm is a set of precise steps. Each step indicates the operation to be performed clearly and unambiguously. The steps are narrated in a precise and simple form. The order of execution of operations is also important. A computer program is an algorithm expressed in a programming language. The steps in the algorithm have corresponding statements in the program. After the problem is defined, the programmer designs the steps or algorithms to solve the problem. The tools popularly used document the solution by the programmers are as mentioned below:

- Flowchart
- Pseudo-code

Flowchart

A flowchart is used to list the precise steps in an algorithm. It consists of geometrical shapes (boxes) of distinct types connected from top to bottom. It indicates the flow of control during program execution. The flow lines have arrows to indicate the direction of the flow of control between the boxes. The operation carried out at each step is written within the box in simple English. Thus, a flowchart is a graphical illustration of the steps involved in arriving at a computer solution to a problem. The flowchart shows the sequence of steps performed and the decision as to which step is to be performed next.

Graphical symbols used in flowcharts

Flowcharts consist of a set of symbols. *Figure 2.1* indicates how to depict start and end operations in a flowchart:

Figure 2.1: *Start and end*

Any computational operation such as assigning value to a variable or adding two numbers can be depicted as given in *Figure 2.2*:

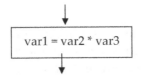

Figure 2.2: *Computational operation*

Quite often in programming we may have to take a decision based on the occurrence of an event. This can be graphically illustrated as given in *Figure 2.3* below:

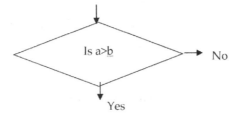

Figure 2.3: *Decision*

Input or output is indicated as a parallelogram as given in *Figure 2.4*:

Figure 2.4: *Input or output*

Furthermore, every program reveals three basic control structures as given below:

- Simple sequence
- Selection pattern
- Repetition pattern

We will discuss them briefly with flowcharts.

Simple sequence

This is the simplest and most often used control structure. Here the computer executes one instruction after another in the order given in the program as given in *Figure 2.5* below.

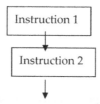

Figure 2.5: *Simple Sequence*

Selection pattern

In this case the computer evaluates a condition. Then, depending on the outcome, the control flows in one of the paths. Once the conditional execution is completed, the control flows rejoin. An example is given below in *Figure 2.6:*

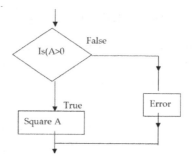

Figure 2.6: *Selection pattern*

Repetition pattern

In this case, on some conditions, the execution of instructions loops back to a previous instruction, as given below in *Figure 2.7:*

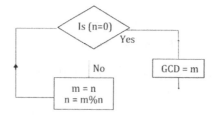

Figure 2.7: *Repetition pattern*

These are the three basic control structures you can find in any program.

Now, let us draw a flowchart for determining whether a triangle whose three sides are given, is right angled or not. We know the technique for determining whether a triangle is right angled. If the square root of the sum of the squares of any two sides is equal to the third side, it is a right-angled triangle. We must check this by taking any 2 sides at a time. The flowchart is given in *Figure 2.8*:

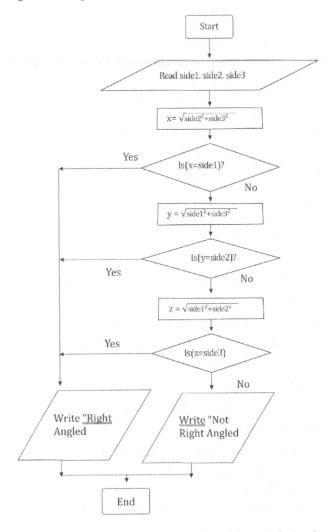

Figure 2.8: Flowchart for checking right angled triangle

Pseudocode

The space related problem in flow charts can be overcome by pseudocode. This is the currently popular tool for documenting algorithms. It might resemble an actual computer code and hence it is known as pseudocode. The definition of pseudocode as given in IEEE standard is given below:

A combination of programming language constructs and natural language used to express a computer program design.

It is a high-level description of the algorithm to solve a problem. We can use the structural conventions of any programming language, such as Python, C, or Pascal. It is intended for human reading rather than machine reading. Pseudocode omits details that are not essential for human understanding of the algorithm, such as declarations. The pseudocode is augmented with simple English-like description details, where convenient, or with compact mathematical notation. The purpose of using pseudocode is that it is easier for people to understand than conventional programming language code. It is commonly used in textbooks and scientific publications that document various algorithms, and in the planning of computer program development, for sketching out the structure of the program before the actual coding takes place. There are no rules governing pseudocode, but it should be easily understandable by an average programmer. The pseudocode could be written in any style, such as simple English, program-style English, etc. A problem requires an algorithmic or step-by-step approach for a solution. The programmer must remember that the computer cannot study the entire problem in one go and give a solution. It must be told to check or calculate one step at a time and finally give the solution. Therefore, it is the programmer who enables the computer to conduct the operations to arrive at a decision. A sample algorithm in pseudocode to find out whether a triangle is right-angled or not is given below:

Sample pseudocode: Algorithm for finding right-angled triangle:

Step 1:   Read the length of the three sides

Step 2:   Store them as side1, side2, and side3

Step 3:   Find the square root of the (side2 square + side3 square)

Step 4:   If it is equal to side1, go to step 10

Step 5:   Else, find the square root of (side1 square + side3 square)

Step 6:   If it is equal to side2 go to step 10

Step 7:   Else, find the square root of (side1 square + side2 square)

Step 8:   If it is equal to side3, go to step 10

Step 9:   Else, print, "The sides do not form a right-angled triangle" and go to Step 11.

Step 10:   Print, "The sides form a right-angled triangle"

Step 11:   End

An algorithm should take care of the termination of a program. Termination of a program can be indicated by End.

Compare the pseudocode with the flowchart in *Figure 2.8*.

Flowchart versus pseudocode

Beginners may use flowcharts, but professionals use pseudocode. We will now discuss the differences between the two.

Flowchart

It is easy to understand and explain. Since it occupies a lot of space, it is not suitable for larger programs. Sometimes the designers are forced to omit steps to fit it on a page. Hence, professional programmers do not prefer flowcharts.

Pseudocode

It is easy to develop and maintain. The pseudocode can be developed using any programming language constructs. If we do so, it reduces the time taken for the conversion of an algorithm to program code later. The pseudocode occupies less space and takes less time to document. But, if not properly indented and aligned while writing, it may be difficult to understand the program logic. The modern and professional programmers prefer pseudocode to document the design of the program.

Testing algorithm

When an algorithm is developed, it should be assessed with the chosen inputs. For this purpose, one must determine the expected output for each input. Therefore, an algorithm consists of data or inputs, a procedure that uses the data and leads you to a conclusion, and lastly, the communication of the conclusion/decision/information. If we look at the example of the right-angled triangle, the sides of the triangle are inputs; checking the square root of the sum of the square of two sides with the third side is the procedure and the conclusion of whether the given triangle is right-angled or not is the output. In the above, if we give input as 3, 4, 5, the output will be as per step 10. If we give input as 4, 5, 6, we will get the output as per step 9. Therefore, testing confirms that the actual output is the same as expected. We can evaluate algorithms by using a pen and paper and noting down what happens at each step.

Simple rules governing algorithms

The following list provides a list of rules about algorithms. It may be used as a checklist to confirm that the algorithm is correct and complete:

- The steps in the algorithm shall be convertible to computer instructions. Each step in the algorithm may be converted to one or more instructions in the computer language.

- The algorithmic steps shall be definite. It shall not be ambiguous. It cannot contain vague statements or inconclusive statements.

- The algorithm steps shall be implementable manually by a human being.

- An algorithm may receive zero or more inputs.

- The result of an algorithm is one or more output.

- An algorithm shall terminate at some point in time. It shall not contain an endless loop.

- An algorithm must be well structured with the first instruction on top of the program.

- It may contain alternate endpoints depending on some context but must end.

Good programming practices

In the following sections, tips for building quality into the product and writing better programs are discussed.

Divide and conquer

One of the popular methods for problem-solving is to divide and conquer. This means that the problem must be divided into smaller problems, each of which must be solved to get the complete solution. Some of the problems where this strategy is adopted are:

- Binary search

- Merge and quick sort

- Matrix multiplication

Program design

Top-down and bottom-up design are two popular approaches for program development. Both approaches have merits. The approaches are discussed briefly in this section.

Top-down and bottom-up design

Any problem can be dealt with in two ways, that is, top-down or bottom-up. A simple example is given here to illustrate the concept. Sorting an array of numbers involves the following:

- Comparison

- Exchange

At the top level, an algorithm must be formulated to carry out sorting using the above operations. We will not bother at this stage as to how to implement these two operations, although it is simple in this case. Once the algorithm is confirmed, the algorithms for comparison and exchange are formulated before the implementation. Therefore, in this approach, one begins from the top-level without bothering about the minute details of the implementation to start with. Divide and conquer strategy is relevant in this methodology.

The bottom-up approach is the reverse. The lower-level tasks are first carried out and are then integrated to provide the solution. In this method, lower-level structures of the program are developed first, and then progressively higher-level structures are created. Here, the algorithms for exchange and comparison will be formulated before formulating the algorithm for the whole problem.

Therefore, either the top-down or bottom-up methodology can be adopted for dividing the problem into smaller modules and then solving it. In the top-down methodology, the overall structure is defined before getting into detail. However, in the bottom-up approach, the details are worked out first before defining the overall structure.

Data organization and data structures

Data is as important as the program or the procedure. Every program can operate only on a specific set of well-defined data elements. Such data elements and their range should be determined before the program development starts. The most important task at this stage is to determine the data structure, that is, type of data elements and how these are organized. Most programming languages support integers, floating-point numbers, and other derived data types. It is, therefore, essential to determine the data types that a program will support. No program can work for all data types. Therefore, adequate attention should be paid to the design of the data structure for each program.

Construction of loops

Loops are very handy when dealing with repetitive calculations. For instance, if one must find out the sum of the first **n** natural numbers, it will be tiresome even for a computer to do it without the use of loops. If 100 numbers are to be added without loops, this will require 100 instructions with one addition at a time or one instruction with 100 data to be added in one go. However, with the help of a loop, it can be achieved in the following manner:

```
Initial value of sum = 0
Initial value of number = 1
Repeat the following 100 times:
      sum = sum + number
      number = number+1
```

Loops make programming easier and save on the number of instructions. Therefore, they are used in all programming languages. Loops are to be constructed with clear initial conditions and clear terminating conditions.

The problem of finding the sum of the first 100 natural numbers can be implemented as illustrated in the following pseudocode:

```
number = 1
sum = 0
while (number <=100):
        sum = sum + number
        number = number + 1
```

This is an example of a **while** loop in Python. Whatever follows the *while* will get executed repeatedly till the condition is satisfied, that is, **number<= 100**.

Writing programs

In the following sections, tips for building quality and writing a better program are discussed.

Modular design

A good program is one which will contain the main program, which calls sub-programs to carry out specific tasks. The subprograms do what the main program directs them to do. Each language gives different names to subprograms. In Python, they are called functions. The greater the number of functions, the faster will be the development of the entire program. The quality of the program will also be enhanced when the program is made modular, as mentioned above with functions. Each function will receive input and may return some output to the called program. By dividing the program into several functions, the problem can be divided and conquered. This facilitates focus on small problems and dealing with one problem at a time.

Choice of variable names

There are rules for naming variables used in a program. Most programming languages allow even a single character for the name of a variable. In Python, there is no limit to the number of characters in a variable name. Programmers generally dislike typing long names and end up with single-character variable names. Such single character variables reduce the readability of a program. Therefore, meaningful names should be formed for the variables. For example, variable `Mark` can be called `mark` itself, whereas employee can be named as `employee` or *emp*; to indicate account, the variable name `acct` can be formed, but not simple `a`; the name for quantity may be `qty` rather than `q`; the variable name for average may be `avg` but an `a`. In short, the variable name should be indicative of the contents of the variable.

Documentation of programs

It would be very difficult to understand one's program if it is made up of one large program without modularization, with short variable names, and without adequate comment statements. Therefore, it would be next to impossible to understand somebody else's program without adequate documentation. Most programming languages make provision for comment statements. Comment statements should be used liberally to document what the program is doing at each major step. Some programmers introduce too many comment statements to get more money from the buyer since they get paid on the basis of number of lines of code they deliver. But this is not the right approach. The comment statements should be sufficient to understand what the programs/functions carryout. At the end of program development, it would be better to get from the developer a listing of the program along with a short write-up on what the program does, preferably at each module.

Program testing

A program developed is not complete unless it is tested thoroughly and found to function properly. Therefore, programs are to be tested. Once a program has been developed, it must be tested with test data. In the case of the program for finding whether the given sides will make a right-angled triangle, one can supply Pythagorean triples as well as non-*Pythagorean triples* and check whether the program concludes correctly whether a right-angled triangle can be constructed or not. In this example, there are only two possible conclusions. However, in complex problems, there will be many conclusions, and the test data should be such that all possibilities are checked. Sample inputs should be supplied to the program to check whether the output meets the requirements.

Before proceeding to test the program, it would be better to determine the valid inputs, which would give valid outputs. It would also be a good idea to test the program with invalid inputs, that is, inputs that may lead to error conditions. Invalid inputs are those that are beyond the range of input or data types different from those specified etc. In such cases, it would be of interest to know whether the program gives proper message and continues without terminating abruptly. This is called gracious degradation. This concept may be difficult for beginners to comprehend, but they could try to look for inputs, which will lead to error conditions. Some examples are divided by zero and factorial of a negative number. The test results are to be documented so that at a later point in time, the same test cases can be executed to demonstrate the correct performance of the program.

Sample algorithms

Now let us look at some sample algorithms, which are often required for problem-solving using computers.

Exchanging values of two variables

We come across a need to swap values contained in two variables in many applications, such as sorting. If we simply interchange the values, one of the values will be lost. For instance, if we want to swap values contained in **var1** and **var2** and if we do as given below, what happens:

```
var1 = var2
var2 = var1
```

In the above example, no doubt the contents of **var2** will be transferred to **var1**. But, when we come to the second statement, **var2** will get the current value of **var1**, which is nothing but the original value of **var2**. Thus, the value contained originally in var1 will be lost. To avoid this, we need to declare another variable of the same type, say temp. Now, we can achieve swapping in 3 steps as given below:

```
temp = var1
var1 = var2
var2 = temp
```

Here, the original value of **var1** is stored in **temp**. Now, **var2** is transferred to **var1**. Thus, **var1** contains the original value of **var2**. Then the contents of temp, which is nothing but the original value in **var1**, is transferred to **var2**. Thus, swapping of values contained in 2 variables needs 3 steps and declaring another variable of the same type. The complete algorithm to swap 2 integers is given below:

```
Swap ( var1, var2)
Step 1:  Read var1 and var2
//create temp as another variable and assign a value of zero to it
Step 2:  temp = var1
Step 3:  var1 = var2
Step 4:  var2 = temp
Step 5:  Write var1 and var2
Step 6:  End
```

Algorithms may receive input data, which are given in parentheses following the name of the algorithm as above. Note that the above algorithm receives two inputs and gives two outputs (Write). The algorithm terminates after writing the values, indicated by the End statement. Now, try to apply the simple rules discussed in the previous section to the above algorithm and confirm that this algorithm possesses all the characteristics of an algorithm.

We have not used any notation for scripting the algorithm. As we go along, we will reduce the description part of the steps by indicating the operations to be carried out symbolically. As such, there is no need to use any syntax for documentation of the algorithms.

Decimal base to binary base conversion

The base of a number system is also called a radix. While a programmer will be comfortable with decimal numbers, the computer system uses a binary number system internally. Let us evolve an algorithm for the conversion of a decimal number to a binary number. This algorithm deals with whole numbers only.

Let us recall how the conversion takes place with an example.

Let us convert 19 into binary:

```
2  |19
2  |9 - 1
2  |4 - 1
2  |2 - 0
2  |1 - 0
0 - 1
```

The equivalent of 19 in binary is 10011.

Therefore, when we divide by 2, the first remainder is the **Least Significant Bit** (**LSB**) and the last remainder is the **Most Significant Bit** (**MSB**). For simplicity, let us assume that we convert them into 8-bit numbers.

The algorithm below gives the method of converting a decimal number to an array of bits:

```
Dec_to_Bin (num)
```

Step 1 :　　Store the decimal number in variable *num*

Step 2 :　　Declare an array *bin* of size 8 to store 8 bits

Step 4 :　　i=0

```
while(i<=7):
        bin[i] = num % 2
        num = num//2                    // integer division
        i=i+1
```

Step 5:　　while(i>=0): //i is 7 now

```
        Print(bin[i])
        I=i-1
```

Step 6:　　End

Python language is sensitive to indentation. Of course, the Integrated Development Environments provide help in the right indentations.

The algorithm receives the decimal number **num**. We are using a while loop in the above program. When the associated condition is satisfied, in this case (i<=7), the block of statements following the **while** will be executed. The binary numbers are written as part of the *while* loop. We can take a few decimal numbers to check whether the algorithm does the conversion of a decimal number to a binary number correctly.

Reversing digits of a natural number

Suppose the natural number is 78654, then after reversing the digits, it will become 45687. We will now write an algorithm to reverse the digits of a given natural number:

```
Reverse (num)
```

Step 1:   Read num

Step 2:   reverse = 0

Step 3:   while (num > 0):

                        reverse = reverse * 10 + (num % 10)

                        num = num//10   # // indicates integer division

Step 4:   Write reverse

Step 5:   End

Greatest Common Divisor

We will see the algorithm developed by the Greek mathematician *Euclid* for finding the **Greatest Common Divisor (GCD)** of two integers. The algorithm is given below:

```
GCD ( m,  n)
```

Step 1:   Read two integers m and n

Step 2:   If m is not greater than n

                        swap(m,n)

Step 3:   temp=0

Step 4:   while n! = 0:

                        temp = m % n

                        m = n

                        n = temp

Step 5:   Write GCD = m

Step 6:   End

Python language uses == to check whether a is equal to b and uses ! = to check whether a is not equal to b. The algorithm receives two integers and writes GCD after checking.

The above algorithm can be written in a much simpler manner using recursive functions. Since it is too early to discuss recursion, the algorithm has been implemented as above. Nevertheless, the algorithm works correctly.

Prime numbers

As we know, a prime number is one which is not evenly divisible by any other number other than by itself and 1. For instance, 2, 3, 5, 7, 11 are all prime numbers. Let us now write an algorithm to find out whether a given number is prime or not. Look at the algorithm below:

```
Prime ( num)
Step 1:       Read num
Step 2:       div = 2
Step 3:       prime = 1
Step 4:       while ((div * div <= num) and (prime ! = 0)):
                    if  num % div = = 0:
                            print ("num is divisible by div")
                            prime = 0
                      else:
                            div = div + 1
Step 5:       if prime ==1:
                    print (num is prime)
              else:
                      print (num is NOT prime)
Step 6:       End
```

The algorithm receives **num** and prints whether the number is prime or not.

Factorial of a given number

We know that factorial of a given number n is given by:

$$!n = 1 \times 2 \times 3 \ldots \times n.$$

The following algorithm will find the factorial of a given number:

```
factorial ( num)
Step 1:       Read num
Step 2:       if num==0:
                      factorial = 1
```

```
            else:
                    factorial=1
                    var=1
Step 3:         while (var <= num):
                    factorial = factorial * var
                    var = var + 1
Step 4:         print factorial
Step 5:         End
```

Note that factorial of 0 =1. Python does not require the declaration of the type of variable. It dynamically understands the type and operates on it as we will see in later chapters.

Finding the maximum and minimum numbers in a list

The list has a specific meaning in Python, and we will discuss it in detail later. It can be assumed to be an array of numbers for the time being. We wish to find the maximum and minimum in the list or the array. An algorithm is given below, which finds both the maximum and minimum in the array simultaneously:

```
Algorithm MaxMin(array[])
Step 1:         max=min=array[0]
Step 2:         for i=1 to n-1, step1:
                    if array[i]>max then max=array[i]
                    if array[i]<min then min =array[i]
Step 3:         print max
Step 4:         print min
Step 5:         End
```

The function receives the array as argument. We initialize two variables **max** and **min** with the first element in the list, that is, **array[0]**. Then in the **for** loop for each subsequent element in the array, we do the following:

If the next element is greater than **max**, **max** will be the next element; if not we do not disturb **max**. Similarly, we then check that if the next element is less than min, then the new min will be the next element; if not, we do not disturb **min**. In this manner, we traverse the entire list, and then we print **max** and then **min** in the list. Try this with sample data to understand better.

Inserting a card in a list of sorted cards

Let us take an example where there are **n** number of cards; they can be playing cards or simple integers. The cards are already sorted. We must insert a new card. To understand the problem easily, let us assume that the list consists of three numbers as given below.

[1, 2, 4]

Let us assume that we wish to insert 3. Then, compare this number with other numbers in the list one by one. If the number in the list is greater than the key (card to be inserted) then insert the key there. The algorithm is as follows:

```
Algorithm insert(key, array[])
Step 1:        i=0
Step 2:        while (i<n):
                      if (array[i] >key):
                              array[i]=key
                              break
                      else:
                              i=i+1
Step 3:        End
```

Guess an integer number in the given range

This is a game. The computer generates a random integer number in a given range. A **random** function is available in Python to generate it. Let us direct the program to generate a random number in the range from 100 to 200 and hide it from the user. The user is then asked to guess the number. If the user can guess the number correctly, he or she wins the game; if not, he or she, loses the game.

After every unsuccessful guess, the program informs the user whether the guessed number was lower or higher than the actual random number generated in the computer. In the algorithm, the random integer is called the **number**, and the value guessed by the user is called **guess**:

```
Algorithm Guess(number)
Step 1:        Computer generates the random integer number in the given
range
Step 2:        Read number
Step 3:        Read guess
Step 4:        if guess > number
                      print "Your guess is too high"
```

```
        if guess < number
                print "Your guess is too low"
        else
                if guess==number
                        print ("congratulations")
Step 5:     End
```

You can play this game with your friends.

Recursion

All the algorithms we discussed are functions. Some functions used iterations, and some did not. There is another methodology in programming called recursion where a function calls itself. This concept is difficult to understand unless explained through examples. Every program can be written without using recursion, but the reverse is not true. Some problems, however, are suitable for recursion. For instance, the factorial problem was solved without recursion by using a while loop. The program can be solved using recursion as shown in the algorithm below:

```
main function
Step 1:     Enter a positive integer n
Step 2:     if(n<0):
                print ("Enter a positive number")
                Stop
            else:
                result= factorial(n)// calling factorial function
Step 3:     Print result
Step 4:     End
factorial(n)
Step 1:     If n==0:
                return 1
            else:
                f=n*factorial(n-1)
Step 2:     return f
```

Now let us analyze how the program proceeds. We get a positive integer n from the keyboard. To find factorial n, we call function **factorial (n)**, where **factorial** is the function for finding the factorial of number n. If n= 0, then **factorial** will be 1.

Assume that we want to find out the factorial of 2, and **factorial (2)** is called. In the function **factorial**, since n is greater than 1, n * fact(n-1) is returned; that is, 2 * fact 1 is returned to the result. Result = 2 * fact(1). This intermediate result is stored somewhere and can be called a runtime stack. The stack is an array that stores values and gives the last element first. Writing into the stack is popularly called push and getting information from the stack is called pop. We have not defined any stack, and therefore we can assume that the system does this for us. After pushing the intermediate result into the stack, the program calls **factorial(1)**, which returns 1. Now the intermediate result is popped and the value of **factorial** 1 is substituted to get the factorial of 2 as 2.

Let us now call factorial 5. We call **factorial** and get back the following:

$result = 5 * factorial(4)$ -   [1]

Now **factorial(4)** is called to get 4 * factorial(3). Substituting this in [1] we get:

$$result = 5 * 4 * facorial(3)$$

Then **factorial (3)** again is called to get 3 * factorial (2) and so on till we get **factorial(1)** which will be returned as 1. Therefore, we get factorial 5 as 5 x 4 x 3 x 2 x 1. Such repetitive calling of the same function is called recursion. Thus, recursion keeps the program size small, but understanding recursion is not easy. If the program can be visualized as recursive, it will result in a compact code. Recursive functions can easily become infinite loops. What will happen if **n** is entered as a negative number? The program will get into an endless loop. Therefore, to avoid such eventualities, we have a statement if (n<0), which prints a statement. This will ensure that if a negative number is entered, the program will terminate gracefully.

Generation of the Fibonacci sequence

There are a number of sequences in mathematics, and Fibonacci is one such sequence. Its first element is 0, and the second is 1. Thereafter, the next element is the sum of the previous two numbers. For instance:

fib[0] = 0

fib[1] = 1

fib[2] = fib[1] +fib[0] = 1+0 = 1

fib[3] = fib[2] +fib[1] = 1+1 = 2

fib[4] = fib[3] +fib[2] = 2+1 = 3

fib[5] = fib[4] +fib[3] = 3+2 = 5

If the total number of elements in the series is given, then the series can be computed. The algorithm is simple:

fib (i)

Step 1:   fib[0] = 0, fib[1] = 1, i = 2

```
Step 2:              print fib[0] and fib[1]
Step 3:              while (i<20):
                         fib[i] = fib[i-1] + fib[i-2]
                         print fib[i]
                         i =i+1
Step 4:              End
```

This program will calculate the first 20 Fibonacci numbers. This is achieved by the while loop.

Towers of Hanoi

The Towers of Hanoi is a puzzle. In this puzzle, there are three towers called *source, destination*, and *temp*. The source is stacked with several circular disks with varying diameters. Each disk has a hole in the center through which the disks can be inserted in the towers, that is, poles. The source is stacked with the largest disk in the bottom and the smallest disk on top as shown in the figure below. The other two towers are empty initially:

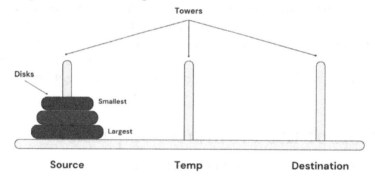

Figure 2 9: Towers of Hanoi

The game is to transfer the disks from source to destination by observing the following rules:

- Only one disk can be moved at a time.

- We cannot place a disk of larger diameter on top of a disk with a smaller diameter.

- The disk removed can be put only on one of the three poles immediately, not even temporarily on an additional pole or ground.

The goal is to transfer all the disks in source to the destination by moving one disk at a time and without violating the rules of the game as above.

Let us try to understand the rules of the puzzle through examples. Assume that there are two disks called 1 and 2 on the source, Disc 1 is on top and Disc 2 at the bottom. The following steps are involved in the transfer of the discs from source to destination following the rules:

1. Transfer 1 from S (Source) to T (Temp)

2. Transfer 2 from S to D (Destination)

3. Transfer 1 from T to D

Thus in 3 steps, we could transfer the disks from source to destination, by observing all the rules.

Let us now assume 3 disks in the source, one top of another as given below. The diameter of disk 3 is larger than 2, which is larger than 1:

1

2

3

The steps involved in transferring the three discs from source to destination by observing the rules are given below:

1. Transfer 1 to D

2. Transfer 2 to T

3. Transfer 1 from D to T

4. Transfer 3 from S to D

5. Transfer 1 from T to S

6. Transfer 2 from T to D

7. Transfer 1 from T to D

This is a 7-step process. The transfer of 2 disks took (2^2-1), that is, 3 steps, the transfer of 3 disks took (2^3-1), that is, 7 steps.

Now observe what we have done and how we have achieved the transfer of disks from source to destination without violating the rules. We have followed a set pattern. Observe that when there were two disks, we transferred the largest disk at step 2 from source to destination when there were three steps. When there were 3 disks, we took 7 steps and exactly at the 4th step we transferred the largest disk from S to D. Therefore, if there are n disks, divide the problem into two:

1. Transfer (n-1) disks from source to temp.

2. Transfer the nth disk to the destination.

We see from the examples that when the nth disk is transferred, the (n-1) disks are at temp stacked in proper order. Now the task is to transfer the (n-1) disks from temp to destination using source as the temp. The second step can now be solved recursively using the same algorithm. Look at the algorithm:

```
Hanoi(n, s, d, t)
Step 1:      if(n==1):

                    Move disc from s to d

             else:

                    Hanoi(n-1, s, t,d)

                    Move n from s to d

                    Hanoi(n-1, t, d, s)

Step 2:      End
```

We have divided this program into two parts as explained above and will continue to subdivide it till conquering it. This strategy is known as divide and conquer, which is a very useful technique in solving complex programs. The Towers of Hanoi problem is a good example of recursion and divide and conquer.

Conclusion

This chapter is important both for the novice and experienced programmers alike. We briefly discussed the use of examples for problem solving, the divide and conquer technique, and the top-down and bottom-up design.

The chapter also discussed variable naming conventions, rules governing algorithms, systematic program design, and recursion.

To give a feel for problem-solving using computers, 12 algorithms were evolved and discussed in this chapter. More complex algorithms will be discussed in the rest of the book.

Points to remember

- Programs are developed to provide solutions to simple problems like making a bill in a grocery shop as well as professional applications like software for fly-by-wired technology.

- Every problem must be defined clearly with the inputs, that is, data, expected outputs and the procedure to be adopted for getting the expected output.

- Program development involves the following steps:

    o   Defining a problem

o   Designing a solution to the problem

o   Writing the program

o   Executing the program in a computer system and testing that it works correctly.

- There are three basic control structure patterns in computer programming as given below:

  o   Simple sequence

  o   Selection pattern

  o   Repetition pattern

- Flowchart and pseudocode are the two tools available for the programmer to design a solution to the problem. These tools are useful to capture the algorithm for finding a solution to the given problem.

- Flowcharts occupies space and hence are not suitable for large programs.

- Pseudocode is more suitable for larger and complex programs since it saves space and time in documenting algorithms.

- Divide and conquer strategy can be adopted for some problems like sorting and searching.

- A function calling itself is known as recursion. Recursion is suitable for solving some problems such as Towers of Hanoi, resulting in compact code.

- It is important to adopt top-down or bottom-up design strategies for program development to ensure the quality of programs developed. In the top-down approach the big picture will be clear very early. Both methodologies facilitate work parallelism.

Questions

Choose the most appropriate answer:

1. **Top-down approach:**

   a. Identifies program structure first

   b. Subprograms are built first

   c. Not useful for design

   d. All of the above

   e. None of the above

2. **Pseudocode:**

    a. Is like flowchart

    b. Gives step by step of program execution

    c. Should strictly be in a programming language

    d. All of the above

    e. None of the above

3. **Variable names should be:**

    a. As short as possible

    b. Fixed length

    c. Meaningful

    d. All of the above

    e. None of the above

4. **An algorithm:**

    a. Must end

    b. Contains computable steps

    c. Follows rules

    d. All of the above

    e. None of the above

5. **The basic control structures in programming include:**

    a. Repetition

    b. Selection

    c. Simple sequence

    d. All of the above

    e. None of the above

6. **The number of poles in Towers of Hanoi problem is:**

    a. 1

    b. 2

    c. 3

    d. None of the above

7. **In Towers of Hanoi with 3 discs, the largest disc is moved from source to destination at:**

    a. 8th step

    b. 4th step

    c. 2nd step

    d. None of the above

8. **Factorial of 4 is:**

    a. 24

    b. 48

    c. 6

    d. None of the above

9. **GCD(252, 36) is:**

    a. 18

    b. 4

    c. 36

    d. None of the above

10. **In the problem of inserting a key in a list of sorted cards, if the number in the array is ....the key (card to be inserted) then insert the key there. Fill in the blanks:**

    a. equal to

    b. greater than

    c. less than

    d. None of the above

- Write short notes on the following:

    o Flowchart versus pseudocode

    o Program design and implementation issues

    o The rules governing algorithms

    o The importance of loops and rules for their design

    o Variable naming convention

- o Comment statements

- o Top-level design

- o The basic model of computation

- o Problem definition

- o Use of examples for problem-solving

- o Divide and conquer

- Match the following:

A	B
Prime number	1. A function calling itself.
Pseudocode	2. Not divisible by any number other than itself and 1.
Flowchart	3. Combination of programming language and natural language.
Recursion	4. Used for documenting
Comments	5. Boxes with text connected together

- Solve the following problems using algorithms given in this chapter. Write what happens in each step:

- o Binary equivalent of decimal number 1024

- o Reverse of 7826

- o GCD (21, 84)

- o Whether number 313 is prime

- o Factorial of 13

- o Find out 15th Fibonacci number

- o Roots of a quadratic equation, a=8, b=-5, c=22

- o Finding sum of digits in a number, 98345678

- o Inserting number 45 in the following array

- o [12, 23, 33, 44, 46, 120]

- o List transfers in the Towers of Hanoi when there are 7 disks.

## CHAPTER 3

Numeric Computations and Console Input

Introduction

In this chapter, we will study the atomic elements, such as identifiers and keywords, which we need to write a Python program. We will write programs to carry out numeric computations with integers, real numbers, and complex numbers. We will also discuss operators, including bit-wise operators, operator precedence, and arithmetic assignment operators. We will understand how to receive input from the console, that is, keyboard, when we are executing the program.

Structure

The chapter covers the following topics:

- Tokens
- Identifiers
- Keywords
- Literals
- Python literal types
- Numeric data types

- Integer operations

- Real number operations

- Scientific notation

- Complex numbers

- Type Boolean

- Expressions and operator precedence

- Augmented assignment operators

- Type conversion

- Console input

- Random numbers

- Bitwise operators

Objectives

After completing the chapter, the reader will understand the tokens of the Python language, which they will use appropriately while developing Python programs. They will understand the various operators the language supports and the importance of operator precedence. The reader will be able to write interactive programs by receiving input through the keyboard.

Tokens

A programming language defines a set of unique tokens for writing computer programs. A program can be written using one or more of the tokens of the language. We will study some of the tokens of the Python language in this chapter. The major tokens of Python language are given below:

- Identifiers

- Keywords

- Constants or literals

- Operators

There are certain other building blocks of a program that do not form part of any of the four tokens listed above. Some of them are given below:

- Blanks or white spaces

- Horizontal tabs

- Newline characters

- Comments

We will look at them in this chapter.

Identifiers

The name of any object, item, function, and class is an identifier. Just as the name of a person, street, or city helps in the identification of a person or a street or a city, the identifier in Python language assigns names to programmable entities such as files, functions, constants, variables, etc. Python defines a set of rules for coining the identifiers. They are:

- An identifier should be a sequence of lower case (or) upper case (or) digits (or) a combination thereof.

- The identifier may start with lower case or upper case letters (It must not start with digits.).

- The identifier name should not be a reserved word. Reserved words are the words reserved for specific purposes by Python.

- Only underscore (_) is allowed to be used as a special character in the identifier names.

- There is no limit to the length of the identifier.

For instance, *print* is the name of a function available with the Python language system to display text on the console monitor. The term *print* has been reserved for the name of a function, and it is an identifier coined by Python. The user should not use it for any other purpose. Any function name, either defined by the language or by the user, is an identifier. Therefore, identifiers can be constructed with alphabets (A..Z), (a..z) 0..9. Besides, an underscore can also be used in identifiers. Unless otherwise specified, however, small letters are usually used for identifiers. Usually, a programmer will not assign long names to an identifier. Typically, the length of an identifier may be 4 to 8 characters. The identifier should be meaningful and easy to infer its meaning. For instance, the meaning of the name, address, street, and tel_no are easy to infer and are neither too long nor too short.

Keywords

These are also known as reserved words of Python, meaning that they have specific meanings to the Python interpreter. They are assigned by Python for specific purposes. They should be used for giving specific instructions to the computer. These words cannot be used for any other purpose, such as naming a variable. Python is a concise language containing only 35 reserved words, and this is one of its strengths. Common tasks such as *print*, *input*, etc. are implemented through library functions in Python, giving relief to programmers and reducing the size of code as compared to other programming languages. This makes the task of programming rather simple. The keywords of Python are given in *Table 3.1*. We will use most of them in the book:

False	await	else	import	pass
None	break	except	in	raise
True	class	finally	is	return
and	continue	for	lambda	try
as	def	from	nonlocal	while
assert	del	global	not	with
async	elif	if	or	yield

Table 3.1: *Keywords in Python language*

Literals

Literals are used to define both variables and constants. In every program, we use different data types such as name, register number, marks, etc. Some of them, like name and register number, will be constants, and others, like marks, may be variable. They must be assigned to an identifier for use in our programs. Variables and constants are fundamental data types. A variable can be assigned only one value at a time but can change value during program execution. A constant on the other hand, as the name indicates, shall not be assigned a different value during program execution. For instance, if PI has been declared as a constant = 3.14, it shall not be reassigned any value in the program. Programs may declare constants. Variables are similarly useful for any programming language. If a *mark* has been declared as a variable, then it can be changed in the program to any value. This is one difference between a variable and a constant. To distinguish named constants from variables, the identifier of constants are formed using upper case letters. For example:

- PI
- SIGMA

Variable names are, on the other hand, formed by lowercase letters:

- mark
- attendance
- passenger

In Python, constants are usually implemented using variables whose values should not be modified during the program's execution. Unlike some other programming languages that have built-in support for constants, Python does not have a specific constant keyword or mechanism. Instead, developers typically use variable names written in uppercase with underscores to indicate that a variable's value shall be treated as a constant (although the value can still be changed, it is considered a convention to treat it as constant). Therefore, Python constant is only a convention and not a rule.

Constants and variables are stored in memory locations during program execution. Memory consists of many storage cells. For instance, the notebook we are using has 8 gigabytes of primary memory space. Each byte in the memory has an address expressed in hexadecimal numbers. During program execution, we will be using variables and constants and will be storing them in the memory locations of the computers. To handle them with minimum effort, we will coin a name for each variable. This name assigned corresponds to an address in the memory of the computer system expressed in hexadecimal number notation. However, the programmer does not have to know the exact address in a hexadecimal number. We address it by the name coined by us during storage. The operating system knows the address of the constant or variable. For instance, the computer during one execution may store, say *num* at location 0x1000. When we reference *num* later, the program will retrieve the current value of *num* from location 0x1000. When we execute the program again *num* may be stored in some other location, say 0x6666. The programmer need not bother about this since, for each execution of the program, the operating system stores a constant or variable in a chosen location and remembers the location until completion of the program execution. Once the program execution is over, the computer will not remember where a particular constant or variable was stored since they will all be deleted.

Python literal types

Python supports the following types of literals:

- Numeric
- String
- Boolean
- List
- Tuple
- Dictionaries
- Sets

We will discuss some of them in this chapter.

Numeric data types

The following numeric types are supported in Python:

- Integer (binary, decimal, octal, and hexadecimal)
- Real numbers: Floating point and scientific notation

- Complex numbers
- Boolean

One of the important points to be noted is that there is no need to declare the type of variables or constants in the Python programs. Python handles it elegantly. If there is no decimal point in a number, it is treated as an integer, and if there is a decimal point, it is treated as a floating-point number. Interpreting whether a number is an integer or a real number, the language stores them differently. However, the storage mechanism is not transparent to the programmer. Let us look at some example programs now.

Integer operations

Open IDLE Shell on your computer, click **File** and select **New File** and type the following:

```
# Program E3x1
# Integer operations
x=5
y = 2
z=0.5
print(x+y)
print(x-y)
print(x*y)
print(x//y)
print(x/y)
print(y**z)
print(x%y)
```

We know the line starting # is a comment statement and will not be executed. This is only for information of the human reader. Save the file as **E3x1.py**. Now press **Run** in IDLE.

The result of the execution of the program is as follows:

```
=============== RESTART: E:/Py programs/Chapter  3/E3x1.py ================
7
3
10
2
2.5
1.4142135623730951
1
```

You can easily verify the correctness of the result of the program. For instance, 2**0.5 is square root of 2 and it is 1.414.

Real number operations

Real number means a floating-point number. We will repeat the same operations using floating-point numbers. We do not specifically say whether the number is an integer or floating-point number. The Python system interprets it correctly always.

Run IDLE from your computer. Type the following in new file:

```
# Program E3x2 Real number operations
x=5.0
y = 2.0
z=0.5
print(x+y)
print(x-y)
print(x*y)
print(x//y)
print(x/y)
print(y**z)
print(x%y)
```

Save the file as **E3x2.py**. Now press **Run** in IDLE.

The result of the execution of the program is as follows:

```
================ RESTART: E:/Py programs/Chapter  3/E3x2.py ================
7.0
3.0
10.0
2.0
2.5
1.4142135623730951
1.0
```

Scientific notation

The real numbers can also be written in scientific notation. Python Scientific notation is a way of writing a large or a small number in terms of powers of 10. Python's REPL will display values as scientific notation when they are bigger than 1×10^{15} or smaller than $1\times10^{-4.}$

If the number is greater than 1e-4 or less than 1e15, it is represented in decimal form by REPL. For instance, in the scientific notation, 7.0 is equivalent to 7E0, 453 is 0.453e3 or 4.53E2 or 45.3e1, and 0.5 is 5e-1. Note that both uppercase E and lowercase e can be used in scientific notation. 45.3E1 is nothing but 45.3 *10^1.

Let us confirm this in IDLE shell in the interactive mode:

```
var1=0.000006
print(var1)
6e-06
var2= 4.5
print (var2)
4.5
var3=150000
print(var3)
150000
var4=12345678912
print(var4)
12345678912
var4=1e16
print (var4)
1e+16
var5=1e6
print(var5)
1000000.0
```

Real numbers are always stored as numeric values. **The values are never stored in the form of** *scientific notation.* Only while printing the floats (depending on the conditions) is it **shown in the form of scientific notation** (the actual value always remains in float value).

Complex numbers

Python supports complex numbers. Type the following program and save as **E3x3.py**:

```
# Program E3x3
# Complex Numbers
x=5.0 + 4.5j
y = 2.0
print(x+y)
print(x-y)
```

```
print(x*y)
print(x.real)
print(x.imag)
  print(x.conjugate())
```

Pressing *F5* or **Run**, IDLE gives the following result:

```
=============== RESTART: E:/Py programs/Chapter  3/E3x3.py ================
(7+4.5j)
(3+4.5j)
(10+9j)
5.0
4.5
 (5-4.5j)
```

This program demonstrates the use of the following built- in functions of Python:

- real

- imag

- conjugate ()

Note that conjugate means that the sign of the imaginary part in a complex number is toggled as the result of the program indicates.

We call these functions in conjunction with an object by using what is known as dot operator (for example, x.imag). In this case, it is x. This is the methodology used by objects to call functions or methods in **Object-Oriented Programming** (**OOP**) languages.

Type Boolean

Python supports the type of Boolean or bool. The two outcomes of a Boolean expression as given below:

- True or 1

- False or 0

Any non-zero integer will be considered as True and zero as False.

Type the program E3x4 by opening a new file in Python and saving it in the same name:

```
# Program E3x4
# Demonstration of Boolean
x=True
```

```
y = False
print(x)
print(y)
x=5<2
print(x)
y=5>2
print(y)
```

On execution, the program gives the following result. Note that 5<2 is False and 5>2 is True:

```
================== RESTART: E:/Py programs/Chapter 3/E3x4.py
==================
True
False
False
True
```

Expressions and operator precedence

The following is an equation in Mathematics:

$$Y= ax^2 +bx+c$$

It is an expression in Python language too. An expression is of the following form:

Variable=expression

The expressions contain independent variables like x and constants like a, b and c. The variable is a dependent variable depending on the values of the above.

Most languages define operator precedence to avoid ambiguity while evaluating expressions. However, there are no separate operator precedence rules for Python. We can assume the same rules for evaluating mathematical expressions for Python as well. The rules of precedence in mathematics are given below for ready reference:

- Operators contained within inner parentheses are evaluated first, followed by other parentheses.

- When more than one operator is present in an expression the following is the order of precedence:

    o   Exponentiation (**)

    o   Multiplication (*)

    o   Float division (/)

o   Integer Division (/ /)

o   Remainder (%)

o   Addition (+) and subtraction (-)

o   If more than one operator of the same precedence exists in an expression then they are evaluated from left to right if the operator is not exponentiation. If the operators are exponentiation, then we evaluate from right to left. This is confirmed by the following example:

```
>>> 3**2**4
43046721
>>> (3**2)**4
6561
>>> 3**(2**4)
43046721
```

Note that the last calculation above matches with the first, confirming that when we evaluate multiple exponentiation operators in an expression, we must evaluate from right to left.

Let us now evaluate an expression and confirm the result through IDLE in the interactive mode:

```
y= 5+4*8-(9*2 -2**(3-1))+16//4%3
5+4*8-(9*2 -2**2)+16//4%3
5+4*8-(9*2 -4)+16//4%3
5+4*8-(14)+16//4%3
5+32-14+16//4%3
5+32-14+4%3
5+32-14+1
37-14+1
23+1
y=24
```

The above is confirmed in REPL and shown below.

```
>>> y= 5+4*8-(9*2 -2**(3-1))+16//4%3
>>> print(y)
24
```

The result of the execution of the above expression confirms the result we obtained manually.

Augmented assignment operators

We come across several expressions. For instance, marks obtained by a student is increased by a number to take care of the toughness of the examination as given below:

mark=mark+5

Such expressions can be written in a different style when the one of the variables in the **Right-Hand Side (RHS)** includes the variable in the **Left-Hand Side (LHS)**. The following example will make it clear:

The general form is *exp1 = exp1 + exp2.*

This can be also written as *exp1 + = exp2.*

Some examples are given in *Table 3.2*:

Simple form	Augmented assignment form
a = a+b	a += b
a = a+1	a += 1
a= a–b	a – = b
a = a–2	a – = 2
a = a*b	a*= b
a = a*(b+c)	a*= b+c
a = a/b	a / = b
a = a/2	a / = 2
d = d – (a+b)	d – = a+b

Table 3.2: Augmented assignment operators

The following operators can be combined with assignment operator(=) to derive augmented assignment operators:

+, -, *, /, //, % , **

Let us carry out a program to demonstrate augmented assignment operators:

```
# Program E3x5.py
# Augmented assignment operators
x=5
y=2
x+=y
print(x)
```

```
x-=y
print(x)
x*=y
print(x)
x//=y
print(x)
x/=y
print(x)
x**=y
print(x)
x%=y
  print(x)
```

When the program is executed, we get the output as given below:

```
================ RESTART: E:/Py programs/Chapter 3/E3x5.py ================
7
5
10
5
2.5
6.25
0.25
```

Let us now try to understand and analyze each output:

```
x=5
y=2
x+=y
```

The above statement means *x=x+y;* hence new value of *x=7*. Now we have the statement:

```
  x-=y
```

This means, *x=x-y*, that is, *7-2=5*. New value of *x=5*.

Now, the next statement is:

```
  x*=y
```

This means *x=x*y=5*2=10*. The result confirms it. In this manner we can verify the other results.

Look at the program below:

```
# Program E3x6.py
# Augmented assignment operators
x=5
y=2.0
x+=y
print(x)
x-=y        # x=x-y
print(x)
x*=y    # x=x*y
print(x)
x+=2.5 # x=x+2.5
print(int(x))
print(round(x)) # round the value of x
x+=0.1
  print(round(x))
```

The result of the program is given below. Analyze the output and understand the operations. You may note 12.5 is rounded to 12 and 12.6 to 13:

```
================ RESTART: E:/Py programs/Chapter 3/E3x6.py ================
7.0
5.0
10.0
12
12
13
```

Type conversion

We observed that if one of the operands is a float value, then we get the result of the operation in the float. That is exactly type conversion. This is an implicit conversion. We can also convert explicitly. We can convert a float to an integer explicitly by prefixing *int* as given below:

int(float_num)

Here are some type conversions allowed in Python:

- **int()**: converts any data type into integer type
- **float()**: converts any data type into float type

- **hex()**: converts integers to hexadecimal

- **oct()**: converts integer to octal

- **bin()**: converts integer to binary

- **str()**: converts the specified value into a string

- **ord()**: converts the one character string like "S" to Unicode code point (83)

- **chr()**: converts the Unicode code point to one character string ('S').

We will come across more in the rest of the book.

Similarly, we can use the round function to find the nearest number. These concepts will be clear from the following results obtained in the interactive mode of Python:

```
>>> var1=6*7.5  # result will be float
>>> var1
45.0
>>> var2=9*8.5
>>> var2
76.5
>>> int(var2)# returns integer part of real
76
>>> round(var2)# rounds to the nearest whole number
76
```

The *int* prefix truncates the fractional part. On the contrary, round gives the nearest whole number. For instance:

```
>>> round(76.5001)
  77
```

Console input

We were giving data as part of the program itself. This forces the user to rewrite the program with new values, when he wants to test the program with new input data. Is this not a cumbersome process? Will it not be interesting if we can give the input at run time when the program is executing? Yes, we can do it and type the input data during program execution. It enables the user to give the values as he desires instead of preprogrammed values. Let us write a program to find the area of a square. To find the area of a square we need the value of the side. We can receive the value entered as given below:

```
side=input ("Enter the value of the side:  ")
```

We use the built-in function **input** to accept a string entered by the user without evaluating the value. The function continues to read the string entered till it encounters a newline character.

The user-entered value will be received as a string. But we need a numeric value. The built-in function **eval** is used to evaluate the numeric value of the string. Thus, we use functions **input** and **eval** to receive user input and it evaluates the value as the program below illustrates:

```
# Program E3x7.py
# getting input from the user
# prompt the user to enter a value
side=eval(input("Enter value of the side:   "))
area=side*side
print('area =', area)
```

In the above program, we get the value of the side through the input statement as a string. Then we convert it to a number using the function **eval()**. After the area is found, it is printed. The 'area=' will be printed truthfully. It is followed by printing the area. The program was executed twice, once with the side in integer and then with side as a real number. Look at the result of the program given below:

```
=============== RESTART: E:/Py programs/Chapter  3/E3x7.py ===============
Enter value of the side:   11
area =
121
>>>
=============== RESTART: E:/Py programs/Chapter  3/E3x7.py ===============
Enter value of the side:   15.1
area =
228.01
```

Now we will write a program to receive two numbers and get the quotient and remainder. To receive two numbers, we have to get the input twice, as the program below illustrates:

```
# Program E3x8.py
# getting two inputs from the user
# prompt the user to enter the number
x=eval(input("Enter value of the nymber:   "))
# prompt the user to enter divisor
y=eval(input("Enter value of the divisor:   "))
```

```
print('quotient =')
print (x//y)
print('remainder =')
  print (x%y)
```

When we wish to receive two numbers, we get the input twice. The quotient is obtained by integer division and the remainder by the modulus operator. Look at the result of the program below:

```
================== RESTART: E:/Py programs/Chapter 3/E3x8.py
==================
Enter value of the nymber:   22
Enter value of the divisor:   5
quotient =
4
remainder =
2
>>>
================== RESTART: E:/Py programs/Chapter 3/E3x8.py
==================
Enter value of the nymber:   33
Enter value of the divisor:   7
quotient =
4
remainder =
5
```

Let us now write a program to find the area of a right-angled triangle. We get the base and height from the user in one go. The values we receive are assigned to the respective variables as per the order specified. The area is calculated and printed. The program is given below:

```
# Program E3x9.py
# Area of a right-angled triangle
base, height=eval(input('Enter the base and height '))
area=0.5*base*height
print('area= ', area)
```

It is a simple program. We have been receiving one input at a time.

In this program we received the two values entered by the user in one statement. The result of the program is given below:

```
==================== RESTART: E:/Py programs/E3x9.py ====================
Enter the base and height 3, 4
area=  6.0
```

We can also receive more than one input at a time using a function **split()**. We know that the **input** function returns strings. In the previous program we used **eval** to convert the string to numbers. We can even convert strings to *int, float* by prefixing the respective types. While **eval** converts strings to appropriate number types, the type conversion will convert to the type desired by the user. Let us look at an example. Here we are going to receive four integers:

```
# Program E3x10.py
# getting four inputs from the user
# prompt the user to enter four numbers
x=input("enter 4 numbers separated by comma:  ").split(',')
first_num=int(x[0])
second_num=int(x[1])
third_num=int(x[2])
fourth_num=int(x[3])
print(first_num)
print(second_num)
print(third_num)
print(fourth_num)
```

We invoke the split function followed by the **input** function. The **split()** function returns a list. The four numbers we are going to enter will be stored in a list. The **first_num** as **x[0]**, **second_num** as **x[1]**, **third_num** *as* **x[3]**, and the **fourth_num** *as* **x[4]**. We convert them to integers by prefix of **int** to the strings returned by the **input** function. In the last four statements, we print them. The result of the program is as follows:

```
=============== RESTART: E:/Py programs/Chapter  3/E3x10.py ===============
enter 4 numbers separated by comma:  11, 22, 33,44
11
22
33
44
```

Now we will write a program to receive different data types such as *int, float* and *complex* from the keyboard. The program is given below. Since the statement spills over to next line in line number 3, an escape character \ is used to continue in the next line:

```
# Program E3x11.py
# getting an int, a float and a complex from the user
```

```
x=input("enter an int, a float and a complex separated by\
comma:  ").split(',')
first_num=int(x[0])
second_num=float(x[1])
third_num=complex(x[2])
print(first_num)
print(second_num)
print(third_num)
```

The result of the program is as follows:

```
================ RESTART: E:/Py programs/Chapter 3/E3x11.py ===============
enter an int, a float and a complex separated by comma:  10, 34.99, 2+4j
10
34.99
(2+4j)
```

Here, we convert the strings returned by the **input** function to the respective types. We discussed the feature of console input in this chapter. As we have seen, the **print** function prints to console monitor. We will discuss more about console output in the next chapter.

eval()

The type conversion with *int, float,* and *complex* worked for numbers. It will not work for non-integer string. The **eval** function converts any string into a number. It can be used for evaluating expressions as the following indicates:

```
>>> eval('75+25')

100
```

If we try typing the conversion of the above with the *int prefix*, it will not work. But when the string contains leading zeros **eval** will not work, but *int* will, as the following indicates:

```
>>> int('0045')

45
```

So, you have to use **eval** or **int,** depending on the situation.

Random numbers

There is a module called *random*. Random numbers are the ones which change every time. We can use it to generate random numbers. We can use **randint(a,b)** function in the module **random**. The function returns a random integer between *a* and *b,* both numbers included. We can also generate a random float *r* such that 0<=r<=1 using **random.random**.

Let us write a program:

```
1.  '''Program E3x12.py'''
2.  # random number generation
3.  import random
4.  print(random.random())
5.  print(random.randint(0,9))
6.  print(random.randint(100, 200))
7.  print(random.random())
```

By now, you know that the first line is a multiline comment, and the second line of the program is a line comment. Then we import module **random** in the third line. In line 4, we pass **random.random()** to the print function to print a random float between 0 and 1. At line 5, we generate a random integer between 0 and 9, both inclusive; at line 6, we generate and print a random integer between 100 and 200, and in the last line, we generate a random float between 0 and 1. The result of the program is given below:

```
0.7504057774115697

9

119

0.5808726609815922
```

Note that the result will be different for each execution and will also be different for the student since we are generating random numbers.

Bitwise operators

A byte consists of 8 bits. A bit is a binary digit 1 or 0. We can carry out operations on the bits in the byte using bitwise operators. Some of the bitwise operators and their names are given *Table 3.3*:

Operation	Symbols and examples
OR	a | b - a or b
AND	a & b - a and b
Complement	~a - complement of a
Left shift	a<<3 - shift bits in a by 3 positions

Operation	Symbols and examples
Right shift	a>>3 - shift bits in a by 3 positions
Exclusive OR	a^b - an exclusive OR B

Table 3.3: Bitwise operators

Let us carry out the operations manually before we check with a program. We will take decimal numbers and convert them to binary numbers for manual operations. However, in the program, this process will not be transparent to the user:

Let a = 45 which is 00101101 in binary.

Let b = 89 which is 01011001 in binary.

OR operation – a | b

The output will be a 1 if at least one of the bits in the numbers is 1. Therefore, a | b will be 01111101, which will be 125, as shown in the following table:

a	45	0	0	1	0	1	1	0	1
b	89	0	1	0	1	1	0	0	1
a | b	125	0	1	1	1	1	1	0	1

Table 3.4: a | b with OR operation

AND operation a&b

The output will be 1 only when both the inputs are 1. Hence the a&b will be 00001001, which will be 9.

Complement ~a

 In complement operations, 0 will become 1 and vice versa. The complement of *a* 00101101 will be 11010010. Since the **Most significant bit (MSB)** is 1, this is a negative number. The negative numbers are given in 2's complement notation. To get the number, we have to do the following:

- Omit MSB and find 1's complement of the rest 7 bits. To get 1's complement subtract 1 from the number. In this process, we will get 1's complement of the number.

- To get the number take the complement of above.

To get 1's complement subtracting 1 from other 7 bits and we get 1010001. Let us find 1's complement of this to get the number. The result will be 0101110. So, this will be 46 and it is a negative number and so the result is -46.

The left shift a<<4

a is 00101101.

Let us shift *a* by 4 bits to the left. The result will be 001011010000, which will be 720 in decimal.

Right shift a>>2

Let us do the right shift of a by 2 bit. The result will be 00001011, which will be 11 in decimal.

Exclusive OR of a^b

The output will be 1, if either a or b is 1 and not both.

a = 45 which is 00101101 in binary.

b= 89 which is 01011001 in binary.

a^b = 01110100   which is 116 in decimal.

Let us verify the results through a Python program. It is given below:

```
# Program E3x13.py
# Bit-wise operations
a=45
b=89
print('binary of a=', bin(a)) # prints the binary value of a
print('binary of b=', bin(b)) # prints the binary value of x
print(('a OR b=', a|b)) #prints a OR b
print(('a AND b=', a&b)) # prints a AND b
print(('complement of a =',~a)) # prints complement of a
print(('shifting a by 4 bits to the left=', a<<4))
print(('shifting a by 2 bits to the right=', a>>2))
print(('exclusive OR of a b =', a^b))
```

The result of the program is given below. It confirms our calculations as above:

```
==================== RESTART: E:/Py programs/E3x13.py ====================
  binary of a= 0b101101

  binary of b= 0b1011001

  ('a OR b=', 125)

  ('a AND b=', 9)

  ('complement of a =', -46)

  ('shifting a by 4 bits to the left=', 720)

  ('shifting a by 2 bits to the right=', 11)

    ('exclusive OR of a b =', 116)
```

Bit-wise operations will be useful in scientific applications.

Conclusion

In this chapter, we have learned the major tokens of the language with which we can design a program. We also discussed various types of literals used in Python 3. We saw examples of numeric computation with different types of operands. We also noted that Python understands the types of constants and variables with the values contained in them. An introduction to Boolean type was given. Augmented assignment operators, bit-wise operators were used in programs. We used the input function to get the user entered value as a string. The conversion from string to a number is achieved by prefixing eval to the input function. We invoke the split function followed by the input function to return more than 1 variable entered by the user as a list. We discussed type conversion and generated random numbers in this chapter.

In the next chapter, we will discuss Unicode formats, which help us to use many of the natural languages in the world in computing. We will discuss strings, collection of characters and string methods. The reader will learn more about console output and formatted printing.

Points to remember

- A program can be written using one or more of the basic building blocks, that is, tokens of the language.

- The major tokens of Python language are given below:

    o   Identifiers

    o   Keywords

- o   Constants or literals
- o   Operators

- An identifier should be a sequence of lower case (or) upper case (or) integers (or) a combination thereof.

- The identifier should start with the lower case (or) upper case letters (It must not start with digits).

- The identifier name should not be a reserved word.

- Only underscore (_) is allowed to be used as a special character in identifier names.

- The length of the identifier is unlimited.

- Python is a concise language containing only 35 reserved words.

- Literals are used to define both variables and constants.

- A variable can be assigned only one value at a time but can change value during program execution. A constant on the other hand, as the name indicates, cannot be assigned a different value during program execution.

- Python supports the following types of literals as given below:
  - o   Numeric
  - o   String
  - o   Boolean
  - o   List
  - o   Tuple
  - o   Dictionaries
  - o   Sets
  - o   Class

- The following numeric types are supported in Python:
  - o   Integer (binary, decimal, octal, and hexadecimal)
  - o   Float
  - o   Complex
  - o   Bool

- One of the important points to be noted is that there is no need to declare the type of variables or constants in the Python programs. If there is no decimal point in a number, it is treated as an integer and if there is a decimal point it is treated as a floating-point number.

- The real numbers can also be written in scientific notation. For instance, 7.0 is equivalent to 7E0, 453 is 0.453e3 or 4.53E2 or 45.3e1 and 0.5 is 5e-1. Note that both upper case E and lower-case e can be used in scientific notation.

- Python supports the type of Boolean or bool.

- The general form is augmented assignment operators is exp1 + = exp2.

- We can convert a float to an integer by prefixing *int* as given below:

- int (float_num)

- Similarly, we can use the round function to find the nearest number. The *int* prefix truncates the fractional part. On the contrary, round gives the nearest whole number.

- When we use *the input* function, the user entered value will be received as a string. This conversion from string to a number is achieved by prefixing *eval* to the input function.

- We invoke the split function followed by the input function to return more than 1 variable entered by the user as a list.

- The type conversions with *int, float,* and *complex* worked for numbers. It won't work for non-integer string and expressions. The *eval* function converts any string into a number. It can also be used for evaluating expressions.

- To generate a random integer or float we have to *import* the *random* module.

- We can carry out operations on the bits using bitwise operators.

Questions

Choose the most appropriate answer:

1. **Tokens include:**

    a. Keywords

    b. Identifiers

    c. Literals

    d. All of the above

    e. None of the above.

2. **Keywords include:**

   a. print

   b. int

   c. False

   d. All of the above

   e. None of the above.

3. **Python literals include:**

   a. class

   b. list

   c. Tuple

   d. All of the above

   e. None of the above

4. **The conjugate of 25-3j is:**

   a. 25+3j

   b. -25-3j

   c. -25+3j

   d. All of the above

   e. None of the above

5. **The result of 16-4.0 is:**

   a. 12

   b. 12.0

   c. Will get runtime error

   d. All of the above

   e. None of the above

6. **eval function converts typed text as:**

   a. string

   b. int

   c. number

   d. All of the above

   e. None of the above

7. **The result of 3*2**3 is:**

    a. 24

    b. 18

    c. None of the above

8. **16 & 9 is equal to:**

    a. 16

    b. 9

    c. 0

    d. None of the above

9. **The prefix of binary numbers is:**

    a. 0x

    b. 0o

    c. 0b

    d. None of the above

10. *split* **function:**

    a. Returns a list of number

    b. Splits a number

    c. None of the above

- Write short notes on the following:

    o Token

    o Numbers in Python

    o Identifier

    o Keywords

    o Python literal types

    o The function eval vs. int

    o Input function

    o Augmented assignment operators

    o Bit-wise operator

    o Three ways of getting 3 real numbers

- Match the following:

A	B
Identifier	1. Gets a string
True	2. Keyword
Reserved words	3. Gets a number
Input	4. Keywords
eval	5. Starts with alphabets

- Write programs for the following:

  o Get 10 real numbers from the user and find their average.

  o Receive decimal number from the user and convert it to octal, hexadecimal, and binary using library functions.

  o Get radius of a circle from the user and find area and perimeter.

  o Get 2 decimal numbers from the user and find the following:

    ❖ OR

    ❖ AND

    ❖ Exclusive OR

  o Get an octal number from the user and shift left by two bits. Shift the shifted number by 2 bits. Comment on the result.

  o Generate random numbers.

  o Calculate the value of the following expression and verify it with the program:

  o $Y=(9+2)*2**4 - 3$

  o Get the length and breadth of a rectangle from the user and find its perimeter and area.

  o Convert the above program to find area of a square and rhombus.

CHAPTER 4
Unicode, Strings and Console Output

Introduction

Computers are multi-lingual, and Python programs can handle textual data written in any of the languages supported by the Unicode consortium, including English. We will understand the basics of Unicode in this chapter. Strings in Python are arrays of bytes representing Unicode characters. They are widely used in programming and are an important data type. The programmers give input through the keyboard and get output displayed on the monitor. Both these devices are collectively known as consoles. In this chapter, we will discuss console output and console input of a string.

Structure

The chapter covers the following topics:

- Character set
- String
- Finding types
- The str trype
- Multi-line strings

- Escaping quotes within string

- Escape sequences

- The index in a string

- Substring: Slicing

- Immutable strings

- Repetition

- String methods

- Methods for modifying strings

- Replace Substrings with replace()

- ord() and chr() functions

- Reversing a string

- Console input of a string

- Console output

- Formatted printing

- String module constants

- Sequence types

- Converting string to bytes

Objectives

After completing this chapter, the reader will understand Unicode code points, the characteristics of strings, and Python methods for string manipulation. The student will learn how to get input through keyboard, print the output in the console monitor and various formatting printing methods. We will know how to convert strings to bytes.

Character set

Python adheres to the de facto International Standards about the use of characters in Python programs. ASCII and Unicode set the standards for characters used in computing.

ASCII code

In the early days of computing, the programming languages supported **American Standard Code for Information Interchange (ASCII)** character sets with 7-bit encoding.

The character set consisted of the characters such as:

- (a ..z)

- (A..Z)

- (0..9)

- Commonly used symbols such as +, -, *, /, %, etc.

Each character is encoded with a number ranging from 0 to 127, thus giving ASCII code for 128 characters. The computers store alphanumeric characters and other characters by assigning a unique number to each character. For instance, in ASCII, the number 65 symbolizes **A**, and the number 90 represents **Z**.

Unicode

Before the Unicode was finalized, there were many different systems for character encodings, that is, for assigning numbers to various characters. These earlier character encodings were limited and did not cover characters of all the world's languages. Even for a single language like English, no single encoding covered all the alphanumeric characters, punctuations, and technical symbols in common use. Pictographic languages, such as Japanese, challenged these earlier encoding standards.

Early character encodings also conflicted with one another. That is, two encodings could use the same number for two characters or different numbers for the same character. Because of this situation, a computer might have to support many different encodings. When data is passed between computers and different encodings, it increases the risk of data corruption or errors.

Furthermore, character encodings existed only for a few languages. However, many languages lacked character support altogether.

Unicode was evolved by the Unicode Consortium to support many popular languages spoken by people worldwide, such as English, French, German, Hindi, Tamil, Telugu, Kannada, Malayalam, etc. A Unicode character starts with \u, followed by 4 hexadecimal digits starting from \u0000 to \uFFFF. Thus, each character is represented by a number from 0 to 65,535 in hexadecimal notation. For instance, the symbol for the letter A is represented by character number 65, which in hexadecimal notation is U+0041, and the letter Z by U+5A, whose decimal equivalent is 90. In Unicode, A..Z have been grouped under Latin uppercase letters.

Unicode is the universal character encoding maintained by the Unicode Consortium. This encoding standard provides the basis for processing, storing, and interchange of text data in any language in all modern software and information technology protocols. The formulation of Unicode allowed people to seamlessly use other Indian and international languages in computing and communications. For more details, visit **https://home. unicode.org/**.

The Unicode Consortium is the authority for Unicode Standards. Their goal is to standardize universal character sets with its standard **Unicode Transformation Format (UTF)**. The Unicode standard is implemented in HTML, XML, Java, JavaScript, E-mail, ASP, PHP, etc. The Unicode standard is also supported in many operating systems and all modern browsers.

As of May 2019, Unicode version 12.1 contains over 137,000 characters, including different scripts, including English, Hindi, Chinese, and Japanese, as well as emojis. These characters are each represented by a Unicode code point. So, Unicode code points refer to actual characters that are displayed. These code points are encoded to bytes and decoded from bytes back to code points. For example, The Unicode code point for alphabet a is U+0061, the emoji ' 😊 is U+1F60A, and omega (Ω) is U+03A9.

Unicode is implemented in different formats. The most used encodings are UTF-8 and UTF-16, which are briefly discussed below:

- **UTF-8:** A character in UTF-8 can be from 1 to 4 bytes long to encode every code point. UTF-8 can represent any character in the Unicode standard. UTF-8 is backward compatible with ASCII. The first 128 characters of Unicode (which correspond one-to-one with ASCII) are encoded using a single octet with the same binary value as ASCII, making valid ASCII text a valid UTF-8-encoded Unicode text. All English characters just need 1 byte — which is quite efficient. We only need more bytes if we are sending non-English characters. It is the most popular form of encoding and is the default encoding in Python 3. UTF-8 is the preferred encoding for e-mail and web pages.

- **UTF-16:** 16-bit Unicode Transformation Format is a variable-length character encoding for Unicode, capable of encoding the entire Unicode repertoire. This encoding is suitable for Asian text as most can be encoded in 2 bytes each. It is bad for English as all English characters also need 2 bytes here. UTF-16 is used in major operating systems and environments, like Microsoft Windows, Java, and dot NET.

- **UTF-32:** It is fixed to 4 bytes. All characters are encoded in 4 bytes, so it needs a lot of memory. It is not used very often.

Let us give the Unicode as a string and find what they represent. Look at the listing below for Hindi followed by English characters:

```
>>> '\u0906'
'आ'
>>> '\u0978'
'ॸ'
>>> '\u0908'
'ई'
>>> '\u0051'
```

```
'Q'
>>> '\u0052'
'R'
```

Let us write some Tamil characters on the screen:

```
>>> '\u0b85'
'அ'
>>> '\u0B89'
'உ'
```

As seen above, every character has an equivalent Unicode, which starts with **\u**.

In the following section, we will discuss strings.

String

In Python, strings are arrays of bytes representing Unicode characters, consisting of not only English characters, but characters from any natural language supported by Unicode. The number of characters in a string may vary from zero to any number. There is an empty string with no characters in it. All strings we create are objects of the built-in class *str*.

We will use interactive mode in REPL or IDLE to learn the language conveniently. The listing from the screen when interactive mode was used in IDLE is given below. The array of characters should be enclosed within single or double quotation marks on both sides and assigned to a string variable. We assign **love** to a string variable **string1** and print it. Then we assign **everyone** to variable **string2** and then print it. The variable **string1** is enclosed within single quotes, and variable string 2 within double quotes. So, the strings can be enclosed within a pair of single quotes or double quotes, but only one of them for a specific string. Do not put a single quote before the first character in the string and double quote at the end, and vice versa, which will lead to syntax errors. Look at the following example:

```
>>> string1='love'
>>> print(string1)
love
# string1, string2, and string3 are string variables
>>> string2=" every one"
>>> print (string2)
 every one
```

String concatenation

We use + to add two numbers. Similarly, we can use the overloaded + operator to add or concatenate two strings as given below:

```
>>> string3=string1+string2
>>> print(string3)
Love every one
```

We will write a program for string concatenations. It is given in the program below:

```
# Program E4x1.py
# printing strings
var1='Ganesh'
var2='karthik'
var3=str(27)
var4=str(15.5)
print('var1='+ var1)   # Concatenating
print('var2='+ var2)   # Concatenating
print('var3='+ var3)   # Concatenating
print('var4='+ var4)   # Concatenating
```

We create 2 string variables, **var1** and **var2**. Then we convert **var3**, which is an integer, and **var4**, which is a float, into strings. In the print statements, the variables and their identifiers are concatenated using the + sign. Since the variables are strings, we could carry out concatenation. We cannot concatenate a string with any other type, such as an integer or float. Here, we have carried out a conversion of integer 27 and float 15.5 to strings. Hence, concatenation was possible. The result of the program is given below:

```
===================== RESTART: E:/Py programs/E4x1.py =====================
var1=Ganesh
var2=karthik
var3=27
var4=15.5
```

Finding types

Python has a built-in string class named **str** with many interesting features. Let us now try to find out the data type of the strings and other data types in the interactive mode. For this purpose, we use a library function **type()** defined in the Python language. Note that **string1**, **string2**, and **string3** are as already defined in the previous section:

```
>>> type(string1)
<class 'str'>
```

```
>>> type(string2)
<class 'str'>
>>> type(string3)
<class 'str'>
>>> a=5+7j
>>> type(a)
<class 'complex'>
>>> b=7
>>> type (b)
<class 'int'>
>>> c=9.0
>>> type(c)
<class 'float'>
>>> d=True
>>> type(d)
<class 'bool'>
```

From the above, the strings are of type **<class 'str'>**, or in other words, they are objects of **<class 'str'>**. Similarly, **int**, **float**, **complex**, and **bool** are built-in types and are objects of the respective built-in classes defined by the language. We came across the following built-in classes in the above interaction with the Python interpreter:

- str

- int

- float

- bool

- complex

Due to the dynamic typing system of Python, when we assign 5 to a variable, it is automatically considered an object of class **int**. Similarly, when we assign 5.0, it is automatically considered to be an object of class **float**. All the strings are objects of the **str** class.

The str class

In Python, there is no explicit *String* class. The standard way to represent strings in Python is by using the **str** class. The **str** class is a built-in class in Python that represents sequences of Unicode characters. It is used to manipulate and work with textual data. Here are some key points about the **str** class: When we refer to the *string class* in Python, we are usually talking about the class **str** itself. In Python, **str** is the built-in string class, and instances of this class represent Unicode strings. When we create a string in Python, we are creating an object of the **str** class.

The str type

The term *type* refers to the category of the object (for example, str, int, float). The term *class* refers to the definition of the type, including its methods and attributes. The **str** is a built-in type in Python that represents a sequence of characters. When we create a string literal (for example, string1 = "Hi"), we are creating an instance of the **str** type. The **str** type is implemented as a class in Python, and strings are instances of this class. We can use the **str()** constructor to create a string object explicitly, like **string1 = str("Hi")**.

When we mention the **str** type, we are referring to the type of a particular object. In Python, everything is an object, and each object has a type. The **str** type is associated with objects that represent Unicode strings.

In summary, the **str** is the class that defines and provides operations for string objects in Python, and the **str** type is the type associated with instances of this class. In everyday usage, we will often see both terms used interchangeably to refer to the concept of working with strings in Python.

The **str** type can be used to convert numbers into strings as given below:

```
>>> a=str(75.5) # float converted to a string
>>> a
'75.5'
>>> a=str(100)  # integer converted to a string
>>> a
'100'
```

Take a look at an interesting example below. The expression is evaluated and assigned to **var**. Then it is converted to string:

```
>>> var=100+8.9 + 4-3j
>>> str(var)
'(112.9-3j)'
```

Notice from the above that when we convert numbers to strings, they are enclosed within single quotes.

In the following, we concatenate strings of width 1. See the result:

```
>>> str('a' +'b')
'ab'
```

Multi-line strings

Sometimes the length of the string may exceed one line. Such multi-line strings can be assigned in 3 different ways:

- By using triple quotes
- By enclosing the string within parentheses
- Using an escape character \

We will look at all three methods of executing statements in the Interactive mode in IDLE.

Method 1: Using triple quotes

The strings were enclosed between single quotes and double quotes when their lengths did not exceed a line. But if the length of the string exceeds a line, then we can enclose such strings with triple quotes as the following interaction indicates:

```
>>>str1='''This is
a
multi-line
string'''
>>> print(str1)
```

When we press *Enter*, we get the following output on the monitor:

```
This is
a
multi-line
string
```

Method 2: Enclosing the string within parentheses

We can create a multi-line string variable by enclosing it within parentheses, as given below:

```
>>>str2=('This is the second
method of creating                                          a
a multi-line string')
>>> print(str2)
```

When the *Enter* key is pressed, we get the following output:

```
This is the second
method of creating                                          a
multi-line string
```

Method 3: Using an escape character \

In this method, we add the escape character \ at the end of every line except the last line, as indicated below:

```
>>> str3='this is \
        the \
        third method'
>>> print(str3)
```

On the execution of the above, we get the result as given below. We got the string, but not in the original form:

```
this is         the         third method
```

We can use any of the three methods discussed above to create strings, which may cross over to the next line.

Escaping quotes within strings

Sometimes, a string may have a single quote or double quote within a string. It may be misleading to the interpreter, and it will treat it as the end of the string. To avoid misunderstanding and retaining single or double quotes, there are two ways as given below:

- Using escape character \.

- Treating the string as a raw string by prefixing lowercase r or uppercase R before the string. The raw string is also useful to treat the backslash character (\) as a literal character.

Look at the listing below:

```
>>> str2='I don\'t like'
>>> str2
"I don't like"
>>> str3=r"I don't like"
>>> str3
"I don't like"
```

Escape sequences

The characters' escape sequences and their purpose are given in *Table 4.1*. We will use them for printing functions:

\b	Backspace
\t	Tab
\n	Linefeed
\f	Formfeed
\r	Carriage return
\\	Backslash
\'	Single quote
\"	Double quote

Table 4.1: Character escape sequences

The index in a string

A string is an array of characters. The index of a string starts at 0 and if the length of a string is n characters, the index of the last character in the string is $(n-1)$. The elements of a string can be accessed by the index value. Let us check this in the interactive mode with IDLE:

```
str1="Cyndrella"
>>> str1[1]
'y'
>>> str1[4]
'r'
>>> str1[7]
'l'
>>> str1[8]
'a'
>>> str1[0]
'C'
```

As we can see, the first character, C, is retrieved by the index [0] and the last character by the index [8]. There are 9 characters in the string.

We can also use the negative index to traverse from the end of the string. Note that str1[-0] is the same as str1[-9] and str1[0], which is the character C for the above string.

str1[-1] is the last character a.

str1[-2] is one before that, which is l.

Since there are 9 characters in all, the address of the first character is **str1[-9]** with the negative index.

Look at the listing below, which confirms the above.

```
>>> str1[-0]
'c'
>>> str1[-1]
'a'
>>> str1[-2]
'1'
>>> str1[-8]
'y'
>>> str1[-9]
'c'
```

Substring: Slicing

A substring is some part of a string. Suppose there are 10 characters in a string. There can be 10 substrings with 1 character each per sub-string. Then, we can take two characters at a time and form substrings, but we cannot alter the order of substrings, the reason for which will be discussed very shortly. Neither can we leave out a character in between. If we start at position 2 and go up to 4, we cannot leave any character. Then, we can take 3 characters at a time and create substrings. As an exercise, calculate the total number of substrings we can create out of a string with 10 characters.

The selection of one or more characters from a string is called slicing.

The general form of slicing is given below:

```
string_object[start_index: end_index+1]
```

string_object[2:7] will return the slice of the string from index 2 to index 6.

We can slice strings as given below:

```
>>> str1='mango box'
```

When we try to access the string as given below, we will get the string from 0th position up to (8-1) 7th position:

```
>>> str1[0:8]
'mango bo'
>>> str1[-1] # finding the value at the first position from the end of the
string
'x'
>>> str1[-9] # finding the value at the first position from the end of the
string
```

```
'm'
>>> str1[7] # finding the value at 7ᵗʰ position.
'o'
```

Note carefully that when we count from the start of the string, the index starts from zero. When we traverse from the end, the index starts from -1.

During slicing, when the starting index is missing, it is assumed to be zero. The following operation will get us the string from the beginning till index 8:

```
>>> str1[:9]
'mango box'
```

When the ending address is given, we slice up to index (end-1). If the ending index is missing, we slice up to the last character:

```
>>> str1[4:]
'o box'  # slice from index till end
```

We can always slice giving both starting address and ending address falling within the range of the indices of the string as given below:

```
>>> print(str1[3:5])  # slice from index 3 to (5-1)
go
>>> print(str1[2:5]) # slice from index 2 to 4
ngo
>>> print(str1[3:7]) # slice from index 3 to 6
go b
```

Reversing a string

An object in Python is called iterable if we can get an iterator from it. We will learn about iterators later. Most built-in containers in Python such as list, tuple, string etc. are iterables. Strings can be reversed (like other iterables), by slicing the string. To reverse any iterable, we use [::-1].

The -1 acts as a step argument, by which Python starts at the last value and increments by -1. An example of reversing a string is given below:

```
>>> str1='oh my god'
>>> print(str1[::-1])
dog ym ho
```

This method of traversing a string in the reverse direction is useful in many applications.

Immutable strings

A string cannot be altered after it is created. It can only be accessed for reading and NOT for writing. So it is immutable. If we try to assign a new character to any of the indices of a string, we will get an error. For instance:

```
str1="Rain"
str1[1]='o'
```

If we try to alter the character at index 1, we will get an error. However, we can assign a new string to a string variable. For instance:

```
str1='cloud'
```

This will work. While individual elements of a string cannot be altered, we can reassign a new string to a string variable. The former situation can be handled as given below:

```
str1="Roin"
```

In this case, the original contents of the variable will be lost.

Repetition

It is important to note that there is no separate built-in type for characters in Python. We can assign a single character to a string as given below:

```
str2='m'
```

We can also create an empty string, as shown below:

```
str3=""
```

A character has to be treated in the same way as we handle strings. We can repeat characters and strings as many times as we need, as the following indicates. The following will repeat string **e** 20 times:

```
>>> 'e'*20
'eeeeeeeeeeeeeeeeeeee'
>>> 'elephant'*4   # repeats 'elephant' four times
'elephantelephantelephantelephant'
```

Note that the repetition creates a string again, as indicated by the opening and closing quotation marks.

String methods

Every programming language has many predefined functions associated with it. We studied mathematical functions and other functions in *Chapter 1, Introduction to Python 3.* These functions are called library functions or built-in functions. It will be clear in *Chapter*

6, *Functions and Recursion*, that a function is a group of statements that will carry out an assigned task. In addition, to check characteristics of strings there are several methods defined as given in *Table 4.2*:

islower()	Checks whether all characters in the string are in lowercase.
isupper()	Checks whether all characters in the string are in uppercase.
istitle()	Checks whether the strings in a sentence are in title case.
isalpha()	Checks whether all characters in the string are alphabets.
isdigit()	Checks whether all characters in the string are digits.
isalnum()	Checks whether all characters in the string are alphabets or digits.
startswith()	Checks whether the string starts with a given value.
endswith()	Checks whether the string ends with a given value.

Table 4.2: String methods

Let us try these methods. The listing below gives the successful evaluation of the string methods:

```
>>> str1='elephant'
>>> str1.islower() # Checks whether all characters in str1 are in lc
True
>>> str1.isalpha() # are all of them alphabets
True
>>> str1.isupper()  # are they all in upper case
False
>>> str1.isalnum() # are they alphabets or numbers
True
>>> str1.isdigit()  # are they digits
False
>>> str1.startswith('e') # does it start with e
True
>>> str1.endswith('t') # does it end with t
True
```

The methods above checked the characteristics of strings.

Methods for modifying strings

We have methods for modifying the strings. The following string methods do that:

`upper()`	Converts string to uppercase.
`capitalize()`	Converts the first character to uppercase.
`lower()`	Converts string to lowercase.
`title()`	Converts string to title case.
`swapcase()`	Swap cases in the string.
`find()`	Searches for a value and returns its position.
`replace()`	Replaces one value with another.
`split()`	Split the string at a given string.

Table 4.3: Methods for modifying strings

We will use these methods and see the results to confirm our understanding:

```
>>> str1.find('p')
3
>>> str1.replace('h', 'k') # replace 'h' with 'k'
'elepkant'
>>> str1.split('a') # It splits the string at 'a' and deletes 'a'
['eleph', 'nt']
>>> str1='I own a house'
>>> str1.split('o')
['I ', 'wn a h', 'use']
>>> str1.capitalize()  # first character changed to Upper Case
'Elephant'
>>> str1.upper() # Converts all characters to Upper Case
'ELEPHANT'
# The string str1 remains as 'elephant'
>>> str1.swapcase()# Changes case
'ELEPHANT'
```

We can also use the lower(), upper() and title() methods to modify sentences as given below:

```
>>> str1='These are string methods'
>>> print(str1.title())# convert str1 to title case
These Are String Methods
```

```
>>> print(str1.lower())
these are string methods
>>> print(str1.upper())
THESE ARE STRING METHODS
```

Note that all these operations do not alter the contents of the string **str1**. Look at the following example:

```
>>> str1='aBcDeF'
>>> str1.swapcase() # toggle case
'AbCdEf'
>>> str1
'aBcDeF'
```

Although the **swapcase()** worked alright, the contents of **str1** did not change. This is the case with all the string modifying methods since strings are immutable. While the string methods give the desired output, the original string is available with the original name.

Replace substrings with replace()

To replace substrings, we can use the replace method. This works for any type of string, including a white space.

An example is given below:

```
>>> str1='oh my god'
>>> print(str1.replace('my', 'Great'))
oh Great god
```

The replace method takes two arguments, substring to be replaced and substring replacing it.

ord() and chr() functions

Python allows converting ASCII characters to numbers and vice versa using **ord()** and **chr()** functions.

chr(number) converts number to character.

ord(character) converts characters to numbers. Peruse the listing below:

```
>>> chr(45)
'-'
>>> chr(89)
'Y'
```

```
>>> ord('a')
97
>>> ord('z')
122
```

We will use these functions later.

Reversing a string

An object in Python is called iterable if we can get an iterator from it. We will learn about iterators later. Most built-in containers in Python such as list, tuple, string etc. are iterables. Strings can be reversed (like other iterables), by slicing the string. To reverse any iterable, we use [::-1].

The -1 acts as a step argument, by which Python starts at the last value and increments by -1. An example of reversing a string is given below:

```
>>> str1='oh my god'
>>> print(str1[::-1])
dog ym ho
```

This method of traversing a string in the reverse direction is useful in many applications.

Console input of a string

We know that **input()** function gets a string when it is not prefixed with **eval()** function. Let us write a program to read a string typed using the keyboard. It is given below:

```
# Program E4x2.py
# getting a string typed by the user
# prompt the user to enter a string
strx=input("Enter a string:  ")
print(strx)
```

The user is prompted to enter a string. The string entered is stored as strx. It is then printed. Look at the result of the program given below:

```
===================== RESTART: E:/Py programs/E4x2.py =====================
Enter a string:  shri Rama Jeyam
shri Rama Jeyam
```

Console output

Let us now study console output. The default output device is the console monitor. We will discuss the salient points of printing to the console monitor in the following paragraphs.

The syntax of the print function is given below:

```
print(value(s), sep= ' ', end = '\n', file=file, flush=flush)
```

We will discuss the parameters of the print function in parentheses. The parameters give the general form of the print function. It is important to understand them.

- **Value(s):** Any value, and as many as we like, there is no upper limit. The values will be converted to a string before printing.

- **sep='separator' (Optional):** We can optionally specify how to separate the objects if there is more than one. The default is ' '. We use commas often.

- **end='end' (Optional):** We can optionally specify what to print at the end. The default is newline characters '\n'.

- **file: (Optional):** An object with a write method. Default :sys.stdout. The stdout is the console monitor. We can omit it.

- **flush : (Optional):** A Boolean, specifying if the output is flushed (True) or buffered (False). Default: False. We will omit it conveniently.

The print function returns output to the monitor. Let us write a few programs to understand the print function:

```
'''Program E4x3.py'''
var1='Ganesh'
var2='karthik'
print(var1,'\n', var2, '\n')
```

In the above program, we print **var1** and take the output to the next line through the newline character and then print **var2**, followed by a newline character. Here, we are not concatenating, but it works fine. Look at the result of the program:

```
==================== RESTART: E:/Py programs/E4x3.py ====================
Ganesh
Karthik
```

We have a similar program given below to print one string followed by another. We declare comma as the separator and so the strings will be separated by a comma:

```
'''Program E4x4.py'''
var1='Ganesh'
```

```
var2='karthik'
print(var1, var2, sep=',')
```

===================== RESTART: E:/Py programs/E4x4.py =====================

```
Ganesh,karthik
```

We will now print numbers and strings. The numbers will be converted into a string and printed:

```
#Program E4x5.py
var1='Ganesh'
var2='karthik'
var3=27
var4=15.5
print(var1, var2,var3, var4, sep=',')
```

The result of the program is given below:

===================== RESTART: E:/Py programs/E4x5.py =====================

```
Ganesh,karthik,27,15.5
```

We used comma as a separator in the above program. We will now use the default separator and use other types of *ends*:

```
#Program E4x6.py
var1='Ganesh'
var2='karthik'
var3=27
var4=15.5
print(var1, var2,var3, var4,sep='@', end='#')
print(var1, var2, var3, var4, sep='...', end='$')
```

The result of the program is given below:

===================== RESTART: E:/Py programs/E4x6.py =====================

```
Ganesh@karthik@27@15.5#Ganesh...karthik...27...15.5$
```

In this program, we tried two **sep** and 2 **end** to demonstrate the flexibility of the print function. Since we specified **end**, the **end** we specified was printed at the end instead of the default newline character. Hence when the second **print** statement was encountered the printing continued in the same line after printing all the 4 variables and a # at the end.

Formatted printing

We want to make an attractive and easily understandable presentation of results of the programs. The formatted printing helps in printing with different styles. Several methods of formatted printing are available. They can be grouped into 4 categories as given below:

- Using built-in format method
- Using % for string formatting
- Using **str.format** method
- Using **fstrings**

Using built-in format method

The built-in **format()** method returns a formatted representation of given integers, real numbers, strings and percentages by using the built-in format specifiers. The **format()** function is similar to the string format method. Internally, both methods call **__format__ ()** method of an object or the method defined in the respective class **str**. It is interesting to see that the objects have access to their built-in method, such as **__format__** and **__iter__** (to be discussed later) in Python.

While the built-in **format()** function is a low-level implementation for formatting an object using **__format__()** internally, string **format()** is a higher-level implementation able to perform complex formatting operations on multiple object strings. Let us now use the **format** method with objects.

Floating point numbers

We may wish to get the output in the format of our choice. This facility is important when we deal with floating-point numbers. For instance, in the case of currency, we need exactly 2 digits after the decimal point. We can format a floating-point number as given below:

```
format (item, format-specifier)
```

Let us look at an example below:

```
>>> value=3.1414
>>> print('value =', format(value, '0.2f'))
value = 3.14
```

Here the **value** is first converted to a string and printed as a string. Since we have specified 2 digits after the decimal point, the other digits of the value from the third location after the decimal point are omitted. The **f** is called the conversion code, which sets the formatting for floating-point numbers. Note that the printing of numbers is carried out as strings. As a general rule, the format for floating-point numbers is as given below:

```
width.precision f
```

Here, **width** refers to the total width of the converted string, including the decimal point, and **precision** refers to the number of digits after the decimal point. In the above example, we have specified a width of 0. Let us look at a few more examples:

```
>>> print (format(4567.35, '6.2f'))
4567.35  # total number of digits 6 and 2 digits after (.)
>>> print (format(567.35, '6.3f'))
567.350 # here the total number of digits is 6 and 3 digits after (.)
```

What happens if the width is greater than required? If the total width is more, then the number is printed with leading spaces, as the following indicates. However, the number of digits after the decimal place will be regulated as per the format, and in this case, to 2 decimal places:

```
>>> print(format(123.678, '10.2f'))
    123.68
```

The printing usually starts from the beginning of the line. Here there are leading spaces due to the excess width more than the space required. In the following example, without any harm, it has added a zero at the end of the fractional part since we have specified a precision of 3:

```
>>> print(format(456.56, '7.3f'))
456.560
```

What happens if the width is less than required? Will it truncate the whole part of the number? No, the printing will exceed the total space specified and print the whole number. The number's width is automatically increased, as the following indicates:

```
>>> print(format(123456.679, '8.3f'))
123456.679
```

The total width printed is 10, and the digits before the decimal point are printed fully. We can also specify zero for the width. In that case, the total width is automatically set to the required size as given below:

```
>>> print(format(123.678, '0.2f'))
123.68
```

What happens if we omit the *f*? It prints the number in scientific notation by default as the following indicates:

```
>>> print(format(456.56, '7.3'))
4.57e+02
```

It has rounded the number, which is not desired. So do not forget to add *f*.

Formatting in scientific notation

If we wish to format a real number in scientific notation, we write *e* instead of **f** in the format. Let us see how it prints the above in scientific notation:

```
>>> print(format(456.56, '7.3e'))
4.566e+02
```

This is more precise. We must include either **f** or **e** in the format.

Let us execute 2 more statements of printing in scientific notation:

```
>>> print(format(1234.71, '10.2e'))
  1.23e+03
```

In the above, extra space is available on the left as a leading space. Compare this printing with the next statement where space is given correctly. In the latter case, there is no leading space:

```
>>> print(format(1234.71, '6.2e'))
1.23e+03
```

Formatting as a percentage

Instead of conversion character **e** or **f**, use %. This will convert the number as a percentage, as the following listing illustrates:

```
>>> print(format(0.9, '5.2%'))# we need total 5 spaces incl. 2 for %
90.00%
>>> print(format(0.05, '6.2%'))# 1 extra space gives leading space
 5.00%
>>> print(format(6.2, '6.2%'))# Here 1 is 100%
620.00%
```

Note that the % format multiplies the number by 100. Number 1 means 100%.

Justification while printing

All the above printing is justified, giving us a leading space if the width is more than required. If we want left justification, we have to insert < sign before the format as the following indicates:

```
>>> print(format(0.67, '10.2%'))
    67.00%
>>> print(format(0.67, '<10.2%'))
67.00%
```

In the first **print** above < is absent, meaning that the printing should be right justified. In the next print, it should be left justified due to the presence of < as a prefix to the format specifier. The output brings out right and left justifications, respectively.

Formatting integers

When we specify the format for integers, we specify the width and the type of integer, as well as whether the number has to be displayed with left justification or right justification. To specify type of integer, we use the following format:

- b for binary
- d for decimal
- x for hexadecimal
- o for octal

Let us see some examples, which are given below:

```
>>> print(format(457, '10d'))  # right justified decimal width 10
       457
>>> print(format(457, '<6x')) # left justified hexadecimal width 6
1c9
>>> print(format(457, '<6o')) # octal width 6 left justified
711
>>> print(format(457, '10b')) # right justified binary width 10
 111001001
```

While we give the decimal number in the print statement, it is converted to the specified base of the number format and printed in all the above 4 print statements.

Formatting strings

We use conversion character *s* to format a string. We can even omit s as the following examples indicate. To right-justify a string we add **>** sign and to left justify we add **<** sign. If the string is longer than the width specified, the width is automatically increased. Look at the following example:

```
>>> print(format('wonderful weather', '>22')) # right justified
     wonderful weather
>>> print(format('wonderful weather', '<22')) # left-justified
wonderful weather
>>> print(format('wonderful weather', '>10')) # less space
wonderful weather
```

When the width specified is less than the size of the string, the width is automatically increased to suit the requirement.

Use of %s as a place holder

In the following program, the conversion character %s (the C language fame) is used to write a formatted string. We initially define the variables and assign them values. We have inserted %s wherever we wish to insert the variables, and the variables themselves are given in parentheses at the end of the string with a prefix of %. Look at the program below:

```
# program E4x7.py

# formatted printing
name='saxena'
year='second'
str1 = 'name is %s and year is %s' % (name, year)
print (str1)
```

In the above program, we have inserted a conversion character as in C language. But the syntax is different in Python. Note the presence of % before the variables. When we print it in the console monitor, which is a standard output device, we get the following result:

```
======================= RESTART: E:/Py programs/E4x7.py
=======================
name is saxena and year is second
```

Note the ease of formatted printing.

Using str.format method

The **str.format()** is one of the string formatting methods in Python 3. It enables substitutions and value formatting. This method lets us concatenate elements within a string through positional formatting.

Passing variables to the placeholder

The formatters permit us to put one or more replacement fields and placeholders. The placeholders are defined by a pair of curly braces inside a string. We are calling the **str. format()** function to print the strings with variables substituted. The values we wish to put into the placeholders and concatenate them with the string are passed as parameters to the format function. The value could be an integer, floating-point number, and string. We know that all strings in Python are constants since strings are immutable.

A program to demonstrate the format is given below. The previous program is rewritten with format function. The use of %s does not need a format function, as the previous program demonstrated:

```
# program E4x8.py
# formatted printing
name='saxena'
year='second'
str1 = "name is {} and year is {}"
print (str1.format(name,year))
```

Formatters work by putting in one or more replacement fields or placeholders — defined by a pair of braces {} — into a string and calling the **str.format()** method. We will pass into the method the value we want to concatenate with the string.

The result of the program is given below:

```
==================== RESTART: E:/Py programs/E4x8.py ====================
name is saxena and year is second
```

Note that the variables passed are placed in the placeholders sequentially.

Passing values to the placeholders

Let us now write a program with 5 place holders and pass the actual values instead of variables as in the previous example to the **str1.format** function. It is given below. The place holders will be substituted with strings passed to the format function:

```
# program E4x9.py
# Multiple placeholders
str1 = "name is {} and {}{} year {} {}"
print (str1.format("krishna", 'studying ', 'fourth', 'at', 'SRM'))
```

The result of the program is given below:

```
==================== RESTART: E:/Py programs/E4x9.py ====================
name is krishna and studying fourth year at SRM
```

Positional arguments

In the last two programs, the placeholders { } were empty. Python replaced the values passed to the **format()** functions in the place holders in the correct order. We can even insert the index or the positional order in the placeholders instead of keeping them blank. The values that are passed to the **format()** function are tuple data types and each value contained in the tuple can be called by its index, which starts with 0. These index numbers can be placed in the curly braces that serve as the placeholders in the string to be printed. Let us write a program to understand positional arguments:

```
# program E4x10.py
# positional arguments
```

```
str1 = "name is {0} and {1}{2} year {3} {4}"
print (str1.format("krishna", 'studying ', 'fourth', 'at', 'SRM'))
```

In the above program, placeholders are not empty. We have placed the index of the values passed to the format function. The index of the string in the first position is 0, and that of the last string is 4. Note that the indices need not appear in the string in the same order. Depending on the need the indices can be placed at the appropriate placeholders. Look at the results of executing the program:

```
==================== RESTART: E:/Py programs/E4x10.py ====================
name is krishna and studying fourth year at SRM
```

The difference between the previous program and the above is that the index of the values passed to the format function are placed within the braces. Formatted printing gives the user flexibility in printing.

Using formatters for variable substitution can be an effective way to concatenate strings and organize values and data. Formatters represent a simple way for passing variable substitutions into a string and are useful for making sure output is readable and user-friendly.

Using Python string module and Template class

Python has a string module. The module has a class called **Template**. We can use the Template for formatted printing. This class is used to create a string template for simpler string substitutions as described in **Python Enhancement Proposal** (**PEP 292**). The **Template** class supports new rules for string substitution. Once the Template has been created, substitutions can be performed.

Here is a program. The **from** keyword is used to import only a specified section from a module. In this case we template from string:

```
# program E4x11.py
# Template
from string import Template
s = Template('${name} was born in ${country}')
print(s.substitute(name='Gandhi', country='India'))
s=Template('${name} plays ${sport}')
print(s.substitute(name='Dhoni', sport='Cricket'))
print(s.substitute(name='Viswanathan Anand', sport='Chess'))
```

In the program, we import the **Template** class from the string module at line 3. At line 4 we create **Template** and pass a string to it with **${name}** and **${country}** as place holders. In between, there is a string. We substitute the place holders with **s.substitute** method

'Gandhi' and *'India'* respectively and print it. At line 5 we created another template. At line 6 and line 7 we print substituting the placeholders preceded by $ sign. The result of the program is given below.

```
===================== RESTART: E:/Py programs/E4x11.py ====================
Gandhi was born in India
Dhoni plays Cricket
Viswanathan Anand plays Chess
```

Note that we created the following variables in the program above:

- name
- country
- sport

Using fstring

Python Enhancement Proposal (PEP 498) introduced a new formatted printing methodology for strings commonly known commonly known as fstrings (because of the leading **f** character preceding the string literal). The idea behind fstrings is to make string interpolation simpler.

To create an fstring, prefix the string with the letter **f** and pass it to a **print** function. The string can be formatted in the same way as we did with **str.format()**. The fstrings provide a concise and convenient way to embed Python expressions inside string literals for formatting. A simple example follows:

```
name="John"
greeting =f"Hello, {name}"
print(greeting)
Hello, John
```

We will look at two more examples of using fstring.

Checking whether a string is a palindrome or anagram

A word is a palindrome if we get the same word when we read it in the reverse. The code for checking whether a word is palindrome is given below:

```
>>> str1='malayalam'
>>> if str1==str1[::-1]:
        print(f'{str1} is a palindrome')
```

In the above, we use:: -1 to reverse the string as discussed in the example for reversing a string. When the reversed string is equal to the original string, we print that the string is a palindrome. Note that we are using formatted printing indicated by **f** prefix to the concatenated string argument. The curly braces are placeholders for the string literals. The result of executing the code is given below:

```
malayalam is a palindrome
```

If two words have the same characters, they are called anagrams. For instance, listen and silent are anagrams. To find whether two strings are anagrams, we sort the words and check for equality as shown below:

```
>>> str1='listen'
>>> str2='silent'
>>> if sorted(str1)==sorted(str2):
        print(f'{str1} and {str2} are anagrams')
```

Again, we are using formatted printing, which simplifies the printing process. We use 2 placeholders for the 2 strings. The result of executing the above in Python interpreter is below:

```
listen and silent are anagrams
```

String module constants

String module contains the set of alphabets, numbers, punctuation marks etc. defined in Python. Let us look at such constants defined in the string module by executing the following program:

```
# program E4x12.py
import string
# string module constants
print(string.ascii_letters)
print(string.ascii_lowercase)
print(string.ascii_uppercase)
print(string.digits)
print(string.hexdigits)
print(string.punctuation)
```

The result of the program follows:

```
==================== RESTART: E:/Py programs/E4x12.py ====================
abcdefghijklmnopqrstuvwxyzABCDEFGHIJKLMNOPQRSTUVWXYZ # ASCII chars
abcdefghijklmnopqrstuvwxyz # ASCII lower case
```

```
ABCDEFGHIJKLMNOPQRSTUVWXYZ # ASCII upper case
0123456789 # ASCII digits
0123456789abcdefABCDEF # ASCII hexadecimal digits
!"#$%&'()*+,-./:;<=>?@[\]^_`{|}~  # Punctuation marks
```

The output of the program gives the constants of the **string** module. They are ASCII lowercase alphabets, uppercase alphabets, digits, hexadecimal digits and punctuation marks.

Sequence types

Sequences allow us to store multiple values in an organized and efficient fashion. The elements of the sequences can be accessed by indices. Python supports six sequence types as given below:

- Unicode strings
- Lists
- Tuples
- bytearray
- bytes
- Range objects.

The strings, tuples, bytes and range are immutable sequences. The lists and bytearray are mutable sequences. The bytes function returns a "bytes" object, which is an immutable sequence of small integers in the range $0 <= x < 256$. They are printed as ASCII characters when displayed. The bytearray returns a new array of bytes. The bytearray type is a mutable sequence of small integers in the range $0 <= x < 256$. The range type represents an immutable sequence of numbers and is commonly used for looping a specific number of times in for loops. We will use the range function in the next chapter. The list and tuple will be discussed in the later chapters.

Converting string to bytes

Conversion from string to bytes is required in file handling and Machine Learning. In Python 3 strings are **str** type and they are Unicode code points. If we want to store these **str** type strings in files we convert them to bytes type. Default encoding is UTF-8 instead of ASCII. We convert strings to bytes and write to files and we convert bytes to string when we read from the file.

The **bytes()** is a built in function and returns a bytes object. It can convert various objects into bytes objects. The syntax of the **bytes** function is given below:

```
bytes(x, encoding, error)
```

x: A source to use when creating the bytes object. A string is of interest now.

Encoding: The encoding of the string e.g. UTF-8

Error: Specifies what to do if the encoding fails - optional.

We will discuss two ways in which string can be converted to bytes.

Method 1: Using bytes(str, enc)

Strings can be converted to bytes using the **bytes** function. This function is available in the Library. It calls the encode function for converting the string to the specified encoding. The program is given below:

```
'''Program E4x13.py'''
# Conversion of strings to bytes
str1='God is Love'
print("The string for conversion : " + str(str1))
# Conversion
byt1 = bytes(str1, 'utf-8') # converts str1 to bytes in UTF-8 format
print('bytes=  ', byt1)
print("bytes string: " + str(byt1))
print("type : " + str(type(byt1)))
```

The result is given below. The function **bytes()** essentially adds **b** to the string:

```
==================== RESTART: E:\Py programs\E4x13.py ====================
The string for conversion: God is Love
bytes=   b'God is Love'
bytes string: b'God is Love'
type : <class 'bytes'>
```

Note that the *bytes* and *bytes string* are preceded by b'. The type of *byt1* is bytes.

Method 2: Using encode

We can convert string to byte using the encode method. In Python 3, the **encode()** method is used to encode a string into a specific byte encoding. Strings in Python are Unicode by default, but when you need to store or transmit text data, it often needs to be converted to a sequence of bytes in a specific character encoding, such as UTF-8, UTF-16, or ASCII.

The basic syntax of the **encode()** method is as follows:

```
encoded_bytes = string.encode(encoding, errors='strict')
```

The **encode()** method encodes the string, using the specified encoding. If no encoding is specified, UTF-8 will be used:

- **string:** The string to be encoded.

- **encoding:** The character encoding to use for the encoding process. It's a string specifying the encoding, such as 'utf-8', 'utf-16', 'ascii', etc.

- **errors (optional):** Specifies how to handle encoding errors. The default is 'strict', which raises a UnicodeEncodeError if an error occurs. Other options include 'ignore', 'replace', 'xmlcharrefreplace', etc.

The following program converts string to bytes using method 2:

```
'''Program E4x14.py'''
# Conversion of strings to bytes
str1='God is Love'
print("The string for conversion : " + str(str1))
# Conversion
byt1 = str1.encode('utf-8')
print('bytes=  ', byt1)
print("byte string: " + str(byt1))
print( "type : " + str(type(byt1)))
```

The result of the program is given below:

```
===================== RESTART: E:/Py programs/E4x14.py ====================
The string for conversion : God is Love
bytes=   b'God is Love'
byte string: b'God is Love'
type : <class 'bytes'>
```

Note that we get identical results as the previous program. In both the programs we converted strings to type **bytes**.

Conclusion

These are the days of computing in many natural languages thanks to the acceptance of Unicode worldwide. In this chapter, we learned Unicode transformation formats, UTF-8 and UTF-16 for multi-lingual computing. We understood that a string is an array of Unicode characters of type **str** and it is immutable. In this chapter we also learned various string methods, and more importantly slicing. We learnt several methods of formatted printing available in Python. We came across a new class, called **Template**, residing in the string module. We learned how to use a template for string substitutions as described in Python Enhancement Proposal (PEP 292). We also studied examples of *fstrings* added in the Python Enhancement Proposal (PEP 498).

In the next chapter, we will learn about various types of operators, such as relational and logical operators, and use them for implementing conditional branching of the program with **if**, **elif** and **else** keywords. We will also discuss iterations and repeated execution of statements using keywords.

Points to remember

- Each ASCII character is represented by a 7-bit ASCII code. The decimal equivalent of the ASCII codes corresponds to numbers ranging from 0 to 127, thus giving ASCII code for 128 English characters.

- Unicode is the universal character encoding, maintained by the Unicode Consortium.

- A Unicode character starts with \u followed by 4 hexadecimal digits starting from \u0000 to \uFFFF.

- **UTF-8:** A character in UTF8 can be from 1 to 4 bytes long. UTF-8 is backward compatible with ASCII. UTF-8 is the preferred encoding for e-mail and web pages.

- **UTF-16:** 16-bit Unicode Transformation Format is a variable-length character encoding for Unicode, capable of encoding the entire Unicode repertoire. UTF-16 is used in major operating systems and environments, like Microsoft Windows, Java and .NET.

- A string is an array of Unicode characters, consisting of not only English characters but characters from any Natural language supported by the Unicode consortium.

  o The number of characters in a string may vary from zero to any length.

  o It should be enclosed within single or double quotation marks on both sides and assigned to a string variable.

- Multi-line strings can be assigned in 3 different ways:

  o By using triple quotes

  o By enclosing the string within parentheses

  o Using an escape character \

- We can use the overloaded + operator to concatenate two strings.

- Strings are of type <class 'str'> or in other words they are objects of <class 'str'>.

- The *str* function can be used to convert numbers into strings.

- Retaining single and double quote inside the string can be achieved by:

  o Using escape character \

  o Treating the string as a raw string by prefixing r before the string

- The character escape sequences are given in *Table 4.1*.

- The index of a string starts at 0 and if the width of a string is n characters, the index of the last character in the string is (n-1). The elements of a string can be accessed by the index value.

- Strings are immutable.

- The selection of one or more characters out of a string is called slicing.

  o The general form of slicing is given below:

  string_object[start_index: end_index+1 :Step]

  The default step size is 1.

- It is important to note that there is no separate type for characters in Python. We can assign a single character to a string.

- We can repeat characters and string as many times as we need.

- String methods are given in *Table 4.2*.

- Methods to modify strings are given in *Table 4.3*.

- Python allows converting ASCII characters to numbers and vice versa using ord() and chr() functions:

  o chr(number) converts the number to a character.

  o ord(character) converts a character to number.

- The syntax of the print function is given below:

  print(value(s), sep=' ', end ='\n', file=file, flush=flush)

  o Value(s): Any value, and as many as we like, there is no upper limit. The values will be converted to the strings before printing.

- The print function returns output to the console monitor.

- Formatting printing:

  o Several methods of formatted printing are available. They can be grouped into 4 categories as given below.

- o Using built-in format method
- o Using '%' for string formatting
- o Using str.format method
- o Using Template class in string module
- o Using fstrings
- There is module called string. It is a built-in module, and we must import it to know the constants and classes defined in the module.
- A new class, called Template, resides in the string module. We can use a template for string substitutions as described in Python Enhancement Proposal (PEP 292).
- The 6 sequence types in Python were listed.
- The bytes () function returns an immutable bytes object:
  - o It can convert strings into bytes objects.

Questions

Choose the most appropriate answer:

1. **The first 128 characters of Unicode:**
   a. Have same binary value as ASCII
   b. Coded with a single octet
   c. Is compatible with UTF-8
   d. All of the above
   e. None of the above

2. **Variable-length character encoding is followed in:**
   a. UTF-8
   b. UTF-16
   c. None of the above

3. **A string:**
   a. is an array of characters
   b. enclosed within quotes
   c. can have zero characters
   d. All of the above
   e. None of the above

4. **Multi-line strings can be assigned by:**

   a. Using triple quotes

   b. Enclosing the string within parentheses

   c. Using \

   d. All of the above

   e. None of the above

5. **The index of 'p' in elephant is:**

   a. -5

   b. 5

   c. 4

   d. None of the above

6. **if str1='banana', substring 'nan' can be obtained by:**

   a. str1[-2:-4]

   b. str1[:]

   c. str1[3:5]

   d. None of the above

7. **In str1 above, find('b') will return:**

   a. 1'

   b. 0

   c. -1

   d. None of the above

8. **In formatted printing, '10.3f' means, the non-fractional part of the number can occupy:**

   a. 7 places

   b. 6 places

   c. 10 places

   d. None of the above

9. **In formatting integers, the character o refers to:**

   a. Octal

   b. Decimal

   c. Hexadecimal

   d. None of the above

10. **function ord():**

    a. converts a character to number

    b. converts a number to character

    c. None of the above

11. **ord('b') will return:**

    a. 97

    b. 98

    c. 99

    d. None of the above

- Write short notes on the following:

  o ASCII Character set

  o Unicode

  o UTF8 and UTF 16

  o Multiline string

  o Forward Indexing and reverse indexing

  o Slicing

  o Formatted printing methods

  o *bytes* function

  o The string module and its uses

  o String methods

- Match the following:

A	B
Template	1. Left justification
UTF-16	2. Starting address 0
Bytes function	3. Variable length
<	4. Import from string
str1[:8]	5. Returns byte object

- Write programs for the following:

  o To get the list of English alphabets and digits supported in Python.

  o To print all the vowels of the Hindi language.

  o To find the type of the following:

  o 78.5, 67, 3+4j, 'string'

  o Write a template for displaying the name and marks obtained by 10 students in a class.

  o To convert a string to bytes in 2 ways.

  o Get 3 strings from the console and concatenate them.

  o Get a real number from the console, round it, and convert and print it as an integer, octal, hex, and binary numbers.

  o Use formatted printing to print all the 7 days of the week in the following format:

  o Monday is day 1 of the week

  o Print the first 100 natural numbers with width 5, as left justified first and then right justified.

  o To convert the following string into bytes:

    ❖ 'Two little ducks'

    ❖ "Hard work pays"

CHAPTER 5

Selection and Loops

Introduction

Different segments of codes can be selected for execution, satisfying certain conditions. The conditions are checked using relational and/or logical operators in an expression. The outcome of evaluating the expressions containing the conditions coined using the operators will be True or False. When we wish to execute a few operations repeatedly, we use the iteration or loop keywords. This chapter deals with creating loops.

Structure

This chapter covers the following topics:

- Structuring programs
- Relational operators
- Logical operators
- Selection constructs
- Nested selection constructs
- Ternary operator

- Iterations

- Generation of mathematical tables

- Keywords *break* and *continue*

Objectives

This chapter will explain the three basic structures found in programs. We will discuss the use of the keywords *if, elif,* and *else* to implement selecting appropriate code segments for execution based on certain conditions. We will also discuss ternary operators for selection in simple situations of selection. The chapter covers *for* loop and *while* loop for executing a set of instructions repeatedly as long as the condition expression remains True. The use of keywords *break* and *continue* in loops is also demonstrated.

Structuring programs

In the early days of computing, programming was an art, and the quality of the program depended only on the ability of the individual chosen for programming. In the modern world, we must break the myth and reduce dependence on individuals. Structured programming is a programming paradigm aimed at improving the clarity and quality and, at the same time, reducing the development time of a computer program by making extensive use of the structured control flow constructs of selection (if/else) and repetition (while and for), block structures, and subroutines. The subroutines are known by other names, such as functions, procedures, and methods. In this chapter, exposure will be given to structured control flow constructs of selection and repetition.

Two computer scientists, *Corrado Bohm,* and *Giuseppe Jacopini* proved that any computer program could be written only with the following three program structures:

- Sequences

- Decisions

- Loops

In structured programming, program flow control is advised to be restricted to the three structures or to a structure derivable from a combination of the basic three. Thus, a structured program should not use GOTOs. Programming languages such as C, C++, Golang and C sharp allow GOTO statements, which alter the program flow abruptly. Python does not support the GOTO construct. The result is a program built of modules that are independent of each other but interdependent to solve the problem. In turn, this gives confidence to a programmer that the code contains fewer logic errors and will be easier to debug and change in the future if a need arises. This observation is a precursor to the evolution of a methodology for modern programming, known as structured programming. Structured programming is the name given to good programming practices.

It is a preferred methodology for programming in procedure-oriented languages such as C. Python is both a procedure-oriented and Object-Oriented- Programming language like C++. Structured programming consists of guidelines for designing programs with built-in quality and reliability.

In this chapter, we will discuss conditional selection and conditional iteration (repetition or looping) constructs supported by Python. In both cases, we will check whether a condition turns out to be true or not, and accordingly, the program execution will take different paths of program execution. To check whether a condition is true or not, Python provides relational operators, logical operators, and Boolean data type, which can contain values True and False.

Relational operators

When we wish to construct selection and loop programming elements, we need relational operators and logical operators. The relational operators are used to check the relationship between two numeric operands, strings or expressions. The relational operators of Python are given below:

- Greater than (>). For example, x > y means, Is x greater than y?

- Less than (<). For example, x < y means, Is x less than y?

- Greater than or equal (> =). For example, x > = y means, Is x greater than or equal to y?

- Less than or equal (< =). For example, x < = y means, Is x less than or equal to y?

- Equal (==). For example, x==y means, Is x equal to y?

- Not Equal (!=). For example, x!=y means, Is x not equal to y?

The result of this comparison will lead to a Boolean outcome: True or False. Let us now use the interactive mode to confirm the functioning of relational operators. Look at the listing below:

```
>>> x=8  # x assigned a value of 8
>>> y=6
>>> x>y  # Is x greater than y?
True
>>> x<y
False
>>> x==y
False
>>> x!=y # Is x not equal to y?
```

```
True
>>> x>=y  # Is x greater than or equal to y?
True
>>> x<=y
False
"C">"c"
False
"coin"=="coin"
True
"meity"<="Meity"
False
"meity">="Meity"
True
```

From the above example, we have understood the use of all 6 relational operators. Also, note that the value of the lowercase alphabet is higher than the uppercase alphabet. Notice that to check equality between two numbers, we use double equal to (==), and for assignments, we use one equal to sign.

Logical operators

We may need to combine multiple conditions in a program. For instance, if we wish to find natural numbers, we may check whether a number is positive and whether it is a whole number. If both conditions are True, we call it a natural number. To combine two or more conditions, we need logical operators. Python provides three logical operators, as given below:

- and
- or
- not

and operator

The operator **and** is used to check, for instance, whether both condition 1 and condition 2 are True. If any of the two conditions is false, the result will be False. Let us try this in the interactive mode of Python. It is given below.

We first assign number **25** to variable **age** and **male** to variable **gender**, as shown:

```
>>> age=25
>>> gender='male'
```

```
>>> if age>=25 and gender=='male':
        premium=1000
        print('premium=', premium)
```

```
premium= 1000
```

In the above example, we are checking two conditions as given below:

```
age>=25
```

```
gender=='male'
```

We have an **if** statement where we combine the above 2 conditions with a logical operator **and** as shown below:

```
age>=25 and gender=='male'
```

It is followed by a colon(:). In the next statement, we assign 1000 to **premium** and then print *premium* in the next line. It prints **premium =1000**. We have also used two relational operators, >= and ==, in the above example. Let us now look at the operation of the **or** operator now.

or operator

The operator **or** is used to check whether condition 1 or condition 2 is True. If both two conditions are false, then the result will be False. Here, after assigning values to **age** and **gender**, we check two conditions as given as part of the **if** statement. The conditions and their Boolean output are given below:

- **age<=25**. It is False since age is assigned 30.

- **gender=='female'**. It is True.

  ```
  >>> age=30
  >>> gender='female'
   >>> if age<=25 or gender=='female':
          premium=750
          print('premium=', premium)
  ```

  ```
  premium= 750
  ```

Since one of the two conditions is True, we get **premium=750** since we are using the **or** operator. We also used two relational operators, <= and ==, in the above.

The above are binary operators, meaning that they operate on 2 operands. The **not** operator is a unary operator that operates on a single argument.

not operator

The function of the operator **not** is like the complement operator. If a condition is True, the result will be False, and vice versa.

Here, we are continuing with the assignments in the previous paragraph. The comparison **gender=='male'** will be False. Since we are prefixing it with **not**, **not gender=='male'** will return True, and hence premium is printed 1250:

```
>>> if not gender=='male':
        premium=1250
        print('premium=', premium)


premium= 1250
```

The **not** negates the outcome of a relational and/or logical expression.

Selection constructs

Python provides the following three keywords to implement conditional branching:

- if
- elif
- else

We have used **if** in the standalone mode. There are two companions to **if**, that is, **elif** and **else**. In any given situation for conditional branching, there will be one if, zero, or more **elif** and optionally one **else**.

The syntax of the selection constructs follows:

```
if (condition 1 == True):  # parentheses not necessary
        statement(s) # on the Tab type 1 or more statements
elif (condition 2 == True): # parentheses not necessary
        statement(s)    # on the Tab type 1 or more statements
# we can have more than one elif with different conditions
else:
        statement(s)  # on the Tab type 1 or more statements
```

Note the following statements with regard to the syntax given above:

- Conditional statements need not be enclosed in parentheses.
- Conditional statement should be terminated by : (colon)

- Statement(s) means one or more statements typed on the Tab in one line after another. Indentation is not optional but a must.

- **if (condition 1 == True)** can be simply written **if(condition 1)**

- **if condition 1 == False** could be written as **if (not condition 1)**

- The above two apply to **elif** also.

- There can be more **elif** with different conditions.

- **elif** is optional. It need not be there.

- **else** is also optional.

- In the three examples given in the above paragraph, **elif** and **else** were not there. Those are the simplest selection statements.

- The statements following **if**, **elif**, and else should be typed on the next tab of the respective definitions. This is critical. Otherwise, we will get a syntax error.

Finding whether a number is positive

Let us write a program to understand the selection constructs of Python. The program is given below:

```
'''Program E5x1.py'''

x=-6

if x>0:
    print('positive number')
elif x==0:
    print('zero')
else:
    print('negative number')
```

In the program, a comment statement has been included within a pair of triple quotes in the first line. The program has all three keywords of the selection constructs of Python. At line 2, we assign -6 to *x*. In line 3, we have the **if** statement followed by a colon. That ends the definition of **if**. In the **if** statement, we check whether x is greater than zero. If the condition is True, we **print ('positive number')**.

If **x** is NOT greater than zero, our program jumps to the definition of **elif**. There, we check whether **x==0**. If so, we **print('zero'.)**

If both **if** and **elif** statements return **False**, that is, *x* is not greater than or equal to zero, then the program control moves to the **else** block. There, we **print('negative number')**.

Since we have initialized x with -6, the *else* part will operate and **print('negative number')**. This is how the program works.

The result of the program follows:

```
========================= RESTART: E:/Py programs/E5x1.py
=======================
negative number
```

Swap case

Let us write a program to get an English alphabet typed by the user. If the user types a lower-case alphabet, the program should convert it to upper-case and vice versa. If they do not type either an uppercase or lower-case alphabet, we display an error message.

In Unicode and ASCII, the characters (a..z) and (A..Z) are stored contiguously. They have a numeric value associated with them. If we subtract 32 from the numeric value of say,' *a'*, we will get the numeric value of '*A'* and so on up to 'z'. Hence, when we add 32 to the numeric value of '*A'*, we will get the numeric value of '*a'*. We will use this fact to swap the lowercase to the upper-case alphabet and vice versa.

The program is given below. In the third line of the program, we get the user input of an English character and will store it as a string named **alpha**. In the fourth line, we check whether it is a lowercase letter. If so we get the numeric value of the alphabet with the **ord()** function. Then, in the next line, we get the alphabet whose numeric value is less than 32 of the typed alphabets.

A similar thing is repeated in the next **elif** block for the conversion of uppercase letter to lowercase. If the user enters a non-alphabet, the conditions in both **if** and **elif** statements will turn out to be False. As a result, the **else** block will be invoked, which prints the error message.

```
'''Program E5x2.py'''
# to change case
alpha=input('enter an English character :')
if alpha >='a' and alpha<='z' :
    y=ord(alpha)
    print(chr(y-32))
elif alpha >='A' and alpha<='Z' :
    y=ord(alpha)
    print(chr(y+32))
else:
    print('invalid character')
```

The result of the program is given below:

```
==================== RESTART: E:/Py programs/E5x2.py
====================
enter an English character :g
G
>>>
==================== RESTART: E:/Py programs/E5x2.py
====================
enter an English character :A
a
>>>
==================== RESTART: E:/Py programs/E5x2.py
====================
enter an English character :9
invalid character
```

The above program illustrates the use of **if**, **elif**, and **else** blocks and also gives us a method to swap English alphabets from lower case to upper case and vice versa.

Finding the largest of three numbers

Let us write a program to find the largest of three numbers. For the sake of simplicity, the numbers are defined in the program itself.

Look at the program. Notice that on top of the program, we have a multiple assignment statement **x=y=z=12**. This is allowed in Python. All three variables are set equal to 12. In the **if** statement, we check whether **x** is greater than **y** and **x** is also greater than **z**. If the condition evaluates to be True, we print: **x is the largest**. Then, in the first **elif** statement, we check whether **y** is greater than **x** and **y** is also greater than **z**. If the condition evaluates to be True, we print: **y is the largest**. Then, in the second **elif** statement following the first **elif**, we check whether **z** is greater than **x** and **z** is also greater than **y**. If the condition evaluates to be True, we print: **z is the largest**. If all three conditions turned out to be false, the numbers should be equal, then the **else** block will be executed. It will then **print('all 3 numbers are equal')**:

```
'''Program E5x3.py'''
x=y=z=12
if x>y and x>z:
    print('x is largest')
elif y>x and y>z:
    print('y is largest')
```

```
elif z>x and z>y:
    print('z is largest')
else:
    print('all 3 numbers are equal')
```

The result of the program is given below:

```
======================= RESTART: E:/Py programs/E5x3.py
=======================
all 3 numbers are equal
```

Since we initialized all three numbers to 12, the **else** block is executed skipping the **if** and 2 **elif** blocks.

However, because of the availability of logical operators, the length of the program will be larger.

Nested selection constructs

We can nest **if..else** blocks. A program has been written to illustrate the concept and is given below. Let us look at the program. In the program, we wish to receive the three numbers from the user. We ask the user to enter 3 numbers at line 3. The first number typed will be received as **x**, the second number as **y**, and the third number as **z**. See the simplicity of console input in Python. The input function will receive the numbers typed as strings. Hence, we use the **eval** function to convert them to numbers.

In the first **if** block in the program, we check whether **x==y==z**. This is allowed. It first evaluates *if* **x==y** and gets a result. If that is False, then there is no need to compare further. If a comparison turns out to be True, the interpreter will proceed to compare with **z**, and if it is False, the **if** statement will return False. Note that any non-zero number is True, and zero is False in Python, like in other languages such as C and C++.

The first **if** is followed by an **else**. If all three numbers are not equal, the control goes to the *else* block where there is one **if** and 2 **elif**. The logic for the rest of the program is the same as the previous program. Here, what we essentially do is that we check whether all 3 numbers are equal; if not, we check one by one to find out which number is the largest.:

```
'''Program E5x4.py'''
# nested if-else
x, y, z=eval(input('Enter 3 numbers:'))
if(x==y==z):
    print('all 3 numbers are equal')
else:
    if x>y and x>z:
```

```
        print('first number is largest')
    elif y>x and y>z:
        print('second number is largest')
    elif z>x and z>y:
        print('third number is largest')
```

The result of the program is given below:

```
====================== RESTART: E:\Py programs\E5x4.py
======================
Enter 3 numbers:67, 98, 11
second number is largest
>>>
====================== RESTART: E:\Py programs\E5x4.py
======================
Enter 3 numbers:99, 12, 9
first number is largest
>>>
====================== RESTART: E:\Py programs\E5x4.py
======================
Enter 3 numbers:4, 4, 4
all 3 numbers are equal
```

The program demonstrated nested **if..elif..else**. In fact, the **else** is followed by **if** and 2 **elif** statements. The nesting sometimes may lead to logical errors, and hence, the programmer should evaluate the expressions carefully.

Ternary operator

Ternary operators are popular in other programming languages also. We can use it in smaller problems as the following example will illustrate. Ternary operators are more commonly known as conditional expressions or conditional operators in Python. It allows the programmer to test a condition in a single line replacing the multiline if-else, resulting in compact code. It is called a ternary operator since there are 3 parts of the operator. A condition part is in the middle, and action results from the condition on either side, as illustrated below:

<statement 1> <condition> <statement 2>

If the condition is True, **<statement 1>** will be executed, and if it is False, <statement 2> will be executed.

Four examples of conditional operators are as follows:

```
>>> result=25%3
>>> print('divisible' if result==0 else 'not divisible')
```

The above example finds the remainder when 25 is divided by 3. In the next statement, **if result==0** is True, we print **'divisible'**. If it is False, we print **'not divisible'**. The result of the conditional expression follows:

```
not divisible
```

In the conditional expression below, we test whether the remainder is zero when 25 is divided by 5 in the expression itself. If it is True, we print **'divisible'**, and if not, we print **'not divisible'**:

```
>>> print('divisible' if 25%5 ==0 else 'not divisible')
```

```
divisible
```

In the following conditional expression, we find the remainder when divided by 2. If it is zero, we print **'even',** and if not **'odd'**:

```
>>> print('Even' if 36%2==0 else 'odd')
Even
```

In the following example, we find **c** as **a%b**. If the remainder is 1, **c** is true and will print **'odd'**. If the remainder is zero, **c** turns out to be false, and in that situation, **'even'** will be printed:

```
>>> a=77
>>> b=2
>>> c=a%b
>>> print('odd' if c else 'even')
Odd
```

Another example is given below. If the number is less than 10 **isLesser** will be True, otherwise it will be False:

```
>>> x=25
>>> isLesser=True if x<10 else False
>>> print(isLesser)
False
```

Ternary operators evaluate something based on a condition being True or False. It facilitates testing a condition in a single line. The ternary operators can be used in simple situations as mentioned above.

Iterations

Python supports the following keywords for executing a set of instructions repeatedly as long as a condition remains *True*:

- while

- for

While loop

The syntax of **while** loop is given below:

```
while condition:
    statement(s)1
else:
    statement(s)2
```

When the condition turns out to be **True**, the **statement(s)1** will be executed. If it is **False statement(s)2** will be executed. Note the following with reference to the above syntax:

- There can be more than one statement(s).

- Note the colon in the definition of *while* (at the end of the *while* statement)

- It is mandatory to place the statement(s) at the first Tab after the starting location of *while*.

- The **else** block is optional.

The **while** loop is executed till the condition is False.

Let us now write a program to find the sum of the first 10 natural numbers:

```
# Program E5x5.py
# Finding sum of 10 natural numbers
sum=0
x=1
while x<=10:
    sum=sum+x
    x+=1
else:
    print( sum)
```

Let us analyze the program. We initialize **sum** to zero and then **x** to 1 at the third and fourth lines of the program, respectively. In line 5, we enter the **while** loop. The statements in the

while block will be executed so long as **x** is less than or equal to 10. Each iteration of the **while** loop starts after the colon and ends before the **else**. In the **while** loop we add **x** to **sum** and then increment *x* which is 2 after the first iteration of the **while** loop. Since **x** is not more than 10, the statements will be repeated until **x= 10**. In each iteration, the new value of **x** is added to the sum. The loop will iterate 10 times, adding 1,2,.., 10 to **sum** each iteration successively. When **x** becomes 11 the **else** part is executed. In the **else** part we print the sum. The result of the program is given below:

```
======================= RESTART: E:/Py programs/E5x5.py
=====================
55
```

Testing whether a number is prime using while loop.

Let us write a program to test whether a given number is prime or not. An algorithm to find whether a number is prime or not is given in *Chapter 2, Algorithmic Problem Solving* with a description. Read it and then read the program below implementing the algorithm:

```
'''Program E5x6.py
finding whether a given number is prime'''
div=2
prime=1
num=eval(input("Enter the number to be checked for prime: "))
while div*div<=num and prime:
    if(num%div==0):
        print(num, " is divisible by ", div)
        prime=0
    else:
        div = div+1
if(prime):
    print(num, " is prime")
```

The algorithm is translated into the program. The **while** loop iterates when both conditions are true. When we find that a number is divisible, we assign 0 to **prime** and the iteration stops. Note that in the program, if the first **if** turns out to be **True**, the **if** in the last statement will be **False**. Let us check the correctness of the program by testing it with a prime number and a divisible number:

```
======================= RESTART: E:/Py programs/E5x6.py
=====================
Enter the number to be checked for prime: 111
111  is divisible by  3
>>>
```

```
======================== RESTART: E:/Py programs/E5x6.py
========================
Enter the number to be checked for prime: 31
31   is prime
```

The range function

The range is one of the six sequences. The **range** function returns an immutable sequence object of integers in the form of a list. We will use it in the **for** loop to keep count of the number of iterations.

For loop

The syntax of **for** loop is given below:

for var in range(x):

      statement(s)1

else:

      statement(s)2

The **range** is a built-in function in Python. It contains a list of numbers in the given range from 0 to (*x*-1). When the variable **var** is within the range of numbers, the **statement(s)1** will be executed. If it is False, that is, **var** is outside the range, then **statement(s)2** will be executed. Note the following with reference to the above syntax:

- There can be more than one statement(s).

- Note the colon in the definition of **for** (at the end of the *for* statement)

- It is mandatory to place the statement(s) at the first Tab after the starting location of **for**.

- The **else** block is optional.

- The **for** loop starts with the first number in the range, which is zero and continues till range-1.

- The number in the range is stepped up by 1 in each iteration.

- Note the use of keyword **in** before **range**.

Let us write a simple program. The program is given in Python Tutorial:

```
'''Program E5x7.py'''
# Demonstration of for loop
for var in range(10):
    print (var)
```

The **range** is given as 10. The numbers in the **range** start from 0 and will proceed up to 9. The **var** is printed and stepped up by 1 each time until it reaches and includes the value of 9. The result of the program is given below:

```
======================= RESTART: E:/Py programs/E5x7.py
=======================
0
1
2
3
4
5
6
7
8
9
```

The **for** loop advances the iterator through the **range** automatically after every iteration. It stops only when no number is left in the **range**. Now, let us use the for loop to solve the same problem of finding the sum of the first 10 natural numbers. The **for** loop will iterate when the counter **x** is in the range specified with the range function, as shown:

```
# Program E5x8.py
# Finding sum of 10 natural numbers
sum=0
for x in range(1, 11):
    sum=sum+x
else:
    print( sum)
```

Here, the **range** function has 2 parameters. When the range has 1 parameter, the range starts from 0. When there are 2 parameters, the **range** starts from the start index, that is, the first number, and goes up to the second index -1. The function **range (x,y)** returns a sequence of integers x, x+1...y-1.

Be aware that Python is sensitive to Tabs. Note carefully where the first alphabet of statements at the 5th and 7th lines of the above program are placed. If we do not place them in those places, we will get errors. Note that **in** is a Python keyword. The result of the program follows:

```
======================= RESTART: E:/Py programs/E5x8.py
=======================
55
```

Variations in range function

range(x) is the same as **range(0,x)**.

range(x,y, i) - **i** is the increment step. For instance, (20, 40, 2). This function will give values from 20 to 38 in steps of 2.

The value of i is 1 by default.

Let us look at an example:

```
# Program E5x9.py

print ('even numbers in the range 10 to 19')
for x in range(10, 20, 2):
    print(x)
```

The result of the program follows:

```
======================== RESTART: E:/Py programs/E5x9.py
======================
even numbers in the range 10 to 19
10
12
14
16
18
```

Note that the range will start from a lower value but will stop 1 number below the upper value. This is why the number 20 was not printed. The loop will terminate when x=19.

The for loop using list

Instead of range in the **for** loop, we can use a list as shown below:

```
for var in list:
        statement(s)1
else:
        statement(s)2
```

We will study **list** soon. In the meantime, assume that the list is like an array.

Finding maximum and minimum numbers in a list

In *Chapter 2, Algorithmic Problem Solving,* we studied an algorithm for finding maximum and minimum numbers in a list. Let us write a program implementing the algorithm for finding the maximum and minimum numbers in a list. It is given below.

In this program, we will initialize both the **max** and **min** with 0th element of **list1**. Then the first **if** checks whether every other number (var) is greater than **max** and if so, assign that value to **max**. Similarly, the second **if** checks whether every other member (var) is smaller than **min** and if so, assign that value to **min**. When the list1 is exhausted, we print the largest and smallest values in the list:

```
'''Program E5x10.py'''
# Finding largest and smallest numbers in list
list1=[111, 333, 456, 77, 9]
max=min=list1[0]
for var in list1:
    if (var > max):
        max = var

    if var <min:
        min=var


else:
    print('largest=', max)
    print('smallest=', min)
```

The result of the program is given below:

```
======================= RESTART: E:\Py programs\E5x10.py
=======================
largest= 456
smallest= 9
```

Generation of mathematical tables

A program to generate mathematical multiplication tables is given below. We have assigned **a** as 1, and in the 6th line, we ask the user to enter their choice about which table they want. The user can enter any positive number. This is assigned to **b**. The **for** loop will iterate 20 times with **a** from 1 to 20. In the **for** loop, we find the product and print one line for each iteration, as shown:

```
'''Program E5x11.py
use for - You can generate multiplication
tables of your choice using this program'''
product=0
b=eval(input('Enter which table you want : '))
```

```
for a in range(1,21):
    product = a*b
    print(a,'X',b,'=',product)
```

The result of the program where we wanted the table for 15 is given below:

```
======================= RESTART: E:\Py programs\E5x11.py
=======================
Enter which table you want : 15
1 X 15 = 15
2 X 15 = 30
3 X 15 = 45
4 X 15 = 60
5 X 15 = 75
6 X 15 = 90
7 X 15 = 105
8 X 15 = 120
9 X 15 = 135
10 X 15 = 150
11 X 15 = 165
12 X 15 = 180
13 X 15 = 195
14 X 15 = 210
15 X 15 = 225
16 X 15 = 240
17 X 15 = 255
18 X 15 = 270
19 X 15 = 285
20 X 15 = 300
```

Keywords break and continue

The keywords **break** and **continue** are discussed in this section.

When the loop is iterating, **break** will terminate the iteration abruptly. On the contrary, the **continue** keyword will skip the current iteration. The following program illustrates the concept of **break**:

```
# Program E5x12.py
# Finding factorial of a given number
```

```
fact=1
x=1
num=eval(input("Enter the number to find factorial:"))
while x<=num:
    fact=fact*x
    if fact>20000:
        break
    x+=1
else:
    print(fact)
```

If factorial (fact) exceeds 20000 at some stage, the program execution stops abruptly without any message. Look at the result carefully. The factorial of 8 and above exceed 20000. Whenever it exceeds, the program execution stops abruptly without any message as the result of the program indicates:

```
======================= RESTART: E:\Py programs\E5x12.py
=======================
Enter the number to find factorial:5
120
>>>
======================= RESTART: E:\Py programs\E5x12.py
=======================
Enter the number to find factorial:8
>>>
======================= RESTART: E:\Py programs\E5x12.py
=======================
Enter the number to find factorial:7
5040
```

Now let us write a program to find odd numbers less than 10. It is given below:

```
# Program E5x13.py
# Finding odd numbers less than 10
x=0
while x<10:
    x+=1
    if x%2==0:
        continue
    else:
        print(x, "is odd number")
```

What is happening in the program? In the **while** loop, x is incremented to 1. If the remainder when we divide x by 2 is 0, the iteration will be skipped due to the **continue**, which takes program control to the top of the loop. In the first iteration, when x becomes 1, the remainder is 1, and hence, the program jumps to the else block, and "1 is odd number" will be printed. Then we get to the top of the **while** block and increment x to 2. Since the remainder will be zero, the iteration will be skipped. The **continue** keyword there will take us to the top of the **while** loop and x will be incremented to 3 and so on. The result of the program is given below:

```
======================= RESTART: E:\Py programs\E5x13.py
=======================
1 is odd number
3 is odd number
5 is odd number
7 is odd number
9 is odd number
```

Keywords learnt in this chapter

Let us recount the keywords discussed in this chapter. It is 13, as detailed below:

- if
- elif
- else
- and
- or
- not
- while
- for
- True
- False.
- in
- break
- continue

We have used 13 out of 35 keywords in this chapter.

We have made only a beginning in using selection and repetition concepts. We will use the concepts learned in the entire book.

Conclusion

Python programs comprise sequences of instructions, decision-making blocks, and loops. In this chapter, we learned how to use if, elif, and else keywords to branch to different code segments. The branching constructs rely on the use of relational and logical operators, which were illustrated through programs. We also used nested if, as well as ternary operators. Quite often, we need to execute a few instructions repeatedly, which are called iterations or loops. We constructed loops using **for** and **while**. We used the *break* and *continue* as part of loops. The keyword *in* was used in conjunction with loops and range functions.

In the next chapter, we will discuss functions and recursion – a function calling itself.

Points to remember

- Any computer program could be written only with the following three program control structures:
  - o Sequences
  - o Decisions
  - o Loops
- There are six relational operators to compare numbers, strings or expressions.
- There are three logical operators such as **and**, **or**, and **not** to combine multiple conditions.
- The outcome of applying relational operators and/or logical operators is one of the following:
  - o True
  - o False
- The syntax of the selection constructs is as follows:

```
        if (condition 1 is True):  # parentheses not necessary
            statement(s) # on the Tab type 1 or more statements
    elif (condition 2 is True): # parentheses not necessary
            statement(s)    # on the Tab type 1 or more statements
    # we can have more than one elif with different conditions
    else:
            statement(s)  # on the Tab type 1 or more statements
```

- We can have a multiple assignment statement such as x=y=z=12. This is allowed in Python.

- We can nest **if..else** blocks.

- Ternary operators are more commonly known as conditional expressions or conditional operators in Python. It allows the programmer to test a condition in a single line replacing the multiline if-else, resulting in compact code.

- Python has the following keywords for executing a set of instructions repeatedly when a condition is true:

  o while

  o for

- The syntax of **while** loop is given below:

```
while condition:
            statement(s)1
else:
            statement(s)2
```

  When the **condition** turns out to be True the **statement(s)1** will be executed. If it is False **statement(s)2** Will be executed.

- The syntax of **for** loop is given below:

```
for var in range(x):
            statement(s)1
else:
            statement(s)2
```

- The **range** is a built-in function in Python. It contains a list of numbers in the given range from 0 to *x-1*. When the variable *var* is within the range of numbers, the **statement(s)1** will be executed. If it is False **statement(s)2** will be executed.

- range(x) is same as range(0,x).

- range(x,y, i) - i is the increment step. For instance, (20, 40, 2). This function will give values from 20 to 38 in steps of 2. The value of i is 1 by default.

- Instead of range in the *for* loop, we can use a list as shown below:

```
for var in list:
            statement(s)1
else:
            statement(s)2
```

- **else** is optional everywhere.

- The keywords **break** and **continue** have the following uses.

  o When the loop is iterating, the **break** will terminate the iteration abruptly. On the contrary, the **continue** keyword will skip the current iteration.

Questions

Choose the most appropriate answer.

1. **Given x=6 and y=6.0, which of the following comparison will be True:**

    a. x>y

    b. x>=y

    c. x<y

    d. None of the above.

2. **Boolean outcomes are:**

    a. True

    b. False

    c. All of the above

    d. None of the above.

3. **Given that we have grade A for marks above 90 and grade B marks otherwise. If marks obtained are 90, the grade awarded will be:**

    a. A

    b. B

    c. None of the above

4.
```
age=25
gender='male'
if age>=25 and gender=='male':
        premium=1000
else:
        premium = 500
print(premium)
```
In the above program If gender ='Female', it will print:

    a. 500

    b. 1000

    c. premium

    d. None of the above

5. **Which of the following is a unary operator:**

    a. and

    b. not

    c. >=

    d. All of the above

    e. None of the above

6. **The continue statement:**

    a. Terminates the program

    b. A place holder

    c. Takes to top of the loop

    d. All of the above

    e. None of the above

7. `while     :`

        `x=x+1`

will result in:

    a. Syntax error

    b. Run-time error

    c. Endless loop

    d. None of the above

8. *else*: **block after for is:**

    a. Mandatory

    b. Optional.

    c. None of the above

9. **for x in range(len(array)) will iterate till:**

   a. len(array)

   b. len(array)-1

   c. len(array-1)

   d. None of the above

10. **The starting number of x in range(x) is:**

    a. 0

    b. 1

    c. None of the above

- Write short notes on the following:

  o How if and while statements fit in structured programming?

  o Write the syntax of while and give an example to illustrate the concept.

  o Write the syntax of for and give an example to illustrate the concept.

  o Write the syntax of if, elif and else and give an example to illustrate the concept.

  o Structuring programs.

  o Compare while and for.

  o Conditional expression.

  o Use of range and list with for loop.

  o Write the following code with while loop:
  ```
  sum=0
  for x in range(1, 11):
          sum=sum+x
  ```

- Match the following:

A	B
and	1. skips the current iteration
break	2. logical operator
elif	3. relational operator
==	4. terminates iteration
continue	5. follows if

- Write programs for the following:

  o The Lucas sequence is 1, 3, 4, 7, 11, 18, 29.

  o The third number is the sum of the previous two numbers. Write an algorithm and a program to print out the first ten numbers of a Lucas sequence.

  o Given that in a sequence, the next number is obtained by adding the last four numbers repeatedly, write a program to generate the first 20 numbers of the sequence. Given also that the first four numbers are 0, 0, 1, and 1.

  o Write a program that will print the natural numbers which are evenly divisible by:

    11, 13, 19, 23, 37.

  o Write a program to print the value of the number in words when the number entered is in the range of 0 to 999.

  o To find out whether a triangle is scalene, isosceles, or equilateral from the sides given.

  o To find even numbers up to 100.

  o To toggle the upper case to lower case and vice versa of alphabets in a word.

  o In a company the basic pay of employees ranges from Rs.5000 to Rs.20000. The formula for HRA and DA are given below:

Basic pay	DA	HRA
₹ 5000 -10000	50% of basic pay	₹ 5000
₹ 10001 -15000	40% of basic pay	₹ 10000
₹ 15001-20000	30% of basic pay subject to a minimum of Rs.6000	₹ 15000

Write a program to find out the salary = Basic pay + DA + HRA, given the basic pay.

Join our book's Discord space

Join the book's Discord Workspace for Latest updates, Offers, Tech happenings around the world, New Release and Sessions with the Authors:

https://discord.bpbonline.com

CHAPTER 6

Functions and Recursion

Introduction

Structured programming has evolved to reduce the chances of errors in programming and improve the quality of programs. The functions promote structured programming. A host of predefined and tested functions exist as part of the Python standard library, which is used by programmers wherever needed. In addition, users develop their own functions to carry out specific tasks. Functions are standalone and can be used in a variety of application programs. The chapter explains fruitful functions and void functions. A function may call one or more functions. It may call itself, which is called recursion. This chapter will be looking at both functions and recursions in detail.

Structure

The chapter covers the following topics:

- Features of structured programming
- Benefits of structured programming
- Built-in functions
- User-defined functions
- General form of function

- Illustrative programs

- Fruitful functions

- Return values

- Another fruitful function

- Runtime stack

- Boolean functions

- Divisibility of a number

- Local and global scope of function parameters

- More function concepts

- Recursion

- Case study: Towers of Hanoi

Objectives

The chapter explains the built-in or library functions and user defined functions. It illustrates the two constituents of a function –function call and function definition. The function definition, in turn, consists of the function header and function body. The chapter covers variable length arguments and their applications. The runtime stack stores intermediate results of execution of the current function before calling another function. The chapter covers recursion extensively and gives interesting programs like the Towers of Hanoi.

Features of structured programming

We will continue the discussions we had in the previous chapter on structured programming. Structured programming demands that the program should be constructed using independent modules or functions or sub-routines. In Python, functions are one of the key enablers of structured programming. The primary purpose of structured programming is to create the right programs the right first time and every time. It enables the design of a program that is understandable, testable, and easily modifiable. Structured programming encourages dividing an application program into a hierarchy of modules or autonomous elements, which may, in turn, contain other such elements. Within each element, code may be further structured using blocks of related logic designed to improve readability and maintainability.

Recall that the top-down design model involves designing the overall program structure first, followed by designing individual functions. Each function is coded as a separate module. The modules are tested individually and later integrated with other modules.

The modules should be designed in such a manner that they have one entry point and one exit point for each function. This modularization has many advantages. One of them is that the modules can be reused in other programs.

Since the top-down structured design is advocated during the high-level design of the program, several functions would have been identified with clear specifications. Therefore, many programmers can work in parallel, designing one module each, enabling work parallelism. Furthermore, the programmers will understand the role of each of the functions in the overall program structure since they have access to the big picture from the top-level design document very early in the project. Structured programming facilitates divide and conquer of the problem, thereby helping in focusing on one problem at a time rather than on smaller problems. All of these lead to quick turn-around time for the development of the software.

Benefits of structured programming

The benefits of structured programming are summarized as follows:

- **Reusability:** Reusability is facilitated by the modular design of the program. Each function is a good candidate for reusability in different programming projects.

- **Ease of debugging:** Since each function is specialized and performs only one task, the functionality can be checked individually. Small codes will be easier to debug rather than larger programs. Since there will be clarity of the specifications of each function, a wrong understanding will be avoided while developing and testing the program.

- **Enhanced understanding:** Structured programming advocates adequate comment statements and documentation. It also advocates coining meaningful names for the functions as well as variables and constants. All of these facilitate ease of understanding of the complete program.

- **Ease of maintenance:** The time taken to locate the module that contains errors will be much shorter in modular structured programs. Since the functions are cohesive and there is a lesser coupling between functions, the side effects of maintenance will also be minimal.

Due to its advantages, structured programming has become popular in the procedure-oriented programming paradigm. The main objective of structured programming is to plan and develop the software as a collection of functions. Python, an open-source language, was developed to enable this concept. Structured programming also means that the execution of statements progresses linearly. There is no back-and-forth traversal while executing the program. The program uses a single entry and single exit pattern. Therefore, structured programming results in understandable programs.

Built-in functions

Python contains several built-in functions. They are also called library functions of Python. What is a built-in function? These functions are pre-written and tested and available when we download Python. We have already used some of them, such as **input()**, **eval()**, **print()**, **isalpha()**, **format()**, mathematical functions, etc. However, for the availability of the library function **print()**, we would have to write a routine whenever we want to print anything as part of the program. This would increase the length of the code, affect readability, and increase complexity. Therefore, it would be better to use the tested library functions as far as possible to facilitate a modular programming paradigm.

User-defined functions

Like other programming languages, we have a **main()** function in Python. In the programs we wrote, we did not specify the **main** function for brevity. Although we did not specify, the **main** function is present in every program implicitly. The **main** is the place from where the program execution starts. We write the program in such a manner that the main function calls other functions as needed for carrying out specific tasks. Each function may, in turn, call other specialized functions wherever required. Such a program will be easy to understand, debug, and maintain. To improve the quality of programming, we should, therefore, use functions wherever required. The functions supplied with the Python language are the built-in functions. Users can write additional functions, which are called user-defined functions.

We now know that each function performs a specified task. Arguments or data may be passed to the function, and the function performs some specified actions. Before we go into more detail, let us understand the usage of functions. Assuming that we want to reverse a number in a program, we split the program into two parts. The **main** function gets the number to be reversed. It passes the number to a function called **reverse**, whose specialized and only job is to get the number, reverse it, and send back the reversed number to the function that calls it.

The **main** function passes on a number to reverse whenever it wants to reverse it. The **reverse** function reverses the number and sends it back to the **main** function. Thus, the task is perfectly partitioned with perfect understanding and protocol. Later on, if some other function wants to reverse a number, it can bank upon the capability of already tested **reverse** function and use it. This is the advantage of modular programming.

General form of function

A function consists of two parts:

- Function definition
- Function call

Function definition

The function definition, in turn, consists of two parts namely function header and function body.

Function header

The function header starts with the keyword **def**. It is followed by the function named **main()** or other function name chosen by the programmer and list of formal parameters in parentheses and is terminated with a colon (:). Remember that there can be only one function named **main()** in the program, but there can be any number of other functions named otherwise. An example of a user defined function is given below:

```
def sum(num1, num2):
```

The function name in this example is **sum**. The parameters **num1** and **num2** are called formal parameters. It indicates the number of arguments to be passed to the function when invoked. The parameters we pass to the function from elsewhere in the program are called actual parameters or arguments. If no parameter needs to be passed for the execution of the function, then the list of parameters will be missing, but the parentheses should still be present.

Function body

The function body is where we put the code to carry out the specific task. The function may return a value to the called function. In such a case, we will have a statement with the **return** keyword. Some functions may explicitly return a variable, and some may not. Still, a return statement may be required in value returning functions. The function terminates when the **return** statement is executed. An example given shortly will make the concept clear.

Function call

We may call a function either directly or indirectly. What do we mean by indirectly? The function call being made as part of the print statement is an example of an indirect function call. The function call may be assigned to a variable as another example of an indirect function. We call a function at any place in the main function or other function without assigning a function to a variable or the function not becoming part of an expression. In such a case, the function is called directly. When we call the function, we pass actual arguments or values. Calling a function is also known as a function reference.

In normal cases, there must be a one-to-one correspondence between the number of formal parameters specified in the function header and the actual arguments sent. Let us look at an example.

Sum of two numbers

Let us write a program to add two numbers.

Let us assume that we wish to get two numbers from the user in the main function. Pass them to a function **sum**. Add them in the **sum** function. Return the value to the **main** function and print it in the **main** function. The algorithm for solving the problem is given below:

```
main function
Step 1:        define function sum
Step 2:        get 2 numbers
Step 3:        call sum and pass the 2 values
Step 4:        get the sum from the function sum
Step 5:        print the value of the sum
function sum
Step 1:        get the value
Step 2:        add them
Step 3:        return the value to the main
```

Here, we have divided the problem. Let us give numbers to the statements to understand how the program works. The statement numbered program is given below.

As we know the statements at line 1 and line 2 are comment statements (written in two different ways beginning with triple quotes and # respectively), which will be ignored during the execution of the program, and it is for the information of the reader. Refer to the following figure:

Figure 6.1: *Function to find sum of two numbers*

In line 3 in the above program, the definition of the function *sum* is given. It starts with a **def** keyword followed by the name of the function **sum**. The formal arguments are declared as **num1** and **num2** within the parentheses. Note that the function definition or the header ends with a colon in line3.

The body of the function **sum** is given at lines 4 and 5. In line 4, we are adding **num1** and **num2** and assigning to the **total**. In line 5 we return **total**. The definition of function **sum** ends there. Blank lines have been inserted at line 6 and line 7 for better readability.

Line 8 is a comment statement. The header of function **main()** is at line 9, preceded by the def keyword and followed by the colon. It does not receive any arguments. In lines 10 and 11, we direct the user to 'enter an integer'. The numbers entered will be stored as strings by the *input* function. We wish the program to work with the values of any type of number. That is the reason we have used the **eval** function, which converts the strings to numbers. We convert the entered string to a number using the **eval()** function. If we intend to find the sum of integers alone, we can replace eval with an int, which will convert the entered string to integers.

In line 12, we have written a print function with 2 arguments. The first one is a string, which will appear as it is when we print, and the second one calls the function **sum** with arguments (a, b). Line 13 is left blank, and in line 14, we have the main function call.

Let us discuss how the program functions. In the above program, there are 2 functions **sum** and **main**. The program starts executing from the function with the name **main** in line 14. This, in turn, passes control to the function **main()** in line 9 and the function starts executing. In line 10 and 11, the program prompts the user to enter an integer each time and the integers entered are stored in variables **a** and **b** respectively. In line 12 the program encounters function **sum** and hence the function **sum** is invoked with the values entered by the user.

Now the control passes to line 3 and **num1** is assigned the first value received and **num2** is assigned the second value received. In line 4 the total is found, and it is returned to line 12. The print function prints the string followed by the value returned by the function **sum**. Now, the job of the **main()** function is completed, and the control is returned to the user. Recall that in this program, we are invoking called function indirectly. We are also clear with the formal parameters, the placeholders, **num1**, and **num2**. The actual parameters are the values typed by the user and received in variables **a** and **b**. The **main()** and **sum()** have each function header and function body, respectively.

The result of the program follows:

```
========================= RESTART: E:/Py programs/E6x1.py
=======================
enter an integer: 12
enter an integer: 36
sum of the numbers= 48
```

Now, whenever we wish to find the sum of two numbers, int, float, or complex, using the same program, we can run the program again. Execution of the program with three different input types is given below:

```
======================= RESTART: E:\Py programs\E6x1.py
=======================
enter an integer: 23
enter an integer: 37.0
sum of the numbers= 60.0
>>>
======================= RESTART: E:\Py programs\E6x1.py
=======================
enter an integer: 4+3j
enter an integer: 3+4j
sum of the numbers= (7+7j)
>>>
======================= RESTART: E:\Py programs\E6x1.py
=======================
enter an integer: 24.5
enter an integer: 34.5
sum of the numbers= 59.0
```

Calling functions multiple times

We now propose that the program gets *a & b* values, gets their **sum1**, gets *c & d*, and gets their **sum2**, and then both the sums are passed to the function to get their total. The program calling **add** function more than once is given below:

```
'''Program E6x2.py'''
# called function
def sum(num1, num2): # function header
    total=num1+num2
    return total
# calling function
def main():
    a=eval(input('enter a number: '))
    b=eval(input('enter a number: '))
    sum1=sum(a,b)
    print('sum of the numbers a and b=', sum1)
```

```
    c=eval(input('enter a number: '))
    d=eval(input('enter a number: '))
    sum2=sum(c,d)
    print('sum of the numbers c and d=', sum2)
    print('sum of sum1 and sum2', sum(sum1,sum2))
if __name__=='__main__':
    main() # main function call
```

In the previous program, we had a **main()** after the definition of the main function. The program execution starts from the **main** function. In the future programs we will be importing other programs called modules. They may have **main** also. However, the name of the imported module will not be *main*.

When the program is executed, the runtime environment notes the definition of function **main**. When it parses the **if** statement, it checks the name of the module being executed. If it is main, then it calls the main function in the current module being executed. The purpose of the last 2 statements in the above program is to ensure that the main function in the current module is executed and not from the imported modules. Note that this is the safest way of calling the main function and not as in the previous program. However, in the rest of the programs in this book, we omit this **if** statement for the sake of brevity.

The result of the program is given below:

```
.======================== RESTART: E:/Py programs/E6x2.py
========================
enter a number: 3+5j
enter a number: 6+7j
sum of the numbers a and b= (9+12j)
enter a number: 7+12j
enter a number: 3
sum of the numbers c and d= (10+12j)
sum of sum1 = sum2 (19+24j)
```

The program and the result indicate some interesting things. We are calling function **sum** twice with the following assignment statements and then printing them:

```
        sum1 = sum( a, b )
        sum2 = sum( c, d)
```

In the third time, we call the function **sum** indirectly by passing **sum1** and **sum2** as part of the print function. Thus, the program goes back and forth between **main** & **sum** as given below:

```
        main()
```

```
        sum (a, b)
            main()
                        sum (c, d)
                main()
        sum (sum 1, sum 2)
        main()
```

Had we not used the function sum, we would have had to write statements of **sum** 3 times in the main program. Such a program would be large and difficult to read. In this method, we have to code for **sum** only once, and hence the program size is small. This is one of the reasons for the usage of functions. The functions we wrote above are user-defined.

Calling more functions in a program

We have seen a program, which calls a function thrice. We will now discuss a problem, which calls three functions.

Problem:

The user gives a four-digit number. If the number is odd, then the number must be reversed. If it is even, then the number is to be doubled. If it is evenly divisible by three, then the digits are to be added. Now let us write the algorithm for solving the problem:

```
Step 1:      get the number.
Step 2:    If the number is odd we call the reverse function.
Step 3:    else multiply the number by 2 and hence call multiply.
Step 4:    If the number is evenly divisible by 3 call add-digits.
```

These are the steps. Writing a function to multiply by 2 is simple. We will look at the algorithm for the other two steps now.

Reverse function

The algorithm for the reverse is given below:

```
    Step 1 :     rev= 0
    step 2 :     do while ( number > 0 )
                        rev = rev * 10 +  (number % 10 )
                        number = number/10
    Step 3 :     return (rev).
```

addDigits function:

```
Step 1 :      sum = 0
Step 2 :      while number > 0
              sum = sum + (number % 10)
              number = number / 10
Step 3 :      return (sum)
```

Let us see how the above algorithm adds digits and works.

Let us give 4321 as the number:

```
Step 1 :      sum = 0
Step 2 :      Iteration 1
              sum = 0 +  modulus of  (4321/10)
              = 0 + 1 = 1
              number = 4321/10 = 432
          Iteration 2
              sum = 1 + modulus of (432/10)
                  =  1 + 2
After 4 iterations
      sum =1+2+3+4
Step 3: sum is returned.
```

The above algorithm is implemented in the program below. The result of the program follows:

```python
# Program E6x3.py
# called function reverse
def reverse(number): # function header
    rev=0
    while(number > 0):
        rev = rev * 10 +  (number % 10 )
        number = number//10
    return rev
# called function multiply
def multiply(number):
    print('double of the number=', 2*number)
# called function addDigits
```

```python
def addDigits(number):
    sum = 0
    while number > 0:
            sum = sum + (number % 10)
            number = number // 10
    return (sum)


# calling function
def main():
    num=eval(input('enter a number: '))
    if num%2==1:
        print('reverse of the typed number=', reverse(num))
    else:
        multiply(num)
    if num%3==0:
        print('sum of digits=', addDigits(num))


main() # main function call
```

The result of the program is given below:

```
======================== RESTART: E:\Py programs\E6x3.py
======================
enter a number: 4231
reverse of the typed number= 1324
======================== RESTART: E:\Py programs\E6x3.py
======================
enter a number: 3933
reverse of the typed number= 3393
sum of digits= 18
======================== RESTART: E:\Py programs\E6x3.py
======================
enter a number: 4236
double of the number= 8472
sum of digits= 15
```

The program works correctly. The reader may go through the program and the results obtained. We have tried different types of return statements as well as coded 3 called functions in this program. The function **multiply()** does not return any value but the other two called functions have return values. Something interesting is happening in the above program. When we entered the number 4236 since it is not odd, the function multiply is called and after executing it there is no return statement. Even when there is a **return** statement, program control is returned to the called function. Although there is no return statement, the program control transfers to the next statement in the called function. That is how the program could call **addDigits()** function.

The void function

A function without an explicit **return** statement is called a **void** function. You might have wondered how the control returned to the **main** function in the case discussed just now. The secret is that the **void** functions return a special value called *None* to the called function. Only that facilitated return to the **main** function in the above situation.

Illustrative programs

We will write a few programs to understand the concept of Python functions.

Exchange the value of two variables

First, let us write a program to exchange the value of two variables. In *Chapter 2, Algorithmic Problem Solving-* we studied an algorithm to exchange (swap) values. We will implement the algorithm as a Python program. It is given below.

We let the user enter two variables in the main function. We call function **swap** and pass these to values of variables to it. The function **swap** exchanges the two variables and prints it. The program is given below:

```python
# program E6x4.py
# Exchange the Value of 2 variables
def swap(var1, var2):
    print('original value of var1=', var1, 'var2=', var2)
    temp=var1
    var1=var2
    var2=temp
    print('new value of var1=', var1, 'var2=', var2)
def main():
    x=input('Enter a variable:')
    y=input('Enter a variable:')
    swap(x, y) # calling swap function
main()
```

The result of the program is given below:

```
======================= RESTART: E:/Py programs/E6x4.py
=======================
Enter a variable:26.5
Enter a variable:45
original value of var1= 26.5 var2= 45
new value of var1= 45 var2= 26.5
```

In the **main** function we get two values and call function **swap** with the same values. The values have been exchanged by the **swap** function and printed by the same function successfully as the results indicate. In this program, there is no need for **swap** function to return values.

Distance between two points

Distance between the two points (x1, y1) and (x2, y2) is given by the formula:

Distance = Square root of (((x2 - x1)**2) + ((y2-y1)**2)))

For instance, let point 1 is (3, 4), and point 2 is (7, 2).

Then *(x2-x1)**2=(7-3)**2 = 42 = 16* and *(y2-y1)**2= (2-4)**2 = (-2)**2 = 4.*

now *16 + 4 =20*, and the square root of *20* is 4.47.

Therefore, the distance between (3, 4) and (7, 2) is 4.47.

The program below finds the distance between two given points. The main function receives the coordinates of the two points and passes them to function **dist**, which finds the distance using the formula above:

```
# Program E6x5.py
# Finding distance between two points
def dist(x1, y1, x2, y2):
    result= (((x2 - x1 )**2) + ((y2-y1)**2) )**0.5)
    print("distance between",(x1,y1),"and",(x2,y2),"is : ",result)
def main():
    x1=int(input("enter x1 : "))
    y1=int(input(«enter y1 : «))
    x2=int(input(«enter x2 : «))
    y2=int(input(«enter y2 : «))
    dist(x1, y1, x2, y2)
main()
```

The result of the program is given below:

```
======================= RESTART: E:/Py programs/E6x5.py
=======================
enter x1 : 3
enter y1 : 4
enter x2 : 7
enter y2 : 2
distance between (3, 4) and (7, 2) is :  4.47213595499958
```

Check the correctness of the result.

Finding square root of a positive number

As we know, Python is rich in libraries. To use mathematical functions, we import **math** library. The square root of a positive number is obtained by using **math.sqrt(x)** as the following program illustrates:

```
# Program E6x6.py
# Finding square root of a number
import math
x=eval(input("Enter a positive number for finding square root :"))
print(math.sqrt(x))
```

In the above program, the user input is converted to a number using the eval function. The execution of the program gave the following results.:

```
===================== RESTART: E:\Py programs\E6x6.py =====================
Enter a positive number for finding square root :25
5.0

===================== RESTART: E:\Py programs\E6x6.py =====================
Enter a positive number for finding square root :169
13.0
```

The results are correct.

Finding square root without using math function

Python library function **math** made it simple to find the square root of a given number. We will write a program for finding square root of a positive number assuming that **math** function is slow. The program is given below. In the program, we wish to find out the square root of x. A function **Sqrt(x)** has been defined for this purpose. We have used upper case S to distinguish from the library function **sqrt**.

We start with an initial **last_guess** of half the value of the number x, 25 whose square root we are finding. In the while loop *guess* will be equal to *(12.5 +25/12.5)/2 =7.25*

Now the difference between guess and last_guess will be (12.5-7.25). Therefore, the last_guess will be 7.25 and the while loop repeats these operations till the error is less than 0.000001. Once the difference is less than the threshold, the guess is returned to the main function, where it is printed:

```
# Program E6x7.py
# Finding the square root of a number without using math function
def Sqrt(x):
    last_guess= x/2.0
    while True:
        guess= (last_guess + x/last_guess)/2
        if abs(guess - last_guess) < .000001: # example threshold
            return guess
        last_guess= guess
def main():
    x=eval(input('Enter number whose square root is needed :'))
    print(Sqrt(x))


main()
```

We get the number **x** from the user and call function **Sqrt(x)**. The result of the program is given below:

```
===================== RESTART: E:\Py programs\E6x7.py =====================
Enter number whose square root is needed :25
5.0
>>>
===================== RESTART: E:\Py programs\E6x7.py =====================
Enter a positive number for finding square root :7.5
2.7386127875258306
===================== RESTART: E:/Py programs/E6x7.py =====================
Enter number whose square root is needed:95.75
9.785192895390463
```

Fruitful functions

In one of the previous programs, observe that the function **reverse** returned value through **rev** and **addDigits** returned value through the variable **sum**. These variables are local to the functions, and we call them local variables. Some functions may not return values explicitly. However, the program execution control goes back to the called function in both cases. Functions returning values are called *fruitful functions*. In a fruitful function, the return statement includes a return value. In such cases, we evaluate the return expression and then return it immediately as the result (the fruit) of this function to the called function.

Return values

We have already executed some fruitful functions. In the following sections, we will discuss some more fruitful functions.

The following code calculates the perimeter of a rectangle. In the function, we can write a return statement as given below:

```
def perimeter(length, breadth):
    return 2*length*breadth
```

The above code can be written in a reader-friendly manner as given below:

```
def perimeter(length, breadth):
    peri=2*length*breadth
    return peri
```

Sometimes we may have multiple return statements, one in each branch of a conditional statement as the following functions illustrate:

```
# Program E6x8.py
# Finding power
def power (x, y):
    if y==0:
        return 1
    elif y==1:
        return x
    else:
        return pow(x,y)
def main():
    x1=int(input(«enter x1 : «))
    y1=int(input(«enter y1 : «))
    print(power(x1, y1))
main()
```

The function **pow(x,y)** is a built-in library function. In the above program there are 3 return statements. The result of the program is given below:

```
==================== RESTART: E:/Py programs/E6x8.py ====================
enter x1 : 2
enter y1 : 0
1
==================== RESTART: E:/Py programs/E6x8.py ====================
enter x1 : 2
enter y1 : 1
2
==================== RESTART: E:/Py programs/E6x8.py ====================
enter x1 : 2
enter y1 : 4
16
```

The code, where the flow of execution can never reach, is called dead code, or unreachable code. In a fruitful function, it is a good idea to ensure that every possible path through the program hits a return statement as shown in the above program.

Another fruitful function

Let us write another fruitful function. This program is for finding the area of a triangle whose length for all three sides are given. The program is given below:

```python
# Program E6x9.py
# Finding area of triangle
import math
def area(a, b, c):
    s=half_perim(a,b,c)
    area1 = math.sqrt(s*(s-a)*(s-b)*(s-c))
    return area1


def half_perim(x,y, z):
        return (x+y+z)/2


def main():
    x1=int(input(«enter x1 : «))
    y1=int(input(«enter y1 : «))
    z1=int(input("enter x1 : "))
```

```
    print(area(x1, y1, z1))
main()
```

We import the math function in this program to find the square root. We have defined two functions in this program in addition to **main()**. We have a function named **area** and **half_perim**, both receiving three numbers. In the main function, we ask the user to type 3 numbers, which we convert to **int**. Then in the last line of the main function, we call the function **area**. The function *area* receives three values. In the line after the function definition of the area, we call the other function **half_perim** and assign it to **s**. The three arguments of function **half_perim** are the same as that was received by the function **area**. The **half_perim** finds half the perimeter of the triangle and returns to variable *s* in the function *area*. In the next line, we calculate the area using Heron's formula, return to the main function, and print there.

We could have received all three sides in one statement. Modify the program to do that. The result of the program is given below:

```
===================== RESTART: E:/Py programs/E6x9.py =====================
enter x1 : 18
enter y1 : 30
enter x1 : 24
216.0
```

Runtime stack

The runtime stack is a data structure that is used in Python during execution of programs. Python needs this runtime stack to maintain information about the state of the program as it executes. A stack is a data structure that lets the program push and pop elements. We push elements onto the top of the stack, and we pop elements from the top of the stack. In simple terms, if we store 3, 4, and 5 one after another in a stack, then when we retrieve (pop) the stored items, 5 will be retrieved first, 4 thereafter, and finally 3. This is a **Last In First Out (LIFO)** data structure.

A runtime stack data structure is used during the execution of the function calls. Whenever a function is invoked then the calling function is pushed into the stack and the called function is executed. When the called function completes its execution and returns, then the calling function pops from the stack and is executed. Calling function execution starts only after called function execution is completed.

When we execute functions, the system uses the run-time stack to store intermittent values. For instance, when a function f1 calls f2, the system creates an activation record for f1 and stores the variables, arguments, and other needed information in the Run-time stack. Similarly, the record of f2 will also be saved in the runtime stack before it passes control to a function, if any, called by it. Once it returns control to the called function f1, the stored data pertaining to f1 will be retrieved, and program execution will resume. In this manner, the data pertaining to the calling functions are stored for use later. Anyway, all these are handled by the system, and it is not transparent to the programmer.

In the program just executed, a function call is made from the main function to Function1 (area). Now, the state of the main function is stored in the runtime stack, and execution of the main function will be continued when Function1 returns. Fucntion1 Calls Function2 (half_perim). The state of Function1 is stored in the stack, and execution of Function1 will be continued when Function 2 returns control after completing its task. This is how functions work by using the runtime stack to store data about the calling functions.

Boolean functions

We can write a Boolean function. This is nothing new, but like any other Python function. We call them Boolean functions to make known that the function returns either True or False outcome.

Divisibility of a number

A Boolean function **is_evenly_divisible** is written here to find out whether any given integer is evenly divisible by any other integer.

In the **main** function, we get console input of two numbers **x** and **y**, and convert them to type **int**. Then we call the function **is_evenly_divisible(x,y)**. If the remainder on dividing **x** by **y** is zero, we return **True**, if not we return **False**. Depending on the return value, we write a message. If the number **x** is evenly divisible by **y**, we say so. The program is given below:

```
# Program E6x10.py
# Boolean Function
# Boolean functions
def is_evenly_divisible(x, y):
    if x % y == 0:
        return True
    else:
        return False
def main():
    x=int(input("Enter an integer:"))
    y=int(input("Enter an integer:"))
    z=is_evenly_divisible(x,y)
    if z==True:
        print(x,'is evenly divisible by ', y)
```

```
    else:
        print(x,'is NOT evenly divisible by ', y)
main()
```

The result of the program follows. We can check with any divisor:

```
==================== RESTART: E:/Py programs/E6x10.py ====================
Enter an integer:15
Enter an integer:3
15 is evenly divisible by  3
```

Since 15 is evenly divisible by 3, we got the above message. Since 26 is not evenly divisible by 5 (remainder=1), we get the following message:

```
==================== RESTART: E:/Py programs/E6x10.py ====================
Enter an integer:26
Enter an integer:5
26 is NOT evenly divisible by  5
```

The purpose of such programs is evident from their names. An important point is that the program can be used with any divisor and not any particular divisor.

Local and global scope of function parameters

The variable defined in a function is called a local variable. Local variables can be accessed only within the function. Global variables are the ones that are defined and declared outside all functions, usually on top of the program. They can also be defined anywhere with *global* prefixes. The global variables will be visible in all functions. A word of caution at this stage: global variables are to be avoided in structured programming.

If a variable with the same name as the global variable is defined inside the scope of a function as well then it will print the value given inside the function only and not the global value.

Any variable that is changed or created inside of a function is local if it has not been declared as a global variable. To tell Python that we want to use the global variable when there exists a local variable with the same, we must use the keyword global, as can be seen in the following example. To summarize, the scope of the local variable is local to the function unless otherwise specified by the keyword global. The global variable will be visible all through the program but will give way to the local variable of the same name. The program for understanding global and local variables is given below.

```
# Program E6x11.py
# global and local scope
```

```
x = 5
# Uses global because there is no local 'x'
def fun1():
    print('Inside fun1() : ', x)
# Variable 'x' is redefined as a local
def fun2():
    x = 7
    print( 'Inside fun2() : ',x)
# Uses global keyword to modify global 'x'
def fun3():
    global x
    x = 9
    print('Inside fun3() : ',x)
def main():
    print ('global : ',x)
    fun1()
    print ('global : ',x)
    fun2()
    print ('global : ',x)
    fun3()
    print ('global : ',x)
main()
```

Let us check what happens in the program step by step. The execution always starts from the **main** function.

In the second line of the **main** function, the value of the variable **x** will be the global variable, and it will print 5 since the value of the global variable is defined at the top of the program as 5.

Then the **main** calls function **fun1** at the third line. Since **fun1** does not have a local variable, it prints the global variable **x**, which is 5. After printing, it returns control to the main function. At line 4, the program will print 5, the global variable. In line 5, the **main** function calls **fun2**. Here the local variable is redefined and printed as 7. Inside the function, it will be printed as 7. It has not affected the global variable *x* and hence the value of the global variable is printed as 5 on line 6 of the **main** function. In line 7, we call **fun3**. Here, since we want to modify the global variable, we prefix **global** to **x** and assign the value of 9 and hence 9 will be printed. In line 8, also **x** will be printed as 9 since the global variable has been modified by **fun3**.

The result of the program is given below:

```
==================== RESTART: E:\Py programs\E6x11.py ====================
global :  5
Inside fun1() :  5
global :  5
Inside fun2() :  7
global :  5
Inside fun3() :  9
global :  9
```

The result is as we anticipated in the above discussions.

More function concepts

In the following sections, we will study some interesting function concepts such as positional arguments, default arguments and variable length arguments.

Positional arguments

In Python, we do not specify the types of formal parameters when we define a function. However, the arguments should be passed in the correct order. In the example below, we have to pass a string, float, and integer, in that order, to function **chng** although it is not so specified in the function header. These arguments may be called positional arguments, default arguments and variable length arguments.

```
'''Program E6x12.py'''
# called function
def chng(x,y,z): # function header
    print(x+'kumar', y+4, z*z)
# calling function
def main():
    a='krishna'
    b=9.8
    c=7
    chng(a, b,c)
main() # main function call
```

The result of the program is given below:

```
==================== RESTART: E:/Py programs/E6x12.py ====================
krishnakumar 13.8 49
```

In the above program, the actual arguments were received in the correct order as required and hence the program worked correctly. If we had changed the positional order, there would have been a problem.

Default arguments

Sometimes we assign a predefined value to the arguments in a function. If we call a function and if the number of arguments is less than the number of formal parameters, then the default arguments will be taken. In the program below the default, the arguments are y=10 and z=20. In the first call, we have:

chng(9)

x=9, and the other two are default values. Therefore sum=39.

The second call is **chng(23,65)**.

Therefore, z will be assumed to be 20 and the sum will be 108.

There should be no doubt in the third call since all the 3 variables are specified.

Look at the program and result now:

```
'''Program E6x13.py'''
# Default arguments
# called function
def chng(x,y=10,z=20): # function header
    print(x+y+z)
# calling function
def main():
    chng(9)
    chng(23, 65)
    chng(2,3,4)
main() # main function call
```

The result of the program is given below:

```
==================== RESTART: E:/Py programs/E6x13.py ====================
39
108
  9
```

An important rule to be noticed with regard to default arguments is as follows:

Assume that the function receives 3 arguments. If we call the function with 1 argument, then the argument will be received as value for the first argument. If we call the function with 2 arguments, then the two arguments will be received as values for the first and second arguments.

Variable length arguments

Python provides a wonderful facility whereby we can decide the number of arguments at runtime. If we had declared a variable length argument, the function would receive any number of arguments. This applies to both the type of arguments discussed in the last two sections. The default arguments are known as keyword arguments and the positional arguments are called non-keyword arguments.

*args and *kwargs

We can pass a variable number of arguments to a function using special symbols. There are two special symbols as given below:

- *args (Non keyword arguments)

- **kwargs (Keyword arguments)

We need not use the same name as given above. We can use any name but should be preceded by the * and ** respectively. The names - args and kwargs - are a convention and good to follow these names.

We use ***args** and ****kwargs** as an argument in the functions when we are not sure about the number of arguments to pass to the function or when we want to pass variable number of arguments at different times.

Python *args

The variable ***args** will allow us to pass variable number of non-keyword arguments to function. In the function, we should use an asterisk * before the parameter name to pass variable length arguments. The arguments are passed as a tuple (like an array, to be discussed in *Chapter 8, Tuples, Sets and Dictionaries*) and these passed arguments make a tuple inside the function with same name as the parameter excluding asterisk *.

Now, we will write a program to pass a variable number of non-keyword arguments. It is given below:

```
'''Program E6x14.py'''
# variable length arguments
# called function
def called(*args): # function header
    for var in args:
        print(var)
```

```
    print("\nData type of argument:",type(args))
# calling function
def main():
    called(9)
    called(23, 65)
    called(2,3,4)
    called(45, 67.8, 'subhash')
main() # main function call
```

The result of the program is given below:

```
==================== RESTART: E:\Py programs\E6x14.py ====================
9
Data type of argument: <class 'tuple'>
23
65
Data type of argument: <class 'tuple'>
2
3
4
Data type of argument: <class 'tuple'>
45
67.8
subhash
Data type of argument: <class 'tuple'>
```

Notice that each time we passed varying number of arguments, that is, 1, 2, 3, 3 arguments respectively to the function called and the program worked correctly. The type of arguments is immaterial since Python is dynamically typed language. The result also confirms that args is of type tuple.

Python **kwargs

Python passes variable length non-keyword argument to function using **args** but we cannot use this to pass keyword argument. We use ****kwargs**, which allows us to pass the variable length of keyword arguments (****kwargs**) to the function.

In the function, we use the double asterisk ** before the parameter name to denote this type of argument. The arguments are passed as a dictionary (to be discussed in Chapter *8, Tuples, Sets, and Dictionaries*), and these arguments make a dictionary inside the function with the name the same as the parameter, excluding the double asterisk **.

Let us write a program with keyword arguments. You will be able to understand it better after you complete *Chapter 8, Tuples, Sets, and Dictionaries*. In the program, we define a function fun that receives **kwargs as a formal parameter to receive a variable number of arguments. In the first **print** statement, we type kwargs. In the **for** loop, we print the keys and values in the dictionary. We use formatted printing. The first-place holder will print the key and then the value. We call the function **fun** with 3 key-value pairs the first time and with 5 key-value pairs next time:

```python
# Program E6x15.py
# Keyword arguments
def fun(**kwargs):
    print("\nData type of argument:",type(kwargs))
    for key, value in kwargs.items():
        print("{} is {}".format(key,value))
def main():
    fun(Firstname="ram", Age=27, Phone=123456)
    fun(Firstname="Sita", Lastname="ram", Country="India", Age=25,
Phone=43210)
main()
```

The result of the program is given below:

```
==================== RESTART: E:/Py programs/E6x15.py ====================
Data type of argument: <class 'dict'>
Firstname is ram
Age is 27
Phone is 123456
Data type of argument: <class 'dict'>
Firstname is Sita
Lastname is ram
Country is India
Age is 25
Phone is 43210
```

The **kwargs** facilitate passing variable number of keyword arguments. The result also confirms that **kwargs** is a type dictionary.

Recursion

Recall that recursion is a function calling itself. We will now look at algorithms that could be recursively solved.

Euclid GCD recursive program

Please refer to the algorithm for finding the **Greatest Common Divisor (GCD)** discussed in *Chapter 2, Algorithmic Problem Solving.* GCD is the greatest common divisor that will divide both the given numbers evenly. The popular Greek mathematician Euclid developed the algorithm for the same. Hence, this algorithm is also known as Euclid's GCD algorithm. The algorithm given in *Chapter 2, Algorithmic Problem Solving* is not recursive. We will now convert the algorithm given in *Chapter 2, Algorithmic Problem Solving,* as a recursive algorithm. It is given below:

```
gcd(m,n)
if(n==0):
    return m
 else:
    return(gcd(n, m%n))
main()
Get the two numbers
If (n>m):
    Swap(m,n)
Result=gcd(m,n)
Print (result)
```

The above is a recursive algorithm for finding the GCD of two numbers. Let us implement the algorithm in a program, which is given below:

```
 E6x16.py - C:/Users/Subbu/Desktop/E6x16.py (3.10.10)
File  Edit  Format  Run  Options  Window  Help
 1  '''Program E6x16.py'''
 2  # Finding Greatest Common Divisor of 2 given numbers
 3  # called function
 4  def gcd(num1, num2): # function header
 5      if(num2==0):
 6          return num1
 7      else:
 8          return(gcd(num2, num1%num2))
 9
10
11  # calling function
12  def main():
13      a=eval(input('enter an integer: '))
14      b=eval(input('enter an integer: '))
15      if b>a:   # swap the numbers
16          temp=a
17          a=b
18          b=temp
19      result = gcd(a,b)
20      print('gcd of', a,'and', b,'= ', result)
21
22  main() # main function call
23
```

Figure 6.2: Program for finding GCD

In the **main** function, two numbers **a** and **b** whose GCD is to be found is received, at lines 13 and 14 respectively. At line 15, If **b** is greater than **a** then the numbers are swapped to ensure *a* is greater than *b*. Let us say **a** is 14 and **b** is 42, after swapping **a** will be 42 and **b** 14. Now in the main function, we call **gcd(42,14)** and assign it to **result** at line 19.

Now the control transfers to the GCD function. There, 42 will be **num1** and 14 **num2**, in the above case. At line 5, we check whether **num2==0**. Since it is false, control goes to line 8. It returns **gcd(14, (42%14=0))**. Now control goes to line 4. At line 5, since num2−−0, it returns num1, which is 14, to the called function, which is **main**. This is assigned to **result** in line 19 and printed in line 20. This is how the program works. The results of the program when executed twice are as follows:

```
===================== RESTART: E:/Py programs/E6x16.py =====================
enter an integer: 15
enter an integer: 25
gcd of 25 and 15 =  5
enter an integer: 36
enter an integer: 12
gcd of 36 and 12 =  12
```

From the main function, we passed two integers to the function GCD. If the second integer is zero, then the first integer automatically becomes the GCD. If not, we call the function recursively. Even if the second number is larger than the first, the algorithm works, as the result of the program indicates. Even if the second number is larger than the first one, the program will work without swapping, but it will take one more iteration. So, you can omit the swapping portion if you like.

Let us carry out two more programs to understand recursion better.

Recursive factorial program

We studied the recursive factorial algorithm in *Chapter 2, Algorithmic Problem Solving*. Let us convert the algorithm to a Python program now. It is given below:

```
# Recursive Factorial Program E6x16b
def fact(n):
    if n==0:
        return 1
    elif n==1:
        return 1
    else:
        return (n*fact(n-1))
def main():
```

```
    num=eval(input("Enter the number whose factorial to be found "))
    print('factorial of', num, '=', fact(num))
main()
```

The results of the program are given below:

```
=================== RESTART: E:\Py programs\E6x16b.py ===================
Enter the number whose factorial to be found 5
factorial of 5 = 120
>>>
=================== RESTART: E:\Py programs\E6x16b.py ===================
Enter the number whose factorial to be found 0
factorial of 0 = 1
>>>
=================== RESTART: E:\Py programs\E6x16b.py ===================
Enter the number whose factorial to be found 1
factorial of 1 = 1
>>>
=================== RESTART: E:\Py programs\E6x16.py ===================
Enter the number whose factorial to be found 20
factorial of 20 = 2432902008176640000
```

Tail recursion

Look at both the functions **gcd** and **fact** discussed above. In both the functions, the recursive calls to the functions are made at the end or tail of the functions. Hence such recursions are called tail recursion.

Calculating the exponential value in Python

In mathematics, the exponential value of a number is equal to the number being multiplied by itself for a given number of times. The number to be multiplied by itself is called the *base* and the number of times it is to be multiplied is the *exponent*.

Python allows users to calculate the exponential value of a number in several ways as described below:

- **Using** `**` **operator**: The double asterisk, `**` operator is a shortcut to calculate the exponential value. Let us take a look at how this can be used in the following code:

  ```
  >>> base = 4
  >>> exponent = 5
  ```

```
>>> print ("Exponential Value is: ", base ** exponent)
Exponential Value is:  1024
```

- **Using built-in function pow( ):** In addition to the ** operator, Python has included a built-in **pow()** function, which allows users to calculate the exponential value. The function takes as input the base and exponent and returns the corresponding value. Let us try it out in the interactive mode as given below:

```
>>> import math
>>> base = 3
>>> exponent = 4
>>> print ("Exponential Value is: ", math. pow(base, exponent))
Exponential Value is:  81.0
```

- **Using exp( ) function:** The **exp()** function in Python allows users to calculate the exponential value with the base set to e.

  Note: The e is a mathematical constant, with a value approximately equal to 2.71828.

  The math library must be imported for this function to be executed.

  The function takes input from the exponent value. We calculate the exponential value using **exp()** function in the interactive mode as given below:

```
>>> import math
>>> exponent = 4
>>> print ("Exponential Value is: ", math.exp(exponent))
Exponential Value is:  54.598150033144236
```

- **Using recursion:** Although this program can be written with a while loop, we will do this using recursion to give another experience of using recursion to solve a problem with the least number of lines of code. The program takes a base and an exponent and finds the exponential value using recursion. Remember the exponent value should be an integer to avoid runtime issues. The algorithm for finding recursion is given below.

  o In the main function, receive the base and exponent from the user.

  o Pass the numbers as arguments to a recursive function **expo(base, pow)** to find the power of the number.

  o Give the condition that if the exponent value is equal to 1, return the *base* number.

  o If the exponent value isn't equal to 1, return the *base* number multiplied with **expo(base, pow-1)**.

    o   Print the final result.

    o   End

The program follows:

```
# Program E6x17.py
# Finding exponentiation of a number
def expo(base,pow):
    if(pow==1):
        return(base)
    elif(pow!=1):
        return(base*expo(base,pow-1))
def main():
    x=eval(input("Enter base: "))
    y=int(input("Enter integer for exponential value: "))
    print(expo(x,y))


main()
```

The result of the program is given below:

```
==================== RESTART: E:/Py programs/E6x17.py ====================
Enter base: 2
Enter integer for exponential value: 10
1024

==================== RESTART: E:/Py programs/E6x17.py ====================
Enter base: 4.5
Enter integer for exponential value: 4
410.0625
```

Study and note the following in the program above:

- The user enters the base and exponent value.
- The numbers are passed as arguments to a recursive function **expo** to find the exponential value.
- A condition is given that if the exponent is equal to 1, the base number is returned.
- If the exponent is not equal to 1, the base number multiplied with the expo function is called recursively with the arguments as the base and exponent value minus 1.
- The final result is printed in the main function.
- Note that the exponent has to be strictly integer.

Case study: Towers of Hanoi

We studied the algorithm for the Towers of Hanoi in *Chapter 2, Algorithmic Problem Solving*. Let us try to implement the program now. The program is given below. Read the algorithm in *Chapter 2, Algorithmic Problem Solving,* and compare the steps:

```
# Program E6x18.py
# Towers of Hanoi program
def xfer(n, s,  d, temp):
        if(n==1):
            print('transfer disk ', n, 'from ',s, 'to ',d)
        else:
                # transfer n-1 disks from source to temp
            xfer(n-1,s,temp,d)
                # transfer n from source to destination
            print('transfer disk ', n, 'from ',s, 'to ',d)
    # transfer n-1 disks from  temp to destination
            xfer(n-1, temp, d, s)


def main():
    n=eval(input('enter the number of disks to play with: '))
    print('The moves follow: ')
    xfer(n,'s', 'd','t')
main()
```

The result of the program is given below for three disks and four disks:

```
==================== RESTART: E:/Py programs/E6x18.py ====================
enter the number of disks to play with: 3
The moves follow:
transfer disk  1 from  s to  d
transfer disk  2 from  s to  t
transfer disk  1 from  d to  t
transfer disk  3 from  s to  d
transfer disk  1 from  t to  s
transfer disk  2 from  t to  d
transfer disk  1 from  s to  d
==================== RESTART: E:/Py programs/E6x18.py ====================
enter the number of disks to play with: 4
```

The moves follow:

```
transfer disk  1 from  s to  t
transfer disk  2 from  s to  d
transfer disk  1 from  t to  d
transfer disk  3 from  s to  t
transfer disk  1 from  d to  s
transfer disk  2 from  d to  t
transfer disk  1 from  s to  t
transfer disk  4 from  s to  d
transfer disk  1 from  t to  d
transfer disk  2 from  t to  s
transfer disk  1 from  d to  s
transfer disk  3 from  t to  d
transfer disk  1 from  s to  t
transfer disk  2 from  s to  d
transfer disk  1 from  t to  d
```

Some points to be noted in the above program are given below:

The program in the main function asks the user to enter the number of disks to play with. (The number entered should be a positive number, if not we have to modify the program.) Then the main function invokes the function **xfer** and passes the value entered by the user. In the **xfer** function if the number of disks is 1, then the disk is transferred from s to d. If the number is not 1 the else block is invoked, and the problem is solved recursively.

Conclusion

In this chapter, we covered in detail how to create user defined functions. We covered void functions and fruitful functions. We used local and global variables in our program. We discussed positional, default, keyword/non-keyword and passed variable length arguments to the functions. We discussed the several ways in which Python allows users to calculate the exponential value of a number.

We wrote a program to find GCD and the factorial of a given number recursively. We solved the Towers of Hanoi puzzle recursively.

In the next chapter, we will discuss lists, one of the most power-packed containers of Python.

Points to remember

- The functions supplied with the Python language are the built-in functions. Users can write additional functions, which are called user-defined functions. Similar to other programming languages, we have a **main()** function in Python from where the program execution starts. We write the program in such a manner that the main function calls other functions as needed for carrying out specific tasks. Each function may, in turn, call other specialized functions wherever required.

- The function header starts with the Python keyword def. It is followed by the function named **main()** or other function name given by the programmer and list of formal parameters in parentheses and is terminated with a colon (:).

- The function body is where we put the code to carry out the specific task. The function may return a value to the called function. In such a case, we will have a statement with the return keyword. The function terminates when the return statement is executed.

- We can call a function multiple times.

- We can call multiple functions in a program.

- A function without a return statement is called void function. The void functions return a special value called None to the called function.

- To use mathematical functions, we import the math library.

- In a fruitful function, the return statement includes a return value. In such cases, we evaluate the return expression and then return it immediately as the result (the fruit) of this function to the called function.

- When we execute functions, the system uses a runtime stack to store intermittent values. It is handled by the system, and it is not transparent to the programmer.

- We name a Boolean function to sound that it returns a Boolean constant.

- The arguments should be passed in the correct positional order.

- Sometimes we assign a predefined value to the arguments in a function. If we call a function and if the number of arguments is less than the number of formal parameters, then the default arguments will be taken.

- Python provides a wonderful facility whereby we can decide the number of arguments at function invocation time. If we had declared a variable-length argument, the function would receive any number of arguments given by the user at each time of execution.

- We discussed keyword arguments and non-keyword arguments.

- Recursion is a function calling itself.

- Some points to be noted in the Towers of Hanoi program are given below:

  o The program in the main function asks the user to enter the number of disks to play with. The number entered should be a positive number. Then the main function invokes the function xfer and passes the value entered by the user. In the xfer function if the number of disks is 1, then the disk is transferred from s to d. If the number is not 1 the else block is invoked calling the function recursively.

Questions

Choose the most appropriate answer.

1. **Python is a:**

   a. Dynamically typed language

   b. Statically typed language

   c. All of the above

   d. None of the above.

2. **A function definition consists of:**

   a. Function name

   b. Formal parameters

   c. def keyword

   d. All the above

   e. None of the above.

3. **Recursion is:**

   a. A function calling more than one function

   b. A function calling another function

   c. A function calling itself

   d. All of the above

   e. None of the above

4. **Exponential value of a number could be found using:**

   a. **

   b. pow()

    c. recursive function

    d. All of the above

    e. None of the above

5. **The function sqrt(x):**

    a. Finds square of x

    b. Finds square root of x

    c. All of the above

    d. None of the above

6. **void function means:**

    a. No explicit return statement

    b. Returns None

    c. All of the above

    d. None of the above

7. **Runtime stack is:**

    a. User-defined

    b. Does not exist in Python

    c. Manages function calls and returns

    d. All of the above

    e. None of the above

8. **Recursive programs are suitable for:**

    a. Towers of Hanoi

    b. Factorial

    c. GCD

    d. All of the above

    e. None of the above

9. **When a number is evenly divisible by another number, the remainder should be:**

    a. Can be anything

    b. 1

    c. 0

    d. All of the above

    e. None of the above

10. **When we specify variable length argument, the number of arguments passed should be:**

    a. Any number

    b. 0

    c. 1

    d. All of the above

    e. None of the above

- Write short notes on the following:

    o **kwargs

    o Positional arguments

    o Variable-length arguments

    o Recursion

    o Fruitful function

    o Void dunction

    o Boolean function

    o Mathematical functions

    o Scope of variables

    o 3 ways of finding base raised to the power exponent

- Match the following:

A	B
sqrt()	1. keyword
Formal parameters	2. passed while calling a function
Actual arguments	3. where program execution starts
main()	4. mathematical function
def	5. place holders

- Write programs for the following:
    - o Find GCD without recursion.
    - o Find the sum and product of 4 numbers typed by the user.
    - o Find factorial without recursion.
    - o Find maximum and minimum numbers in a list in a function named maxi and mins.
    - o Pass the radius of a circle to a function and calculate the area and perimeter and print them.
    - o Generate a random integer in the range (100, 200) and test whether the number is prime or not.
    - o Find Fibonacci numbers in a called function.
    - o Function returning grades for marks obtained as per the rule below.
      A – greater than 90
      B – greater than 75 but up to 90
      C- greater than 60 but up to 75
      D- greater than or equal to 50 but up to 60
      F- less than 50
    - o Convert decimal number to a binary number, octal number and hexadecimal number.
    - o Find the output of the following program:

    ```python
    x = 5
    def fun1():
            global x
            x=x-2
            print(x)
    def fun3():
            x = 9
            print(x)
    def main():
            print (x)
            fun1()
            print (x)
            fun2()
            print (x)
            fun3()
            print (x)
    ```

Join our book's Discord space

Join the book's Discord Workspace for Latest updates, Offers, Tech happenings around the world, New Release and Sessions with the Authors:

https://discord.bpbonline.com

CHAPTER 7
Lists

Introduction

One of the strengths of Python is the availability of ubiquitous containers. The containers are data structures that enable systematic and easy handling of data. Python provides four versatile and powerful containers. The list is one of them, which will be discussed in this chapter. A list can hold zero or more data items of the same or different types. The containers are designed to be portable. Three interesting case studies are given in this chapter to help the reader understand the concepts pertaining to lists.

Structure

The chapter covers the following topics:

- Containers
- Array
- List
- Mutable sequence
- Mutable
- Slicing

- Getting Python keywords online

- List concatenation

- Nesting of lists

- Built-in functions

- Difference between functions and methods

- Console input

- List methods

- Use of keyword in

- Loops in list

- List comprehension

- Aliasing list

- Cloning lists

- Passing list and returning list

- Arrays in Python

- Sum of an array of numbers

- Case study: Circulate the values of n variables

- Caution about tabs

- Case study: Linear search

- Case study: Binary search

Objectives

In this chapter, we will learn how to declare and define a list – a collection of commas-separated values within square brackets. We will learn how to extract part of a list through slicing. We will be discussing list concatenation and nesting of lists. We will also study the use of the built-in library functions and methods specific to lists. We will also learn cloning and aliasing lists. We will understand how to pass a list as an argument and return a list from a function in this chapter.

Containers

One of the reasons why Python is so highly regarded as a rapidly developing language is because of its advanced data containers and methods for working with them. Containers are software objects. Containers are objects that hold an arbitrary number of other objects. They are compound data types in contrast with simple int or float types. A container puts together an entire runtime environment, such as an application, and all its dependencies, libraries, other binaries, and configuration files needed to run it, bundled into one package. This enables the seamless porting of software objects. They facilitate software to run reliably when moved from one computing environment to another. This could be from a developer's laptop to a test environment and perhaps from a physical machine to a virtual machine in a private or public cloud.

Python provides the following four container classes and associated methods, which makes the language powerful. The classes are discussed in *Chapter 9, Introduction to Object-Oriented Programming*:

- List

- Tuple

- Dictionary

- Sets

These data types provide ease of organizing and handling large data, which we come across in ML and big data analytics. We will study lists in this chapter and other compound data types in the next chapter.

Array

Suppose we are writing a program for student marks. If there are 100 students in a class, then we need 100 variables to store their marks. In such cases, an array comes handy. We can use variable **marks[i]** and store the marks of 100 students in it. In mathematics, **marks[1]** will store the marks of the first student and **marks[40]** that of the 40th student. However, in programming, **marks[0]** will correspond to the first student and **marks[39]** that of the 40th student. Thus, array is a collection of items of the same data type. A string is a special array and a collection of characters. The arrays can also be considered a container containing multiple data items of the same type. Although Python supports arrays, lists are elegant data structures with several built-in functions and methods to manipulate them.

List

The most versatile of the containers is the list. A list, like an array, consists of multiple data items. However, lists can hold multiple data types, for instance, numbers and strings. It is the convention in Python to store only items of the same data type in a list. There can be duplicate data items in a list. For instance, marks obtained by two students in an examination may be the same. A number of students get centum, which a list can store.

A list can be written as a collection of comma-separated values (items) between square brackets. Let us define 2 lists as given below:

```
names=['ram', 'lakshman', 'sita', 'mathi']
marks=[100, 100, 100, 60]
```

The advantage of Python is that we do not have to declare a type of list beforehand and then assign values to it, like we do in other programming languages. If a collection of data items are comma-separated and enclosed between square brackets, Python recognizes it as a list. The *list*, like other built-in data types int and float is a built-in class with associated methods.

Let us write a program to create the above lists and print them. In the program, we create a list called **names** and store 4 items. Then we create another list called **marks** and store four items. The first list contains strings and the second numbers. We then print all members of both the lists. The program is given below:

```
'''Program E7x1.py'''
names=['ram', 'lakshman', 'Sita', 'Mathi']
marks=[100, 100, 100, 60]
print(names)
print(marks)
```

The result of the program is given below:

```
===================== RESTART: E:/Py programs/E7x1.py =====================
['ram', 'lakshman', 'Sita', 'Mathi']
[100, 100, 100, 60]
```

The execution of the above program illustrates the following points:

- The lists are assigned names or identifiers.
- Here, the list names is a collection of strings and marks.
- The container can hold duplicate elements.
- The elements of the list are contained within square brackets.
- A comma separates each element.
- We can print the entire list by passing the name of the list to the print, a built-in function.

Let us now understand some properties of lists.

Mutable sequence

The list is a sequence type, like a string. A string contains a sequence of characters, whereas a list is a sequence of any valid data type, including strings, whose elements are accessible by indices. Hence, they are known as **sequence types**. The elements of the list and string can be accessed using the indices. The first element has an index of zero in all sequences in Python. Unlike a string, a list is mutable, and hence, the data items or elements can be replaced by identifying the position to replace an existing element. Furthermore, a new list can be created with the same name as that of an existing list. We will try these concepts in the interactive mode. We can type either Python or IDLE in the Windows search box of the desktop, and the interactive screen will pop up with three statement pointers >>>, as shown:

```
>>> list1=[10,20,30,40] # list created with 5 elements
>>> print(list1[1])  # print element at index 1, second element
20
>>> print(list1)  # print entire list, all five elements
[10, 20, 30, 40]
>>> list2=list1    # copy list1 to list2
>>> print(list2)
[10, 20, 30, 40]
>>> print(list2[1])
20
```

Note that the index of elements starts with zero. When **list1** is copied to **list2**, there will be 1 list pointed to by both the list objects.

Mutable

Unlike strings, the lists are mutable, as the following listing demonstrates. Since lists are mutable, we can add, delete, and modify elements in a list. Look at the execution of statements in the interactive mode. Comments explain the operations carried out:

```
>>> list1=['rose', 'jasmine', 'lotus', 'mullai', 'sivanthi']
# list1 created with 5 flower names
>>> list1[4]='lily' # Replace the existing element 4 with 'lily'
>>> print(list1)
['rose', 'jasmine', 'lotus', 'mullai', 'lily'] # Note the change
>>> list1[3]=[] # deleting element with index 3 - mullai
>>> list1[4]='thulasi'# string replacement
>>> print(list1)
['rose', 'jasmine', 'lotus', [], 'thulasi']
# after deleting and replacing
>>> list1[1]=' '  # replacing element 1 with empty string
```

```
>>> print(list1)
['rose', ' ', 'lotus', [], 'thulasi']   # place holder remains
>>> list1=[1, 2, 3]
>>> del(list1[2])# delete element with index 2
>>> len (list1)
2                       # there are 2 elements after deletion
>>> print(list1)
[1, 2] # confirms
```

Slicing

Slicing is a flexible tool to build new lists out of an existing list. Slicing in Python is a feature that enables accessing parts of sequences like *strings*, *tuples*, and *lists*. We can also use them to modify or delete the items of mutable sequences such as *lists*.

The list shares many properties with string. It supports indexing as above and slicing. As the name suggests slicing is extracting some portion of the list as the following indicates:

```
>>> flowers=['Tulip', 'Daffodil', 'Poppy', 'Sunflower', 'Bluebell', 'Rose'] #
list flowers has 6 items
>>> print(flowers)
['Tulip', 'Daffodil', 'Poppy', 'Sunflower', 'Bluebell', 'Rose']
>>> print(flowers[:2]) # slice from index 0 up to 2, excluding 2
['Tulip', 'Daffodil']
>>> print(flowers[2:])# slice from index 2 till end
['Poppy', 'Sunflower', 'Bluebell', 'Rose']
>>> print(flowers[2:4])
['Poppy', 'Sunflower'] # slice from index 2 to 3 (4-1)
```

The explanations are given side by side for ease of understanding of the reader. Thus, we can slice any portion of the list. Recall that if the starting index is not given, it means the index is 0. If the end index is not given, it means the index is last.

Getting Python keywords online

We do not have to refer to any resource to get a list of Python keywords. We can get it online by printing **kwlist** as the following illustrates:

```
>>> import keyword
>>> print(keyword.kwlist)
['False', 'None', 'True', 'and', 'as',
```

```
'assert', 'async', 'await', 'break', 'class',
'continue', 'def', 'del', 'elif', 'else',
'except', 'finally', 'for', 'from', 'global',
'if', 'import', 'in', 'is', 'lambda',
'nonlocal', 'not', 'or', 'pass', 'raise',
'return', 'try', 'while', 'with', 'yield']
```

As can be seen, there are 35 keywords in Python. This is an excellent facility in Python, and users can find the keywords at any time or whenever in doubt.

List concatenation

A new list can be added at the end of a list in three ways, as the following illustrates:

```
list2=[1, 3, 5,7]
>>> list2 +[9, 11, 13, 15] # add the list of 4 elements to list2
[1, 3, 5, 7, 9, 11, 13, 15]# method1
>>> list1=[2, 4, 6,8]
>>> list2=[10, 12, 14]
>>> list3=list1+list2 # concatenation method2
>>> print(list3)
[2, 4, 6, 8, 10, 12, 14]
>>> list1+=list2 # method3-shorthand notation of method2
>>> print(list1)
[2, 4, 6, 8, 10, 12, 14]
```

We simply added another list at the end of an existing list. After the concatenation with the overloaded **+** operator, we get a single list. Note that overloading means using operators like + to carry out more complex operations, such as adding two strings, two lists, and so on.

In the second method, we create a new list to store the elements of the concatenated list.

Nesting of lists

It is possible to nest lists, that is, creating a list of lists as the following indicates. Here we retain the original lists and join them together. We do not get a single list:

```
>>>list1 = [10, 20, 30, 40]
>>>list2 = [1, 3, 5, 7]]
>>>list3=[list1, list2] # nesting of list1 and list2
>>> print(list3)
```

```
[[10, 20, 30, 40], [1, 3, 5, 7]]
>>> print(list3[1])
[1, 3, 5, 7]
```

Note carefully the above statement. It means that the list has 2 lists as items with indices 0 and 1, respectively. This is because of the nesting. *list3[1]* refers to *list1*. When we concatenated the lists with the + symbol, we got 1 list with contiguous elements, as in the previous paragraph. But, when we nest it with a comma, the lists maintain their identity. The combined list is a list of 2 lists. Thus, a list can have elements or lists as elements.

Built-in functions

As discussed in *Chapter 1, Introduction to Python 3*, several built-in functions are available in Python, and the list of built-in functions is given in *Appendix 3*. These functions could be used with any Python objects such as *lists*. We will use some of them to carry out useful operations on lists. For instance, we can sort the contents of a list in ascending order. Operations carried out using the built-in functions with lists containing numbers are listed below:

```
>>> list2=[100, 90, 70, 67,114]# list2 created with 5 elements
>>> print(sorted(list2))# sort the list and print
[67, 70, 90, 100, 114] # sorted list
>>> print(list2) # sorting does not alter the original list
[100, 90, 70, 67, 114]
>>> print(sum(list2))# finds the sum of elements and print it
441
>>> print(len(list2))# prints the number of elements in list2
5
>>> print(max(list2))# prints the maximum of the elements
114
>>> print(min(list2))# Prints Minimum of the list
67
>>> print(list2)
[100, 90, 70, 67, 114]
>>> del(list2[1])# deleting element with index 1 - number 90
>>> print(list2)
[100, 70, 67, 114]# deleted 90 from the list2
>>> list1=list2+[10, 20, 30, 40]# adding another list to list2
>>> print (list1)
```

```
[100, 70, 67, 114, 10, 20, 30, 40]
>>> del(list2)  # deletes the list list2
```

We carried out the following operations using built-in functions successfully, as above:

- **sorted()**: This function sorts the numbers in ascending order without disturbing the original list.

- **sum()**: We can find the sum of the elements using the **sum( )** function.

- **len()**: Helps us to get the size of the list in terms of the number of data elements.

- **max()**: As the name suggests, we can find the largest element in the list.

- **min()**: we can find the smallest element in the list.

- **del()**: A chosen element or all the elements can be deleted using this function.

- **Concatenation**: A new list can be added at the end of the list.

Difference between functions and methods

There is a subtle difference between functions and methods in Python. As we know, functions discussed in the previous chapter are **self-contained** and **independent** units. They receive specified inputs and give output. Methods are similar. However, the functions called by classes and objects are called **methods**.

We pass the list as an argument to the built-in function. For instance, **max(list1)**. On the contrary, we call the built-in list methods in conjunction with the **list** object using **dot** operator. This is one difference. The built-in functions are common to all objects, such as tuples and sets, but the methods discussed here are specific to the list only. This is another difference. For instance:

```
>>> list1.append(77)# adding 77 at the end of the list
>>> print(list1)
[100, 70, 67, 114, 10, 20, 30, 40, 77]
```

In the above, we have appended **77** to the end of the list.

Console input

Let us now write a program to get the elements from the keyboard typed by the users and carry out some operations – functions and methods:

```
'''Program E7x2.py'''
ELEMENTS=6 # A constant defined
list1=[]  # Empty list created
for i in range(ELEMENTS): # for loop will run 6 times
```

```
    data=eval(input('Enter a new integer: '))
    list1.append(data)
print(list1)
print(len(list1))  # function len finds length of list1-will print 6
print (sum(list1)) # finds sum of all elements of list1
print (sorted(list1))# sort the elements in list1
print (max(list1)) # Find maximum in the list1
print (min(list1))  # Find the minimum in the list1
```

We get integers from the keyboard 6 times and append the typed number to **list1** using the **append** method. Then, we carry out the functions as specified. The comments, along with the program statement, indicate the function carried out. Result of the program is given below:

```
=================== RESTART: E:/Py programs/E7x2.py ===================
Enter a new integer: 66
Enter a new integer: 55
Enter a new integer: 44
Enter a new integer: 33
Enter a new integer: 22
Enter a new integer: 11
[66, 55, 44, 33, 22, 11]
6
231
[11, 22, 33, 44, 55, 66]
66
11
```

List methods

We will look at some more methods available for Python lists. They are given in *Table 7.1*:

Method	Operation carried out in list objects
list1.remove(var1)	Deletes first occurrence of var1 in list1
list1.pop(ind)	Deletes the item with index ind in list1
list1.insert(ind1, var2)	Inserts var2 at index ind1 in list1
list1.count(num)	Counts the number of times num appears in list1
list1.extend(list2)	Appends all elements in list2 to list1

Method	Operation carried out in list objects
list1.index(var3)	Returns the index of number var3
list1.reverse()	Reverses the elements in list1
list1.sort()	Sorts the elements of the list in ascending order

Table 7.1: *List methods*

Note that there is a built-in function *sorted* and a method *sort*. The difference lies in the methodology to invoke them. While we call the built-in function *sorted* as **sorted(list1)**, we call the method *sort* as **list1.sort()**.

We will now execute some methods in the following program. Read the comments in each statement and look at the result of the program to understand the methods:

```
'''Program E7x3.py'''

list1=[111, 13, 123, 89, 71, 11, 89, 13]  # list created

print(list1)

list1.remove(13)  # Removes first occurrence of 13 in the list1

print(list1)

list1.pop(4)    # Removes element with index 4 from list1

print(list1)   #

list1.insert(2,33) # insert 33 at index 2

print (list1)

print(list1.count(89)) # counts the number of times 89 appears in list1

list2=[10, 20, 30]

list1.extend(list2) # appends list2 to list1

print(list1)

list1.reverse()

print(list1)

print(list1.index(111))
```

The result of the program is given below:

```
=================== RESTART: E:\Py programs\E7x3.py ===================
[111, 13, 123, 89, 71, 11, 89, 13]
[111, 123, 89, 71, 11, 89, 13]
```

```
[111, 123, 89, 71, 89, 13]
[111, 123, 33, 89, 71, 89, 13]
2
[111, 123, 33, 89, 71, 89, 13, 10, 20, 30]
[30, 20, 10, 13, 89, 71, 89, 33, 123, 111]
9
```

Note the difference between *remove* and *pop*. Similarly, note the difference between *extend* and *list concatenation*. The availability of several built-in functions and methods is a boon to the programmer. Let us interact some more with the interpreter:

```
>>> list1=[] # empty list created
>>> list1.append(10)# add 10 to the list
>>> list1.append(20)# add 20 at the end of the list
>>> print(list1)
[10, 20]
>>> list1.pop()# remove the last item in list
20
>>> print(list1)
[10]
```

> Note that append adds an item at the end of a list and pop removes the last item in the list.

Use of keyword in

We used keyword **in** with **for** loop. We can also use keyword **in** to check whether a string or object is in a list. Look at the following example:

```
>>> list1=['sunday', 'monday', 'tuesday', 'thursday']
>>> print('tuesday' in list1)
```
True

We are checking whether **'tuesday'** is in **list1**. Since it is in the list, we get the result as **True**.

Loops in list

There are a number of ways in which loops can be constructed involving lists. We will see one by one.

Method 1

Here, we use the keywords **for** and **in**. The program is given below. We can use any valid identifier instead of **i**:

```
'''Program E7x4.py'''
# loop method 1
flowers=['lily', 'rose', 'jasmine', 'sunflower']
for i in flowers:
    print (i)
```

We create a list named **flowers**. Then for every **i** in flowers, we print **i**. The **for** loop iterates 4 times since there are 4 elements in **flowers**. The result of the program is given below:

```
================== RESTART: E:/Py programs/E7x4.py ==================
lily
rose
jasmine
sunflower
```

Method 2

We can also use indices of the list instead of variables, as given in the following program. Note the difference between the previous program and this. Here we use the **range** function and **len** functions. The **len** function returns the number of elements in the list. The **range** function returns a sequence of numbers, as shown:

```
'''Program E7x5.py'''
# loop method 2
flowers=['lily', 'rose', 'jasmine', 'sunflower']
for i in range (len(flowers)):
    print(flowers[i])
```

Note the variation in the **print** statement. The result of the program is given below:

```
================== RESTART: E:/Py programs/E7x5.py ==================
lily
rose
jasmine
sunflower
```

Method 3

We will use **while** instead of **for** and write a loop. Here we set up a counter **i** and for the first time, print the first element with **i** =**0**. Then, we will increment it and print the list element till it is less than the length of the list. The program and the result follow:

```
'''Program E7x6.py'''
# loop method 3 with while
flowers=['lily', 'rose', 'jasmine', 'sunflower']
n=len(flowers)
i=0
while(i<n):
    print(flowers[i])
    i=i+1
```

The result of the program is given below:

```
=================== RESTART: E:/Py programs/E7x6.py ===================
lily
rose
jasmine
sunflower
```

Method 4

Instead of giving the name of the list in the **for** loop, we can give the list itself as shown below:

```
>>> for element in [10, 20, 30]:
    print(element)
10
20
30
```

List comprehension

Comprehensions are constructs that allow sequences to be built in one line from other sequences. Let us first try to understand why comprehension is useful. For instance, one can either explicitly create a list containing squares of five natural numbers, as given below:

```
Squares = [0, 1, 4, 9, 16]
```

The second method of creating the above list is to use a **for** loop to create a list, as given below:

```
>>> squares=[]
>>> for num in range(5):
       squares.append(num*num)

>>> print(squares)
[0, 1, 4, 9, 16]
```

The third way to create a list is by using a single line of code:

```
>>> squares = [num*num for num in range(5)]
>>> print(squares)
[0, 1, 4, 9, 16]
```

The one-liner above is called a **list comprehension**. Notice the compactness.

A list comprehension is of the following form within square brackets:

```
[expression for var in sequence [optional for and/or if]]
```

It is given within square brackets containing an expression followed by a **for** and one or more **for** and/or **if**.

Another example is given below. In the program, we create a list **numbers1** with 5 numbers. After printing the list, we create another list called **numbers1**. Here, we square each element **num** if it is even. There are only 2 even numbers: 2 and 4. Therefore **numbers1** will contain their squares, namely, 4 and 16. After printing the list, we create another list, **numbers2**. Here, if the number is odd, we cube them and do not consider even numbers. Since there are 3 odd numbers, 1, 3, 5, their cubes form the list **numbers2**:

```
'''Program E7x7.py'''
# list comprehension
Numbers1=[1, 2, 3, 4, 5]
print(numbers)
numbers1=[num**2 for num in numbers if num%2==0] # square even    # numbers
print(numbers1)
numbers2=[num**3 for num in numbers if num%2==1] # cube odd numbers
print(numbers2)
================== RESTART: E:/Py programs/E7x7.py ====================
[1, 2, 3, 4, 5]
[4, 16]
[1, 27, 125]
```

Note that the contents of the original list are lost when we carry out **list comprehension**.

Let us try and see some more examples of creating lists with the help of list comprehension.

Creating Pythagorean triplets

This is another interesting application of list comprehension. A Pythagorean triple consists of three positive integers **a**, **b**, and **c**, such that $a^2 + b^2 = c^2$. We usually write such a triplet as **(a,b,c)**, for instance **(3,4,5)**:

```
>>> [(a,b,c) for a in range(1,20) for b in range(1,20) for c in range(1,20)
if a**2 + b**2 == c**2]
[(3, 4, 5), (4, 3, 5), (5, 12, 13), (6, 8, 10), (8, 6, 10), (8, 15, 17),
(9, 12, 15), (12, 5, 13), (12, 9, 15), (15, 8, 17)]
```

Notice the simplicity of selecting Pythagorean triples – *a*, *b*, *c*.

We can do the looping with list comprehension as given below. We will discuss more list comprehensions in the next section:

```
'''Program E7x8.py'''
# loop method 4 with list comprehension
flowers=['lily', 'rose', 'jasmine', 'sunflower']
[print (flow) for flow in flowers]
```

The result of the program is given below:

```
================== RESTART: E:/Py programs/E7x8.py ====================
lily
rose
jasmine
sunflower
```

Aliasing list

In Python, **aliasing** happens whenever one variable's value is assigned to another variable, because variables are just identifiers that store references to values. In computer programming, aliasing refers to the situation where the same memory locations are accessed using different names. Let us write a program to learn this concept. In the program, we create **list1** with 5 numbers. Then, we assign **list1** to **list2**. Now **list1** and **list2** share the same memory address. We now append number **16** to **list1** and not to **list2**. When we look at the result of the program **list2** also has the sixth element **16** exactly like **list1**. This is because of aliasing:

```
'''Program E7x9.py'''
# list aliasing
list1=[1, 2, 3, 4, 5]
list2=list1
print(list2)
```

```
list1.append(16)
print(list1)
print(list2)
=================== RESTART: E:/Py programs/E7x9.py ===================
[1, 2, 3, 4, 5]
[1, 2, 3, 4, 5, 16]
[1, 2, 3, 4, 5, 16]
```

Cloning lists

Aliasing does not make a copy of one object to another. It results in two objects sharing the same memory space. The result is that when we modify one object, it affects the other. On the contrary, in cloning, we copy one object to another. If we copy one list to another, then 2 list objects will be created, and they will be independent. So, a change made to one object will not affect another. This is called **cloning**. It is achieved through slicing. Let us write a program.

In the program, the line numbers have been added after program execution for the sake of explaining. In *line 3*, we create **list1** with the first 5 natural numbers. In the next statement (*line 4*), we are slicing the **list1**, omitting both the starting address and ending address for the slicing. This means **list2** will also contain all the numbers. This is a cloning method. How do we check that it is cloning and no aliasing? Recall that in aliasing, when we make changes to one list, it affects the other in the same way. That means if we add an element to one list, it automatically gets added to the second one. Similarly, if we delete an element, it gets deleted in both lists. In cloning, we have two objects, so, changes made to one object will not affect another. After copying, the lists will be stored in different locations so that after copying they are independent. Let us check that.

In *line 5*, we delete the element of **list1** with index 1, that is, number 2. Now **list1** will be **[1, 3, 4, 5]**.

In *line 6* we print **list2**. From the result of the program, we can find that **list2** is not affected and it has the first 5 natural numbers intact.

In *line 7*, we append **16** to **list2**. Therefore, **list2** will have 6 numbers as against 4 in **list1** as the result confirms.

This is the difference between **aliasing** and **cloning**:

```
E7x10.py - E:\Py programs\E7x10.py (3.10.11)
File  Edit  Format  Run  Options  Window  Help
 1 |"Program E7x10.py"'
 2 # list cloning
 3 list1=[1, 2, 3, 4, 5]
 4 list2=list1[:] # slicing
 5 del(list1[1])
 6 print(list2)
 7 list2.append(16)
 8 print(list1)
 9 print(list2)
10
```

Figure 7.1: Difference between aliasing and cloning

The result of the program is given below:

```
================== RESTART: E:/Py programs/E7x10.py ===================
[1, 2, 3, 4, 5]
[1, 3, 4, 5]
[1, 2, 3, 4, 5, 16]
```

Passing list and returning list

A list can be passed as a *parameter* to a function. A function can also return a list as an *argument*. We will experiment the following with an example program.

Transpose of a matrix

Let us write a program for finding the transpose of a matrix. When we find the transpose of a matrix, the row index will become the column index, and the column index will become the row index. For instance, a *3x2* (3 rows and 2 columns) matrix is given below:

```
 2   3
 5   7
11  13
```

When we transpose the matrix, it will become a *2x3* (2 rows and 3 columns) will be created as given below:

```
2 5 11
3 7 13
```

Note that each row can be considered as a list. The above matrix can be written as given below:

```
[[2, 5, 11], [3, 7, 13]]
```

The above can be rewritten in the matrix form as follows:

```
[[2, 5, 11],
 [3, 7, 13]]
```

Now, look at the program *E7x11.py* below:

```
E7x11.py - C:/Users/Subbu/Desktop/E7x11.py (3.10.11)        —

File  Edit  Format  Run  Options  Window  Help
 1 # Program E7x11.py
 2 # Finding Transpose of a given matrix
 3
 4 def transpose(mat1):
 5   mat1_transpose = [[0, 0, 0],
 6           [0, 0, 0]]
 7   for rows in range(len(mat1)):
 8     for columns in range(len(mat1[0])):
 9       mat1_transpose[columns][rows] = mat1[rows][columns]
10   return(mat1_transpose)
11
12 def main():
13   mat0 = [[2, 3],
14         [5, 7],
15         [11, 13]]
16   mat2=transpose(mat0)
17   print("Transposed Matrix is")
18   for elements in mat2:
19     print(elements)
20
21 main()
22
```

Figure 7.2: Program to find transpose of a matrix

We have defined a function **transpose** in *line 4*. It receives a formal parameter **mat1**. In *line 12*, we have defined the **main** function. In *lines 13 to 15*, we define **mat0** as a *3x2* matrix. Three lists can be nested as given below to create the list **mat0**:

```
>>> list1=[2, 3]
>>> list2=[5,7]
>>> list3=[11,13]
>>> list4=[list1, list2, list3]
>>> print(list4)
[[2, 3], [5, 7], [11, 13]]
```

In *line 16*, we call method **transpose** and pass **mat0** as an argument. It is received as **mat1** in *line 4* of the program.

In *lines 5* and *6*, we create **mat1_transpose** as a *2x3* matrix with all values zero.

In *lines 7* and *8* we have nested for loop.

The inner loop at *line 8* finds the number of columns in **mat1** by finding **len(mat1[0])**. It will be 2. 2 is assigned as the range to the inner loop. The inner loop will iterate 2 times for each index value in the outer loop.

The outer **for** loop finds a range of rows at *line 7* and assigns the range in the statement. It is 3. Therefore, the outer **for** loop will iterate 3 times. Then the transpose, that is, changing columns to rows takes place *line 9*. The values of rows and columns of **mat1** and **mat1_transpose** at each successive iteration is given below. One can take a pencil and paper and see how the indices of the numbers change in each matrix and each iteration:

3x2 matrix	2x3 matrix
Matrix=mat1	Matrix = mat1_transpose
Column, row	row, column
1, 1 (number 2)	1, 1
2, 1 (number 3)	2, 1
1, 2 (number 5)	1, 2
2, 2 (number 7)	2, 2
1, 3 (number 11)	1, 3
2, 3 (number 13)	2, 3

Table 7.2: Matrix transpose steps

Then the function **transpose** returns the transposed matrix to **main()**. In the **main** function, the transposed matrix is collected in **mat2** in *line 16*. The received matrix is printed by the statements at *lines 18* and *19*. In the example program, we passed a nested list to the transpose function and it returned a nested list back to the main function. It is as easy as passing a value to a function and returning a value from it.

The result of the program is given below:

```
================== RESTART: E:\Py programs\E7x11.py ==================
Transposed Matrix is
[2, 5, 11]
[3, 7, 13]
```

Arrays in Python

An array is a collection of items of the same data type stored at contiguous memory locations. The array module defines an object type which can compactly represent an array of basic data types such as integers, and floating-point numbers. This makes it easier to calculate the position of each element by simply adding an offset to a base value, that is, the memory location of the first element of the array. Arrays in Python are not arrays in conventional programming languages like *C* and *Java* but are closer to lists in characteristics. A user can treat lists as arrays. Although we consider lists with the same data type, they can hold heterogeneous types such as *numbers* and *strings*, but *arrays* cannot hold heterogeneous elements.

The type of elements of arrays or the type of the array needs to be declared, whereas lists do not need type declaration because they are a part of Python's syntax. This is the reason lists are more often used than arrays. If we want to store a large amount of data, then we should consider arrays because they can store data very compactly and efficiently.

To use arrays in Python, we need to import the standard **array** module. This is because the array is not a fundamental data type like *strings*, *integers*, and so on. Here is how we can import an array module in Python:

```
from array import *
```

Once we have imported the **array** module, we can declare an array as given below:

```
arrayname = array(type, [elements])
```

In the declaration above, **arrayname** is the name of the array. The type indicates the data type, and we are already familiar with elements. The type is specified at object creation time by using a type code, which is a single character. The object types supported by the **array** module in Python and their corresponding type codes are given in the table below:

Type code	Type	Bytes allotted
b	signed char (character)	1
B	unsigned char (character)	1
h	Signed short	2
H	Unsigned short	2
i	Signed int	2
I upper case I	Unsigned int	2
l lower case l	Signed long	4
L	Unsigned long	4
q	signed long long long	8
Q	Unsigned long long	8
f	Float	4
d	Double	8

Table 7.3: Bytes allotted for each type

The types are the codes that are used to define the type of array values. The type **i** indicates that the array elements are integers. Arrays are sequence types and behave very much like lists, except that the type of objects stored in them is constrained by the type code. For instance, an array can be declared as given below:

```
array1= array('i',[2, 3, 5, 7])
```

A list is part of the array. In addition to type code has to be specified. If type code is missing in the above, **array1** will be a list.

Let us write a program using arrays. The program is given below:

```
# Program E7x12.py
# using Python arrays
from array import *
def main():
    a1=array('i',[12, 18, 6, 24, 72])# Integer array declared
    print('originl array is: ', a1)
    a3=a1*3 # repeat elements of array 3 times
    print('array repeated 3 times is: ', a3)
    print(type(a1)) # type of a1
    print(a1[2]) # print the array element with index 2
    for x in a1: # print all elements of array
        print(x)


main()
```

The result of the program *E7x12.py* is given below:

```
original array is:  array('i', [12, 18, 6, 24, 72])
array repeated 3 times is:  array('i', [12, 18, 6, 24, 72, 12, 18, 6,
24, 72, 12, 18, 6, 24, 72])
<class 'array.array'>
6
12
18
6
24
72
```

Read the comments given along with the statements to understand the program. First, we print the array. Then we repeat the array 3 times. We find the type of array as **<class 'array.array'>**. Then after printing the element with index 2, we print all elements with a for loop. The reader will realize that the Python built-in type list is much easier to use. However, there are occasions where arrays may be preferable.

Sum of an array of numbers

A list has a built-in function **sum** to find the sum of the list elements and the array does not have. We will write a program to find sum an array of numbers. In the program, the array is initialized with integers. The for loop adds each element **x** to sum which was initialized to zero at the beginning of the program, as shown:

```
# Program E7x13
# sum an array of numbers
from array import *
def main():
    a1=array('i',[12, 18, 6, 24, 72])# Integer array declared
    print('original array is: ', a1)
    sum=0
    for x in a1:
        sum=sum+x
    print('sum=', sum)

main()
```

The result of the program is given below:

```
================== RESTART: E:/Py programs/E7x13.py ==================
original array is:  array('i', [12, 18, 6, 24, 72])
sum= 132
```

We used a **for** loop in the program. Look at the simplicity of the **for** statement.

Case study: Circulate the values of n variables

Let us take a look at an interesting problem. We have a list. We have to pop out (extract) the first element and append it at the end of the list. This is known as **circulating the elements of a list**. If there are 5 elements in the list and if we repeat it 5 times, we will get the original list again. The program for achieving the same is given below:

```
# program E7x14.py
# Circulate the values of n variables
def circulating(list1):

    for val in range (len(list1)):
```

```
        ele = list1.pop(0)
        list1.append(ele)
        print('circulated list is: ', list1)
def main():
    no_of_elements = int(input("Enter number of values : "))
    list0 = []
    val=0
    while val<no_of_elements:
        ele = int(input("Enter integer : "))
        list0.append(ele)
        val=val+1
    print('original sequence is ')
    print(list0)
    circulating(list0) # calling circulating
main()
```

In the **main** function, we ask the user to specify the **no_of_elements** in the list. Then we create an empty list **list0**. In the **while** loop, we ask the user to enter the value of the element and append to **list0**. If we had specified **no_of_elements** as 5, the loop would iterate 5 times and ask the user to enter the value and append it to **list0**. Then we print the original sequence and call function **circulating** and pass **list0**.

In function **circulating** we receive the list as **list1**. After the definition of function **circulating**, we have a loop with for. We repeat the for loop for **(len(list1))** times, that is, length of the list, number of times. In this case 5 times. In the function **circulating** we do the following 5 times:

- Pop (remove) the first element with index 0.

- Append (add) the element at the end of the list.

- Print the list: We will notice circulation.

The result is given below:

```
================== RESTART: E:/Py programs/E7x14.py ==================
Enter number of values : 5
Enter integer : 11
Enter integer : 22
Enter integer : 33
Enter integer : 44
Enter integer : 55
```

```
original sequence is
[11, 22, 33, 44, 55]
circulated list is:   [22, 33, 44, 55, 11]
circulated list is:   [33, 44, 55, 11, 22]
circulated list is:   [44, 55, 11, 22, 33]
circulated list is:   [55, 11, 22, 33, 44]
circulated list is:   [11, 22, 33, 44, 55]
```

Notice carefully from the result above how the elements are circulating, transferred from the first position to the last position in every iteration. For instance, number **11** reached the last position in the first iteration, **22** in the second iteration, and so on.

Caution about tabs

In Python indenting matters. The programmer cannot indent as he likes since it may lead to semantic errors. The right indenting of every statement is important. **IDLE** does it for us most of the time, but it may be misleading sometimes. The programmer should be alert while indenting statements every time. For instance, notice what happens if the current indent of the **print** statement in *line 7* of the program above is shifted by one tab to the left. The output will be different, and you cannot visualize the circulation of the elements.

Case study: Linear search

Search is the process of finding out whether a given data element is present in an array of data. This problem is encountered in many real-life situations. Searching for a name in a telephone directory or a voter's list are all quite common problems. We may like to search whether an item is present on the list or not.

The user specifies the item to be searched which can be called **key**. The key is compared with each item in the list. The list need not be sorted for linear search. If the item in the list is equal to the **key**, then the item is found. Here the entire list is compared from the beginning till the end. If the item to be searched for matches with an item in the list of data, then the search is stopped, and otherwise, the search is continued till the end of the list. This method of searching is called **linear search**. The algorithm for linear search is given below:

```
Linear Search (list, key)
Define the sorted list ia
item to be searched  = key
len(ia)=n
found  =  false
while ( i <= n - 1)& ( found=false ):
```

```
            if ( ia [i] == x )   then
                found = true
            else:
                i  =  i  +  1
if(found=True):
print (fount at  position i+1)
    else:
        print (Not Found)
End
```

The program, which implements the algorithm for linear search, as a **while** loop is given below:

```
# program E7x15.py
# Linear Search
def read_key():
    key_item = eval(input("Enter the key item to search: "))
    return key_item
def linear_search(search_key):
    ia = [10, 20, 30, 40,50]
    found = False
    n=len(ia)
    i=0
    while (i<n-1) & (found==False):
        if ia[i] == search_key:
            found = True
            break
        else:
            i+=1
    if found:
        print('Item found at location',  i + 1)
    else:
        print("Item not found in the list")
def main():
    key = read_key()
    linear_search(key)
main()
```

The program implements the algorithm given above. The data is part of the function **linear_search** for the sake of simplicity. We read the key in function **read_key**. The function returns the key to the main function. We call the function **linear_search** and pass the **key**. The result is obtained in the function and printed there itself:

```
================== RESTART: E:\Py programs\E7x15.py ==================
Enter the key item to search: 30
Item found at location 3
>>>
================== RESTART: E:\Py programs\E7x15.py ==================
Enter the key item to search: 89
Item not found in the list
```

The program has been written with two functions **read_key** and *linear search* in addition to the **main** function. We can also check whether a string is there in a list using the same program. The program with data changed and the result produced is given below. Note that the list **ia** in this program is unsorted.

```
# program E7x16.py

def read_key():

    key_item = eval(input("Enter the key item to search: "))

    return key_item

def linear_search(search_key):

    ia = ['ram', 'krishna', 'sita', 'mary','vidhya']

    found = False

    n=len(ia)

    i=0

    while (i<n-1) & (found==False):

        if ia[i] == search_key:

            found = True

            break

        else:

            i+=1
```

```
    if found:
        print('Item found at location',  i + 1)
    else:
        print("Item not found in the list")
def main():
    key = read_key()
    linear_search(key)
main()
```

```
=================== RESTART: E:/Py programs/E7x16.py ==================
Enter the key item to search: 'sita'
Item found at location 3
>>>

=================== RESTART: E:/Py programs/E7x16.py ==================
Enter the key item to search: 'mitra'
Item not found in the list
```

Case study: Binary search

There are several search methods. We have already discussed the **linear search** in this chapter. Here we look at **binary search**. An important pre-condition for binary search is that the data is ordered or arranged in ascending or descending order in an array, like names are arranged alphabetically in a telephone directory.

Let us now study the algorithm for the binary search to understand the concept. Here also, we will assume that the array of numbers is arranged in increasing order:

```
Algorithm for Binary Search(search_key)

Read list a

left = 0

right = n-1

found = False

while (left < =right)&(found=False):

mid = (left + right)//2

        if (a (mid) ==search_key):
            found = True
        elif  (a (mid) < search_key)
            left = mid + 1
        else:
```

```
            right = (mid-1)
if (found):
      print ("found")
   else:
      print ("Not found")
End
```

The program and result of the program are given below:

```
# Program E7x17.py
# binary search
def read_key():
    key_item = eval(input("Enter the key item to search: "))
    return key_item


def binary_search(search_key):
    a=[2, 3, 5, 7, 11, 13]
    n=len(a)
    left = 0
    right = n-1
    found = False
    while (left <=right)& (found==False):
        mid = (left + right)//2
        if a[mid] ==search_key:
                    found =True
        elif (a[mid] < search_key):
                    left = mid + 1
        else:
                    right = (mid-1)
    if found==True:
        print('Item found at location',  mid+1)
    else:
        print("Item not found in the list")
def main():
    key = read_key()
    binary_search(key)
main()
```

The above-mentioned program implements the algorithm. In the main function, first we call the function **read_key**. Then we pass the key returned by the function to **binary_serach**. Also note that the tabs and spaces in all Python programs are critical to get a correct running program, both with valid inputs and invalid inputs. Check also with invalid inputs. In the following case check with a number not in the list, strings, and so on. The result of the program is given below:

```
================== RESTART: E:/Py programs/E7x17.py ==================
Enter the key item to search: 7
Item found at location 4
>>>
================== RESTART: E:/Py programs/E7x17.py ==================
Enter the key item to search: 11
Item found at location 5
>>>
================== RESTART: E:/Py programs/E7x17.py ==================
Enter the key item to search: 15
Item not found in the list
```

We implemented the binary search algorithm and tested it with numbers.

Conclusion

In this chapter, we used built-in functions and list-specific methods. There is a subtle difference between functions and methods. We call the built-in list methods in conjunction with the **list** object using **dot** operator. We carried out operations using the Python built-in functions explained in the chapter.

We also carried out operations on the list objects using the list methods and looked at three interesting case studies in this chapter.

In the next chapter, we will study three interesting containers – tuples, dictionaries, and sets.

Points to remember

- We can print the entire list by passing the name of the list to the print, a built-in function.

- We can use slicing to get a part of the list.

- Python keywords can be printed online.

- A new list can be added at the end of a list in three ways.

- It is possible to nest lists, that is, creating a list of lists.

- Loops using lists can be constructed in four different ways.

- A list comprehension is of the following form within square brackets:

  `[expression for var in sequence [optional for and/or if]]`

- In Python, aliasing happens whenever one variable's value is assigned to another variable, because variables are just identifiers that store references to values. In computer programming, *aliasing* refers to the situation where the same memory locations are accessed using different names. The result is when we modify one list it affects the other.

- If we truly copy them then 2 list objects will be created, and they will be independent. So, a change made to one object will not affect another. This is called **cloning**. It is achieved through **slicing**.

- A list can be passed as a parameter to a function. A function can also return a list as an **argument**.

- When we find the transpose of a matrix, its row will become a column, and column will become a row in the transposed matrix.

- An array is a collection of items of the same type stored at contiguous memory locations.

- To use arrays in Python, we need to import the standard **array** module.

Questions

Choose the most appropriate answer:

1. **List object:**

     a. can hold duplicate entries

     b. is mutable

     c. has comma-separated items

     d. All of the above

     e. None of the above

2. **Sequence type includes:**

     a. Dictionary

     b. Sets

     c. Tuple

   d. All the above

   e. None of the above

3. **Cloning is carried out using:**

   a. list1=list2[:]

   b. list1=list2

   c. None of the above

4. **When we delete an element from a list using del keyword:**

   a. The entire list is deleted

   b. The placeholder remains

   c. The length of element reduces by 1

   d. All of the above

   e. None of the above

5. **Executing list1=[1,2,3,4,5] followed by print(list1[:2] will give:**

   a. [4,5]

   b. [1,2]

   c. (1,2)

   d. All of the above

   e. None of the above

6. **Assuming that list1 and lis2 are already defined, list3=[list1, list2]is list:**

   a. Nesting

   b. Concatenation

   c. Copying

   d. All of the above

   e. None of the above

7. **The output of following program is:**

```
a1=array('i',[10, 20, 30, 40, 50])

    sum=0

    for x in a1:

      sum=sum+x

     print('sum=', sum)
```

   a. 50

   b. 150

   c. sum=150

   d. All of the above

   e. None of the above

8. **The output of the following program is:**

```
numbers=[5, 10, 20]

[print (flow) for flow in numbers]
```

   a. 5, 10, 20

   b. 5 10 20

   c. 5

      10

      20

   d. All of the above

   e. None of the above

9. **The output of the following program is:**

```
List1=[30, 45, 10]
print (sorted(list1))
```

   a. [10, 30, 45]

   b. [30, 45, 10]

   c. [45, 30, 10]

   d. All of the above

   e. None of the above

10. **List function is the same as:**

   a. Method

   b. Comprehension

   c. concatenation

   d. All of the above

   e. None of the above

- Write short notes on the following:
  - o Containers
  - o Sequences
  - o Characteristics of lists
  - o Aliasing
  - o Cloning
  - o List comprehension
  - o List loops
  - o Slicing
  - o Nesting of lists
  - o Binary search
- Match the following:

A	B
Cloning	1. list1=list2
Aliasing	2. sum()
Function	3. Type code
Method	4. uses slicing
Array	5. append()

- Write programs for the following:
  - o Rewrite the program for linear search, receiving the list elements from the user.
  - o Rewrite the program for linear search using an array.
  - o Rewrite the program for binary search, receiving the list elements from the user.
  - o Rewrite the program for binary search using an array.
  - o Write a program to add corresponding elements of 2 matrices.
  - o Using list comprehension to:
    - ▪ Create a list whose elements are incremented from an existing list.
    - ▪ Number 5 subtracted from elements of an existing list.
  - o Create a list containing the days of the week. Assuming that Monday signifies day 1, and Sunday day 7, write a program that will print the name of the day given any number in the range 1 to 7.

o   Find out the result of the following program:

```
list1=[1, 2, 3, 4, 5]
print(list1)
list1.remove(2)
print(list1)
list1.append(77)
print(list)
list1.pop(4)
print(list1)
list1.insert(2,33)
print (list1)
print(list1.count(1))
list2=[10, 20, 30]
list1.extend(list2)
print(list1)
list1.reverse()
print(list1)
print(list1.index(5))
```

o   Write a program to double an element if it is odd and triple it if it is even.

o   Write the output of each step:

```
>>>list2=[7, 6, 5, 4, 11]
>>>print(list2)
>>>print(sorted(list2))
>>>print(list2)
>>>print(sum(list2))
>>>print(len(list2))
>>>print(max(list2))
>>>print(min(list2))
>>>print(list2)
>>>del(list2[1])
>>>print(list2)
>>>list1=list2+[10, 20, 30, 40]
>>>print (list1)
>>>del(list2)
```

Join our book's Discord space

Join the book's Discord Workspace for Latest updates, Offers, Tech happenings around the world, New Release and Sessions with the Authors:

https://discord.bpbonline.com

## CHAPTER 8

Tuples, Sets, and Dictionaries

Introduction

We discussed the built-in container list in the previous chapter. We will continue our discussions on three other three popular containers in this chapter. Tuple elements are comma separated and held between parentheses. The tuple is an immutable container, unlike a list, and will preserve data integrity. A set is an unordered collection of heterogenous data types, comma-separated and held between braces. The dictionaries contain key-value pairs and, as the name suggests, can be used to create language dictionaries and telephone directories. All the containers use comprehension to create new containers of the same type. The reader is advised to read this chapter after understanding the concepts given in the previous chapter.

Structure

The chapter covers the following topics:

- Tuple
- Set
- Dictionaries

Objectives

After studying this chapter, the reader will understand the nitty-gritty of the powerful Python containers, the compound data types, each of them useful in certain situations to hold and handle data. We will understand the similarities and differences between *list* and *tuple*. Like lists and tuple can be used to return values from functions. On the contrary, a set is an unordered collection of data items with no duplicate elements. It is handy for eliminating duplicate entries. Set objects support mathematical operations like *union*, *intersection*, *difference*, and *symmetric difference*, which is a unique property of sets.

Tuple

A tuple is one of the useful containers. Let us look at the salient features of tuples defined as follows:

- The tuple is one of the containers, sequences and compound data types.

- The tuple is similar to lists on some aspects listed below:

  o It can hold heterogeneous data types.

  o Tuples can hold duplicate data items in it.

  o The items of tuples can be accessed with indices like a list.

  o Like lists, the tuple elements are separated by commas.

  o Like lists, slicing and repetition are permitted.

  o Like lists, we can use the built-in functions such as *max, min, sum, sorted* and *len.*

The major differences between tuples and lists are given below:

- We use parentheses to hold the elements in a tuple, whereas we use square brackets to hold the elements of a list.

- During an assignment to tuples, even parentheses are not needed.

- Tuples are immutable like *strings*, whereas *lists* are mutable. The elements of tuples cannot be modified.

Let us learn about tuples in the interactive mode of Python. Read them carefully. It would be better to practice it on a laptop.

```
>>> tup1=(10, 20)# contains two numbers
>>> print(tup1)# entire tuple can be printed
(10, 20) # result of above statement
tup5=()    # empty tuple
```

```
>>> print (tup5)
()        # note empty parenthese
>>> tup2=(10, 25.6, 'swamy')# contains heterogeneous data
>>> print(tup2)
(10, 25.6, 'swamy')
>>> print(tup2[2])  # elements can be accessed by specifying index
Swamy      # indices are always given in square brackets
>>> tup3= 10, 25.6, 'swamy'  # parentheses not needed
>>> print(tup3)
(10, 25.6, 'swamy')   # it works
>>> print(type(tup3))
<class 'tuple'>    # type identified as class tuple
```

Tuples are immutable. This means that once a tuple is created, we cannot add new elements, delete elements from it, replace elements or reorder the elements. Let us check.

We get a runtime error, when we try to modify a tuple as the following two examples indicate:

Example 1:

```
>>>tup3[2]=34  # modifying element of tup3 with index 2
Traceback (most recent call last): # runtime error
  File "<pyshell#9>", line 1, in <module>
    tup3[2]=34
TypeError: 'tuple' object does not support item assignment
```

Example 2:

```
>>> tup3[1]=[] # trying to delete item at index 1
Traceback (most recent call last):
  File "<pyshell#10>", line 1, in <module>
    tup3[1]=[]
TypeError: 'tuple' object does not support item assignment
```

Built-in functions

Most of the built-in functions that are used with lists can also be used with tuples. In the following program, we will use some of them:

```
'''Program E8x1.py'''
ELEMENTS=5 # A constant defined
tup1=65, 85, 105, 205, 15 # assignment without parentheses
```

```
print(tup1)
print(len(tup1))  # length of tup1 - should print 5
print (sum(tup1)) # should print 475
print('average= ', sum(tup1)/ELEMENTS) # should be 95
print (sorted(tup1))
print(tup1)# sorted cannot alter tup1
print (max(tup1))# should be 205
print (min(tup1))# should be 15
```

The result of the program is given below. The results are as expected.

```
= RESTART: E:/Py programs/E8x1.py ===
(65, 85, 105, 205, 15) # tup1
5     # length of tup1
475    # sum of elements of tup1
average=  95.0  # average of elements of tup1
[15, 65, 85, 105, 205] # sorted tup1 printed as list
(65, 85, 105, 205, 15) #   tup1 remains as it was
205 # maximum of the elements of tup1
15  # minimum of the elements of tup1
```

Creating tuples from other container types

We can create a list and print it as a *tuple*. Similarly, we can create a string and print it as a tuple as the following indicates:

```
>>> list1=[9, 8, 7, 1, 2]
>>> print(tuple(list1))
(9, 8, 7, 1, 2) # see the parentheses instead of square brackets
>>> str1='beautiful'
>>> print (tuple(str1))
('b', 'e', 'a', 'u', 't', 'i', 'f', 'u', 'l')
```

Although a tuple is immutable, it can hold the immutable string and mutable list as the following demonstrates:

```
>>> tup4=([1,2,3,4], 'swamy')
>>> print (tup4)
([1, 2, 3, 4], 'swamy')
```

There is no change in the contents of **tup4**. Thus, a tuple can be used where we wish to prevent accidental tampering of data in a list or a string.

Built-in functions contd.

Tuple does not support methods such as **append ()** provided by the list. Let us carry out some more operations using built-in library functions:

```
'''Program E8x2.py'''
# Some more Operations using built in Functions
tup1=15, 65, 85, 105, 205 # create a tuple
tup2=('Oh', 'my', 'God')
print('concatenation ', tup1+tup2)
print('duplicate ', 2*tup2)
print('slicing ', tup1[1:3])
print(205 in tup1) # in operator- should get true
for var in tup2:   # printing elements in a tup1
    print(var, end='\n')
print(tup1==tup2) # result should be false
```

Result of the program is given below:

```
=================== RESTART: E:\Py programs\E8x2.py ===================
concatenation  (15, 65, 85, 105, 205, 'Oh', 'my', 'God')
duplicate  ('Oh', 'my', 'God', 'Oh', 'my', 'God') # repetition
slicing  (65, 85) # It won't affect tuple
True  # yes 205 is in tup1
Oh   # Printing using for loop starts here
my
God
False # tup1 is not equal to tup2
```

We have used a **for** loop to print elements in a tuple. Since it is a **for** loop, one element will be printed in each iteration. Contrast this with printing all the elements in one go or printing each element by their indices as shown below:

```
>>> tup1=15, 65, 85, 105, 205
>>> print(tup1[2])
85
```

Additional operations on tuple

Some more useful operations that can be carried out on tuples are given below:

- Creating tuple of tuples

- Embedding a tuple into another
- Unpacking elements of one tuple on another

These operations are performed in the following program. The result of the program is as follows:

```
'''Program E8x3.py'''
# additional operations on lists
tup1=15, 65, 85, 105, 205 # create a tuple
tup2=('Oh', 'my', 'God')
tup3=(tup1, tup2) # creating tuple of tuples
print('tup3= ', tup3)
tup4=(11, 22, tup2, 33) # embedding tup2 in tup4
print(tup4)
tup5=('me', 'you', *tup2, 'thank you') # unpacking tup2
print(tup5)
```

```
=================== RESTART: E:/Py programs/E8x3.py ===================
tup3=  ((15, 65, 85, 105, 205), ('Oh', 'my', 'God'))
# created tuple of tuples
(11, 22, ('Oh', 'my', 'God'), 33) # tup2 embedded in tup4
# unpacked tup2 in tup5
('me', 'you', 'Oh', 'my', 'God', 'thank you')
```

Unpacking of a tuple refers to the process of extracting individual elements or items from a tuple. The individual elements can be assigned to separate variables. This is particularly useful when we have a tuple containing multiple values and we want to work with those values individually. In Python, you can unpack a tuple using a simple assignment statement. The following code will clarify:

```
Python 3.10.10 (tags/v3.10.10:aad5f6a, Feb  7 2023, 17:20:36) [MSC v.1929
64 bit (AMD64)] on win32
Type "help", "copyright", "credits" or "license" for more information.
>>> # Example of tuple unpacking
>>> tuple_example = (1, 2, 3)
>>> x, y, z=tuple_example
>>> print(x)
1
>>> print(y)
2
>>> print(z)
3
>>>
```

Tuple as a return value

When a function returns more than one value, the values can be returned as a tuple. A program is given below to calculate the area, perimeter, and diagonal of a rectangle:

```python
'''Program E8x4.py'''
#   Returning values as a tuple
import math
def rect(l, b):
    area=l*b
    perim=2*(l+b)
    diag=math.sqrt(l*l+b*b)
    return(area, perim, diag)
def main():
    l,b=eval(input('enter length and breadth of a rectangle:'))
    area, perimeter, diagonal=rect(l,b)
    print('area=', area)
    print('perimeter=', perimeter)
    print('diagonal=', diagonal)

main()
```

In the program, we receive user input of the *length* and *breadth* of a rectangle as **l** and **b** in one go in the first line of the **main** function. In the second line of the **main** function, we call function **rect(l,b)** to get the area, perimeter, and diagonal as a tuple from the function **rect()**. Assume that we give two values, 3 and 4, separated by a comma. When the program executes, we will be invoking function **rect(3,4)**. In the **rect** function, **l** will be 3, and **b** will be 4. It will calculate **area**, **perim**, and **diag** as per the formula. Since we have to find the square root to find the diagonal, we import **math**. After calculation, the function **rect** returns all three calculated values as a tuple.

The three values returned as a tuple received in the **main** function are printed separately in the **main** function. There is no confusion about the values and their names. The result of the program is given below:

```
=================== RESTART: E:/Py programs/E8x4.py ===================
enter length and breadth of a rectangle:30,40
area= 1200
perimeter= 140
diagonal= 50.0
```

List as a return value

Like a tuple, a list can be used to return more than 1 value. Let us write a program to calculate the **area**, **perimeter,** and **diagonal** of a *square* and return it as a list. It is given below:

```
'''Program E8x5.py'''
#    Returning values as a list
import math
def sqre(l):
    area=l*l
    perim=4*l
    diag=math.sqrt(2)*l
    return[area, perim, diag]
def main():
    length=eval(input('enter length of a square:'))
    area, perimeter, diagonal=sqre(length)
    print('area=', area)
    print('perimeter=', perimeter)
    print('diagonal=', diagonal)


main()
```

In the program, we receive user input of the *length* of a square as *length* in the first line of the **main** function. In the second line of the **main** function, we call the function **sqre(length)**. Assume that we give a value 10. When the program executes, we will be invoking function **sqre(10)**. In the **sqre** function, l will be 10. It will calculate **area**, **perim**, and **diag** as per the formula. Since we have to find the square root to find the diagonal, we import **math**. After calculation, the function **sqre** returns all three calculated values as a list. In the previous program, the return statement enclosed the three values in parentheses, and hence, they were returned as a tuple. In this program, the **return** statement encloses the three values in square brackets, and hence they are returned as a list. It is simple to understand and implement. The result of the program is given below:

```
================== RESTART: E:/Py programs/E8x5.py ====================
enter length of a square:10
area= 100
perimeter= 40
diagonal= 14.142135623730951
```

Tuples and lists provide convenient mechanisms to return more than 1 value from a function. However, tuple is preferred over the list, since the former being immutable will prevent accidental tampering of returned data.

Set

Python Tutorial published by *Python* **https://docs.python.org/3/tutorial/datastructures. html#sets** defines a set is an unordered collection with no duplicate elements. It is handy for eliminating duplicate entries. Each of the containers has its unique characteristics. Recall that list is mutable and tuple is immutable. Set objects support mathematical operations like *union, intersection*, difference, and *symmetric difference*. This is a unique property of sets.

Let us look at some salient features of sets, one of the built-in compound data types defined in Python.

The list is versatile of all containers in Python and so we contrast a new container with it. Set is similar to lists in many aspects, such as:

- It holds heterogeneous data types.

- This compound data type can include all built-in types.

- Like lists, it is mutable.

- The entire set can be printed just by using the name of the set.

The major differences from the list are:

- A set is an unordered collection of objects. The order of elements of sets at any time may not necessarily be the same as that during insertion/addition. Therefore, items of sets cannot be accessed with indices.

- Unlike lists, sets do not hold duplicate data items in it. If an element is repeated, it will be removed.

- Being unordered, the slicing of sets is not possible.

- Uses curly braces to hold the elements in a set.

We will confirm the concepts through writing a program:

```
'''Program E8x6.py'''
# Sets
s2={'ram', 'lakshman', 'Sita', 'Mathi'} # enclosed in curly braces
print(s2)
s3={121, 24.5, 4+3j, True, 'vin'} # hetrogeneous data type
print(s3)
marks={100, 99, 98, 60, 100} # duplicate item will be ignored
print(marks)
```

The result of the execution of the above is given below:

```
{'lakshman', 'Sita', 'Mathi', 'ram'}# order of insertion not maintained
{True, (4+3j), 24.5, 121, 'vin'}
{98, 99, 100, 60} # duplicate item 100 eliminated
```

The order of insertion of elements in the set is not reflected on execution and the duplicate item **100** has been deleted.

Type set

Let us create a set **st1** and find its type. It is given below:

```
>>> st1={100, 200, 300}
>>> print(type(st1))
<class 'set'>
```

As the result reveals **st1** is an object of the built-in class **set**.

The set function

We can convert the other container types such as *list, tuple* and *string* to sets using the **set** function as the following reveals:

```
>>> st1='oh my god'
>>> se1=set(st1)
>>> print(se1)
{'h', ' ', 'o', 'd', 'y', 'g', 'm'}
>>> st2=(10, 20, 30, 40)
>>> se2=set(st2)
>>> print(se2)
{40, 10, 20, 30}
>>> st3=[1, 2, 3, 5, 7]
>>> se3=set(st3)
>>> print(se3)
{1, 2, 3, 5, 7}
```

A set will not maintain the order of insertion in the original container *string, list* and *tuple*. Hence, the elements may not be in the same order of insertion in some cases as the above illustrates.

Built-in functions

Most of the built-in functions that are available for lists are also available for **sets**. In the following program, we will use some of them:

```
'''Program E8x7.py'''
# Built-in Functions on set
marks={100, 99, 98, 60, 10, 31, 17}
print(marks)
print(len(marks)) # since length is 7 it will print 7
print(sum(marks))  # will print 415
print(min(marks)) # will print 10
print(max(marks)) # will print 100
print(99 in marks)  # returns true
print(16 in marks)  # returns false
print(100 not in marks) # returns false
print(sorted(marks))
print(*marks) # unpacks the elements*
```

The result of the program is given below. The results are as expected:

```
=================== RESTART: E:\Py programs\E8x7.py ===================
{98, 99, 100, 10, 17, 60, 31}
7     # length of set
415# sum of set
10    # Minimum in the set
100# maximum in the set
True      # yes, 99 is in the set
False # 16 is not in the set
False # 100 is in the set
[10, 17, 31, 60, 98, 99, 100] # sorted set printed as list
98 99 100 10 17 60 31 # unpack the elements in the set
```

Note: *marks unpacks the set and gives the elements without braces.

Methods of set class

Set has a few methods that operate on set objects. The program below creates two set objects **marks** and **s1**, enclosed within curly braces. Since set elements cannot be accessed through indices, we have to use the methods to do the task. The following methods have been exploited in the program:

- **update()**
- **add()**
- **remove()**
- **clear**

```
'''Program E8x8.py'''
# Methods of class set
marks={100, 99, 98, 60, 10, 31, 17}
s1={'Joseph', 'Peter', 'Thomas'}
marks.update(s1) #adds s1 to marks
print(marks)
s1.add('Xavier') # adds Xavier to s1
print(s1)
marks.remove(100) # deletes 100 from marks
print(marks)
s1.clear() # Removes all elements from s1
print(s1)
```

Result of the program is given below:

```
=================== RESTART: E:/Py programs/E8x8.py ===================
{98, 99, 100, 10, 'Joseph', 17, 'Peter', 'Thomas', 60, 31}
# marks after updating s1 to marks
{'Peter', 'Xavier', 'Joseph', 'Thomas'} #s1 after adding 'Xavier'
{98, 99, 10, 'Joseph', 17, 'Peter', 'Thomas', 60, 31} # marks after
removing 100
set() # s1 after clear
```

The results confirm our assumptions as given in the comments of the program.

Mathematical operations

We can carry out the following operations on sets. We need two sets to carry out these operations.

- **Union**: It is logical **or** operation. Elements in either list will be identified by this operation.
- **Intersection**: The resulting list will identify elements in both the lists. It is logical **and** operation.
- **Difference**: It contains elements in **list1** but not in **list2**, **list1-list2**.

- **Symmetric difference**: It identifies elements in either of the list, but not both. It is logical **exclusive or** operation on sets.

The following program tests all the above features of sets:

```
'''Program E8x9.py'''
# set operations
marks1={100, 99, 98, 60, 10, 31, 17}
marks2={77, 17, 100, 99, 98, 32, 17}
print("marks1: ", marks1)
print('marks2:' ,marks2)
print(marks1.union(marks2))  # elements in either list
print(marks1|marks2) # will get the same result
print(marks1.intersection(marks2)) # elements in both the lists
print(marks1&marks2)  # same result as above
print(marks1.difference(marks2)) # elements in marks1 and not in marks2
print(marks1-marks2)# same result as above
print(marks1.symmetric_difference(marks2))# elements in either set but not
both
print(marks1^marks2) # exclusive or - same result as above
```

The result confirms all the mathematical operations programmed. The results of pair of lines can be read as follows:

- 3rd and 4th line **marks1 or marks2**
- 5th and 6th line **marks1 & marks2**
- 7th and 8th line **marks1-marks2**
- 9th and 10th line **marks1 exclusive or marks 2**

The result of the program is given below:

```
==================== RESTART: E:/Py programs/E8x9.py ====================
marks1:  {98, 99, 100, 10, 17, 60, 31}
marks2: {32, 98, 99, 100, 77, 17}
{32, 98, 99, 100, 10, 77, 17, 60, 31}
{32, 98, 99, 100, 10, 77, 17, 60, 31}
{17, 98, 99, 100}
{17, 98, 99, 100}
{10, 60, 31}
{10, 60, 31}
```

```
{32, 10, 77, 60, 31}
{32, 10, 77, 60, 31}
```

Checking a set in comparison with other sets

We can check whether a set is a *subset* or *superset* of another. We can also check whether a set is equal to another as the following program indicates:

```
'''Program E8x10.py'''
# set operations
set1={100, 99, 98, 60, 10, 31, 17}
set2={100, 60, 31, 17}
print(set1.issuperset(set2)) # should be True
print(set1.issubset(set2)) # should be False
print(set1==set2) # should be False
```

The first **print** should return true and the other two will turn out to be false as the result indicates:

```
=================== RESTART: E:/Py programs/E8x10.py ==================
True
False
False
```

Set comprehension

Set comprehension is another way of creating new sets from already defined sets. A new set is created from another set. It is programmed in braces containing an expression followed by a **for** keyword and zero or more for and or if keywords.

An example of set comprehension follows:

```
>>> se1={1, 2, 3, 4}
>>> se2={num**3 for num in se1 if num%2}
>>> print(se2)
{1, 27}
```

Dictionary

All of us might have used pocket dictionaries and we know how it is organized. When we search for the meaning of the word, for instance, *jump*, we get its meaning. We can call the word for which we are finding meaning as the *key* and the meaning as the value. Similarly, in Python, we can visualize dictionaries as consisting of key-value pairs.

Dictionaries are also called **maps**. It is also a container object and a compound data type. Some of the features of dictionaries are given below:

- It is not a sequence type like *list* and the *elements* cannot be accessed with indices.

- It enables retrieval, deletion, and addition using the key.

- Keys in the dictionary are unique and immutable but can be deleted.

Some examples of dictionaries

We will look at a few examples of sets. For instance, we can create a set of **autos** as given below:

```
autos={'TN4567': 'madan', 'KA2890:'joseph', 'DBC844':'ganesh'}
```

In the dictionary **autos**, the registration number is the key, and the name of driver is the value. Each key has a corresponding value without exception. For instance, dictionary **days** can be defined as given below:

```
days={'Sunday':11, 'Monday':12, 'Tuesday':13, 'Thursday: 15}
'''in the days dictionary, days are keys and dates are values'''
meaning={'active':'lively', 'docile':'quite', 'smart':'clever'}
```

In the **meaning** dictionary, the keys are the first words, and values are the second words in each of the dictionary elements. Note that each dictionary element is a key-value pair. This is the uniqueness of dictionaries, which is not the case in the other Python containers. In that way, dictionaries are unique.

Let us learn some of the concepts in the interactive mode:

```
>>> days={'sunday':11, 'Tuesday':13, 'Monday':12}# dictionary
>>> print(days['Monday'])# printing element of dictionary using key
12
>>> print(days)# printing all elements of dictionary.
{'sunday': 11, 'Tuesday': 13, 'Monday': 12}
```

Iterations over dictionaries

The dictionaries can be iterated in four different ways as the following section will illustrate.

Method 1

In this method, we specify two parameters **k** and **v** following the **for** construct. The parameter **k** refers to the key, and **v** refers to the value in the dictionary. The **marks. items()** refers to the key-value pairs in the dictionary **marks**:

```
>>> marks={'ram':100, 'sita':99, 'hanuman': 99, 'laksh':100}
```

```
>>> for k, v in marks.items():# iterating over key-value pairs
        print(k,v)
ram 100
sita 99
hanuman 99
laksh 100
```

See that the single quotes around the keys and colon between keys and values are not printed.

Method 2

Here, we omit the second parameter **v**, but it works the same way as *Method 1*:

```
>>> for k in marks.items():
        print(k)
('ram', 100)
('sita', 99)
('hanuman', 99)
('laksh', 100)
```

Note that the strings have quotes surrounding them and the pairs are in parentheses.

Method 3

In this method, we print only the keys. We omit the *items*. This prints all keys and not values:

```
>>> for key in marks:
        print(key)
ram
sita
hanuman
laksh
```

Alternatively, we can give the dictionary in the definition of the **for** loop instead of the name of the dictionary:

```
>>> for key in {'ram':100, 'sita':99, 'hanuman': 99, 'laksh':100}:
    print(key)
ram
sita
hanuman
laksh
```

Method 4

In this method, we print all values:

```
>>> for val in marks.values():
        print(val)
100
99
99
100
```

An interesting point to be noted about dictionaries is as follows:

- To refer to the keys, we used either k, key or keys. We can also use other names like p, q, and r.

- To refer to the values, we used either v, val, or value or values. We can also use other names like p, q, and r.

Using built-in functions with dictionary

We can carry out the following operations in a dictionary:

- Adding a new key-value pair

- Modifying a key-value pair

- Deleting a key-value pair

- Deleting a dictionary object – delete all elements in it

- Finding the existence and non-existence of a key

- Finding the number of pairs

- Maximum key value

- Minimum key value

- Obtaining key insertion order

- Obtaining sorted list of keys

We write a program to make use of the operations with a dictionary:

```
'''Program E8x11.py'''
# Dictionary operations
dct1={1:'Jan', 2:'Feb', 3:'March', 4:'April'}
dct1[5]='May'
```

```
print(dct1) # May will be added
dct1[1]='January' # modifying Jan to January
print(6 in dct1) # checks presence of 6 in dct1
print(6 not in dct1) # Checks absence of 6 in dct1
print(len(dct1))  # prints the number of elements
print(max(dct1)) # prints maximum key value
print(min(dct1)) # prints minimum key value
print(list(dct1)) # prints keys as a list in order of insertion
print(sorted(dct1)) # prints sorted keys as a list
del(dct1[3]) # it will delete key value pair with key =3
print(dct1)
del(dct1) # the object will be deleted and no elements left
print(dct1)
```

The result of the program is given below. In the last line of the program, since we are trying to display a non-existing dictionary object, it throws error.

```
================= RESTART: E:/Py programs/E8x11.py ==================
{1: 'Jan', 2: 'Feb', 3: 'March', 4: 'April', 5: 'May'}
False # checks whether 6 is in dictionary
True  # Checks whether 6 is NOT in dictionary
5       # prints the length of dictionary
5       # maximum key value in dictionary
1       # minimum key value in dictionary
[1, 2, 3, 4, 5]
[1, 2, 3, 4, 5] # sorted keys
{1: 'January', 2: 'Feb', 4: 'April', 5: 'May'}
Traceback (most recent call last):
  File "E:/Py programs/E8x6.py", line 18, in <module>
    print(dct1)
NameError: name 'dct1' is not defined
```

Since we had deleted **dct1** and tried to print it, we are getting a runtime error.

Dictionary methods

In addition to the operations, the dictionary supports the following methods:

- **dictionary.keys()** # keys will be printed as a tuple.
- **dictionary.values()** # values will be printed as tuple.

- **dictionary.items()** # returns a sequence of tuples.
- **dictionary.clear()** # deletes all entries.
- **dictionary.get(key)** # gets the value corresponding to the key.
- **dictionary.pop(key))** # item corresponding to the key will be popped.
- **dictionary.popitem()** # last item will be returned.
- **dct1.update(dct2)** # **dct2** added to **dct1**.

A program using these methods is given below:

```
'''Program E8x12.py'''
# Dictionary Methods
def main():
    dct1={1:'Jan', 2:'Feb', 3:'March', 4:'April'}
    print(dct1) # keys and values of dictionary printed
    print(dct1.keys()) # keys will be printed as tuple
    print(dct1.values()) # values will be printed as tuple
    print(dct1.items())  # items printed as tuple
    print(dct1.get(3))     # will print march
    print(dct1.pop(3))   # march will be printed
    print(dct1.popitem()) # last item will be returned
    dct2={5:'May', 6:'June'} # new dictionary created
    dct1.update(dct2) # dct2 added to dct1
    print(dct1)
main()
```

The result of program is given below:

```
=================== RESTART: E:/Py programs/E8x12.py ==================
{1: 'Jan', 2: 'Feb', 3: 'March', 4: 'April'}
dict_keys([1, 2, 3, 4])
dict_values(['Jan', 'Feb', 'March', 'April'])
dict_items([(1, 'Jan'), (2, 'Feb'), (3, 'March'), (4, 'April')])
March # getting value with key== 3
March # popping item with key==3
(4, 'April')  # popitem - last key: value
{1: 'Jan', 2: 'Feb', 5: 'May', 6: 'June'} # after adding dct2
```

Dictionary comprehension

We can create new dictionaries using the **for** loop. The general form of the **for** is given below:

```
dct2={key:value for(key, value) in dct1.items()}
```

Note that braces are used for dictionary comprehension. Using this form, two new dictionary objects are created in the following program:

```
'''Program E8x13.py'''
# Dictionary comprehension
def main():
    dct1={1:'Jan', 2:'Feb', 3:'March', 4:'April'}
    print(dct1) # keys and values of dictionary printed
    print(dct1.keys()) # keys will be printed as tuple
    dct2={key**4:value for (key, value) in dct1.items()}
# dct2 with new values which are old value^4 will be created
    print(dct2)
    dct3={'Monday':1, 'Tuesday':2, 'Thursday':4}
    dct4={key:value**2 for (key, value) in dct3.items()}
   # dct4 with new values of squared old values created
    print(dct3)
    print(dct4)

main()
```

The result of the program is given below:

```
=================== RESTART: E:/Py programs/E8x13.py ==================
{1: 'Jan', 2: 'Feb', 3: 'March', 4: 'April'}
dict_keys([1, 2, 3, 4]) # keys of dictionary printed as list
{1: 'Jan', 16: 'Feb', 81: 'March', 256: 'April'} # keys to power 4
{'Monday': 1, 'Tuesday': 2, 'Thursday': 4}
{'Monday': 1, 'Tuesday': 4, 'Thursday': 16} # keys squared in above
```

Let us look at another example of creating a new dictionary from another dictionary using dictionary comprehension. It is programmed in braces containing an expression followed by a **for** keyword and zero or more for and or if keywords. An example of dictionary comprehension is given below:

```
>>> dct1={'apple': 100, 'orange': 60, 'banana': 55}
>>> dct2={k:v*1.2 for (k,v) in dct1.items()}
```

```
>>> print(dct2)
{'apple': 120.0, 'orange': 72.0, 'banana': 66.0}
```

Nested dictionaries

The dictionaries can be nested as given below:

```
marks={
'ram':{'maths':89, 'physics':98, 'chemistry':100},
'ravi':{'maths':86, 'physics':95, 'chemistry':90},
'sita':{'maths':89, 'physics':98, 'chemistry':100},
'lak':{'maths':88, 'physics':96, 'chemistry':100}
}
```

Let us try it out in a program:

Look at the program below. We have nested 4 dictionaries named **'ram'**, **'ravi'**, **'sita'** and **'lak'** and we have nested them under the dictionary, *marks*. After nesting them, we print the nested dictionary **marks**.

```
'''Program E8x14.py'''
# Nesting Dictionary
def main():
    marks={
        'ram':{'maths':89, 'physics':98, 'chemistry':100},
        'ravi':{'maths':86, 'physics':95, 'chemistry':90},
        'sita':{'maths':89, 'physics':98, 'chemistry':100},
        'lak':{'maths':88, 'physics':96, 'chemistry':100}
        }
    print(marks)
main()
```

The result of the program is given below:

```
=================== RESTART: E:/Py programs/E8x14.py ==================
{'ram': {'maths': 89, 'physics': 98, 'chemistry': 100}, 'ravi':
{'maths': 86, 'physics': 95, 'chemistry': 90}, 'sita': {'maths': 89,
'physics': 98, 'chemistry': 100}, 'lak': {'maths': 88, 'physics': 96,
'chemistry': 100}}
```

Note: The name of the dictionary precedes the key-value pairs.

Conclusion

In this chapter, we discussed in detail about containers tuple, set and dictionary. All the four containers discussed, that is, list, tuple, set, and dictionary have access to the built-in library functions and methods specific to them. Tuples are like lists on some aspects such as holding heterogeneous data types, holding duplicate data items, accessing elements with indices, slicing and repetition. We also created a tuple of tuples and embedded a tuple into another. We carried out mathematical operations on sets and learned to create new lists, tuples and dictionaries using comprehension.

In the next chapter, we will discuss object-oriented programming.

Points to remember

- Like list, the tuple elements are separated by commas.

- Like list, we can use the built-in functions such as max, min, sum, sorted and len.

- During assignment to tuples, even parentheses are not needed. But we need to put the elements of a list in square brackets.

- Most of the built-in functions used with lists can also be used with tuples.

- We can create a list and print it as a tuple. Similarly, we can create a string and print it as a tuple.

- Some more useful operations that can be carried out on tuples is given below.

    o Creating tuple of tuples

    o Embedding a tuple into another

    o Unpacking elements of one tuple on another

- When a function returns more than one value, the values can be returned as a tuple.

- A set is an unordered collection with no duplicate elements. It is very handy in eliminating duplicate entries.

- Set objects also support mathematical operations like union, intersection, difference, and symmetric difference.

- Set has a few methods which operate on set objects.

    o `update()`

    o `add()`

    o `remove()`

    o `clear()`

- We can carry out the following operations on sets. We need 2 sets to carry out these operations:

  o Union

  o Intersection

  o Difference

  o Symmetric difference

- We can check whether a set is a subset or superset of another. We can also check whether one set is equal to another.

- An interesting point to be noted about dictionaries is given below:

  o To refer to the keys, we can type either k, key, keys, p, q and r.

  o To refer to the values, we can type either v, val, value or values, p, q and r.

Questions

Choose the most appropriate answer:

1. **Tuple is:**

   a. mutable

   b. immutable

   c. None of the above.

2. **tuple1=11, 2,3,5,7,13. The len(tuple1) will return:**

   a. 7

   b. 5

   c. 6

   d. None of the above

3. **In tuple1=11, 2,3,5,7,13. tuple1[2:4] will return:**

   a. (2,3)

   b. (3, 5)

   c. (3,5,7)

   d. None of the above

4. **What is the result of executing the following?**

   `>>>8 in tuple1`

   a. True

   b. False

   c. None of the above

5. **Values can be returned from a function as:**

   a. tuple

   b. list

   c. All of the above

   d. None of the above

6. **Values are held between curly braces in:**

   a. lists

   b. tuples

   c. sets

   d. All of the above

   e. None of the above

7. **Duplicate items are eliminated in:**

   a. sets

   b. lists

   c. tuple

   d. None of the above

8. **Elements cannot be accessed with indices in:**

   a. list

   b. tuple

   c. dictionary

   d. All the above

   e. None of the above

9. **Logical operations are possible in:**

   a. list

   b. dictionaries

c. tuple

d. None of the above

10. **Sequence type is:**

a. lists

b. sets

c. dictionaries

d. None of the above

• **Write short notes on the following**:

o Similarities and differences between tuples and lists

o Tuple built-in functions

o Creating tuples from lists and strings

o Mathematical operations on sets

o List as a return value

o Similarities and differences between tuples and sets

o Different ways of iteration of dictionary

o Set operations

o Built-in functions are common to all the four containers

o Properties common to all four containers

• Match the following:

A	B
Tuple	1. curly braces
Dictionary	2. square brackets
Sets	3. parentheses
List	4. last item returned
popitem()	5. key-value pairs

• Write programs for the following:

o Create a tuple of the first 100 natural numbers using for loop and find their average.

o Create a tuple of the first 100 natural numbers using a while loop and find their average.

o   Create a student record of marks in 5 subjects as a tuple and find the total and average.

o   Repeat the above with dictionaries.

o   To demonstrate tuple and list as return values in a function returning circumference and area of a circle.

o   Create a dictionary for the following data:

Ram	100
Sita	100
Laksh	97
Krishna	78
Gopal	86
Shiv	100

A student record consists of 5 students and their marks in five subjects. Create a dictionary and print the marks obtained by each student in each subject.

o   To count the occurrences of each number in a tuple.

o   To sort a dictionary in ascending order of key and then value.

o   Write a program to carry out the following operations in a=10, 45, 1, 2, 89, 100:

  ▪   sum

  ▪   minimum

  ▪   maximum

  ▪   sorted in ascending order

Join our book's Discord space

Join the book's Discord Workspace for Latest updates, Offers, Tech happenings around the world, New Release and Sessions with the Authors:

https://discord.bpbonline.com

## CHAPTER 9

Introduction to Object-Oriented Programming

Introduction

Python is a versatile high-level and structured programming language. It is a procedure-oriented language. It is also a scripting language. Above all it is a full-fledged object-oriented programming language. Only a few programming languages share such a credit. In the preceding chapters, we executed several functions. The programs were written in a procedure-or function-oriented manner. We also realized that Python is a structured programming language with strict rules for indenting and supporting structured programming concepts such as the decision and iteration constructs and functions. Large programs have been written with these concepts. However, data integrity may be of concern in critical applications in procedure-oriented programs. Furthermore, the concepts discussed so far do not provide facilities for building systems with **graphical user interfaces (GUI)**. This problem can be overcome with object-oriented programming, which we will discuss in this chapter. Python is also an object-oriented programming language implying structured programming as well as protecting data integrity and security.

Structure

The chapter covers the following topics:

- Object-oriented programming

- Advantages of OOP

- Class

- The self

- Object

- Access control

- Object initializer

- Destruction of objects

- The id function and type function

- Carrying out operations on objects

- Class variables versus instance variables

- Operator overloading

- Overloading functions supported in Python

- Overloading binary operators

- Documentation strings

Objectives

After going through this chapter, the reader will understand class, a user-defined type, and objects, which are instances of classes. In OOP, data access is controlled so that a novice does not tamper with them. We will also discuss the advantages of OOP. The language provides object initializers. It also provides destructors to reclaim the memory space allocated when it is no longer required. We will also learn the difference between class and instance variables. The chapter will also discuss the documentation of programs.

Object-oriented programming

Let us examine the three important principles an **object-oriented program** (**OOP**) should support. They are listed below:

- Encapsulation (data hiding)

- Inheritance

- Polymorphism

We will briefly discuss the features that provide object orientation to computer programs.

Encapsulation

Data is synonymous with objects. In the early days of programming, instructions were more important. Inadequate attention was given to protecting the integrity and safety of data due to the nature of **procedure-oriented programming** concepts. This led to losses of space missions and many failures of safety-critical systems. Structured programming was brought to discipline programming to minimize errors in the code. OOP further strengthened programming by emphasizing data and encapsulating them to prevent tampering by unskilled users or programmers. This concept is not new but has been practiced in other engineering products. For instance, take the example of a car. We cannot see the components inside or meddle with them. However, we can drive the car without knowing what is inside. We can carry out all car functions, such as starting the engine, changing gears, pressing the clutch, accelerator, and brake when needed, using the external interfaces provided in the car, without knowing the details of the components used. However, an authorized car mechanic has access to the car's components. He can check and replace them when needed. This is an analogy to the concept of encapsulation of objects in OOP. The objects are open for use but closed for modifications.

Wrapping together data and functions creates the objects in OOP. They are bound together. This represents encapsulation in OOP. We can use encapsulated objects through the designated interfaces only. Thus, the inner parts of the program are sealed or encapsulated to protect from accidental tampering. This feature is not available in conventional procedure-oriented-programming languages where the data can be corrupted since it is easily accessible.

In Python, an OOP language, encapsulation is achieved through classes. A *class* is a blueprint for making an object. It defines the specifications for constructing objects with data and functions. It defines the private or internal working of the objects and their public interfaces. The data, known as **data member(s)** of the *class*, define the state of the proposed object. The functions or methods define its interfaces. We will discuss classes in more detail later.

In Python, a *class* is used for defining two types of members, as given below:

- Data
- Functions

Data are constants and variables that specify the characteristics of the class. Functions, called **methods**, contain a sequence of instructions that operate on the data. An object is a variable of a type *class*. It is a self-contained computing entity with its data and methods. This means an object will have its copy of the attributes, the literals. However, the methods common to all the objects created in the *class* need not be kept in each object. Providing access to the methods may suffice. The attributes of each distinct object will be unique. However, all objects have access to the common methods of the class.

Note carefully that a *class* can give rise to many objects but is not an object on its own. The objects thus created have a common structure, but different characteristics. Thus, two objects of a *class* with different names will have the same variable names, but with different values, that is, they have the same data types but different data. For instance, take the example of two cars of the same model. They are different entities with differences in color, engine number, chassis number, and maybe in fittings. Each car is an object made as per common specifications. In some special cases, two objects can also have the same data. A *class* is a framework for the proper encapsulation of objects. The data members of the objects can be accessed only through the interface available in public.

Inheritance

Inheritance property is akin to human beings. A child inherits the property of his father. He can acquire new properties or modify the inherited ones. Similarly, a new *class* can derive its properties from another existing class. Thus, it becomes a derived *class* of the parent class, called a **base class**. A derived *class* inherits all the properties of the base *class*. Therefore, the degree of encapsulation of the base *class* applies equally to the derived one. More properties can be added to the derived class if needed. The complexity of the derived *class* may grow as the level of inheritance grows. There is no limit to the level of inheritance. Inheritance property aids the reusability of already developed and tested code in new applications.

Polymorphism

Polymorphism is a useful concept in OOP languages. In simple terms, it means one name and many duties. It provides a common interface to carry out similar tasks. In other words, a common interface is created for accessing related objects. A method with a common name may be defined in the base class and its subclasses during inheritance. Python runtime system attaches the appropriate method to an object of any of the base or inherited classes. Since Python is a dynamically typed language, the attachment of each object type at runtime to appropriate methods depending on the context is an inherent characteristic of the language.

Operator overloading

Python also supports operator overloading. The common operators, such as +, –, *, /, and so on, can be programmed to carry out the respective operations on different compound data types, such as containers or user-defined objects, depending on the context in which the operator is used. Such operators are said to be overloaded. This simplifies a program by making the same operators work for different types of objects.

We will discuss *inheritance* and *polymorphism* in the next chapter. Operator overloading is also a type of polymorphism covered in this chapter.

Advantages of OOP

Let us discuss the advantages of object-oriented programming briefly:

- **Reusability**: The object-oriented programs are designed for reuse. Encapsulation, polymorphism, and inheritance facilitate ease of reuse.

- **Maintainability**: Each class is self-contained with data and methods, and the methods are grouped. Therefore, the maintainability of object-oriented programs is high.

- **Natural**: The software objects represent the real objects in the problem domain, and hence, programming is closer to reality.

- **Modular**: Modularity in OOP is obtained by dividing the program into well-defined and closely-knit classes.

- **Extensibility**: The inheritance mechanism facilitates extending the feature of the classes easily.

- **Data integrity**: Avoiding global variables and **goto** statements, binding the data within the class, and providing restricted access ensures data integrity.

Class

What is a **class**? We know many classes in our daily life. Some examples are men, women, students, teachers, chairs, tables, PCs, and so on. Objects of each *class* possess similar characteristics but vary in magnitude. For instance, the height and weight of each man may vary. However, the specifications remain the same. Therefore, all the examples discussed above can be considered as different classes.

A **class** in Python is an important framework for creating user-defined data types. Classes provide convenient mechanisms to the programmer to build their data types apart from the built-in classes such as *int, float, str, complex, bool, list, tuple, set,* and *dictionary*. The class types are convenient to represent real entities. They are needed since built-in types cannot be used to represent real entities so conveniently. They are quite handy to represent various real entities like a bank account, student record, payroll, animals, and other man-made items such as *graphical objects*. A *class* defines both data and methods to operate on them. A *class* gives blueprint for a data type to be created. It is self-contained with data and methods.

A *class* will have a name, usually starting with an upper-case letter. A *class* definition may consist of data and function definitions. The *class* is a keyword.

A simple class

Let us look at an example of a class. It is given below:

```
class Account:

    def get_data(self,s, n, b):

        self.name=s

        self.account=n

        self.balance=b
```

Note that Python is case sensitive and hence **Account** and **account** are identifiers for different entities. Every class is preceded by the **class** keyword. The *class* name tag follows it, followed by a colon. In the above example, the *class* name is **Account**. It is convention that a class name starts with upper case letters. In the above example of **Account** class, a method has been defined after the class definition. A method has to be defined in the first tab. It begins with a **def** keyword. It is followed by a valid identifier as the name for the method, followed by a colon. Here, the method name is **get_data**. It is followed in parentheses by a term **self** and three formal parameters.

The self

What is the significance of **self**? Whenever an object, an instance of a *class* calls a method, the memory address of the object in hexadecimal format gets passed to the method. The address is collected by the parameter *self* in the method. Although it is the convention to use the term *self*, any other meaningful term could also be used. The method **get_data** above has been defined with 3 formal parameters **s**, **n** and **b**. In the body of the method, *s* is assigned to **self.name**, n is assigned to **self.account**, and **b** is assigned to **self.balance**. Note that **name**, **account**, and **balance** are the three attributes of the class **Account** or the data members of the class. There is no restriction on the maximum or minimum for the data members or the methods. The attributes of the object are set by the method indirectly in this case.

Object

Each man or woman or an item is an object of class **man** and class **woman** respectively with unique characteristics. Similarly, an object is an instance of a class or in other words, object is created with the attributes of a *class*. A *class* provides a blueprint for creating objects. It is not stored anywhere, and memory is not allotted to classes since they do not exist physically. On the contrary, objects exist physically, and memory has to be allotted when an object is created. Being an object-oriented programming language, Python has an abundant number of built-in classes in its standard library. For instance:

```
a=12    # a is an object of built-in class int
b=10.5 # b is an object of built-in class float
```

```
c=4+3j  # c is an object of built-in class complex
d='god' # d is an object of built in class str
e=[10, 20, 30] # e is an object of built-in class list
f={3, 5, 7, 11}  # f is an object of built-in class set
```

Everything is an object in Python – the literals, string, functions, containers like *list*, *tuple* and so on. An object can be considered to be a variable of the type *class*, similar to other variables of the built-in classes such as *int*, *str*, *complex*, and so on. In the previous example, **Account** is a user-defined *class*. Every person's account is an object. Each account holder has a name, (account) number, and balance. However, all accounts use the same template. Thus, any number of replicas (objects) can exist for each defined class. This is the relationship between **objects** and a **class**. The relationship is illustrated pictorially below:

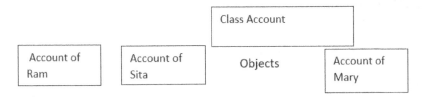

Figure 9.1: Objects or instances of class Account

In *Figure 9.1*, we have a class named **Account**. Below it, we have 3 objects of the class **Account**. The names of the objects are *Ram*, *Sita*, and *Mary*, respectively. While *class* holds a generic data structure, objects hold specific data, as illustrated in the figure. Thus, one *class* can give rise to many objects. Objects have names and their data. The methods will contain program statements. The objects share the methods in the class.

Access control

The access to data and functions of a class could be:

- **Private**: Access is restricted to the specific class.
- **Public**: Access is open to all classes.
- **Protected**: Access is restricted to specific class and inherited classes, which will be explained in subsequent chapters.

If the member methods or data members are declared to be public, then they can be accessed from anywhere. The members, either the data members or the member methods, if declared private, can be accessed only from within the class. The data members should not be declared public since it will defeat the very purpose of data hiding, which is one of the essential requirements of OOP. However, the member methods are usually declared public. Declaring both the methods and data as *private* will shield the class from the outside world and therefore it does not serve any useful purpose. To protect data integrity and security, the data are declared private. The methods are allowed to be accessible from anywhere, from within the class or outside of it. The authorized objects outside the class can access its private data members only through the member methods of the class that are declared *public*. The member methods cannot be accessed from outside if declared *private*. Therefore, the member methods must be declared public for meaningful programs. How do we specify whether a data or method is public, private, or protected? The private data will have a prefix of double underscore (__), also known as **underscore**, as illustrated in the following program. The protected data members will have a prefix of a single underscore. If the underscore prefix is missing, the data or method will be assumed to be public.

Using the concepts learned so far, let us write a program to create a class **Account** and then display the name, account number, and balance of 3 account holders. The program is given below with line numbers for ease of understanding. Let us read line by line and try to understand the program:

```
E9x1.py - E:\Py programs\E9x1.py (3.8.2)                    —    □    ×

File  Edit  Format  Run  Options  Window  Help
 1  # program E9x1.py
 2  # A simple class
 3  class Account:   # class definition
 4      def get_data(self, s, n, b):
 5          self.__name=s
 6          self.__account = n
 7          self.__balance =b
 8
 9      def display(self):   # Method declaration
10          print("Name =", self.__name)
11          print("Account number =", self.__account)
12          print("Balance        =", self.__balance)
13
14  def main():
15      Vinay = Account()    # creating object
16      Vinay.get_data('Ram', 1212, 10000.75)
17      Vinay.display() # calling a function
18
19      # creating second object
20      Karthik = Account()   # creating object
21      Karthik.get_data('Sita', 1213, 24578.90)
22      Karthik.display() # calling a function
23
24  main()
25
26  |
```

Figure 9.2: *Creating objects of Account class*

The first and second lines are comment statements since they start with **#**. They are for information and not for execution. Such documentation is useful to understand the program by others and by the programmer himself later on. Therefore, the insertion of adequate comments in the program is a welcome step.

We have a class definition in *line 3*. Note that the definition ends with a colon. The **class** keyword is in lowercase, and the class name starts with an uppercase letter, which is a convention and not a rule.

In *line 4*, we are defining a method **get_data()** beginning with the **def** keyword. The name of the method is **get_data**. It receives **self** and three formal parameters, and the function definition ends with a colon. Whenever an object calls a method, the address of the calling object is passed implicitly to the method. The address is collected by *self*. The next 3 statements at *lines 5, 6*, and 7 belong to the function **get_data()**. The following are the data members of the class **Account** as implied by the **get_data** method:

- name

- account (Account beginning with uppercase A is the name of the class and account is a data member)

- balance

When an object calls this method **get_data**, the three attributes of the method as listed above are passed to the method. The attributes are, in turn, assigned to the data members of the object in *lines 5, 6*, and 7. In other programming languages such as *C++* and *Java*, the data members are explicitly and directly defined in the *class*. However, that is not always the case with Python. Here, we are defining them indirectly through a method of the class.

In the method **get_data**, we assign the actual arguments to the three data members of the calling object, as given below:

1. **self.__name=s**

2. **self.__account=n**

3. **self.__balance=b**

What does the double underscore signify? It means that the access specifiers for all three data members, **name, account**, and **balance**, are *private*. When an object is created, the actual values of the arguments will be specified. The object's address is received by **self** at the time of creation of the object. An object has to call this method at runtime to assign the values for its data members.

In *line 9*, we have the definition of method *display* preceded by the **def** keyword and ends with a colon. It does not receive any formal parameters. However, *self* within the parenthesis to identify the object calling the function. In the method, we print all the three data members.

You can see the dot operator at several places. The object or the *self*, precedes dot. The *self* refers to the address of the object calling the function, or in other words, the object itself. An attribute or method follows the dot. This implies that the attribute or method is called by an object preceding the dot.

The **display** method prints the values of the three data members of the object, that is, **name**, **account**, and **balance**. The method *display* can be called only after the object has been created with the **get_data** method. Object creation is complete only when its data members get specific attributes or values. The class definition ends at *line 12*. The class has two methods and 3 data members.

The **main()** function is defined in *line 14*. In *line 15*, we create an object **Vinay** of type **Account**. The object created from the **Account** class will have specific values for data. Then, in *line 16*, we pass the actual data of the **name**, **account**, and **balance** of **Vinay** to the function **get_data**. They are received by the respective data members. Each object is a specific instance of the class. Creating an object is also called **instantiation**. The data in the objects are called **instance data**. They are the attributes of the object.

In *line 17*, we invoke the **Vinay.display** function that prints the account details of the object **Vinay**. In *lines 20 to 22*, we repeat the same steps for another object **Karthik**. This time **self** will receive a different address of object **Karthik**. The account details of **Karthik** object will be displayed now.

Some points concerning the program to be noted are given below:

- We created objects outside the class and accessed methods in the class. We could do this because the methods are public. The methods are called by an object using dot notation. For instance, **Vinay.display()**.

- All three data members are declared private with a double underscore prefix. This is the right approach.

- **self** receives the address of the object calling the methods.

- Class ties together data and methods and hence a compound data type.

The result of the program is given below:

```
=====RESTART: E:/Py programs/9Ex1.py =======================
Name = Ram
Account number = 1212
Balance        = 10000.75
Name = Sita
Account number = 1213
Balance        = 24578.9
```

We have successfully executed an OOP and understood the concepts clearly. The objects and special data types are to be created as given in the program.

Note that in creating user-defined objects, we followed the given set pattern:

We first declared the user-defined data type namely **Account** which is a class. Then, we gave the name of its instance as *Vinay*. When we create an object, the system automatically allocates the required memory space for the object. Both the fundamental data variables such as marks and objects, which are variables of type class, are created in a similar manner. In the case of a simple variable, it is just an assignment of memory for one variable. On the other hand, in the case of an object, the assignment of memory should be for all the data members. Furthermore, there is a way of associating the data members with the corresponding objects through the *self*.

Object initializer

In addition to the two user-defined methods seen in the above program, a special method for incorporation into the class exists. It is called the **initializer**. The operation of the object initializer is similar to constructors in some programming languages, such as C++. It is executed whenever we create new objects of that *class*. It is the first piece of code to be executed when we create a new object of a *class*. It is called by the object to initialize an object's attributes or data members on creation. The method is **__init__()**. The name of the method **init** is preceded and followed by double underscores. If we do not define **__init__()**, Python provides an **__init__()** method automatically.

A question may arise, then what is **get_data** method? The **__init__**method initializes the object and **get_data** modifies it. The **__init__** also plays the role when an empty object is created.

Destruction of object

When an object is no longer in use, it should be deleted using **__del__()** method to free up resources such as memory space. This method is called **destructor** in other programming languages, such as C++. The method **__del__()** is called when an object goes out of scope. Note that **del** is a keyword of Python. It is preceded and followed by double underscores when we define a destructor to free up the space occupied by the object no longer needed in the program.

Let us write a program incorporating these two features. Look at the program:

```
 *E9x2.py - E:\Py programs\E9x2.py (3.10.11)*

File  Edit  Format  Run  Options  Window  Help

 1 | # program E9x2.py
 2 | # A complete class
 3 | class Account:  # class definition
 4 |    def __init__(self, s ='', n=0, b=0.0):
 5 |        self.__name=s
 6 |        self.__account = n
 7 |        self.__balance =b
 8 |
 9 |    def get_data(self, s, n, b):
10 |        self.__name=s
11 |        self.__account = n
12 |        self.__balance =b
13 |
14 |    def display(self):  # Method declaration
15 |        print("Name =", self.__name)
16 |        print("Account number =", self.__account)
17 |        print("Balance      =", self.__balance)
18 |
19 |    def __del__(self):
20 |        print('object deleted  '+str(self))
21 |
22 | def main():
23 |    Vinay = Account()  # creating object
24 |    Vinay.get_data('Ram', 1212, 10000.75)
25 |    Vinay.display() # calling a method
26 |
27 |    # creating second object
28 |    Karthik = Account()  # creating object
29 |    Karthik.get_data('Sita', 1213, 24578.90)
30 |    Karthik.display() # calling a method
31 |
32 |    # creating third object
33 |    m= Account()  # creating object
34 |    m.get_data('mary', 1214, 20000)
35 |    m.display() # calling a method
36 |
37 | main()
38 |
```

Figure 9.3: Demonstrating initializer and destructor

In *line 4*, we have defined **__init__** method. **__init__** is a special Python method that is automatically called when memory is allocated for a new object. The sole purpose of **__init__** is to initialize the values of instance members for the new object. Whenever an object is created, its address will be passed on to **self** in **__init__** function. The **__init__** method in this program has been designed with default arguments, **s** assigned an empty string, **n**, and **b** to zero. These default arguments will be assigned to the three data members of new object at *lines 5* to *7*. The object will be initialized with the default arguments.

In *line 23*, when object **Vinay** of type **account** is created, the **__init__** function will be invoked, and the data members initialized with empty string and zeros respectively. Then in *line 24*, we invoke **get_data** function with object **Vinay** with actual arguments. The object **Vinay** will be updated with the actual arguments. In *line 25*, we call **display** function for **Vinay** object to display the data members of **Vinay** object. We repeat the similar actions for object **Karthik** in *lines 28* to *30*. Then for object **m** in *lines 33* to *35* of the program, repeat the task of creating the object and displaying the data members. After that, all the three objects have gone out of scope, and hence **__del__**, the destructor function, is called three times in *line 19*, and in *line 20*, we print a message. Look at the result of the program below:

```
=================== RESTART: E:/Py programs/E9x2.py ===================
Name = Ram
Account number = 1212
Balance       = 10000.75
Name = Sita
Account number = 1213
Balance       = 24578.9
Name = mary
Account number = 1214
Balance       = 20000
object deleted: <__main__.Account object at 0x032EA568>
object deleted: <__main__.Account object at 0x033493E8>
object deleted: <__main__.Account object at 0x033493D0>
```

Notice that the three objects were stored in different locations as revealed by their addresses in the above result. When we execute the program again, we may not get the same addresses for the objects.

The above program has been written in the object-oriented manner with the **__init__** method and **__del__** method. If we do not define them, Python will assign default constructor and destructor. Although we omit them for brevity, it is a good practice to build object-oriented programs with **__init__** and **__del__**.

The id function and type function

When a program is executing, Python assigns a unique **id** for each object. It will not change during the execution of the program. The **id** is an integer. The **id** may change next time we execute the same program. The type of the object can also be found using the **type()** function. Let us insert these functions in the previous program and check.

In the program, as soon as an object is created, we check the **id** and **type** in the **main** function. Then after that, we call the **display** function. Therefore, **id** and **type** will be printed first and then the details of the objects will be printed.

```python
# program E9x3.py
# A complete class
class Account:  # class definition
    def __init__(self, s ='', n=0, b=0.0):
```

```python
        self.__name=s
        self.__account = n
        self.__balance =b
    def get_data(self, s, n, b):
        self.__name=s
        self.__account = n
        self.__balance =b

    def display(self):     # Method declaration
            print("Name =", self.__name)
            print("Account number =", self.__account)
            print("Balance       =", self.__balance)
    def __del__(self):
            print('object deleted: '+str(self))

def main():
    Vinay = Account()   # creating object
    Vinay.get_data('Ram', 1212, 10000.75)
    print('id of Vinay object=', id(Vinay))
    print(type(Vinay))
    Vinay.display() # calling a function
    # creating second object
    Karthik = Account()   # creating object
    Karthik.get_data('Sita', 1213, 24578.90)
    print('id of Karthik object=', id(Karthik))
    print(type(Karthik))
    Karthik.display() # calling a function
    # creating third object
    m= Account()   # creating object
    m.get_data('mary', 1214, 20000)
    print('id of m object=', id(m))
    print(type(m))
    m.display() # calling a function
main()
```

The result of the program is given below:

```
=================== RESTART: E:/Py programs/E9x3.py ===================
id of Vinay object= 57124200
<class '__main__.Account'>
Name = Ram
Account number = 1212
Balance        = 10000.75
id of Karthik object= 57512936
<class '__main__.Account'>
Name = Sita
Account number = 1213
Balance        = 24578.9
id of m object= 57512624
<class '__main__.Account'>
Name = mary
Account number = 1214
Balance        = 20000
object deleted: <__main__.Account object at 0x0367A568>
object deleted: <__main__.Account object at 0x036D93E8>
object deleted: <__main__.Account object at 0x036D92B0>
```

For all the three objects we created, the program prints unique id followed by the type of the object. The type is **Account** class in the main function for all the three objects as displayed.

Carrying out operations on objects

We can make the program more dynamic. For instance, we wish to create an *object* of **Account** class and then deposit an amount. This needs a method in the class, say **crediting**, with a formal parameter to receive the deposit amount. It is then added to the *balance* of the account. The program is given below:

```
# program E9x4.py
# A simple class
class Account:  # class definition
    def get_data(self, s, n, b):
        self.__name=s
        self.__account = n
```

```
        self.__balance =b
    def crediting(self, amount):
        self.__balance+=amount


    def display(self):      # Method declaration
            print("Name =", self.__name)
            print("Account number =", self.__account)
            print("Balance        =", self.__balance)

def main():
    Vinay = Account()    # creating object
    Vinay.get_data('Ram', 1212, 10000.75)
    Vinay.display() # calling a function
    Vinay.crediting(12500)
    Vinay.display()
main()
```

Note that we have to call the methods using the dot operator, which connects the object with the method called.

```
=================== RESTART: E:/Py programs/E9x4.py ===================
Name = Ram
Account number = 1212
Balance        = 10000.75
Name = Ram
Account number = 1212
Balance        = 22500.75
```

Notice the change of balance after the deposit. The same program can be extended for the withdrawal of an amount by the account holder. We need to write a method for the same.

Class variables versus instance variables

Data members can simply be referred to as **variables**. The variables and methods that we used so far can be called **instance variables** and **instance methods**. Although the methods were common to all objects of the class, they could be called only with an **object** and not with the **class**. So far, we had not been defining either a **class** variable or **class** method. The class variables and methods belong to a class. They can be invoked by the class. We distinguish the *class* method and variable by omitting the *self*, the address of the object associated with the variables and methods. If *self* is missing, then it belongs to the *class* and not any of its objects. The *class* variables and methods are accessed with class name prefix as **Account.display()**, where **Account** is the name of a class and **display()** is a class method. A program is given below, which counts the number of objects created.

The program creates a class **Account** with a class variable called **No_of_Accounts**, which is initialized with a value of zero. It is a class variable. Whenever an object is created, the **__init__** function will be called. In the function, after initializing the object's variables, the class variable is also incremented. In the **__init__** function, we increment the **class** variable by 1 whenever a new object is created.

There is no change in the **get_data** method, which is called by *objects* to create them. Then, we have defined a class method **display()**. The absence of **self** indicates that it is a class method. It is followed by the destructor.

In the **main** function, we create an object **Vinay** in the first two lines, and then we call the class method **display()**. Since the **No_of_Accounts** has been incremented to 1, it will display **Number of Accounts= 1**.

In the **main** function, we create the second and third objects and the class method will display **Number of Accounts= 2** and **Number of Accounts= 3** respectively. Since destructor will be called in the end, their messages will follow:

```python
# program E9x5.py
# To demonstrate class variables
class Account:  # class definition
    No_of_Accounts=0  # class data member

    def __init__(self, s ='', n=0, b=0.0):
        self.__name=s
        self.__account = n
        self.__balance =b
        Account.No_of_Accounts+=1

    def get_data(self, s, n, b):
        self.__name=s
        self.__account = n
        self.__balance =b


    def display():  # class method
            print('Number of Accounts=', Account.No_of_Accounts)
```

```
    def __del__(self):
            print('object deleted: '+str(self))


def main():
    Vinay = Account()    # creating object
    Vinay.get_data('Ram', 1212, 10000.75)
    Account.display() # class calling its method
    # creating second object
    Karthik = Account()    # creating object
    Karthik.get_data('Sita', 1213, 24578.90)
    Account.display()
    # creating third object
    m= Account()    # creating object
    m.get_data('mary', 1214, 20000)
    Account.display()


main()
```

The result of the program is given below:

```
==================== RESTART: E:/Py programs/E9x5.py ==================
Number of Accounts= 1
Number of Accounts= 2
Number of Accounts= 3
object deleted: <__main__.Account object at 0x02A3A568>
object deleted: <__main__.Account object at 0x02A993E8>
object deleted: <__main__.Account object at 0x02A99280>
```

Operator overloading

Mathematical operators can be overloaded. A (+) operator adds not only integers but also floating-point numbers; hence we can say that it is already overloaded. We can also program it to add two distances (objects) in feet and inches, and weights in kilograms and grams. However, that needs a procedure. Operator overloading is a procedure and it is another useful methodology in Python. The language allows most of the operators, such as **+**, **-**, *****, **/**, and so on. to be overloaded. As the name suggests, here the conventional operators can be programmed to carry out similar operations on objects. This overloading concept is fundamentally the same, that is the same operators are made to perform similar operations depending on the context.

Python operators work with built-in classes. For example, the (**+**) operator will perform arithmetic addition on two numbers, merge two lists, and concatenate two strings. It is achievable because (**+**) operator is overloaded by **int** class, **str** class, and **list** class respectively. The feature in which Python allows the same operator to have different purposes according to the context in which it is used is called **operator overloading**. Operator overloading means giving extended meaning beyond their predefined conventional operational meaning. In this chapter, we will study the overloading of operators for user-defined objects.

Overloading functions supported in Python

Python supports operator overloading through special functions made available by the language for this purpose. When we use an operator on user-defined data types, then a special function associated with that operator is invoked automatically. For instance, when we use – (minus) operator, the built-in magic method **__sub__** is automatically invoked in which the operation for - operation is defined. Python supports overloading of the following operators with corresponding *magic methods* pre-defined in Python:

Operator	Method
+	__add__(self, other)
-	__sub__(self, other)
*	__mul__(self, other)
/	__truediv__(self, other)
//	__floordiv__(self, other)
%	__mod__(self, other)
**	__pow__(self, other)

Table 9.1: Arithmetic operators

Comparison operators

Operator	Method
<	__lt__(self, other)
>	__gt__(self, other)
<=	__le__(self, other)
>=	__ge__(self, other)
==	__eq__(self, other)
!=	__ne__(self, other)

Table 9.2: Comparison operators

Assignment operators

Operator	Method
+=	__iadd__(self, other)
-=	__isub__(self, other)
*=	__imul__(self, other)
/=	__idiv__(self, other)
//=	__ifloordiv__(self, other)
%=	__imod__(self, other)
**=	__ipow__(self, other)

Table 9.3: Assignment operators

Operator		Method
−	It negates the operand.	__neg__(self)
+	It retains the sign of the operand	__pos__(self)
~	performs a bitwise negation of the operand.	__invert__(self)
not	negates the Boolean value of the operand.	__not__()

Table 9.4: Unary operators

Python facilitates the overloading of such a large number of operators.

Overloading binary operators

We will now carry out overloading of binary operators, which operate on two operands.

Overloaded minus operator

Let us define an operator – (minus) to carry out subtraction of complex numbers. Python has a built-in data type called **complex** (lowercase *c*), and it can be used to subtract two complex numbers straight away. For the sake of simplicity, a class **Complex** to find the difference between 2 complex numbers is given here, which will also subtract complex numbers. As we know, a complex number consists of the real part and an imaginary part. Look at the following program for an overloaded subtraction operator for two complex numbers:

E9x6.py - C:\Users\Subbu\Desktop\E9x6.py (3.10.10)

File Edit Format Run Options Window Help

```
# program E9x6.py
# operator overloading
class Complex:  # class definition
    def __init__(self, r=0, i=0.0):
            self.__real = r
            self.__imag =i

    def __sub__(self,other):
        comp1=Complex()
        comp1.real = self.__real - other.__real
        comp1.imag = self.__imag - other.__imag
        return comp1

    def display(self):  # Method declaration
        print("difference =", self.real, self.imag, 'j' )


    def __del__(self):
        print('object deleted: '+str(self))

def main():
    num1 = Complex(8,7)    # creating object
    num2 = Complex(3,4)
    num3=num1-num2
    num3.display() # calling a function

    num1 = Complex(200.75,27.75)    # creating object
    num2 = Complex(100.25,100.5)
    num3=num1-num2
    num3.display() # calling a function

main()
```

Ln: 1 Col: 0

***Figure 9.4**: Minus operator overloading*

In *line 3*, the class **`Complex`** is defined. In *lines 4* to *7*, we have defined the **`__init__`** method to initialize the objects of type **`Complex`** on creation. The private data members **`self.__real`** and **`self.__imag`** are initialized to zero with default arguments in the method. In *line 8*, we have the definition for **`__sub__`** function. It receives two arguments. The **`other`** refers to the second number that we pass. In the method, we declare **`comp1`** as an object of **`Complex`** class at *line 9*. Then, we subtract the second number **`other.real`** from **`self.real`** in *line 10*. Similarly, we find the difference between imaginary parts in *line 11*. In *line 12*, we return **`comp1`** containing the difference between the 2 numbers. In *line 14*, we have the *display* method followed by the destructor method in *line 18* which deletes the objects, not in scope.

In the **`main`** function at *lines 22* and *23*, we create objects **`num1`** and **`num2`** of class **`Complex`**. In *line 24*, we subtract **`num2`** from **`num1`** using the operator – and assign to **`num3`**. This invokes the magic method **`__sub__`**, and the subtraction of the second object from the first is carried out. The display method (**`Num3.display()`**) is called at *line 25*, with the value returned to the **`main`** function and stored in **`num3`**, and the result is displayed. After displaying the result, the destructor is called automatically since the objects have gone out of scope. We repeat the same process from *line 27* to *30* for another set of complex numbers.

The result of the program is given below:

```
=================== RESTART: E:\Py programs\E9x6.py ===================
difference = 5 3j
object deleted: <__main__.Complex object at 0x0367A568>
```

```
object deleted: <__main__.Complex object at 0x036D9370>
object deleted: <__main__.Complex object at 0x036D92C8>
difference = 100.5 -72.75 j
object deleted: <__main__.Complex object at 0x036D9280>
object deleted: <__main__.Complex object at 0x0367A568>
object deleted: <__main__.Complex object at 0x036D9370>
```

Overloading unary operator

There are four unary operators:

- **Unary positive operator +**: It retains the sign of the operand.

- **Unary negative operator -**: It negates the operand.

- **Unary bitwise NOT operator ~**: It performs a bitwise negation of the operand.

- **Unary logical NOT operator not**: It negates the Boolean value of the operand.

In the following program, we demonstrate the overloading of all the four operators.

```
# Program E9x7.py
# Unary operator example program in Python
# Define a variable
x = 10
# Unary positive operator (+)
result_positive = +x
print("Unary positive operator (+):", result_positive)  # Output: 10
# Unary negative operator (-)
result_negative = -x
print("Unary negative operator (-):", result_negative)  # Output: -10
# Unary bitwise NOT operator (~)
result_bitwise_not = ~x
print("Unary bitwise NOT operator (~):", result_bitwise_not)  # Output: -11
(complement of x in two's complement representation)
# Unary logical NOT operator (not)
y = True
result_logical_not = not y
print("Unary logical NOT operator (not):", result_logical_not)  # Output:
False
```

Go through step-wise in the above program. The program is self-explanatory. The result of the program is below:

```
=================== RESTART: E:/Py programs/E9x7.py ===================
Unary positive operator (+): 10
Unary negative operator (-): -10
Unary bitwise NOT operator (~): -11
Unary logical NOT operator (not): False
```

Overloaded == operator

We will now overload == operator. When we overload == operator, we use the magic method __eq__ in the class. In the following program, we wish to check whether two objects have the same attributes, or in other words, the objects are equal. We also wish to check whether two variables are pointing to the same object. A program is given below to check the characteristics of the objects.

In the FPS system of measurement, the length is measured by feet and inches, 12 inches make a foot. We have defined a class **Length** with 2 data members **ft** and **inch**. The __ init__ method initializes **ft** and **inch** to zero.

We have defined the magic method __eq__. Here, the self refers to the first object and other the second object. These are the formal parameters of the __eq__ method. If the corresponding data members **ft** and **inch** of both the objects are equal, the function __eq__ returns **True**. If not, it returns **False**. This is the function of the overloaded == operator in this program.

In the **main** function, we create 2 objects **len1** and **len2**. Then, we assign **len2** to **len3**. In the first 2 **if** statements, we check whether the given objects are equal. In the next 2 **if** statements, we check whether an object is same as another object or in other words, we check whether the two variables are pointing to the same object. We use keyword **is** to check this.

The program is given below:

```
# Program E9x8.py
# overloading == operator
class Length:
    def __init__(self, ft=0, inch=0):
        self._ft=ft
        self._inch=inch
    def __eq__(self, other):
        if self._ft==other._ft and self._inch==other._inch:
            return True
```

```
        else:
            return False
def main():
    len1=Length(3, 4)
    len2=Length(4,5)
    len3=len2
    if len1==len2:
        print("objects len1 and len2 are equal")
    else:
        print('objects len1 and len2 are not same')
    if len2==len3:
        print("objects len2 and len3 are equal")
    else:
        print('objects len2 and len3 are not same')
    if len1 is len2:
        print('len1 and len2 are pointing to same object')
    else:
        print('len1 and len2 are NOT pointing to same object')
    if len2 is len3:
        print('len2 and len3 are pointing to same object')
    else:
        print('len2 and len3 are NOT pointing to same object')
main()
```

The result of the program is given below.

```
================== RESTART: E:/Py programs/E9x8.py ====================
objects len1 and len2 are not same
objects len2 and len3 are equal
len1 and len2 are NOT pointing to same object
len2 and len3 are pointing to same object
```

The result of the execution of the programs confirm that the overloaded operators have carried out the intended operations. Similarly, we can overload any other basic operators.

Note that we should not directly call the language-defined method such as **__init__()**, **__del__()** and all the magic methods. These methods are called Python at runtime.

Documentation strings

It is also good practice to systematically add documentation in every program we write. We add documentation of the following items for better understanding of the programs:

- class

- module

- method

- function

The documentation may be a single line or multiline comment but should start in the first line below the definition of method or class. Such comments are known as **docstring** and available in the attribute **__doc__**. The following are the rules for incorporating *docstring* in the program:

- Single-line comments should be written within triple quotes.

- Multiline comments should be written with a summary line followed by a blank line. It is followed by a detailed comment.

- We can print the *docstring* using **help()** method.

An example will make the concept clear. Look at the program below:

```python
# program E9x9.py
# docstring
class Account:
    ''' This is the definition of the class
    The class defines bank account'''
    def get_data(self, s, n, b):
        self.__name=s
        self.__account = n
        self.__balance =b

    def display(self):
        ''' this is a method to display object attributes'''
        print("Name =", self.__name)
        print("Account number =", self.__account)
        print("Balance       =", self.__balance)

def main():
```

```
    Vinay = Account()    # creating object
    Vinay.get_data('Ram', 1212, 10000.75)
    help(Account)
    help(Vinay.display())
```

```
main()
```

The result of the program is given below:

```
================== RESTART: E:/Py programs/E9x9.py ==================
Help on class Account in module __main__:
class Account(builtins.object)
 |   This is the definition of the class
 |
 |   The class defines bank account
 |
 |   Methods defined here:
 |
 |   display(self)
 |       this is a method to display object attributes
 |
 |   get_data(self, s, n, b)
 |
 |   ----------------------------------------------------------------
---
 |   Data descriptors defined here:
 |
 |   __dict__
 |       dictionary for instance variables (if defined)
 |
 |   __weakref__
 |       list of weak references to the object (if defined)
Name = Ram
Account number = 1212
Balance        = 10000.75
Help on NoneType object:
class NoneType(object)
```

```
 |  Methods defined here:
 |
 |  __bool__(self, /)
 |      self != 0
 |
 |  __repr__(self, /)
 |      Return repr(self).
 |
 |
 |  ----------------------------------------------------------------
 |  Static methods defined here:
 |
 |  __new__(*args, **kwargs) from builtins.type
 |      Create and return a new object.  See help(type) for accurate
signature.
```

In addition to the *docstring* written by us, the system gives detailed information about the class, methods and so on. defined in the program.

Conclusion

In this chapter, an introduction to OOP, class and object, access control to ensure integrity of data, the very purpose of OOP was given. The conventional operators like arithmetic operators can be overloaded to carry out more complex tasks on objects. Operator overloading means giving extended meaning beyond their predefined conventional operational meaning through the corresponding magic methods. We looked at example programs to illustrate the concept. Python assists in documentation of strings with docstring. We also had a glimpse of initializer and destructor in this chapter. We understood the benefits of object-oriented programming in this chapter. In the next chapter, we will study two important features of OOP – inheritance and polymorphism.

Points to remember

- **Class**: A user-defined prototype for an object that defines a set of attributes and methods that characterize an object of the class. The attributes are data members (class variables and instance variables) and the methods are accessed via dot notation.

- A class defines the specifications for constructing objects with data and functions. It defines the private or internal working of the objects and their public interfaces. The data, known as **data member** (**s**) of the class, define the state of the proposed object. The functions or methods define its behavior.

- Classes provide convenient mechanisms to the programmer to build their data types apart from the built-in classes, such as *int, float, str, complex, bool, list, tuple, set,* and *dictionary*. The class types are convenient to represent real entities.

- A class will have a name, usually starting with an upper-case letter. A class definition may consist of data and method definition(s).

- The class name tag follows class, followed by a colon.

- **Class variable**: A variable that is shared by all instances of a class.

- **Data member**: A class variable or instance variable that holds data associated with a class and its objects.

- **Object**: A unique instance of a data structure that is defined by its class. An object comprises both data members and methods. Wrapping together data and functions creates the objects in OOP. A class can give rise to several objects but is not an object on its own.

- **Method**: A special kind of function that is defined in a class definition. A method begins with a **def** keyword. It is followed by a valid identifier as the name for the method. It is followed in parentheses by the term self and formal parameters, separated by commas and followed by a colon.

- **Instance**: An individual object of a certain class.

- **Instantiation**: The creation of an instance of a class.

- **self**: Whenever an object calls a method, the memory address of the object in hexadecimal format gets passed to the method. The address is collected by the variable self in the method.

- The access to data and functions of a class could be:

  o **Private**: Access restricted to the specific class

  o **Public**: Access open to all classes

  o **Protected**: Access restricted to the specific class and classes derived from it

  The data members should not be declared public since it will defeat the very purpose of data hiding, which is one of the essential requirements of OOP. However, the member methods are usually declared public.

- The initializer is executed whenever we create new objects of that class. The name of the initializer method is **init**, preceded and followed by double underscores.

- When an object is no longer in use, it should be deleted using **__del__()** method to free up resources such as memory space. The method **__del__()** gets called when an object goes out of scope.

- Inheritance property aids the reusability of already developed and tested code in new applications.

- Since Python is a dynamically typed language, the attachment of each type of object at runtime to appropriate methods depending on the context is an inherent characteristic of the language.

- The common operators such as **+**, **-**, *****, **/** and so on. can be programmed to carry out the respective operations on different compound data types such as containers, or user-defined objects depending on the context in which the operator is used. Python defines magic methods to enable operator overloading. We overloaded two operators to illustrate the concept of operator overloading.

- When a program is executing, Python assigns a unique id for each object. It will not change during the execution of the program. The id is an integer. The id may change next time we execute the same program.

- The type of the object can also be found using the **type()** function.

- The class variables and methods can be invoked only by the class. We distinguish the class method and variable by omitting the self-associated with the variable and method.

- **Inheritance**: The transfer of the characteristics of a class to other classes that are derived from it.

- The *docstring* is used to add documentation in the program.

Questions

Choose the most appropriate answer:

1. **Data hiding is achieved through declaring data members as:**

    a. Public

    b. Private

    c. Either public or private

    d. All of the above

    e. None of the above

2. **__init__() is a:**

    a. Class

    b. Method

    c. Data type

    d. All of the above

    e. None of the above

3. **Member methods are usually declared:**

    a. Public

    b. Private

    c. None of the above

4. **The objects are created in:**

    a. The class

    b. Main function

    c. Anywhere in the program

    d. All of the above

    e. None of the above

5. **In inheritance:**

    a. There is a base class

    b. There are derived classes

    c. Derived classes inherit from base class

    d. All of the above

    e. None of the above

6. **Operator overloading is programmed in:**

    a. Main function

    b. Class

    c. __init__

    d. All of the above

    e. None of the above

7. **Operator overloading:**

    a. Does not need __init__

    b. Does not need class

    c. Uses magic methods

    d. All of the above

    e. None of the above

8. **Built-in classes include:**

    a. int

    b. str

    c. list

    d. All of the above

    e. None of the above

9. **Data members should be:**

    a. Private

    b. Public

    c. Methods

    d. All of the above

    e. None of the above

10. **Methods should be:**

    a. private

    b. public

    c. methods

    d. All of the above

    e. None of the above

- Write short notes on the following:

    o Relationship between class and objects.

    o Member methods versus **__init__** method.

    o Use of dot operator.

    o Access specifiers.

    o State how data hiding is achieved in Python.

    o Importance of self.

    o Class variables and methods.

    o Initializer and **__del__** methods.

    o Magic methods.

    o Class definition and method definition.

- Match the following:

A	B
Class	1. Assigns initial values to objects
Object	2. Generally declared public
Data hiding	3. Contains Methods
Methods	4. Private data members
__init__	5. Holds unique data

- Write programs for the following:

  o To credit and debit in a bank account.

  o A library database using class and with the following data items:

    ▪ Title of book

    ▪ Acc number

    ▪ Author

    ▪ Publisher

    ▪ Price

    ▪ Create 10 records

  o Modify the above program to search for a book by title or author or publisher.

  o Create a class **Circle** and methods to find the perimeter and area.

  o Create a class **Cube** and methods to find the perimeter and area.

  o Create a class for car with the following data members and create 10 records.

    ▪ Registration number

    ▪ Place of registration

    ▪ Date of registration

    ▪ Owner name

    ▪ Chassis number

  o With the class above, search car by any of the above attributes.

  o Add complex numbers using operator overloading.

  o Adding and subtracting two lengths in foot and inches.

  o Create a class for finding roots of a quadratic equation by getting a, b and c from the user.

CHAPTER 10

Inheritance and Polymorphism

Introduction

In this chapter, we continue our discussions on **Object-Oriented Programming (OOP)**. One of the objectives of OOP is to facilitate the reusability of already-developed code. The inheritance property of Python makes this happen seamlessly. Polymorphism, another important concept of OOP, can be practiced with Python, leading to run-time polymorphism through which both the base class and derived class can access the method with the same name. Abstract classes are used as interfaces, and we cannot create an object of the abstract class.

Structure

The chapter covers the following topics:

- Reusability
- Inheritance
- Implementing reuse
- The object class
- Diamond problem

- Method overriding

- The isinstance function

- Polymorphism

- Dynamic binding

- Abstract class

- Iterators

- Iterable

- User-defined iterators

- Generators

Objectives

In this chapter, we will understand what reusability is of already developed code, its importance, advantages, and how to carry this out through what is known as the inheritance property of Python 3. All classes in Python are derived from the *object* class in the Python standard library. We will cover three different types of inheritance, that is, single, multiple, and multi-level. When we carry out multiple inheritance, there is a possibility that a derived class inherits the same property from two or more base classes, known as the diamond problem. In this chapter, we will look at the solution to the diamond problem so that a derived class inherits the property from only one class. We also cover containership, another implementation of reusability. We also implement polymorphism, dynamic binding of methods, and abstract class in this chapter.

Iterators in Python are objects that allow us to traverse through a sequence of data or a container, one element at a time, without needing to know the underlying implementation details of that container. They provide a common interface for accessing elements of different data structures like lists, tuples, dictionaries, and more. Generators in Python are functions that enable the creation of iterators. We discuss iterators and generators in this chapter.

Reusability

The term reusability, as the name suggests, is to use already developed, compiled, and tested working programs for a new requirement with the least effort. This will save the time and effort required for developing the programs afresh. Furthermore, errors creep into computer programs easily. A reliable code is one that is thoroughly tested. If such a code can be used again and again in new applications without fear of defects creeping in, then it will increase the productivity of the programmers and improve quality while reducing the cost.

Reusability is rather a revolutionary concept in programming. The ultimate result of this concept will be the availability of off-the-shelf software components (modules) that have been tested thoroughly and certified by independent agencies. However, the development of such components is slow. The goal of software technology is to make many tested components available for use in commercial software development. Then, the development of software applications will be like manufacturing, where the tested components are assembled to create a software system quickly. Only then will software development mature to a stage where there are no delays, no cost overruns, and the quality of the product is beyond doubt. **Object-oriented Programming (OOP)**is the first step towards component technology.

Inheritance

Inheritance in Python is a fundamental concept in OOP that allows a new class (called a subclass or derived class) to inherit attributes and methods from an existing class (called a superclass or base class). This promotes code reuse, modularity, and extensibility in software development. The user-defined types, namely the classes, provide an opportunity for inheritance. Assume that we have developed a module taking into consideration the users' requirements. Usually, the client will require some additional features at the time of delivery after seeing the product. After the completion of the project, adding a new feature in the conventional programming languages is not an easy job. It can lead to new errors and sometimes even failure of the software project in extreme cases. On the contrary, in OOP, adding a new feature after a class has been developed is rather easy. The class, which is already available, is known as a base class. The base class is also known as the superclass or parent class. Adding a new feature may require either adding a new data element or a new function. This can be achieved by extending the class. For this purpose, a new class must be defined as inheriting from the base class. This new class is called a derived class, sub-class or child class in Python. The derived class can inherit some or all the properties of the base class as per requirements. Adding new classes does not require any changes to the base class.

Code reuse is one of the uses of inheritance. However, there are many uses, some of which are listed below:

- **Modularity:** Inheritance helps to organize code into logical hierarchies, making it easier to manage and understand. By defining related classes that inherit from a common superclass, we can group related functionality together and encapsulate implementation details.

- **Polymorphism:** Inheritance enables polymorphism, which allows objects of different classes to be treated uniformly through a common interface. This promotes flexibility and extensibility in code design, as we can write methods that operate on objects of the superclass type without needing to know the specific subclass.

- **Specialization and generalization:** Inheritance allows us to create specialized subclasses that inherit and extend the functionality of a more general superclass. This allows us to capture common behavior in the superclass while providing customization and specialization in the subclasses.

- **Overriding methods:** Subclasses can override methods of the superclass to provide specific implementations that are tailored to their own behavior. This allows us to customize and extend the behavior of existing classes without modifying their implementation directly.

- **Inheritance trees:** Inheritance allows us to create hierarchical class structures, known as inheritance trees, where subclasses inherit from other subclasses, forming a tree-like structure. This enables us to model complex relationships and hierarchies in our application domain.

In the following paragraphs, we will discuss some topics pertaining to inheritance as outlined above.

The deriving of properties through inheritance is akin to that of human beings. The child inherits all or some of the properties of the parent. The child may add his properties. Both the inherited property and the newly acquired property can be used simultaneously by the child. However, the parent is aware of only what he has lent. The child can, in turn, become a parent and lend his properties to his child in a similar manner. This can go on, and in Python, there is no limitation to the number of either the levels of inheritance or the derived classes for a base class. Thus, several possibilities exist about inheritance in Python. They are listed diagrammatically in the following section.

Single inheritance

A single inheritance is a relationship between one parent and one child, as depicted in *Figure 10.1*:

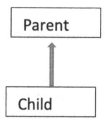

Figure 10.1: Single inheritance

Multilevel inheritance

The inheritance can continue to more than one level, depending on the need. *Figure 10.2* indicates a multi-level inheritance:

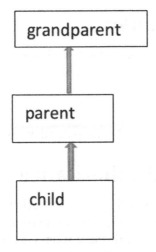

Figure 10.2: Multi-level inheritance

In the multi-level inheritance depicted above, the child inherits from the parent, which again is a derived class of grandparent. Therefore, the child may have some or all the properties of the parent and grandparent.

Multiple inheritance

On the contrary, multiple inheritances refer to a class inheriting the properties of multiple base classes, as illustrated in *Figure 10.3*:

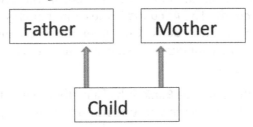

Figure 10.3: Multiple inheritance

In the above case, the child can inherit the properties of both the father and mother, which are both base classes. The child is the only derived class in this case.

It does not mean that a child class can inherit only from 2 base classes as shown in *Figure 10.3*. A derived class can be inherited from any number of base classes.

Implementing reuse

There are two ways of implementing reuse as follows:

- Containership

- Inheritance

In both above ways, we can reuse code and extend an existing class.

Containership and inheritance

We know that a bank has accounts and a class has students. There is a relationship between the two objects, bank and account, and class and students. The bank *has* accounts and a class *has* students. The object bank and account have a *has* relationship. Similarly, the class and students have a has relationship. In such cases, we may use containership to reuse code. Containership is also known as composition.

We also know that a parent is like a grandparent, and a rectangle is like a square. There are like relationships between the parent and grandparent and the rectangle and square. In such cases, we may use the inheritance of a class for reuse.

Containership

We first study containership. When we implement containership, there will be two classes, where one class will borrow features of another class. In the given program, there are two classes: **Bank** and **Account**. The **Account** is the container class in the program, which will contain objects from the class **Bank**. Containership is a concept in object-oriented programming where one class contains an instance of another class as a member. Now, let us read the program line by line.

In line 3, we have a definition of class **Bank**. It has a method named **get_bd** and is defined at line 4. It receives only the self as the argument. In the method, we initialize two data members, **bankName** and **balance**. Since we are defining the data members directly, there is no need to pass the formal parameters to the method. This is another way of initializing objects since, ultimately, an object of the class will call the method for its creation.

It is followed by the method **display_bank** at line number 8. At line numbers 9 and 10, we print the bank name and branch name, as shown in *Figure 10.4*:

```
E10x1.py - E:\Py programs\E10x1.py (3.10.10)
File  Edit  Format  Run  Options  Window  Help
1  # program E10x1.py
2  # A Container class
3  class Bank:
4      def get_bd(self):
5              self._bankName='Bank of India'
6              self._branch='Adayar'
7
8      def display_bank(self):
9          print('bank name =', self._bankName)
10         print('branch name =', self._branch)
11
12 class Account.  # class definition
13     def get_data(self, s, n, b):
14         self.__acName=s
15         self.__accountNum = n
16         self.__balance =b
17         self._obj=Bank()
18         self._obj.get_bd()
19
20     def display(self):  # Method declaration
21         print("Name =", self.__acName)
22         print("Account number =", self.__accountNum)
23         print("Balance      =", self.__balance)
24         self._obj.display_bank()
25
26 def main():
27     vinay = Account()  # creating object
28     vinay.get_data('Ram', 1212, 10000.75)
29     vinay.display()  # calling a method
30
31
32 main()
33
```

Figure 10.4: A container class

We have a definition of class account in line number 12. In line 13, we have defined the method **get_data** with three formal parameters and self. In lines 14 to 16, values are assigned to the three data members of the class **Account**.

In line 17, we create an object **obj** of class **Bank**. In the next line, we call the method **get_bd** with the object **obj**. Thus, we call the method of class **Bank()** in the method of class **Account**. This will add the data members of class **Bank** to the class **Account**. In line 20, we have defined a method **display**. Here, we print the **acName**, **accountNum**, and **balance** of *class* **Account** in lines 21, 22, and 23. At line 24, we invoke object **obj** of **Bank** class and call the method **display_bank**. This is the trick of containership. The called object will print the name of the bank and branch name.

In the main function, at line 27 we create an object **Vinay** of class **Account** and pass actual arguments to create an object of class **Account**. Note that the name of the account is **Vinay** and name of the account holder is **Ram**. Then we call the method **display()** of class **Account**. The called method will also print the **Bank** attribute as the result of the program confirms:

```
==================== RESTART: E:\Py programs\E10x1.py ====================
Name = Ram
Account number = 1212
```

```
Balance       = 10000.75
bank name = Bank of India
branch name = Adayar
```

Let us understand how the program worked. We defined a class **Bank** and in the next line, we defined a method **get_bd** for use during object creation. In the previous chapter, we declared formal parameters in such methods and passed actual parameters while creating an object. For the sake of simplicity and the fact that we are writing this program for all customers of one bank, here we assigned the values to data members of the class in the **get_bd** method itself. Then we defined the container class **Account** and its method **get_data** with three formal parameters to create an object when needed. In the class **Account**, in the **get_data** method, we define an object named **obj** of class **Bank**. Notice that in line 18, we call the method **get_bd** of class **Bank**. Thus, when we create object **Vinay** at line 27 and pass actual parameters at line 28, we will have a container object **Vinay** which not only has the three data members of the class **Account**, but also two data members of the class **Bank**.

In the **display** function of **Vinay** object, we will print its data members followed by the printing of data members of class **Bank** facilitated by its member method at line 24.

We created one object in the previous program. Let us now create three objects in the same program for better understanding. The revised program is in *Figure 10.5* below:

```
1  # program E10x2.py
2  # A Container class
3  class Bank:
4      def get_bd(self):
5          self._bankName='Bank of India'
6          self._branch='Adayar'
7
8      def display_bank(self):
9          print('bank name =', self._bankName)
10         print('branch name =', self._branch)
11
12 class Account:  # class definition
13     def get_data(self, s, n, b):
14         self.__acName=s
15         self.__accountNum = n
16         self.__balance =b
17         self._obj=Bank()
18         self._obj.get_bd()
19
20     def display(self):  # Method declaration
21         print("Name =", self.__acName)
22         print("Account number =", self.__accountNum)
23         print("Balance      =", self.__balance)
24         self._obj.display_bank()
25
26 def main():
27     vinay = Account()  # creating object
28     vinay.get_data('Ram', 1212, 10000.75)
29     vinay.display() # calling a method
30
31     joseph = Account()
32     joseph.get_data('Joseph', 1213, 20000.50)
33     joseph.display()
34
35     sridhar=Account()
36     sridhar.get_data('Sridhar', 1214, 15000.25)
37     sridhar.display()
38
39
40 main()
```

Figure 10.5: A container class creating 3 objects

The result of the program is as follows:

```
================= RESTART: C:/Users/Subbu/Desktop/E10x2.py =================
Name = Ram
Account number = 1212
Balance       = 10000.75
bank name = Bank of India
branch name = Adayar
Name = Joseph
Account number = 1213
Balance       = 20000.5
bank name = Bank of India
branch name = Adayar
Name = Sridhar
Account number = 1214
Balance       = 15000.25
bank name = Bank of India
branch name = Adayar
```

See the convenience. There was no need for us to give the bank name and branch name with the creation of every object. They are given only once in the **Bank** class. We are using this data whenever we create an object of **Account** class. That is the advantage of containership. Here the **Account** class contained the **Bank** object. This program can be used to have the data of all the account holders of a bank.

Note in the above that there are two identifiers – one to denote the object name and the other to denote the name of the Account holder. We create the first object with name **vinay** and the name of the account holder is **Ram**. Then we create the second object with name **joseph** and the name of the account holder is **Joseph**. We create the third object with name **sridhar** and the name of the account holder is **Sridhar**.

Inheritance

Inheritance is a feature of OOP which is used to define a new class, which can use the properties of a base class. The new class is called the derived class or child class, and the class from which this derived class has been inherited is the base class or parent class or superclass. The derived class may include some additional features. This inheritance concept helps to reuse the code.

Single inheritance

In the following, we will address a single inheritance. There will be one base class and 1 derived class. Let us write a program to understand inheritance. Refer to the given program **E10x3.py** at *Figure 10.6*:

```
E10x3.py - C:/Users/Subbu/Desktop/E10x3.py (3.10.11)
File  Edit  Format  Run  Options  Window  Help
 1 # Program E10x3.py
 2 # Single Inheritance
 3
 4 class Youth:
 5
 6     def __init__(self, first, last):
 7         self._first_name=first
 8         self._last_name=last
 9
10     def display(self):
11         print('first name:', self._first_name)
12         print('last name:', self._last_name)
13
14 class Student(Youth):
15
16     def __init__(self, first, last, roll_num):
17         Youth.__init__(self, first, last)
18         self.__roll_num=roll_num
19
20     def display(self):
21         print('first name:', self._first_name)
22         print('last name:', self._last_name)
23         print('roll_num:',  self.__roll_num)
24
25 def main():
26
27     per1=Youth("manoj", "prabhakar")
28     per2=Student("manoj","prabhakar", "IT802")
29
30     per1.display()
31     per2.display()
32
33 main()
34
```

Figure 10.6: Single Inheritance

At line 4, we have defined a base class **Youth**. The **__init__** function of the class has been defined at line 6. The function receives **self** (address of calling object) and two formal parameters, **first** and **last**. The **__init__** function contains 2 data members named **first_name** and **last_name**. They have been declared as type **protected** preceded by single underscore since they may be accessed in the derived class.

The **__init__** function is followed by definition of a function **display()** at line 10. This method displays the first name and last name of the received object at lines 11 and 12.

We have the definition of the derived class **Student** at line 14. It is sub-class of class **Youth** as indicated in the parentheses of the definition of class **Student**. This gives the privilege to the class **Student** for using the properties of class **Youth**.

At line 16, the definition of the **__init__** method of the **Student** class begins. In the header of the **__init__** method, there are 4 formal parameters including **self**. The second and third parameters belong to the base class and the fourth one **roll_num** belongs to the derived class. In the method, we first call *Youth.__init__*, and in the last line of the method, we initialize the data member of the derived class, that is, **roll_num**. The order has to be maintained. Note that **__roll_num** is a private data member.

The **__init__** function of the derived class is also followed by the definition of a function **display()** at line 20. This method displays **first_ name**, **last_name** of the received object at lines 21 and 22 and **roll_num** at line 23. Note that there are two methods, one in the base class and another in the derived class with the same name **display**.

In the main function, we create two objects **per1** and **per2** at lines 27 and 28. The object **per1** is of class **Youth** and **per2** is of **Student**. Then at lines 30 and 31, we call method **display** with the respective objects.

The result of the program is as follows:

```
================ RESTART: C:/Users/Subbu/Desktop/E10x3.py =================
first name: manoj
last name: prabhakar
first name: manoj
last name: prabhakar
roll_num: IT802
```

The first two lines of the result are the contribution of the **display** method of the base class and the last 3 lines are that of the derived class. This program demonstrates the inheritance of the properties of base class in the derived class and also that the derived class builds on the properties (**first_name** and **last _name**) of the base class and adding its own requirements.

Note carefully, the above program has two methods with the identical name, **display**. Both the base class and derived class objects **per1** and **per2** respectively, are called **display** method. The methods appropriate to the objects were dynamically dispatched due to the dynamic typing system of the Python language.

Access types revisited

Observe single underscores or double underscores before the data members in *Figure 10.6* above. Also, in *Chapter 9, Introduction to Object-Oriented Programming*, we discussed public, private and protected data members. The private data members with a double underscore, also called dunderscore, are accessible only within the class while public data members are accessible from everywhere. In this program had we defined private data members with a double underscore in class **Youth** then they will not be visible in class **Student**. We want the data members of the class **Youth** to be protected and be available in the derived class, so we declare them with a prefix of the single underscore and type protected. The data members callable in the derived classes are declared protected. We are not going to use the data members of class **Student** in any other class and so we have declared them private with a double underscore. That is the trick. To summarize, the data members and methods to be visible only in the class in which they are defined are to be declared as private with double underscore. Those members to be visible also in derived classes are declared protected with single underscore prefix to the data members. Generally, the methods are declared public to make them available anywhere. If there is no prefix of underscore to data members, then they can be public. The characteristics of access types are summarized in *Table 10.1*:

Access type	Prefix	Accessible
Public	None	Everywhere
Protected	single underscore	Within the class and derived classes
Private	Double underscore	Within the class

Table 10.1: Access types

Multi-level inheritance

We will now look at multilevel inheritance. A class derives its properties from a base class. The derived class may in turn become a base class for another child class. Since there is a hierarchy of classes, we can call this phenomenon a multi-level inheritance. In the program, we have a superclass **Book**. The **Price** is derived class of **Book** and **Agency** is derived class of **Price**. Or in other words, **Price** is the superclass for the class **Agency**. Look at the given in *Figure 10.7*:

```
# program E10x4.py
# Multi-level Inheritance
# base class
class Book:
    def __init__(self, bookTitle, auth):
        self._title = bookTitle
        self._author = auth

class Price(Book):
    def __init__(self, title, author, price):
        Book.__init__(self, title, author)
        self._price = price

class Agency(Price):
    def __init__(self, title, author, price, publisher):
        Book.__init__(self, title, author)
        Price.__init__(self, title, author, price)
        self._publisher = publisher
    def display(self):
        print('Title: ', self._title)
        print('Author: ', self._author)
        print('Price: ', self._price)
        print('Publisher:', self._publisher)

def main():
    obj3 = Agency('Python', "Subburaj Ramasamy", "550", "BPB")
    obj3.display()
main()
```

Figure 10.7: Multilevel Inheritance

In the program, we have defined a class **Book** and its **__init__** method. It initializes the two data members of the **Book** class. Then we have defined a class **Price** derived from class **Book** as indicated in the class definition. The derived class has its **__init__** method with two formal parameters of the base class and one of the **Price** class. It is followed by the **Book.__init__** method, which initializes the data members belonging to the **Book** class. It is followed by the initialization of the member of the derived **Price** class, that is, **price**.

Then we have defined a derived class of **Price** named **Agency**. The class definition is followed by its **__init__** method with four formal parameters. In the **__init__** method, we call **Book.__init__** followed by **Price.__init__** with the respective parameters. In the last line of the **__init__** method, we initialize the parameter **publisher** belonging to the **Agency** class. Look at the systematic way of expansion of properties (parameters).

The definition of class **Agency** is followed by a method **display(self)**. The method prints the two attributes of the superclass and one each of the derived classes. In the main function, we create an object **obj3** of the class **Agency** with four attributes, one belonging to it and the other three to the inherited classes. Then we call the display method with this object.

The result of the program is as follows:

```
== RESTART: C:/Users/Subbu/AppData/Local/Programs/Python/Python310/E10X4.py ==
Title:  Python
Author:  Subburaj Ramasamy
Price:  550
Publisher: BPB
```

We note the following from the above example:

- Inheritance provides a facility for reusing the classes.

- It helps us to add forgotten or newly arising attributes later.

- It provides a systematic way to extend the code to suit new requirements.

- There is no limit to the levels of multilevel inheritance.

Multiple inheritance

So far, we have been looking at single inheritance, which means that a class derives from one base class. In multiple inheritances, a class derives properties from more than one base class. We write a program to understand multiple inheritance. Here, there are two base classes – **Book** and **Agency**. There is a derived class named **Price**. The class **Price** inherits from both the super classes **Book** and **Agency**. Look at the following program in *Figure 10.8.*

The class **Book** has two attributes, and the class **Agency** has also two attributes. The definition of the derived class **Price** is followed by **__init__** method with five formal parameters: two each for the two super classes and one of the derived class. Followed by the definition of the **__init__** method of the derived class, we call **Book.__init__** and **Agency.__init__** methods. Each has three formal parameters including **self**. Then we initialize the price of the derived class **Price**. This is followed by a display method, which prints all the five arguments received.

In the main function, we create an object **obj3** with values for all the five parameters: two each for both the base classes and one of the derived class. It is followed by a call to the display function called with **obj3**:

```
E10x5.py - C:/Users/Subbu/Desktop/E10x5.py (3.10.10)

File  Edit  Format  Run  Options  Window  Help
 1  # program E10x5.py
 2  # Multiple Inheritance
 3  # base class 1
 4  class Book:
 5      def __init__(self, bookTitle, auth):
 6          self._title = bookTitle
 7          self._author = auth
 8  class Agency:      # base class 2
 9      def __init__(self, namAgency, loc):
10          self._name=namAgency
11          self._location=loc
12
13  class Price(Book, Agency):
14      def __init__(self, title, author, name, location, price):
15          Book.__init__(self, title, author)
16          Agency.__init__(self, name, location)
17          self._price= price
18
19
20      def display(self):
21          print('Title: ', self._title)
22          print('Author: ', self._author)
23          print('Publisher:', self._name)
24          print('location:', self._location)
25          print('Price: ', self._price)
26
27
28  def main():
29      obj3 = Price('Python',"Subburaj Ramasamy", "BPB", "New Delhi", "550")
30      obj3.display()
31  main()
32
```

Figure 10.8: Multiple Inheritance

```
================ RESTART: C:/Users/Subbu/Desktop/E10x5.py ==================
Title:   Python
Author:   Subburaj Ramasamy
Publisher: BPB
```

```
location: New Delhi
Price:   550
```

The above program explains how a class can get properties from two base classes, that is, multiple inheritance.

The object class

There is a built-in class called **object** in Python. All the base classes we program in Python are by default inherited from the built-in **object** class. Other derived classes are inherited from the respective base classes as indicated in parentheses in their class definition. For instance, the definition of the two base classes can be written as follows:

```
class Book(object):
class Agency(object):
```

We were omitting **object** for the sake of simplicity. There is no harm in omitting it since Python assumes that if a class does not specify base class, the **object** as a base class for such classes is implied.

The **object** class provides the following special methods with two leading underscores and two trailing underscores:

- __new__()
- __init__()
- __str__()

We will discuss their operations briefly.

When an object of the class is created then the __**new**__method is automatically called. It, in turn, calls __**init**__ method to initialize the attributes of the object. When we specify __**init**__ method in our programs we are overriding the built-in __**init**__ method.

The __**str**__ method returns a description of the object. Let us write a small program to understand the above.

In the program we define the class **Book** inheriting from built-in superclass **object**. In the **display** method, we have a statement **print(self)**. It will print details about the object calling the method. It is equivalent to saying it in the following ways:

- print(Book)
- print(Book.__str__())

Refer to the following code:

```
# program E10x6.py
# base class
```

```python
class Book(object):
    def __init__(self, t, au):
        self._title = t
        self._author = au
    def display(self):
        print('Title: ', self._title)
        print('Author: ', self._author)
        print(self)


def main():
    obj1 = Book('TQM',"Subburaj Ramasamy")
    obj1.display()
main()
```

The result of the program is given below. It prints the name of the class and location of the object in memory:

```
=================== RESTART: E:/Py programs/E10x6.py ====================
Title:   TQM
Author:   Subburaj Ramasamy
<__main__.Book object at 0x02F1A568>
```

Thus the **__str__** method prints the name the class, function in which the object is created and the memory location address at which the object is located.

Diamond problem

In multiple inheritance, there is quite a big problem called the diamond problem. When we allow multiple inheritance, then we must face the fact that we might inherit the same class more than one source. Refer to the following *Figure 10.9*:

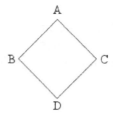

Figure 10.9: The diamond

For instance, if class B and class C inherit from class A and class D inherits from B and C then it potentially gets two copies of class A, one through B and another through C.

In Python as all classes inherit from **object**, multiple copies of **object** are inherited whenever multiple inheritance is used. That is, the diamond problem occurs even in the simplest of multiple inheritance.

In the program one above the last, we implemented multiple inheritance. The class **Price** is inheriting from two base classes, that is, **Book** and **Agency**:

Figure 10.10: *The diamond problem example*

In this case, the classes **Book** and **Agency** have a library class **object** as the superclass although it is not specifically stated. If we draw the inheritance tree it will be as shown in *Figure 10.10*. The tree resembles a diamond shape and hence it is called a diamond problem. It will be clear that the class **Price** will get one copy of class **object** through class **Book**, and another copy of **object** through class **Agency** as follows:

`Left: object   ….>Book…>Price`

`Right: object…> Agency…>Price`

Therefore, which copy of class **object** should be used by class **Price** is the problem. Python has a rule to avoid this ambiguity. The class received from the left superclass should be taken by the class **Price** and that received from the right should be ignored. Usually, the superclass defined first becomes the left superclass, while the one written below it becomes the right superclass. It is the order of the creation of the superclass's. Thus, the diamond problem is resolved.

Method overriding

Method overriding permits us to modify the implementation of a method in the superclass by the derived class. It is the choice of a derived class to change the implementation of any method which is already provided by one of its base classes. To implement, method overriding, the following conditions must be fulfilled. The method that is redefined in the child class should have the same name and signature as in the parent class. An example program implementing method overriding is given below.

It is a simple program. Both the superclass and derived class have a method named **subt** and they have 2 formal parameters. The methods in the parent class and child class performs different operations. In the parent class method, we find *(a-b)* and in the child class, we find *(a-2*b)*:

```
# Program E10x7.py
# Method overiding
class Sup:

    def subt(self, a, b):
        print('The difference of Two numbers = ', a - b)


class Der(Sup):

    def subt(self, a, b):
        print('The difference now = ', a - 2*b )



def main():
    obj1 = Sup()
    obj1.subt(300, 100)
    obj2 = Der()
    obj2.subt(300, 100)


main()
```

First time the method **subt** is called with the super class object and in the next time with subclass object. The result of the program is as follows:

```
======== RESTART: E:/Py programs/E10x7.py =====================
The difference of Two numbers =  200
The difference now =  100
```

Modifying a method of the superclass in the subclass is known as method overriding.

The isinstance function

In larger programs, it may be difficult to keep track of whether an object is of a particular class. In such cases, we can use this function **isinstance** to confirm, as the program illustrates:

```
# Program E10x8.py
# isinstance method
class Sup:

    def subt(self, a, b):
        print('The difference of Two numbers = ', a - b)


class Der(Sup):

    def subt(self, a, b):
        print('The difference now = ', a - 2*b )


def main():
    obj1 = Sup()
    obj2 = Der()
    if isinstance(obj1, Sup):
        obj1.subt(300, 100)
    elif isinstance(obj2, Der):
        obj2.subt(300, 100)

main()
```

In the above program, in the **if** block we check whether **obj1** is an object of class **Sup**. It is so and hence it returns True and so function **subt** will be called in conjunction with **obj1**. The next **elif** will not be evaluated at all in this case. The result of the program is as follows:

```
===================== RESTART: E:/Py programs/E10x8.py =====================
The difference of Two numbers =  200
```

In addition, there is another global function called **issubclass(c1, c2)**. This checks whether c1 is a derived class of c2 and returns True if it is so.

Polymorphism

Recall that in *Chapter 9, Introduction to Object-Oriented Programming*, we discussed operator overloading. It is polymorphism. In Python, operator overloading allows objects to define or redefine the behavior of built-in operators (+, -, *, /, etc.) when applied to instances of a class.

Polymorphism in Python refers to the ability of different objects to respond to the same method or function call in different ways. This allows objects of different types to be treated as instances of a common superclass. Polymorphism is a key concept in object-oriented programming and is supported in Python through method overriding and duck typing.

There are two main types of polymorphism in Python:

- **Compile-time polymorphism:** This is achieved through method overloading and operator overloading. However, Python does not support method overloading in the traditional sense due to its dynamic typing nature.

- **Run-time polymorphism:** This is achieved through method overriding and duck typing. Method overriding occurs when a subclass provides a specific implementation of a method that is already defined in its superclass. Duck typing refers to the concept of treating objects based on what they can do rather than what they are.

While the term *compile-time polymorphism* is commonly associated with statically typed languages like C++ where method overloading is resolved at compile time, in Python, operator overloading, and method overloading are not strictly considered as compile-time polymorphism because Python is dynamically typed and does not have a compilation step in the traditional sense. However, the term compile-time polymorphism could still be used colloquially to refer to the concept of operator overloading in Python, although it does not precisely match the definition in statically typed languages like C++. In Python, the resolution of overloaded operators happens dynamically at runtime based on the types involved in the operation, which aligns more closely with the concept of *run-time polymorphism*.

So, while operator overloading in Python is not typically referred to as *compile-time polymorphism* due to the dynamic nature of Python, you might find it informally mentioned in that context, albeit not technically accurate. It is more commonly associated with *run-time polymorphism* due to Python's dynamic typing and late binding.

The difference between inheritance and polymorphism is that while inheritance is implemented in classes, polymorphism is implemented in methods.

Poly means many, and morphism means forms or, in other words, one name and many forms. It refers to one method name in many classes and is hence callable by many objects. Python is a dynamically typed language, which is its **Unique Selling Point (USP)**. It uses duck-typing. The term duck typing comes from the idiomatic saying, *If it looks like a duck and quacks like a duck, it is probably a duck.* Duck-typing in Python allows us to use any object that provides the methods without the necessity of the object belonging to any class. In duck-typing, an object's suitability is determined by the presence of methods rather than the actual type of the object.

Polymorphism is the concept of a method or an object having more than one form or implementation. The main use of polymorphism in OOP is the ability of objects of different types to respond to the same method call, implementing a specific type of behavior. In a nutshell, Polymorphism is the ability to perform an action on an object regardless of its type. This is implemented by creating a base class and having two or more subclasses that all implement methods with the same signature. (Signature includes the name of the method and the list of the formal parameters.) Any object that manipulates these methods can call the same methods regardless of which type of object it is operating on, without needing to do a type checking first as to which class the object belongs. Polymorphism without inheritance in the form of duck typing is available in Python due to its dynamic typing system. This means that if the classes contain the methods with the same signature, the Python interpreter does not distinguish between them, as the only checking of the calls occurs at run-time. Refer to the following *Figure 10.11*:

```
* *E10x9.py - C:\Users\Subbu\Desktop\E10x9.py (3.10.10)*

File  Edit  Format  Run  Options  Window  Help
 1  # Program E10x9.py
 2  # Polymorphism .
 3  class G_shape:
 4     def perimeter(self):
 5        pass
 6
 7
 8  class Square(G_shape):
 9     def perimeter(self):
10        self._side=5
11        return(4*self._side)
12
13  class Rectangle (G_shape):
14     def perimeter(self):
15        self._length = 10
16        self._breadth = 5
17        return(2 * (self._length+ self._breadth))
18
19  class Circle (G_shape):
20     def perimeter(self):
21        self._radius = 7
22        return(2 * 3.14 * self._radius)
23  def calc_perimeter(input_obj):
24     print(input_obj.perimeter())
25
26
27  def main():
28     gs_obj=G_shape()
29     calc_perimeter(gs_obj)
30     s_obj=Square()
31     calc_perimeter(s_obj)
32     r_obj = Rectangle()
33     calc_perimeter(r_obj)
34     c_obj = Circle()
35     calc_perimeter(c_obj)
36  main()
37
```

Figure 10.11: *Polymorphism*

Look at the example program given above to illustrate Python type Polymorphism.

From lines 3 to 7, we have the definition of the parent class **G_shape** with the definition of a method **perimeter**. This is a parent class and does not serve any purpose other than that it is to be inherited by other classes. The method perimeter in the class is intended to be overridden in subclasses.

The pass statement at line 5 does nothing. It is used as a place holder for future coding. It is used when a statement is required syntactically, but the program requires no action. For instance, if we have a function yet to be developed, but a place is required for it in the program, we can use pass as a placeholder. The pass statement in Python is used when a statement or a condition is required to be present in the program, but we don't want any command or code to execute.

At line 8, we have defined a class **Square** as a sub-class of **G-shape**. At line 9, we have defined a method **perimeter** with the same signature as that of the method in base class **G_shape**. This method overrides **G_shape.perimeter()**. When an object of type Square has its **perimeter** method called, this is the method that will be called rather than that in the parent class. At line 11, the method returns the perimeter of the square with a side equal to 5.

At line 13, we have defined a class **Rectangle** which is also a sub-class of **G_shape**. This method also has method perimeter. Between lines 19-22, we have defined a class **Circle** and its **perimeter** method with the same signature.

In line 23, we have defined a method **calc_perimeter()**. This is the method which implements polymorphism. It receives **input_object**, and at the next line, it calls the **perimeter** method. This method receives an object and will call that object's perimeter method. Note that the object type is not specified. It could be a square, rectangle, circle, or **G_shape** object. It calls the corresponding perimeter method and prints it. This is how Python type polymorphism is implemented.

In the main function, we create an object each of G_shape, square, rectangle and circle classes. Then we call **calc_perimeter** method with each object. The **calc_perimeter** method dispatches the call to the respective **perimeter** method. The **perimeter** method calculates the perimeter of the corresponding method and returns the calculated value to **calc_perimeter**. It prints the value.

The result of the program is as follows:

```
================ RESTART: C:\Users\Subbu\Desktop\E10x9.py ==================
None
20
30
43.96
```

Here polymorphism is implemented through the **calc_perimeter** method. The basic difference between inheritance and polymorphism is that inheritance allows the already existing code to be reused again in a program, and polymorphism provides a mechanism to dynamically decide what form of a method to be invoked at runtime.

Polymorphism in Python facilitates code reusability by allowing different objects to be treated uniformly through a common interface, even though they may have different implementations. This promotes modularity and flexibility in code design.

By designing classes to adhere to a common interface (e.g., by defining shared methods or properties), we can write functions or modules that operate on objects of that interface type without needing to know the specific implementations of those objects. For instance, the **calc_perimeter()** provides a common interface to various objects of the classes in the above program.

This promotes the following aspects of code reusability:

- **Flexibility:** With polymorphism, we can create code that operates on a generic type, allowing us to easily substitute different implementations of that type without changing the code that uses it.

- **Modularity:** We can write code that depends on an abstract interface rather than concrete implementations. This allows us to isolate changes to specific implementations without affecting other parts of the code.

- **Scalability:** Polymorphism allows us to easily extend our codebase by adding new implementations of existing interfaces without modifying the existing code.

Dynamic binding

We implement inheritance with a superclass and one or more sub-classes. The subclass inherits the features of the superclass. Every object of a sub-class can be considered also to be an instance of the superclass. All the classes may each have a method with a common signature. Python determines which method is to be called at run-time. This principle is known as dynamic binding. A program is given below which demonstrates the exploitation of superclass method by sub-classes at runtime.

In the program, **G_shape** is the superclass, **Square** and **Circle** are its derived classes. In the main function, we have defined a method display, which receives a superclass object. The display function has the **object** class method **__str__**, which provides a string description of the object received. We call method **display** with objects of superclass and sub-classes one at a time. Although we defined the method **display** with the superclass object, it works well for the derived classes as well. This is because of the dynamic binding characteristics of Python. This is also a feature of polymorphism. Look at the given program to understand dynamic binding:

```python
# Program E10x10.py
# Dynamic Binding
class G_shape(object):

    def perimeter(self):
        pass
class Square(G_shape):
```

```
        def perimeter(self):
            self._side=5
            return(4*self._side)
class Circle (G_shape):
    def perimeter(self):
        self._radius = 7
        return(2 * 3.14 * self._radius)

def main():
    g_obj=G_shape()
    def display(g_obj):
        print(g_obj.__str__())
    display(g_obj)
    s_obj=Square()
    display(s_obj)
    display(s_obj.perimeter())
    c_obj = Circle()
    display(c_obj)
    display(c_obj.perimeter())

main()
```

The result of the program is given below.

```
==================== RESTART: E:/Py programs/E10x10.py ====================
<__main__.G_shape object at 0x031DA3A0>
<__main__.Square object at 0x031DA430>
20
<__main__.Circle object at 0x031DA490>
43.96
```

This program implements a superclass with two derived classes. The objects of **Square** and **Circle** class, when they need function to display the object characteristics, they look for the method in their respective classes. Since they could not find a match, they went to their superclass and found one and used it to display the details about the corresponding object. This is dynamic binding.

Abstract class

An abstract class permits us to create a set of methods, which should be created within any or all the derived classes derived from the abstract class. A class that contains one or more abstract methods is called an abstract class. An abstract method has a declaration but does not have an implementation. When we want to provide a common interface for different implementations of a component, we use an abstract class.

An object cannot be created from an abstract class. The abstract classes are also called interfaces. The parent class in the above program -E10x10- does not perform any specific action except facilitating deriving sub-classes. Such classes are suitable for declaring as abstract classes. To declare a class as an abstract class, we must specify the following on top of the program:

```
from abc import ABC, abstractmethod
```

In the above, abc: abstract base class. The class **ABC** is present in **abc**. We have to import **ABC** from **abc**. We have to also import abstractmethod.

In addition to it, we must mark the method in the base class as an abstract method using the decorator **@abstractmethod**. The abstract class should contain methods marked as **@abstractmethod**.

Look at the program **E10x11.py**. This is like the program **E10x9.py**, with the following modifications:

- The parent class contains an abstract method.

- The class **Rectangle** is deleted.

The G-shape class cannot be used to create an object since it is an abstract class. However, let us try to create an object **gs_obj** of **G_shape** in the main function and see what happens:

```
# Program E10x11.py
# Abstract class
from abc import ABC, abstractmethod
class G_shape(ABC):
    @abstractmethod

    def perimeter(self):
        pass
class Square(G_shape):
    def perimeter(self):
        self._side=5
        return(4*self._side)
```

```
class Circle (G_shape):
    def perimeter(self):
        self._radius = 7
        return(2 * 3.14 * self._radius)
def calc_perimeter(input_obj):
    print(input_obj.perimeter())


def main():
    gs_obj-G_shape()
    calc_perimeter(gs_obj)
    s_obj=Square()
    calc_perimeter(s_obj)
    c_obj = Circle()
    calc_perimeter(c_obj)
main()
```

As expected, we got a run-time error because we tried to create an object of abstract class as the following indicates:

```
================ RESTART: C:/Users/Subbu/Desktop/E10x11.py ================
Traceback (most recent call last):
  File "C:/Users/Subbu/Desktop/E10x11.py", line 29, in <module>
    main()
  File "C:/Users/Subbu/Desktop/E10x11.py", line 23, in main
    gs_obj=G_shape()
TypeError: Can't instantiate abstract class G_shape with abstract method
perimeter
```

Let us now comment on the statements about the creation of an object of abstract class in the program. We added a # at the beginning of the first and second statements in the program. In other words, we are not going to create an object of the abstract class.

The result of the program after the modification is as follows:

```
================ RESTART: C:/Users/Subbu/Desktop/E10x11.py ================
20
43.96
```

Now, we know how to create an abstract class. By defining an abstract base class, we can define a common **Application Program Interface (API)** for a set of subclasses. This capability is especially useful in situations where a third party is going to provide implementations, such as with plugins, but can also help when working in a large team or with a large code-base.

By default, Python does not provide abstract classes. Python comes with a module that provides the base for defining **Abstract Base classes (ABC)** with a module named ABC.

ABC works by decorating methods of the base class as abstract. A method becomes abstract when decorated with the keyword **@abstractmethod**. The decorator has a specific meaning in Python and is discussed in *Chapter 13, Gems of Python*.

Iterators

The official Python tutorial gives a lucid explanation about iterators. Most of the container objects can be looped over by using a **for** statement. We had iterated over container objects such as lists and tuples using a **for** loop. We may recall and add new ways of iteration of container elements. For instance, the following are examples of iteration with list, dictionary, string and file:

```
for element in [1, 2, 3]:
print(element)
for key in {'one':1, 'two':2}:
    print(key)
for char in "123":
    print(char)
for line in open("myfile.txt"):
    print(line, end='\n')
```

To quote the official Python tutorial *This style of access is clear, concise, and convenient. The use of iterators pervades and unifies Python. Behind the scenes, the for statement calls iter() on the container object*. The **iter** function returns an iterator object that defines the method **__next__()** which accesses elements in the container one at a time. When there are no more elements, **__next__()** raises a **StopIteration** exception which terminates the **for** loop. The same iteration concept can be extended to classes and then it is called a user-defined iterator.

Iterable

In Python, *iterable* and *iterator* are related but distinct concepts:

- Iterable:
    - o An iterable is any object that can be iterated over, meaning it can be used in a loop.
    - o Iterable objects have an **__iter__**() method, which returns an iterator.

- o Common iterable objects include lists, tuples, strings, dictionaries, sets, and more.

- o Iterables can be used directly in a loop, such as **for item in iterable:**.

- Iterator:

  - o An iterator is an object that represents a stream of data and implements the iterator protocol.

  - o Iterators have a **__next__()** method, which returns the next item in the stream.

  - o Iterators also have an **__iter__()** method, which returns the iterator itself (this is necessary for iterators to be considered iterable).

  - o Iterators maintain state and know how to access the next element in the sequence.

  - o Once an iterator has been exhausted (i.e., it has no more elements to return), it raises a StopIteration exception when **__next__()** is called.

  - o Common examples of iterators include the **iter()** function, generator objects, and file objects.

  - o Iterators can be used with the **next()** function or in a loop, such as for item in iterator:.

Here is a summary of the differences:

- **Iterable** objects are those that can be looped over (for example, lists, tuples, dictionaries).

- **Iterator** objects are those that generate values on the fly and maintain an internal state to remember the position of the next value.

In essence, all iterators are iterables, but not all iterables are iterators. Iterables provide the means to create iterators, but iterators are responsible for the actual iteration, maintaining their state, and providing the next value when requested.

User-defined iterators

To create an object as an iterator we have to implement the methods **__iter__()** and **__next__()** to the object. In Python, all classes have a method called **__init__()**, which allows initializing when the object is being created. Similarly, the **__iter__()** method is also available to carry out operations such as initializing but must always return the iterator object itself. The **__next__()** method also allows us to program operations, but, must return the next item in the sequence. If we wish our class to function as an iterator, we have to define **__iter__** and **__next__** in the class. Let us look at an example program implementing both **__iter__** and **__next__** methods.

In the program, we define class **Dec**, which is a derived class of the built-in class **object**. We can even omit the mention of the **object** without affecting the program. Then we have defined **__iter__** method, where we define **num** as 100. This is followed by the **__next__** method. If num is equal to zero we raise an exception **StopIteration**, which will halt the program. If the number is not equal to zero, we decrement **num** by 2 and return. We then declare **even** as an object of **Dec** class and **iter_even** as the iterator of the **even** class. Then we call **next(iter_even)** and print 3 times. Each time **num** will be decremented by 2:

```python
# program E10x12.py
# Iterator
class Dec(object):
  def __iter__(self):
    self.num = 100
    return self
  def __next__(self):
    x = self.num
    if(x==0):
        raise StopIteration
    else:
        self.num -= 2
        return x
even = Dec()
iter_even = iter(even)
print(next(iter_even))
print(next(iter_even))
print(next(iter_even))
```

The result of the program is as follows:

```
======================= RESTART: E:\Py programs\E10x12.py
100
98
96
```

To summarize, in Python, an iterator is a method which implements the iterator protocol. Iterator in Python is simply an object that can be iterated upon. It is an object which will return data, one element at a time. A Python iterator object must implement two special methods, **__iter__()** and **__next__()** , collectively called the iterator protocol.

Generators

Python generators are a simple way of creating iterators. In the last program, to build an iterator, we implemented a class with **__iter__()** and **__next__()** methods, kept track of internal states and raised **StopIteration** exception when there are no values to be returned. All the tasks mentioned above are automatically handled by the generators in Python.

A generator-function is defined as a normal function, but whenever it needs to generate a value, it does so using the **yield** keyword rather than keyword **return**. If a function contains at least one yield statement (it may contain more yield or return statements), it becomes a generator function. A generator is a function that returns an object (iterator) that we can iterate over (one value at a time). It is as easy as defining a normal function but with a **yield** keyword instead of a **return** keyword. Generators use **yield** instead of **return**, to return data from a function. Both **yield** and **return** will return some value from a function. The difference is that while a **return** statement terminates a function entirely, the **yield** statement pauses the function, saving all its states, and later continues from there on successive calls. Each time **__next__()** is called it returns to the place where it was last time.

An iterator for decrement operation with *a generator* is given below. We have a function **Even_gen**, which initializes **num** to 100. After the print statement, we have **yield num**. Then after decrementing **num** by 2, we have another **yield** function. The above step is repeated. In the end, we have a **for** loop where we print the items:

```python
# program E10x13.py
# generator
def Even_gen():
    num = 100
    print('This is printed first')
    # Generator function contains yield statements
    yield num
    num-= 2
    print('This is printed second')
    yield num
    num-= 2
    print('This is printed at last')
    yield num


for item in Even_gen():
    print(item)
```

Note that the **for** loop is not part of the **Even_gen** function and hence it is not typed in the Tab. The 3 **yield** statements return the **num** for printing in the **for** loop. The result of the program is as follows:

```
==================== RESTART: E:/Py programs/E10x13.py ====================
This is printed first
100
This is printed second
98
This is printed at last
96
```

Let us write a program to reverse a string using a generator. In this example, we use the **range()** function to get the index in reverse order using the first for loop. It is as follows:

```
# program E10x14.py
# reversing a string
def reverse(str1):
    length = len(str1)
    for i in range(length - 1, -1, -1):
        yield str1[i]
# For loop to reverse the string
for char in reverse('purposeful'):
            print(char)
```

Note that the second **for** loop is not part of the **reverse** function and hence it does not start in the Tab. The **reverse** in the second **for** loop calls the **reverse** function and passes a string to the **reverse** function. The reversed characters are printed in the second **for** loop. The yield in the generator function returns the reversed string. The result of the program is as follows:

```
==================== RESTART: E:\Py programs\E10x14.py ====================
l
u
f
e
s
o
p
r
u
p
```

A normal function starts execution from first line and continues until we reach a return statement or an exception or end of the function. Any of the local variables created during the function scope are destroyed and not accessible later. In the case of a generator when it encounters a yield keyword the state of the function is frozen and all the variables are stored in memory until the generator is called again. Note that unlike functions, which return a whole list, a generator yields one value at a time which requires less memory.

Let us briefly discuss the salient features of a generator function. It is discussed as follows:

- Generator function contains one or more yield statements.

- When called, it returns an object (iterator).

- Methods like **__iter__()** and **__next__()** are implemented automatically. So we can iterate through the items using **__next__()**.

- Once the function yields, the function is paused and the control is transferred to the caller.

- Local variables and their states are remembered between successive calls.

- Note the unique style of programs and in particular, the **for** statements.

Generator expressions

An expression can be formed using a generator function. A generator expression is like list comprehension. It creates a generator without **yield** statement. The generator expressions are enclosed within parentheses unlike list comprehension enclosed within square brackets. Some examples of generator expressions are as follows:

1. gen1=min(random.randint(100, 200) for n in range (20))

The above generates 20 random numbers between 100 and 200 and finds the minimum. Execution in interactive mode is as follows:

```
>>> import random
>>> gen1=min(random.randint(100, 200) for n in range (20))
>>> print (gen1)
120
```

2. gen2=(n**4 for n in range(10))

In this case the statement generates n^4 for n from 0 to 9. Execution in interactive mode is as follows:

```
>>> gen2=(n**4 for n in range(10))
>>> print (gen2)
<generator object <genexpr> at 0x02F3EA38>
```

```
>>> print (list (gen2))
[0, 1, 16, 81, 256, 625, 1296, 2401, 4096, 6561]
```

In the above **gen2** is converted to list and printed. Thus, generator expressions provide compact code like list comprehension.

Let us look at an example of a generator expression used within a for loop:

```
# Example E10x15.py
# Generator expression within a for loop
numbers = [1, 2, 3, 4, 5]
# Using a generator expression to generate squares of numbers
squared_numbers = (x ** 2 for x in numbers)
# Iterating over the generator expression using a for loop
for squared_number in squared_numbers:
    print(squared_number)
```

In the program **E10x15.py** above:

- We define a list of numbers containing some integers.

- We create a generator expression (x ** 2 for x in numbers) that generates the square of each number in the list.

- We iterate over the generator expression using a for loop.

- During each iteration, the next squared number is generated on-the-fly by the generator expression and printed.

This demonstrates how a generator expression can be used seamlessly within a for loop to produce values lazily as they are needed, without needing to store the entire sequence of squared numbers in memory. The result of the program is given below:

```
==================== RESTART: E:/Py programs/E10x15.py ====================
1
4
9
16
25
```

Conclusion

We learned that in OOP, adding a new feature after a class has been developed is rather easy. The class, which is already available (after thorough testing) is known as a base class. The base class is also known as a superclass or parent class. Adding a new feature may require either adding a new data element or a new function. This can be achieved by extending the program in OOP. For this, a new class must be defined as inheriting the base class. This new class is called a derived class, sub-class, or child class in Python. Adding new classes does not require any changes to the base class.

We discussed three types of inheritances – single, multiple, and multi-level. The diamond problem arises when we implement multiple inheritance, and we found a solution to solve this problem in this chapter. We also discussed three access types – public, private, and protected.

We covered polymorphism with Python extensively. Polymorphism and inheritance facilitate the reusability of Python code. We also discussed iterators, iterables, user-defined iterators and generators in this chapter.

In the next chapter, we will learn about file handling in the era of machine learning and big data analytics.

Points to remember

- A single inheritance is a relationship between one parent and one child.

- In multi-level inheritance, it can continue to more than one level depending on the need.

- On the contrary, multiple inheritances refer to a class inheriting the properties of multiple base classes.

- Containership is also known as composition.

- The *private* data members with a double underscore, also called underscore, are accessible only within the class, while *public* data members are accessible from anywhere.

- The protected data members will be accessible in the derived classes also.

- Generally, the methods are declared public to make them available anywhere. If there is no prefix of underscore to data members, then they can be considered to be public.

- Method overriding permits us to modify the implementation of a method of the superclass by the derived class.

- In larger programs, it may be difficult to keep track of whether an object is of a particular class. In such cases, we can use this function **isinstance()** to confirm. In addition, there is another global function called **issubclass(c1, c2)**. This checks whether c1 is a derived class of c2 and returns True if it is so.

- An abstract class can be a blueprint for other classes.

- The subclass inherits the features of the superclass. Python can attach a subclass object to a superclass method. This principle is known as dynamic binding.

- An iterator is an object, which has implemented both **__iter__()** and **__next__** **()** in it. However, the iterable is also an object which has implemented only **__iter__()**. So, an iterable will be static and point to the same data item when accessed again and again and will not move to next item in the list. However, when we use **__iter__**, **__next__** will be available to fetch the next element. That is the difference between the two.

- Python generators are a simple way of creating iterators. A generator is a function that returns an object (iterator) which we can iterate over (one value at a time). It is as easy as defining a normal function, but with a **yield** statement instead of a **return** statement.

- The generators are powerful and perform differently as compared to normal functions.

- We also used generator expressions to give a compact code like list comprehension.

Questions

Choose the most appropriate answer.

1. **A data member is accessible in the class and inherited class only if declared:**

    a. public

    b. private

    c. protected

    d. All of the above

    e. None of the above

2. **__iter__() is a:**

    a. class

    b. method

    c. data type.

    d. All of the above

    e. None of the above

3. **Methods are usually declared as:**

    a. protected

    b. private

   c. All of the above

   d. none of the above

4. **The minimum number of superclasses for multiple inheritance is:**

   a. 1

   b. 2

   c. All of the above

   d. None of the above

5. **In multilevel inheritance the minimum number of derived classes is:**

   a. 0

   b. 1

   c. 2

   d. None of the above

6. **Container class:**

   a. has object of other class

   b. provides an object to other class

   c. All of the above

   d. None of the above

7. **__next__ () will be invoked with:**

   a. iter

   b. iterable

   c. All of the above

   d. None of the above

8. **Inheritance is implemented through:**

   a. classes

   b. methods

   c. All of the above

   d. None of the above

9. **Polymorphism is implemented through:**

    a. classes

    b. methods

    c. All of the above

    d. None of the above

10. **Reuse is implemented through:**

    a. containership

    b. inheritance

    c. All of the above

    d. None of the above

- Write short notes on the following:

    o   The built-in object class and its methods

    o   protected vs. private

    o   multiple inheritance

    o   The diamond problem

    o   container

    o   Types of inheritance

    o   polymorphism

    o   dynamic binding

    o   generator

    o   Distinguish between iterable and iterator

- Match the following:

A	B
Function	1. like relationship
Generator	2. interface
Container	3. has relationship
Inheritance	4. return
Abstract class	5. yield

- Write programs for the following:
    - o To build a container class student with the university object.
    - o To build a container class Flat (owner, number, telephone) with Apartment object.
    - o Implement polymorphism with the following class hierarchy – person-youth-student.
    - o Implement multiple inheritance with corporate and regional offices as super classes and a local office as derived class.
    - o Build inheritance with square as base class and rectangle as a derived class and with methods to calculate their areas.
    - o To find whether a string is a palindrome or not using generators.
    - o To demonstrate dynamic binding.
    - o Add one more derived class named Address in the program E10x3.
    - o Add class Triangle in program E10x6.
    - o Build a hierarchy of classes – Basic pay, gross salary and net salary of an employee.

Join our book's Discord space

Join the book's Discord Workspace for Latest updates, Offers, Tech happenings around the world, New Release and Sessions with the Authors:

https://discord.bpbonline.com

CHAPTER 11
File Handling

Introduction

In professional applications such as banking, insurance, stock market, and ticket booking, the data must be stored forever and should be retrievable at anytime from anywhere. One way to store such data is in files. Therefore, a Python programmer must understand how Python supports file handling. Python is the preferred language for Machine Learning and Artificial Intelligence. Data handling is crucial in this area, and Python supports it fully. This chapter will demonstrate Python's file-handling features.

Structure

The chapter covers the following topics:

- Files
- Writing to a file
- Reading from a file
- Text and binary files
- Mode parameters
- Copying files

- Appending text
- The **with** for file close
- Case studies
- The **seek** method
- Writing to binary file and then reading
- Java Script Object Notation
- Pickle solution
- Pickle vs. JSON
- Case study
- Command line arguments

Objectives

This chapter covers opening, reading, writing, appending, copying, and closing, text and binary files, and associated methods. Different methods for reading, including implicit reading from a file, are discussed. We will also discuss the popular **JavaScript Object Notation (JSON)** and the pickling solution to encode, write, and then read from files. In the Machine Learning and Big Data Analytics arena, **Comma Separated Values (CSV)** files are used widely, and the same concept is demonstrated in this chapter. The command line arguments and the **shutil** module to copy files are also discussed.

Files

We were carrying out input/output with the console. Big data analytics and Machine Learning deal with large files, and therefore, we should learn how to write and read from files. In this chapter, we will discuss input/output with files. The Python programs we came across in the book were tested with data. All programs need the input data to process in the program and the output information is provided by the computer system to the user. Input and output need a file to store them permanently. The files, in turn, are stored in compartments on computer systems that are managed by the Operating System. Although variables provide us with a way to store data temporarily while the program runs, if we want such data for future use, we should store them permanently on a hard disk or a flash or compact disk.

A file can be identified by the following three attributes:

- Filename
- Its extension
- The location or path, which specifies the location where the file exists.

We will study some techniques to read and write to the files in this chapter.

Writing to a file

We must open files for a specific purpose, such as to read or write, or combination of read and write. To write a file, we must open a file for writing purposes specifically. Before opening the file for writing, we must create a file object. We can assign any arbitrary identifier to the file object such as **outfile**. The programmer can choose any valid identifier. We can open the file in a hard disc drive. Let us choose the name of the file as **d1.txt** since we are proposing to write a text to a text file. The following statement will open a file for writing:

outfile=open ("d1.txt", 'w')

Notice that we need three items for writing, as given below:

- Physical file, in this case, **d1.txt**. The file will be created in the current directory.

- A file object that is associated with the physical file, in this case, **outfile**.

- The mode parameter "w" for writing into the file.

The **open()** is a built-in function in Python to open a file. In the above example, it is assigned to a file object called **outfile**. The name of the file and file mode w (for writing) is passed on as argument to the **open** function. The arguments are given within parentheses.

Checking existence of a file

Before we write, we must make sure that we are writing in a new file and not to an existing file to avoid overwriting any useful information already stored in the file. For this purpose, we should check whether a file already exists or not, and if it is so, we may either **exit** from the execution of the program or the programmer may use other options. To check the existence of the file already, we have to import **os. path** and **sys**. Let us try to understand what it means now. We know that **os** refers to the operating system of the system we are using, which is *Windows10* in this case. The os module is a part of the standard library, or **stdlib**, in Python 3. It comes with the Python installation, but we must import it when needed. The **path** gives a list of directories in our system. We need to **import os.path** to check if the file to be used for writing already exists. The **sys** refers to the system needed to *exit* from the program when a file already exists with the same name. The **isfile()** method will return True if the file exists. If it is an existing file and we do not want to erase the contents, we must skip the assignment of an object to the file for writing by using **exit()** function. The following code should be inserted before we open a file for writing:

```python
import os.path
import sys
if os.path.isfile("d1.txt"):
    print('d1.txt exists')
sys.exit()
```

The **sys.exit()** will terminate the execution of the program when **isfile** function returns true. The program below writes strings to the specified file:

```
# program E11x1.py
# writing to a file
import os.path
import sys
def main():

        filename=input('Enter filename for writing  ')
        if os.path.isfile(filename):
            print('filename exists')
            sys.exit()
        else:
        # open file for writing
            outfile = open(filename, "w")
        # writing
            outfile.write('First line of Text\n')
            outfile.write('Second line of Text\n')
            outfile.write('Third Line of Text\n')
            outfile.close()


main()
```

The result of the program is given below.

```
==================== RESTART: E:\Py programs\E11x1.py ====================
Enter filename for writing  d1.txt
filename exists
>>>

==================== RESTART: E:\Py programs\E11x1.py ====================
Enter filename for writing  e1.txt
>>>
```

Here the user was asked to enter the file name. Since the file **d1.txt** entered by the user already exists, the program execution stopped after printing the message above. Let us choose another file that does not exist in the system. This time the user typed **e1.txt**. Since the file name did not exist, the program execution was successful, and no message popped up.

In the program, we assign the filename entered by the user to the file object **outfile**. We then write three lines of text by calling the built-in function *to write* in conjunction with the file object. The file object and, in turn, the file are closed after writing three lines to the named file. When we executed the program, we did not get any output since we did not expect anything other than an error message if the file already exists. The file **e1.txt** was created in the current directory, as confirmed by the successful execution of the program. The existence of the file was also physically verified in the current directory.

When we use a **print** function, the new line character "\n" is automatically inserted after the string by default, but that is not the case with **write()**. Therefore, a programmer has to insert it specifically if it is desired that the next string should be printed in the next line as carried out in the above program.

Reading from a file

Reading the same file can help check whether we have written to the disk. We need three items for reading from a file, as given below:

- Physical file, in this case, **e1.txt**. The file is in our current directory.
- File object that is associated with the physical file, in this case, **infile**.
- The mode parameter "r" for reading in the file.

To open a file for reading, we create a file object **infile** and call it as given below:

```
infile =open("e1.txt", "r")
```

The program for reading from an existing file is given below:

```
# program E11x2.py
# reading from a file


def main():
    # open file for reading
    infile = open("e1.txt", "r")
    # reading
    print (infile.read())


main()
```

The result of the program is given below:

```
==================== RESTART: E:\Py programs\E11x2.py ====================
First line of Text
Second line of Text
Third Line of Text
```

In the above program, we open the named file for reading, in the read mode, "r". Then we print whatever we are reading using **infile.read()**. Similarly, we wrote using **outfile. write()**. Look at the simplicity of Python for reading and writing. The result of the program confirms that our writing in the above program and reading in this program are both successful.

readline() method

In the above program, we read all the lines in one go. In certain cases, the text file may be large, or we may want to read the content line by line. In that case, we can use the **readline()** method. The **readline()** function reads a single line from the specified file and returns a string that contains a trailing newline character.

The program below shows using the **readline()** function and displaying the returned result:

```python
# program E11x3.py
# reading line by line

def main():
    # open file for reading
    infile = open("e1.txt", "r")
    # reading
    print (infile.readline())

main()
```

The result of the program is given below. It has read only the first line, inspite of there being 3 lines in the file. The newline character '\n' is not printed. It makes the effect of going to next line, but character is not printable.

```
==================== RESTART: E:/Py programs/E11x3.py =====================
First line of Text
>>>
```

If we wish to print all three lines in the file, repeat the print statement three times as shown in the program below:

```python
# program E11x4.py
# reading three lines

def main():
    # open file for reading
```

```
    infile = open("e1.txt", "r")
    # reading
    print (infile.readline())
    print (infile.readline())
    print (infile.readline())
```

```
main()
```

The result of the program is given below. It has printed all the three lines in the file:

```
==================== RESTART: E:/Py programs/E11x4.py ====================
First line of Text
Second line of Text
Third Line of Text
```

Some points to be noted about the **readline** method are given below:

- The **readline ()** method reads a single line from the specified file.

- If used in text mode, then **readline ()** returns a string and returns a byte object in binary mode.

- A "\n", the trailing newline character at the end of the string, is omitted.

- We may provide **size** argument in the **readline()** method, an optional numeric argument.

- If we do not provide the size argument or a negative value is given, then one line will be returned at a time.

- If the size argument is given, then it is the maximum byte count that will be returned. In this case, the newline character will also be included if it lies within the size specified, and **readline()** function may return an incomplete line.

Let us read 7 bytes using the *size* method in **readline()** method. The program is given below:

```
# program E11x5.py
# reading 7 bytes

def main():
    # open file for reading
    infile = open("e1.txt", "r")
    # reading
    print (infile.readline(7))
```

```
main()
```

The result of the program is given below. It has printed 7 characters in the first line.

```
==================== RESTART: E:/Py programs/E11x5.py ====================
First l
```

readlines() method

Note the s suffix to readline in the above. We can read all lines in one go if we use **readlines
()** function. Each line will be treated as an element in a container list with an appended newline character. The program to read all lines in the text is given below:

```
# program E11x6.py
# reading all lines together

def main():
    # open file for reading
    infile = open("e1.txt", "r")
    # reading
    print (infile.readlines())

main()
```

The result of the program is given below:

```
==================== RESTART: E:/Py programs/E11x6.py ====================
['First line of Text\n', 'Second line of Text\n', 'Third Line of Text\n']
>>>
```

We invoke the **readlines** method connected to the file object by the dot operator. It also reads the newline character at the end of each line, as the result indicates.

Implicit reading

So far, we have been calling the **read**, **readline** or **readlines** functions in conjunction with the respective file objects explicitly. We can do it implicitly without calling the **read**, **readline** or **readlines** methods, as the following program demonstrates:

```
# program E11x7.py
# implicit method for reading

def main():
```

```
# open file for reading
infile = open("e1.txt", "r")
# reading
for line in infile:
    print (line)
```

```
main()
```

We are neither calling **read**, nor **readline** nor **readlines** method in the program. Once the file object is assigned to open a file in read mode, we can read it implicitly as given in the program. We print the contents of the file if there are contents in the file. This is an implicit reading methodology since we do not use any of the read methods. The **in** keyword is used to check if a value is present in a sequence (list, range, string, etc.). The **in** keyword is also used to iterate through a sequence in the **for** loop. In the above program, the sequence is nothing but the file object **infile** and, in turn, the file it points to.

As discussed in *Chapter 4, Unicode, Strings and Console Output*, an object in Python is called iterable, if we can get an iterator from it. The *for* loop calls the **__iter__()** method of the file object **infile**. This method returns an iterator object. The iterator object has a method **__next__()**, which returns the next item in the file. When all the items in **infile** have been iterated, call to **__next__()** raises a **StopIteration** exception which terminates the for loop. *The line* in the program is just a variable like **var**, **i**, etc. The reader can replace the *line* with other variable names. The result of the program is given below:

```
===================== RESTART: E:/Py programs/E11x7.py =====================
First line of Text
Second line of Text
Third Line of Text
```

An important point to note is that the **read()** method reads all the data from the file and returns it as one string. The **readline()** method reads a line or part thereof from the file and returns it as one string. The **readlines()** method reads all the data from the file and returns it as a list of strings.

Text and binary files

We wrote to a text file and read it, now let us talk about the types of files. There are two types of files, as given below:

- Text file
- Binary file

As common sense dictates, if we want to write 789 in the text mode, we will need three characters or 24 bits. When we write the same number in the binary mode, we will need less space. Another interpretation is that all files created with Notepad on Windows or vi editors on UNIX are text files, and others are binary files.

Mode parameters

We have seen that the appropriate mode parameters must be specified to read from a file or to write to a file. In addition to 'r' for reading and 'w' for writing, there are several other modes, a list of which is given below in *Table 11.1*:

Mode	Function
"r"	Read mode
"w"	Writing mode. Create a file if not existing. If existing overwrites the file
"a"	Append mode
"rb"	Reading mode in binary
"r+"	Reading and writing at the same time
"rb"	Reading and writing mode in binary
"wb"	Writing mode in binary
"w+"	Reading and writing mode
"wb+"	Reading and writing in binary mode
"ab"	Appending in binary mode
"a+"	Appending and reading mode
"ab+"	Appending and reading mode in binary

Table 11.1: File mode parameters

Essentially there are five operations in file handling as given below:

- Read
- Write
- Append
- Read and write
- Append and read

We carry out these operations in text and binary files. The append operation means writing after the current contents of the file without overwriting them.

Copying files

To carry out copying, we need a source file and a destination file. The following steps are involved in copying files:

- Open-source file for reading and assign file object **infile** to it.

- Check the destination file. If it exists, exit.

- Otherwise, open the destination file for writing and assign file object **outfile** to it.

- For every line in the source file, write to the destination file through the respective object.

- To check if we have written, open the destination file in the read mode.

- Print the contents of the destination file.

- Close both **infile** and **outfile**.

```
# program E11x8.py
# copying from a source file to a destination file
import os.path
import sys


def main():
    # open file for reading
    infile = open("e1.txt", "r")
 # open file for writing

    if os.path.isfile("e2.txt"):
        print('e2.txt exists')
        sys.exit()
    else:
        outfile=open("e2.txt", "w")
    # copying
        for line in infile:
            outfile.write(line)
    # checking contents of destination file
    outfile = open("e2.txt", "r")
    print(outfile.read())
    infile.close()
    outfile.close()
```

```
main()
```

The result of the program is given below:

```
===================== RESTART: E:/Py programs/E11x8.py =====================
First line of Text
Second line of Text
Third Line of Text
```

In this program, we have written to the file **e2.txt** from **e1.txt**. If we run the program again, *an exit* will be triggered since the file already exists, and the program will terminate. Hence, if you want to run the program again, change the name of the file for writing every time.

Appending text

We can add text at the end of the current contents of a text file. The following program illustrates the concept of appending. We will use **e2.txt** file which already contains three lines of text, for this experimentation.

```python
# program E11x9.py
# appending to a file

def main():
    # open file for appending
    outfile = open("e2.txt", "a")
    outfile.write("appending fourth line\n")
    outfile.write('appending fifth line\n')
    outfile.close()
    # reading
    infile=open("e2.txt", 'r')
    print (infile.read())
    infile.close()

main()
```

The result of the program is given below:

```
===================== RESTART: E:\Py programs\E11x9.py =====================
First line of Text
Second line of Text
```

```
Third Line of Text
appending fourth line
appending fifth line
```

We opened the file in append mode, wrote two lines, and then closed it. After this, the same file was opened in read mode. Now, read the entire contents of the file through **infile** file object and after reading, close the file.

Note that except for the change of mode parameter from "w" to "a", there is no difference between writing and appending. We use the same write function in both modes. However, since we are appending to an existing file, we do not check the existence of the file; rather, we write to an existing file.

The with for file close

We learned to close files through the respective file objects as soon as the file is no longer needed. If we do not close the file, Python's garbage collector system may close it. To be sure that the file is closed after the work, we can open files using the keyword **with** as given below:

```
with open ("e2.txt", "w") as outfile:
```

The **with** ensures that the file object is closed. The program E11x7 is modified using with and given below:

```
# revised program E11x7.py
# implicit method for reading

def main():
    # open file for reading
    with open("e1.txt", "r") as infile:
    # reading
        for line in infile:
            print (line)

main()
```

The result of the program is given below.

```
================== RESTART: E:/Py programs/revisedE11x7.py ==================
First line of Text
Second line of Text
Third Line of Text
```

The opening of the file **with** will ensure closing the file as soon as the file is no longer needed.

Case studies

This section will discuss some case studies related to file handling.

Counting occurrence of each word in a text file

Sometimes it may be required to count the occurrence of each unique word in a text file. To count the occurrence of each word, we create a dictionary object that stores each unique word as a key and its count of the number of occurrences of the word as the corresponding value. We iterate through each unique word in the file and add it to the dictionary with a count of 1 the first time. If the word is already present in the dictionary and if it repeats, we increment its count by 1 for every repetition. Look at the implementation in the program window in *Figure 11.1*:

```
*E11x10.py - C:\Users\Subbu\Desktop\E11x10.py (3.10.10)*
File Edit Format Run Options Window Help
 1  # program E11x10.py
 2  # counting  each word in a text file
 3
 4  def main():
 5      filename=input('Enter file name: ').strip()
 6      infile=open(filename, "r")
 7
 8      dict1=dict()
 9
10      for line in infile:
11  # Remove the spaces and new line characters
12          line=line.strip()
13
14          line=line.lower()
15  # split the line into words
16          words=line.split(" ")
17
18          for word in words:
19  # Check if the word is already in dictionary
20              if word in dict1:
21                  dict1[word]=dict1[word]+1
22              else:
23  # Add the word to dictionary with count=1
24                  dict1[word] =1
25
26      for key in list(dict1.keys()):
27          print(key, ":", dict1[key])
28
29
30  main()
31
```

Figure 11.1: Counting occurrence of words

We exploited the feature of dictionary to count the number of occurrences of a word in a file. Each unique word is a key in the dictionary.

Let us analyse what happens in the program (*Figure 11.1*), line by line. In *Line 4*, the main function has been defined. In *Line 5*, the *filename* is received from the user. In *Line 6*, we open the file filename in the read mode and assign it to the file object in file. In *Line 8*, we create an empty dictionary called **dict1**.

In this case, we read the contents of the file implicitly. At *Line 10*, we have a **for** loop, which iterates till there are contents in the file and we carry out the following:

- At *Line 12*, we carry out the strip of each *line* in the text file and assign it to the line. A line is a variable. The **strip** is a method that eliminates specific characters from the beginning and the end of a string. By default, it removes any white space characters, such as spaces, tabs, and newline characters.

- At *Line 14*, we convert the text in the line to lowercase alphabets.

- At *Line 16*, we carry out **line.split(" ")**, which separates the words and assign them to a list containing *words*. Now *words*, a list, contains all the words in the file we opened for reading.

- At *Line 18*, we have a **for** loop. It will iterate until all words are exhausted in the list *words*. Here, *word* is like a counting variable like **i**. We can even use **i** or **var** instead of *word*.

- At *Line 24*, each new word will be stored as a **key** in **dict1** with a value of 1.

- At *Lines 20 and 21*, when the word repeats, the value corresponding to the key will be incremented by 1. On *Lines 26 and 27*, the value of each word will be printed.

The result of the program is given below:

```
==================== RESTART: E:/Py programs/E11x10.py ====================
Enter file name: e2.txt
first : 1
line : 9
of : 3
text : 3
second : 1
third : 1
appending : 6
fourth : 3
fifth : 2
```

A summary of steps in the word count program are given below:

1. Open the file for reading.

2. Create an empty dictionary.

3. Remove the leading spaces and new line characters using **strip ()** method.

4. Convert all words to lower case using **lower ()** method.

5. Split the words using split (' ')

6. Check every word in the file.

7. If it is a new word create an entry in the dictionary with the word as the key and count as 1.

8. If the word is repeating increment the count of the word.

9. When there are no more words in the file print the word and corresponding count.

A similar method can be used for counting characters in a file.

Counting occurrence of each alphabet in a text file

A program for counting the occurrence of each character in a file is given *Figure 11.2* below:

```
# *E11x11.py - C:/Users/Subbu/Desktop/E11x11.py (3.10.11)*
File Edit Format Run Options Window Help
1 # program E11x11.py
2 # counting  character in a text file
3
4 def main():
5     filename=input('Enter file name: ')
6     infile=open(filename, "r")
7 # print the contents of the file
8
9     dict1=dict()
10
11     for var in infile:
12         print(var)
13 # Remove the  spaces and new line characters
14         var=var.strip()
15
16         var=var.lower()
17 |
18         for ch in var:
19 # Check if the character is already in dictionary
20             if ch.isalpha():
21                 if ch in dict1:
22                     dict1[ch]=dict1[ch]+1
23                 else:
24 # Add the character to dictionary with count=1
25                     dict1[ch] =1
26
27     for key in list(dict1.keys()):
28         print(key, ":", dict1[key])
29
30
31 main()
32
```

Figure 11.2: Counting characters in a file

We get the name of the file to read from the user at *Line 5* of the program, open it and assign to an object **infile** at *Line 6*. In *Line 9*, we create an empty dictionary **dict1**. We have defined an iterator with a **for** loop at *Line 11*. Till there are contents in the file, it carries out the following operations in each iteration:

- Print contents in the file (so that we can cross-check the result) at *Line 12*.

- The program removes white space characters, such as spaces, tabs, and newline characters, at *Line 14*.

- Converts the characters to lowercase at *Line 16*.

In *Line 18* we have defined another iterator with a **for** loop. The iterator with **for** is a convenient mechanism to scan files. Till there are contents in the file, it carries out the following operations in each iteration.

In *Line 20*, the program checks if the character read, is an alphabet with **isalpha()** and if **isalpha()** returns True, we carry out the following:

1. Check at *Line 21*, if **ch** is already in **dict1** (check whether the character is repeating)

    - If true i.e. the character is repeating, at *Line 22*, we increment the value corresponding to the key (character) in dictionary.

2. If (**ch in dict1**) is *False* then it means that the character is encountered for the first time. In such a case **else** block will be invoked at line 23.

3. When the alphabet is encountered for the first time, In *Line 25*, we create a new key value pair with key equal to the alphabet examined as above and value assigned as 1. Try to understand the logic.

The above steps repeat till the file is read fully.

After exhausting all characters, we reach line 25 and we print the characters and the respective count of occurrence of each alphabet in the file.

The result of the program is given below. The three lines in the file under examination have been printed first, followed by the count of occurrences of each character is printed.

```
==================== RESTART: E:/Py programs/E11x11.py ====================
Enter file name: f1.txt
abcdef ghijk lmnopq rstuvw xyzFirst line of Text
Second line of Text
Third Line of Text
a : 1
b : 1
c : 2
d : 3
```

```
e : 8
f : 5
g : 1
h : 2
i : 6
j : 1
k : 1
l : 4
m : 1
n : 5
o : 5
p : 1
q : 1
r : 3
s : 3
t : 9
u : 1
v : 1
w : 1
x : 4
y : 1
z : 1
```

Such a difficult program could be written easily because of the built-in features of Python.

The seek method

When we read the contents of a file or write contents to it, the **seek** method is used for moving the file object to a specified position in the file. The **seek** method is useful for manipulating file objects. While reading through a file, the system maintains a fileposition pointer corresponding to the location of the next character to read. When we read or write next time, it will start from the next character in the file. Sometimes, it is necessary to read from a file sequentially, that is, from the beginning, several times during program execution. In such cases, each time, we must reposition the fileposition pointer to the beginning of the file which can be achieved by calling the **seek** method in conjunction with the file object as in **infile. seek(0)**. The syntax of the **seek** method follows:

```
file_object.seek(offset, reference)
reference = 0 means beginning of the file
```

```
1= current position in the file
```

```
2=end of file
```

In a text file, 0 and 1 can only be used. For instance:

```
file_object(64,0)  # moves to position 64 from beginning of file.
```

Files opened in binary mode can use all three numbers 0, 1, and 2. For instance,

```
File_object.seek(-64, 2)  # moves 64 positions from end of file
```

```
File_object.seek(-64, 1)  # moves 64 positions to the left from current
position
```

```
File_object.seek(10, 0)  # moves 10  positions from beginning  of file
```

Writing to binary file and then reading

Look at the program below. At the third line of the program, we assign a file object called **outfile**. We *open a* file named "b1" in the mode "wb+". "wb+" signifies reading and writing in binary mode. It means that the file object will be used for writing to a binary file and reading from it. We then write three numbers in 3 steps. Now we carry out the following operation of the **for** loop:

- **outfile.seek(i)**: We move the file pointer to the ith position. During the first iteration to the 0th position and at 12th iteration to the 11th position.

- **print(outfile.tell())**: We print the position in the file currently.

- **print(outfile.read(1))**: We read one character at a time from the file. 0th character will be read, that is, b'1' will be read first and printed. In the 9th iteration, b'9' will be read and printed. From the 10th iteration onwards, a blank will be printed since we wrote only 9 numbers.

```
# program E11x12.py
# Writing to a binary file and reading
outfile=open("b1", 'wb+') # for reading and writing
outfile.write(b'123')
outfile.write(b'456')
outfile.write(b'789')
for i in range (12):
    outfile.seek(i)
    print(outfile.tell())
    print(outfile.read(1))
outfile.close()
```

Notice the starting position of the **close** statement. Put it in the first Tab and watch the fun. The result of the program is given below:

```
=================== RESTART: E:\Py programs\E11x12.py ===================
0
b'1'
1
b'2'
2
b'3'
3
b'4'
4
b'5'
5
b'6'
6
b'7'
7
b'8'
8
b'9'
9
b''
10
b''
11
b''
```

Note the results carefully. We get the file positioned first and followed by the byte. In the binary mode, the numbers are preceded by b and enclosed within single quotes. The program reads 1 byte at a time and the file pointer also moves 1 position at a time. Since we are reading 1 byte at a time, it will read and print 1 byte at a time. Because of this, we could not get back the original 3-digit numbers as we wrote and, we got one byte at a time. We modified the program to get back the original numbers. The program is given below.

We have made the following modifications:

We write 3 bytes at a time thrice. We modified the range function in the **for** loop. The range function has 3 parameters. It start with 0 and end with (12-1) but with a step of 3. During the first time, the pointer will be at 0th position, then at 3rd position and so on. During the first iteration it reads the first three bytes 123 and prints it. In the second iteration the program goes to the 4th position and reads the bytes 456. We have programmed to read 3 bytes at a time. That is all the changes made:

```python
# program E11x13.py
# Writing to a binary file and reading
outfile=open("b1", 'wb+') # for reading and writing
outfile.write(b'123')
outfile.write(b'456')
outfile.write(b'789')
for i in range (0,12,3):
    outfile.seek(i)
    print(outfile.tell())
    print(outfile.read(3))
outfile.close()
```

The result of the program is given below. We got back the numbers we wrote as a whole and not one character at a time.

```
==================== RESTART: E:/Py programs/E11x13.py ====================
0
b'123'
3
b'456'
6
b'789'
9
b''
```

Java Script Object Notation

Till now, we were writing text or numbers to files and reading them. Now, we would like to write containers like lists, Tuples, etc. to files. Conventional file **read** and **write** methods are rather complicated for this. We can use **JavaScript Object Notation (JSON)** to make it easier to write and read containers.

Since its inception, JSON has become the de facto standard for information exchange. It is used to transport data from one system to another. In Python, we use JSON to store and exchange data. It is a standardized format the community uses to pass data around like **Extensible Markup Language (XML)**. JSON was inspired by a subset of the JavaScript programming language dealing with object literal syntax. JSON has long since existed as a standard because it is easy both for humans and machines to create and understand.

JSON supports primitive types, like strings and numbers, as well as nested lists, dictionaries, and objects. Python comes with a built-in package called JSON for encoding and decoding JSON data. We can use it in our programs by inserting the following statement:

```
import JSON
```

Serialization and deserialization

The process of encoding to JSON is called a serialization process. This term refers to the transformation of data into a series of bytes (hence serial) to be stored or transmitted across a network. Naturally, deserialization is the reciprocal process of decoding data that has been stored or delivered in the JSON format. The JSON encoding is for writing data to disk, while decoding is for reading data into system memory.

Serializing JSON

The JSON library uses the **dump()** method for writing data to files. There is also a **dumps()** method (pronounced as "dump-s") for writing to a Python string. Python objects are translated to JSON format as illustrated as per the conversion shown in *Table 11.2* below:

Python	JSON
Dictionary	Object
list, tuple	Array
str	String
int, float	Number
True	True
False	False
None	Null

Table 11.2: Conversion of Python objects to JSON

Deserializing JSON

In the JSON library, we will find **load()** and **loads()** for turning JSON encoded data into Python objects. Just like serialization, there is a similar conversion table for deserialization.

The libraries we use to interact with cloud-based services such as *Twitter*, now renamed as X, communicate with our applications via JSON objects. JSON is a text-based, human, and computer-readable data interchange format. JSON converts Python data into appropriate JSON types before writing to a file. Similarly, it converts JSON types read from a file into Python types. Let us look at a program to write and read a list into a text file:

```
# program E11x14.py

# writing and then reading a list using json
```

```
import json
def main():
    # open file for writing and reading
    with open("d2.txt", "w+") as iofile:
        list1=[2, 3, 7, 11, 13, 19, 23]
        json.dump(list1, iofile) # writing
        iofile.seek(0)
        list2=json.load(iofile)
        print(list2)
    iofile.close()


main()
```

In the program we import *json*. We open file **d2** as a read and write file with file object **iofile**. Usage of **with** prefix to open to ensure closing of the files at the end may be noted. The **list1** is written (dump) into the file. We then move the file pointer to the beginning by specifying **seek(0)**. It is then read by the **load** command. Thus, we dump (write) and then load (read). The result of the program follows:

```
==================== RESTART: E:\Py programs\E11x14.py ====================
[2, 3, 7, 11, 13, 19, 23]
```

We have successfully written a list to a file using JSON. Now let us write a program to write and read a tuple using json. Here we *dump* a tuple **tup2** into the file and load (read) and print it. The program and the result are given below:

```
# program E11x15.py
# writing and then reading a tuple using json
import json
def main():
    # open file for writing and reading
    with open("d2.txt", "w+") as iofile:
        tup1=('Ram',189923, 4000.55)
        json.dump(tup1, iofile) # writing
        iofile.seek(0)
        tup2=json.load(iofile)
    print(tup2)
    iofile.close()


main()
```

The logic in the program is similar. In the previous program, we wrote a list, but here we write a tuple to a file using JSON and read back. The usage of JSON simplifies writing to a file and reading from it. The result of the program is given below:

```
==================== RESTART: E:/Py programs/E11x15.py ====================
['Ram', 189923, 4000.55]
```

As given in *Table 11.2,* when we serialize a tuple, JSON converts it into an array. So when we de-serialize, we got a list as the result of the program indicates.

We now will write a dictionary into file and read it back using json. The program and the result it produced on execution are given below:

```python
# program E11x16.py
# writing and then reading a dictionary using json
import json
def main():
    # open file for writing and reading
    with open("d2.txt", "w+") as iofile:
        dct3={'Jan':1, 'Feb':2, 'March':3, 'April':4}
        json.dump(dct3, iofile) # writing
        iofile.seek(0)
        dct3=json.load(iofile)
    print(dct3)
    iofile.close()


main()
```

Here again, the logic is the same. We are writing a dictionary to a file using JSON. The result of the program is given below. We got back the output as a dictionary, no change of form as the previous example.

```
==================== RESTART: E:/Py programs/E11x16.py ====================
{'Jan': 1, 'Feb': 2, 'March': 3, 'April': 4}
```

Serializing and de-serializing to and from strings

We can use strings instead of files to write and read. We use **json** object **dumps** (note s at the end) to serialize and **loads** for deserialization. Let us write a program to carry out the input/output with list, tuple, and dictionary objects in the same program. The program and the result are given below:

```python
# program E11x17.py
# writing into string and then reading from it using json
```

```
import json
def main():
        list1=[2, 3,5, 7, 11, 13, 17]
        tup2=('mohan', True, 11, 4.8)
        dct3={'Jan':1, 'Feb':2, 'March':3, 'April':4}
        str1=json.dumps(list1)# writing list1 to str1
        str2=json.dumps(tup2) # writing tup2 to str2
        str3=json.dumps(dct3) # writing dct3 to str3
        i=json.loads(str1)
        j=tuple(json.loads(str2))
        k=json.loads(str3)
        print('list1=', i)
        print('tup2=', j)
        print('dct3=', k)


main()
```

Result of program:

```
list1= [2, 3, 5, 7, 11, 13, 17]
tup2= ('mohan', True, 11, 4.8)
dct3= {'Jan': 1, 'Feb': 2, 'March': 3, 'April': 4}
```

Since we typecast **str2** to tuple before printing, we got the **tup2** as a tuple.

Pickle solution

Pickle is used for serializing and de-serializing Python objects similar to JSON. The important difference between JSON and pickling is that the JSON library of Python performs the translation of Python objects into JSON objects and vice versa. The pickle converts all objects to byte streams, 0s and 1s.

Any object in Python can be pickled so that it can be saved onto the disk drive. The pickle serializes the object first before writing it to a file. The process of converting Python objects such as lists and dictionaries to byte streams (0s and 1s) is called pickling or serialization or flattening, or marshaling. The idea is that this byte stream contains all the information necessary to reconstruct the object in another Python script. To do that, we import pickles. Like JSON, pickle has two methods. The first one is a **dump**, which dumps an object to a file object, and the second one is load, which loads an object from a file object for reading.

Let us demonstrate pickling for a list object with a program. It is given below:

```
# program E11x18.py
```

```
# pickling
import pickle
def main():
        x=['This', 'is', 'pickling', 'problem']
        outfile=open("b2", 'wb') # open for writing
        pickle.dump(x,outfile)
        outfile.close()
        infile=open("b2", 'rb')
        y = pickle.load(infile)
        print(y)
        infile.close()
main()
```

In the above program after importing **pickle**, we create a list with 4 strings. We *dump* this to the file "b2". After closing the file, we open the same file for reading in binary mode. We then download the list with **load** function and print it. The result of the program is given below:

```
======== RESTART: E:/Py programs/E11x18.py =====================
['This', 'is', 'pickling', 'problem']
```

The program shows us how to import the pickled object and assign it to a variable. *Pickling* is the process whereby a Python object hierarchy is converted into a byte stream, and *unpickling* is the inverse operation whereby a byte stream (from a binary file or bytes-like object) is converted back into an object hierarchy. What are its applications? They are given below:

- It is useful when we wish to *dump* some objects while coding in the python shell. So after dumping whenever we restart the python shell we can import the pickled object and de-serialize it.

- Sending Python data over a TCP connection in a multi-core or distributed system

- Storing Python objects in a database

The advantages and disadvantages of pickling are given below:

- **Advantages**

  o   Easy to use and does not require several lines of code.

  o   The pickled file generated is not easily readable and thus provides some security.

- **Disadvantages**

o Languages other than Python may not be able to reconstruct pickled Python objects.

o Risk of unpickling data from malicious sources.

Pickle versus JSON

JSON is a format for data-interchange and is easily readable by humans. Although it was derived from JavaScript, JSON is standardized and language independent. This is a major advantage over pickle. It is secure and faster than pickle.

However, if we only need to use Python, then the pickle module is still a good choice for its ease of use and ability to reconstruct complete Python objects.

An alternative is cPickle. It is similar to pickle, but written in C. It is faster. Both produce the same byte streams, which means that Pickle and cPickle are compatible.

Case study: CSV files

Exchanging data through text files is quite common. One of the popular formats for exchanging data is the CSV format. A **Comma Separated Values (CSV)** file is a plain text file that uses specific structuring to arrange tabular data. Since it is a plain text file, it can hold only actual text data—in other words, printable ASCII or Unicode characters. CSV files use a comma to separate each specific data value. The CSV file looks like the following:

```
column 1 header, column 2 header, column 3 header
first row data 1,first row data 2,first row data 3
second row data 1,second row data 2,second row data 3
```

The data required for the next program, a CSV file, is shown below:

```
Country,Age,Salary,Purchased
France,44,72000,No
Spain,27,48000,Yes
Germany,30,54000,No
Spain,38,61000,No
Germany,40,,Yes
France,35,58000,Yes
Spain,,52000,No
France,48,79000,Yes
Germany,50,83000,No
France,37,67000,Yes
```

The student can generate the above data as a CSV file in many ways. The easiest way is to type the above in Excel spreadsheets and save it as a CSV file with comma delimited.

Include the header as the first record and other rows as each successive records but omit all the commas.

The first row contains column headers. As you can see there are 4 columns. This data pertains to customers who bought a car. The first column gives the country of origin of the customer, 2nd column gives the age, 3rd column gives the annual salary and the 4th column whether the customer purchased a car during the year – Yes or No.

Each data element is separated by a comma. The first row identifies each piece of data—in other words, the name of a data column. Every subsequent row after that is actual data. In general, the separator character is called a delimiter, and the comma is not the only one used. Other popular delimiters include the tab (\t), colon (:), and semi-colon (;) characters. Properly parsing a CSV file requires us to know which delimiter has been used.

The CSV library provides functionality to both read from and write to CSV files. The CSV library contains objects and other code to read, write, and process data from and to CSV files. Look at the program below:

```python
# Program E11x19.py
# Reading CSV files
import csv
# Open the CSV file
with open('data.csv', 'r') as infile:
    # Create a CSV reader object
    csv_reader = csv.reader(infile)


    # Iterate over each row in the CSV file
    for row in csv_reader:
        # Each row is a list of values separated by commas
        print(row)
```

In the above program we *import csv*. Then we open **data.csv** as **infile** using **with** to ensure closing of the file at the end. Then we assign **infile** to **csv_reader**. Then in the **for** loop, we print each row. The result of the program is given below:

```
= RESTART: E:/Python final after copy editing/Python Program Files/
revised program E11x19.py
['Country    Age,Salary,Purchased', 'age', 'salary', 'Purchased']
['France     4 ,72000,No', '44', '72000', 'No']
['Spain', '27', '48000', 'Yes']
['Germany    30  5400', '30', '5400', 'No']
['Spain', '38', '61000', 'No']

['Germany', '50', '83000', 'Yes']
```

Command line arguments

We have been assigning source file name and destination file name as part of the program. There is a facility to specify them at runtime. We can give the name of the file, which contains the name of the program, followed by the source file and destination file as command line arguments when the program is executed. The command-line arguments need not be file names alone, but any valid identifier. To use command-line arguments, we have to import **sys**.

The **sys** is a basic module shipped with Python. Its approach is similar to the C library using **argc/argv** to access the arguments. The *sys* module implements the command line arguments through a simple list named **sys.argv**.

Each list element in **argv** represents a single argument. The first item in the list, **sys.argv[0]**, is usually the name of the Python program file, which we have written. The rest of the list elements, **sys.argv[1]** to **sys.argv[n]**, are the command line arguments. As a delimiter between the arguments, a space is used.

The equivalent of **argc** of C language is just the number of elements in the list. To obtain this value, use the Python **len()** operator. Look at the program below to read command line arguments:

```python
# program E11x20.py
# command-line arguments
import sys


def main():
    print('number of arguments=', len(sys.argv))
    print("argument 0 - file name is", sys.argv[0])
    print("argument 1 - ", sys.argv[1])
    print("argument 2 - ", sys.argv[2])


main()
```

In the program, we assume that we will give 2 arguments in addition to the name of the program file. In the command prompt, we type the file name followed by 2 numbers, all separated by space. The **argv[0]** is the name of the file. Here, we gave **argv[1]=100** and **argv[2]=200**. The result of the program is given below:

```
C:\>E11x20.py 100 200
number of arguments= 3
argument 0 - file name is C:\E11x15.py
argument 1 -  100
argument 2 -  200
```

Since the total number of arguments are 3, the **len()** is 3.

File copy from source to destination

When we wish to copy a file while executing the program, we give the name of the program file as argv[0], the source file as argv[1], and the destination file as **argv[2]**. To understand the program, we have to understand **getopt** and **shutil**. They are discussed below.

getopt module

The **sys** module splits the command line strings. The Python **getopt** module goes a bit further and extends the separation of the input string by parameter validation. It enables the **sys** module to process input data properly. To do so, both the **sys** module and the **getopt** module have to be imported. Importing both **sys** and **getpot** ensures that the arguments are validated before the execution of the file copy program.

shutil module

In Python 3, **shutil** is a built-in module that provides a higher-level interface for file operations. It stands for *shell utilities* and offers functions for copying, moving, archiving, and removing files and directories. It's often used for tasks involving file and directory manipulation that go beyond the basic file operations provided by the **os** module.

The **shutil** module in Python is used for simplifying the process of copying. The **shutil.copy()** method in Python is used to copy the content of the source file to the destination file. The source must represent an existing file, but the destination can be a file and must be writable. If the destination is a file and already exists, then it will be replaced with the source file; otherwise, a new file will be created. Now, look at the program below:

```python
# program E11x21.py
# file copy
import sys, getopt
import shutil

def main():
    source=sys.argv[1]
    dest=sys.argv[2]
    shutil.copyfile(source, dest)
    outfile=open(dest, 'r')
    print(outfile.read())
main()
```

In the program, we import the following libraries:

- **sys**, **getopt**
- **shutil**

In the main function, we assign **argv[1]** as the source and **argv[2]** as the destination file. We then use **shutil.copyfile** to copy the source file to the destination. To confirm that we have copied the file properly we read the contents of the destination file.

The **getopt** module in Python is used for parsing command-line options and arguments. It is commonly used when writing scripts or programs that need to handle command-line inputs in a structured and flexible manner.

When we are copying files, **getopt** might be used in a script or program that performs file operations to handle options such as specifying the source and destination paths, setting different copying modes (for example, overwrite, append, skip), or enabling verbose output to show progress.

Using **getopt** allows developers to define and handle command-line options easily and efficiently, making their scripts more user-friendly and versatile. It helps in parsing command-line arguments in a standardized way, which simplifies the process of handling user inputs.

The **sys** module provides access to some variables used or maintained by the Python interpreter and to functions that interact strongly with the interpreter. It doesn't specifically handle command-line argument parsing like **getopt**.

The **getopt**, on the other hand, is specifically designed for parsing command-line options and arguments. It helps in handling command-line arguments passed to a script or program.

While **sys.argv** can be used to access command-line arguments directly, **getopt** provides a more structured way to parse command-line options, which can be helpful in more complex scenarios. However, using getopt is a choice made by the developer based on the requirements of the script or program they are writing.

The result of the program below confirms the true copy of source file.

```
c:\>E11x21.py d1.txt e1.txt
First line of Text
Second line of Text
Third Line of Text
```

See the ease of copying files using command line arguments.

Conclusion

In this chapter we learnt how to read, write, append, copy and close text and binary files. The **readline()** method reads a single line from the specified file.

We can also read all the lines. For this purpose, we use **readlines()** method. Each line acts as an item in the list with an appended newline character.

We can read implicitly on opening the file without calling either the **read** or **readline** or **readlines** method in the program.

A case study on counting words in a text file and another case study on counting occurrence of alphabets in a text file were given in this chapter. We also learnt how to traverse in a file and read by using seek and tell methods.

We also used pickling solution for file handling and learnt how to use command line arguments. We used **shutil** module to simplify copying files.

Exceptions do occur while executing programs. We will discuss exception handling in the next chapter.

Points to remember

- We need three items for reading from and writing to a file as given below:
  - o Physical file
  - o File object that is associated with the physical file.
  - o The mode parameter "r" for reading from a file and "w" for writing to a file.

- There are two types of files as given below:
  - o Text file
  - o Binary file

- Appropriate mode parameters have to be specified to read from a file or to write to a file. In addition to 'r' for reading and 'w' for writing, there are several other modes, a list of which is given in *Table 11.1*.

- Essentially there are five operations in file handling as given below:
  - o Read
  - o Write
  - o Append
  - o Read and write
  - o Append and read

- We carry out these operations in text and binary files. The append operation means writing after the current contents of the file without overwriting them.

- To carry out copying we need a source file and a destination file.

- Sometimes we may forget to close a file after reading or writing which may lead to loss of data. To be doubly sure that the file is closed after the work, we can open files using **keywords**. The keyword **with** ensures that the file object is closed.

- While reading through a file, the system maintains a fileposition pointer representing the location of the next character to read. When we read or write next time, it will start from the next character in the file. We can modify it using the seek method.

- `print(outfile.tell())` prints the position in the file currently.

- The process of encoding to JSON is called serialization. This term refers to the transformation of data into a series of bytes (hence serial) to be stored or transmitted across a network. Naturally, deserialization is the reciprocal process of decoding data that has been stored or delivered in the JSON standard. Encoding is for writing data to disk, while decoding is for reading data into memory.

- The JSON library uses the `dump()` method for writing data to files. There is also a `dumps()` method (pronounced as "dump-s") for writing to a Python string. Python objects are translated to JSON as illustrated as per the conversion shown in *Table 11.2*. In the JSON library, we will find `load()` and `loads()` for turning JSON encoded data into Python objects.

- Pickle is also used for serializing and de-serializing Python objects like JSON.

- In CSV files, each data element is separated by a comma. The first row identifies each piece of data—in other words, the name of a data column. Every subsequent row after that is actual data.

- When we execute programs for file copy with command line arguments, we can give the name of the file, which contains the name of the program, followed by the source file and destination file. To do this we have to import sys.

- The **sys** module splits the command line strings. The Python **getopt** module goes a bit further and extends the separation of the input string by parameter validation. It enables the sys module to process input data properly. To do so, both the *sys* module and the **getopt** module have to be imported.

- The **shutil** module in Python is for simplifying the process of copying files. The **shutil.copy()** method in Python is used to copy the content of the source file to the destination file or directory.

Questions

Choose the correct option:

1. **The** *isfile* **on an existing file will return**:

    a. False

    b. True

    c. None of the above

2. **Files require:**

   a. file name

   b. extension

   c. location

   d. All of the above

   e. None of the above.

3. **Reading from a file requires:**

   a. file object

   b. file name

   c. mode parameter

   d. All of the above

   e. None of the above.

4. **Open function is required for file**

   a. reading

   b. appending

   c. writing

   d. All of the above

   e. None of the above

5. **Valid file operations include**

   a. reading

   b. writing

   c. appending

   d. All of the above

   e. None of the above

6. **Implicit reading from a line needs the use of :**

   a. readline

   b. readlines

   c. read

   d. None of the above

7. **The file modes permitted are:**

   a. Append and read

   b. Read and write

   c. Append

   d. All of the above

   e. None of the above

8. **seek (0) means read from:**

   a. character 0

   b. beginning

   c. end

   d. All of the above

   e. None of the above

9. **Encoding is for:**

   a. serializing

   b. deserializing

   c. None of the above

10. **To handle command line arguments, the following need to be imported:**

   a. sys

   b. getopt

   c. All of the above

   d. None of the above

- Write short notes on the following:

   o File object

   o Four types of reading from a file

   o JSON encoding and decoding

   o Writing to and reading from strings using JSON encoding

   o Pickling

   o CSV file creation and reading

o JSON vs pickle

o appending

o The **shutil** module in Python

o Command-line arguments and counting of the total number of arguments passed

- Match the following:

A	B
readline()	1. Needed to open a file
readlines()	2. Read and write mode
File object	3. Load
"w+"	4. Reads all lines
Decoding	5. Reads one line at a time

- Write programs for the following:

o Write a program to check the existence of a file and write the first 100 Natural numbers to a binary file.

o Write a program to read from the file line by line.

o Write a program to append the next 100 Natural numbers to the binary file created at 1.

o Write a program to write the following bytes three digits at a time and find the position of each digit:

❖ b'976

❖ b'432

❖ b'568

❖ b'123

o Write a program to count the occurrence of each character in a text file.

o Create a CSV file with 26 the rows, each row corresponding to lower case alphabet starting from *a* and ending with *z*. Write a program to read them and print.

o Write the following list to a file using JSON encoding and read and print:

o ('rose', jasmine', 'lotus', 'red', 'blue', 'green')

o Repeat the above by writing to strings and reading using JSON.

o   Repeat the same with pickling.

o   Write the following to a file in your system:

   ❖   To-day is a rainy day

   ❖   To Great souls

   ❖   To rejoice themselves

   ❖   To carry on

o   Write a program to copy the file to a destination file and read line by line without importing any library functions or modules like the `shutil`. Obtain the names of the source file and Destination file from the command line.

Join our book's Discord space

Join the book's Discord Workspace for Latest updates, Offers, Tech happenings around the world, New Release and Sessions with the Authors:

https://discord.bpbonline.com

CHAPTER 12
Exception Handling

Introduction

We have written several programs and successfully executed them so far. The Python interpreter checked the program for errors. On clean interpretation, we assumed that there would be no errors thereafter and went ahead and executed the program. In all the programs written so far, after clean interpretation, we did not expect any problems to occur at runtime. We are confident that the program will execute as expected. If there were still errors, we left it to the runtime system for handling and halting program execution if required. The errors occurring during runtime and halting the program abruptly are called exceptions. This approach may be fine for experimental programs. If the software is meant to handle aircraft landing and if a runtime error occurs and the system halts, then there will be chaos. In such situations, we will desire that the software continues its other operations, and we will certainly not like the abrupt halting of the program. Therefore, in critical software systems, we should anticipate the run-time errors and find a way of resolving the problems while the software continues to run. In such cases, we may also like to continue with the rest of the program after handling the errors. The objective of handling such unforeseen errors or exceptions is to enable programs to deal with exceptions gracefully and facilitate the program to continue its operations without abrupt halt. We will understand how to handle exceptions and run-time errors in this chapter.

Structure

The chapter covers the following topics:

- Some standard exceptions
- Handling exceptions
- The syntax for exception handling
- Reading file with exception handling
- The finally keyword
- Word count program with exception handling
- Multiple except
- Use of else
- Value error
- Raising exceptions
- Case study

Objectives

Python provides several standard exception classes. We will understand how to use them in our programs to successfully handle run-time errors without causing abrupt halting of the program. We will also develop our own exception classes in this chapter. We will add more value to the programs by adding techniques to display the cause of errors. We will develop expertise in handling keywords for exception handling.

We will also understand the different types of errors thrown on exceptions. We will also rewrite file handling with an exception handling mechanism.

Some standard exceptions

There are many causes for an exception to occur and there are many types of exceptions. Python provides some standardized exception classes, which can be called in the programs we write to handle exceptions. A list of some of the standard exception classes is given in *Table 12.1*. Note that the numbers given are serial numbers and do not represent the error numbers assigned by Python. For instance, Python assigns Err no. 2 for IOError.

S. No	Exception classes
1.	BaseException: Base class for all exceptions, the root class for exceptions
2.	Exception: Subclass of above and superclass for other exception classes

S. No	Exception classes
3.	StopIteration: Raised when the next() method of an iterator does not point to any object.
4.	SystemExit: Raised by the sys.exit() function.
5	StandardError: Subclass of Exception class and Base class for all built-in exceptions except StopIteration and SystemExit.
6	ArithmeticError: Subclass of above and Base class for errors at S.No. 6, 7, and 8 that occur during numeric calculations.
7	OverflowError: Raised when a calculation exceeds the maximum limit for a numeric type.
8	FloatingPointError: Raised when a floating-point calculation fails.
9	ZeroDivisionError: Raised when a division or modulo by zero takes place for all numeric types.
10	SyntaxError: When the program violates the syntax
11	LookupError: Base class for errors at S.No 12 and 13
12	IndexError: Raised when an index is not found in a sequence.
13	KeyError: Raised when the specified key is not found in the dictionary.
14	NameError: Raised when an identifier is not found in the local or global namespace.
15	OSError: Errors occurring due to OS functions
16	IOError: Raised when an input/output operation fails, such as the print statement or the open() function when trying to open a file that does not exist.
17	IndentationError: Raised when indentation is not specified properly.
18	TypeError: Raised when an operation or function is attempted that is invalid for the specified data type.
19	ValueError: Raised when the built-in function for a data type has the valid type of arguments, but the arguments have invalid values specified.
20	RuntimeError: Raised when a generated error does not fall into any of the predefined categories.

Table 12.1: Type of standard exception classes

In addition to the standard exception classes, the programmers can devise their own exception classes for handling exceptions that may occur in the programs. For instance, a banking application software may raise an exception when the customer is withdrawing an amount, which will reduce the balance below the minimum amount required to be maintained in the account.

Handling exceptions

The syntax error will be caught by the Python interpreter. If there is a syntax error the program will not run. The runtime errors may occur despite our best programming skills and efforts. Such errors that occur during runtime or after clean interpretation are called exceptions. The exceptions can be handled in many ways:

- **Doing nothing**: This will happen by default – in such a case the program execution will terminate causing loss of data and maybe cause some damage. Hence, it should be avoided.

- Another way could be just displaying the error message on the screen and proceeding further- other ways could be directing the user to re-enter values or try again or do something.

- It is the responsibility of the programmer to anticipate the exceptions either due to the user's action or the anatomy of the program leading to runtime error with some input data or other system-related issues. An intelligent programmer, by experience, will be able to visualize such incidents occurring and handle them with the facility provided by Python for exception handling.

The syntax for exception handling

Although Python has fewer keywords, it has allocated the following four keywords for exception handling:

- try

- except

- finally

- raise

These keywords are used extensively for exception handling.

Exceptions are nothing but runtime errors after clean interpretation or during actual execution of the program. The exception occurs due to unforeseen errors occurring during program execution. We have to plan and provide remedial action so that the program does not stop abruptly. This is known as exception handling. To do this, we have to anticipate exceptions in the program that we are writing.

We anticipate exceptions to occur and build the code as following:

```
try:

    <body>

            except < Exception type>:

            <handler>
```

The code with a possibility to throw an exception is given in the <body> of the try block. When an exception occurs, if the exception matches built-in exception types and matches with that given after the except keyword, the corresponding handler is activated. Note that when an exception occurs, execution of the rest of the statements in the <body> will be skipped, and program control goes to except.

In the last chapter on file handling, we wanted to make sure that we are not writing to an existing file since otherwise the existing contents will be deleted. So checked whether a file existed and if so we called **sys.exit()** and aborted the program. We will now write a program for reading from a file with exception handling. One of the exceptions in reading a file is that the file does not exist. If a file does not exist, we have to stop reading and give the error message and exception type.

Reading file with exception handling

Suppose we are trying to read from a file that does not exist, when we try to open the file for reading, it will throw an exception. Let us write a program to read a file, the name of which is entered by the user. *Figure 12.1* depicts the code:

```
# program E12x1.py
# reading from a file

def main():
    # open file for reading
    while True:
        try:
            file_name=input('Enter filename for reading. ').strip()
            infile= open(file_name, 'r')
            break
        except IOError as ioe:
            print ("Error: can\'t find file or read data")
            print(ioe)
            print(ioe.args)


    # reading
    print (infile.read())

main()
```

Figure 12.1: Exception handling when opening file

We anticipate that the reader will make a mistake while typing the file name. Therefore, the program has a while loop to repeatedly prompt the user to enter a file name till he is successful in typing the name of an existing file. The try and except blocks between lines 7 to 14 are in the while loop. The try block begins at line 7. At line 8, the user entered file name is assigned to **file_name**.

At line 9, the file, **file_name** is opened with file object infile. If the file opening is successful, the program exits the while loop at line 10 because of the break keyword. The user will not be prompted again to enter a file name. When the user types the correct file name, no exception will be thrown, and control goes to the next line after the except block, that is. line 16. The file will be opened at line 16 and printed at line 18. The program control will go to line 16 only when there is no exception.

When the file name is incorrect an exception will be thrown and the except block beginning at line 11 will be executed skipping the break statement in the process. The exception will be caught by the IOError built-in exception class and an object ioe will be created. We print the error statement, ioe, and ioe. args in the exception block. If there is an exception, the break will not act and the user will be asked to enter the file name again.

The result of the program is as follows:

```
===================== RESTART: E:\Py programs\E12x1.py =====================
Enter filename for reading: d1
Error: can't find file or read data
[Errno 2] No such file or directory: 'd1'
(2, 'No such file or directory')
Enter filename for reading: c1
Error: can't find file or read data
[Errno 2] No such file or directory: 'c1'
(2, 'No such file or directory')
Enter filename for reading: e1.txt
First line of Text
Second line of Text
Third Line of Text
```

We had devised remedial measures in the form of **try..except** block in the program. Hence, on the first two occasions, since the file did not exist, the unforeseen thing had happened and reported by Python runtime. In the next time since the correct file name was given, it was read and contents printed.

To summarize, statements expected to go wrong at runtime should be placed in the **try** block. The statements in the **try** blocks will be executed and if an exception occurs the statements in the **except** block will be executed. In case of no exception, the **break** statement will come into action and the **while** block will be terminated and taking program control to line 16.

If the exception is triggered by **open** due to the non-availability of the file, the break will be skipped and **except** block will be activated. After catching the exception, the execution continues from the **try** block again.

We anticipated the **IOError** exception. If the exception thrown by the program does not match programmed exceptions, the program execution will be terminated displaying stack trace. However, that will not be a graceful exit from the program.

The finally keyword

The **try** block can have an optional block **finally**. This block is generally used to release external resources. In all circumstances, whether an operation was successful or not, we must clean up the resources before the program terminates. These actions (closing a file, GUI, or disconnecting from network) are performed in the finally **clause**. We can also give other useful information in the **finally** block.

Here is an example of file operations to illustrate this:

```
try:
    f = open("test.txt", encoding = 'utf-8')
    # perform file operations
finally:
    f.close()
```

This type of construct makes sure that any file that is open during the program execution is closed even if an exception occurs.

The previous program to read from a file is repeated with **finally** block and given below:

```
# program E12x2.py
# reading from a file
def main():
    # open file for reading
        while True:
                try:
                        file_name=input('Enter filename for reading:\ ').strip()
                        infile= open(file_name, 'r')
                        break
                except IOError as ioe:
                        print ("Error: can\'t find file or read data")
```

```
                print(ioe)
                print(ioe.args)
        finally:
                print('We have handled the exception')


    # reading
        print (infile.read())


main()
```

The result of the program will be as follows:

```
==================== RESTART: E:\Py programs\E12x2.py ====================
Enter filename for reading: e1
Error: can't find file or read data
[Errno 2] No such file or directory: 'e1'
(2, 'No such file or directory')
We have handled the exception
Enter filename for reading: e1.txt
We have handled the exception
First line of Text
Second line of Text
Third Line of Text
```

Note that we have placed the keyword **finally** in the **while** block. It will always be executed whether there is an exception or not. We have also used the **strip** function in this program. The **strip ()** method removes any leading (spaces at the beginning) and trailing (spaces at the end) characters. This ensures that the correct file name is derived from the user entry.

Word count program with exception handling

The above concept can be extended to any program involving reading files. The same *word count* program seen in the previous chapter is given below including the exception handler. The new code for the exception handler is in boldface. Since we want to execute the program again and again till the correct file name is entered, we have put the exception block in a **while** block.

```
# program E12x3.py
# word count in a text file
```

```python
def main():
    while True:
        try:
            filename=input('Enter file name: ').strip()
            infile=open(filename, "r")
            break
        except IOError:
            print(filename, ' does not exist')

    dict1=dict()    # Empty dictionary
    for line in infile:
        line=line.strip()
        line=line.lower()
        words=line.split(" ")
        for word in words:
            if word in dict1:
                dict1[word]=dict1[word]+1
            else:
                dict1[word] =1
    for key in list(dict1.keys()):
        print(key, ":", dict1[key])

main()
```

The result of the program is given below. The first time, a wrong file name was given, and the next time of execution, a correct file name was given.

```
Enter file name: dx1.py
dx1.py  does not exist
Enter file name: d1.txt
python : 3
is : 2
an : 1
interesting : 1
language : 1
fast : 1
```

```
be : 1
careful : 1
while : 1
indenting : 1
programs : 1
```

When the program was executed the first time, a non-existing file name was given and the exception handler was activated and the program displayed the message "**dx1.py does not exist**". In the second iteration since the correct file name **d1.txt** was typed, we got the result right.

The salient points to be noted about exception handling are as follows:

- If we suspect a code that is likely to cause exception, place the code in the **try** block.

- Each **try** block is followed by one or more except blocks to catch the exceptions.

- If an exception is not raised, control goes to the first line just after the except blocks.

- If an exception occurs at run time in the **try** block, the exception is raised and statements in the **try** block from that point of throwing an exception will be skipped.

- In case of multiple except blocks, one for each type of exception, the exception handler that matches the exception is invoked.

- If the actual exception does not match any of the programmed exceptions, the built-in exception handler catches the exception and prints a stack trace, and aborts the program. To avoid such a situation, it is advisable to program a default **except** for block for unknown exceptions rather than allowing the run-time system to abort the program. A simple **except**: will catch any exception that is not caught by any other exception handler in the program. It catches all exceptions, if not caught already by any other exception handler.

Multiple except

We put the code that may throw an exception in the **try** block. A code is likely to cause different types of exceptions. Therefore, we may provide multiple **except** blocks one for each possible type of exceptions and one as a default for the unknown exception. In this program below, we have provided for the following exceptions for a single try block:

- ZeroDivisionError

- unknown error

Look at the following program. We are carrying out the division in the **try** block, followed by two **except** blocks and a finally block.

```
# program E12x4.py
# divide

def main():

        try:
            var1=eval(input('enter an integer: '))
            var2=eval(input('enter an integer: '))
            var3=var1/var2
            print('var3= ', var3)
        except ZeroDivisionError as er1:
            print('Divison by zero')
            print (er1.args)
            print(er1)

        except:
            print('unknown error')
        finally:
            print('program execution completed')

main()
```

Note that we are carrying out a float division and hence the result will be a real number. The result of the program is as follows:

```
==================== RESTART: E:/Py programs/E12x4.py ====================
enter an integer: 10
enter an integer: 0
Divison by zero
('division by zero',)
division by zero
program execution completed
>>>
==================== RESTART: E:/Py programs/E12x4.py ====================
enter an integer: 10
enter an integer: a
unknown error
```

```
program execution completed
>>>
```

```
==================== RESTART: E:/Py programs/E12x4.py ====================
enter an integer: 10
enter an integer: 2
var3=  5.0
```

```
program execution completed
```

When the divisor was *a*, it was not programmed exception. Hence the default and catch all **except** class caught the exception and unknown error was printed. The finally block executes whether an exception occurs and not and it prints a message after the program execution is completed every time.

Use of else

Use of **else** in exception handling programs is optional. Let us write a program to use **else** in the exception handling program. We wish to carry out the integer division. A program is given below. It can throw **ZeroDivisionError** or unknown error or it will be print the quotient. In this program, the **else** part will be executed when there is no exception. In such cases, it will give a message and also the quotient.

```python
# program E12x5.py
# use of else

def main():

    try:
        var1=eval(input('enter an integer: '))
        var2=eval(input('enter an integer: '))
        var3=var1//var2

    except ZeroDivisionError as er1:
        print('Divison by zero')
        print (er1.args)
        print(er1)

    except:
        print('unknown error')
    else:
```

```
        print('no exception. result=', var1//var2)
```

```
main()
```

The result of the program when it was executed 3 times is as follows:

```
==================== RESTART: E:/Py programs/E12x5.py ====================
enter an integer: 4
enter an integer: ui
unknown error
>>>
==================== RESTART: E:/Py programs/E12x5.py ====================
enter an integer: 7
enter an integer: 0
Divison by zero
('integer division or modulo by zero',)
integer division or modulo by zero
==================== RESTART: E:/Py programs/E12x5.py ====================
enter an integer: 10
enter an integer: 2
no exception. result= 5
```

During the last trial, since there was no exception, we got the result as above. Note that when the else is part of try- except –else, block, the else block will be executed only when there is no exception.

Value error

We should be expanding our knowledge base in exceptions to devise suitable strategies for exception handling. In addition to **ZeroDivisonError**, there is an exception called **ValueError**, which is thrown when the data type passed is not as per the expected syntax. The following program for Integer Division adds this exception class:

```
    # program E12x6.py
    # ValueError
def main():

        try:
            var1=int(input('enter an integer: '))
            var2=int(input('enter an integer: '))
```

```
                    var3=var1//var2


            except ZeroDivisionError as er1:
                print('Divison by zero')
                print (er1.args)
                print(er1)
            except ValueError as ive:
                    print('ValueError Exception')
                    print(ive)
                    print(ive.args)
            else:
                    print('no exception. result=', var1//var2)


main()
```

The result of the program is as follows:

```
==================== RESTART: E:\Py programs\E12x6.py ====================
enter an integer: 15
enter an integer: a
ValueError Exception
invalid literal for int() with base 10: 'a'
("invalid literal for int() with base 10: 'a'",)
>>>
==================== RESTART: E:\Py programs\E12x6.py ====================
enter an integer: 15
enter an integer: 0
Divison by zero
('integer division or modulo by zero',)
integer division or modulo by zero
>>>
==================== RESTART: E:\Py programs\E12x6.py ====================
enter an integer: 16
enter an integer: 8
no exception. result= 2
```

We executed the program thrice. The **ValueError** exception occurred when we entered a character instead of an integer, Note that when we get the result in the **else** block, there has been no exception of any kind.

Raising exceptions

Let us write a program to use the **raise** keyword for an exception. This program expects a positive number from the user. If the user enters a negative number, an exception will be thrown. If the user enters a non-digit, **ValueError** exception will be thrown. The program is as follows:

```
# Progran E12x7
# using raise for exception
try:
    x=int(input('enter an integer: '))
    if x<0:
        raise Exception("negative number")
    elif not type(x) is int:
        raise ValueError("Only integers are allowed")
except ValueError as er1:
        print('invalid type')
        print (er1.args)
        print(er1)

except:
        print('unknown error')
```

When a non-number was entered, an exception was raised by the keyword **raise**, and the exception matched with **ValueError**. When the user entered a negative number, the exception was raised by the **raise** keyword and caught by catch-all **except** block since it did not match with other exceptions. The result of the program is as follows:

```
===================== RESTART: E:/Py programs/E12x7.py =====================
enter an integer: a
invalid type
("invalid literal for int() with base 10: 'a'",)
invalid literal for int() with base 10: 'a'
>>>
===================== RESTART: E:/Py programs/E12x7.py =====================
enter an integer: -8
    unknown error
```

Note that whenever we throw an exception with **raise** keyword, it is caught by appropriate exception handlers.

Case study: Custom exception

This case study builds a custom exception class. The following program is familiar to you:

```
E12x8.py - C:/Users/Subbu/Desktop/E12x8.py (3.10.11)
File Edit Format Run Options Window Help
 1 class BalanceErrorException(RuntimeError):
 2     pass
 3 class Account:   # class definition
 4     def get_data(self, s, n, b):
 5         self.__name=s
 6         self.__account = n
 7         self.__balance =b
 8
 9     def debiting(self, amount):
10         self.__balance-=amount
11         if self.__balance < 10000:
12             self.__balance+=amount
13             raise BalanceErrorException
14
15     def display(self):   # Method declaration
16         print("Name =", self.__name)
17         print("Account number =", self.__account)
18         print("Balance        =", self.__balance)
19
20 def main():
21     Vinay = Account()   # creating object
22     Vinay.get_data('Ram', 1212, 17000)
23     Vinay.display() # calling a function
24     while True:
25         try:
26             x=eval(input('Enter amount to be withdrawn: '))
27             Vinay.debiting(x)
28             break
29         except:
30             print('insufficient balance')
31             print('withdrawal denied')
32         finally:
33             Vinay.display()
34 main()
```

Figure 12.2: Custom exception

We have added exception clauses to it. We are adding a method of *debiting* in the program. The bank has a policy that a minimum balance of ₹ 10000 should be maintained by the account holder. Let us have a look at the above program.

The **BaseException** class is at the top of the Python built-in exception classes. We can define a custom exception class by extending the class **BaseException** or any of its subclasses provided by Python. We are defining our exception class **BalanceErrorException** as a subclass of **RuntimeError** subclass of **BaseException** class at line 1. At line 2 we pass, or in other words, we do nothing.

At line 3, we define class **Account**. Between lines 4 to 7, we have defined a method **get_data** to initialize the name, account (number), and balance.

At line 9, we have defined a method *debiting*, which receives an amount (proposed to be withdrawn) as a parameter. At line 10 we subtract the amount to be withdrawn from the *balance*. At line 11, we check if the new balance is less than 10000. If it is so i.e. the balance is less than 10000, we do the following:

- At line 12, we restore the balance

- At line 13, we raise **BalanceErrorException**

If the balance is not less than 10000, we don't do the above two actions.

Between lines 15 to 18, we display the details of the account.

At line 20, we have defined the main function. At line 21, we create an object **Vinay** of **Account** class. At line 22, we initialize the attributes of **Vinay** object. Note that the name of the object is **Vinay**, and the name of the account is **Ram**. In line 23, we display the details of the account pointed to by **Vinay** object

At line 25, the try block begins. At line 25 we ask the Teller to enter the amount proposed to be withdrawn. Then at line 26, we call the method debiting, passing the amount to be withdrawn as an argument, and the action now shifts to the method debiting.

If the balance after debiting the amount is less than 10000, the withdrawal is canceled, and an exception is raised, and program control is transferred to the except clause at line 29. In lines 30 and 31, messages are printed. Then clause finally at line 32 is executed. At line 33, the display function is called, and it prints the account details of the **Vinay** object. No amount is debited due to the restoration of balance at line 12 since the withdrawal is denied.

What happens if the balance after debiting is not less than 10000. The if block between lines 12 to 13 will be skipped, and control returns to break at line 28. The break terminates the while loop, except the block is skipped and finally is executed, displaying the details of the **Vinay** object.

The result of the program will be as follows:

```
===================== RESTART: E:/Py programs/E12x8.py ====================
Name = Ram
Account number = 1212
Balance       = 17000
Enter amount to be withdrawn: 12000
insufficient balance
withdrawal denied
Name = Ram
Account number = 1212
Balance       = 17000
Enter amount to be withdrawn: 5000
Name = Ram
Account number = 1212
Balance       = 12000
```

The first time the account holder wanted to withdraw 12000 and since it was denied, he withdrew 5000 next time.

Thus, we have built a custom exception defined by the user.

Knowing the cause of the error

In the last program, we did not directly print the amount of withdrawal that caused the exception. We can add the code to print the inputs that cause an exception. For this purpose, we must add code in the user-defined custom exception class.

We are now writing a program to find the perimeter of a triangle. A triangle cannot be formed if the triangle inequality rule is not fulfilled. The triangle inequality rule states that the sum of the lengths of any two sides should be greater than the length of the third side. If the triangle inequality rule is not fulfilled, we have to raise an exception since the result will not be valid. In the following program, at line 4, we define a class **TriangleInequalityException** as a derived class of the library exception subclass **RuntimeError**. At line 5 we define the **__init__** method which receives 3 formal parameters in addition to, self. The three parameters are assigned to side1, side 2, and side3 at lines 6 to 8.

At line 9, we define the class **Triangle**. A method **get_data** is defined at line 10. In the method, the data members side1, side 2, and side3 are initialized at lines 11 to 13. In line 15, we define method **perim**. Between lines 16 to 18, we check whether the sum of the lengths of any two sides is less than the length of the third side. Even if any of the conditions is True, **TriangleInequalityException** will be raised. The arguments of the exception are the 3 sides of the triangle. If all the 3 conditions are false, the perimeter of the triangle will be returned at line 21 in the else block. Refer to the following figure:

```
# program E12x9.py
# Custom Exception

class TriangleInequalityException(RuntimeError):
    def __init__(self,s1, s2, s3):
        self.side1=s1
        self.side2=s2
        self.side3=s3
class Triangle:  # class definition
    def get_data(self, s1, s2, s3):
        self.side1=s1
        self.side2=s2
        self.side3=s3

    def perim(self):
        if self.side1 + self.side2 < self.side3 or\
            self.side2 + self.side3 < self.side1 or\
            self.side1 + self.side3 < self.side2:
            raise TriangleInequalityException(self.side1,self.side2,self.side3)
        else:
            return (self.side1 +self.side2+self.side3)
def main():
    tgle=Triangle()
    while True:
        try:
            x, y, z=eval(input("Enter the 3 sides of the triangle :"))
            tgle.get_data(x,y,z)
            print('perimeter= ', tgle.perim())
            break
        except TriangleInequalityException as tie:
            print('sides', tgle.side1, tgle.side2, tgle.side3, 'cannot form')
            print(tie.args)

main()
```

Figure 12.3: To know the cause of the error

In the main function, we create an object **tgle** of class **Triangle**. We have designed the program to run till the user gives the valid sides of the triangle and hence we have a while loop at line 24. In the try block beginning at line 25, we receive the lengths of 3 sides entered by the user at line 26. At line 27, call the **get_data** method with the object **tgle** and the length of sides given by the user. At line 28, we call the method **perim** with the object **tgle**. If in the **perim** method an exception is raised, it will be caught by except at line 30 and the messages will be printed.

If no exception is thrown in the **perim** method, control will return to line 28, and perimeter will be printed. The break will exit the while loop and program execution will stop.

The result of the execution of the program will be as follows:

```
===================== RESTART: E:\Py programs\E12x9.py ====================
Enter the 3 sides of the triangle :2,3,7
sides 2 3 7 cannot form a triangle
(2, 3, 7)
Enter the 3 sides of the triangle :3,5,1
sides 3 5 1 cannot form a triangle
(3, 5, 1)
Enter the 3 sides of the triangle :10, 3, 4
sides 10 3 4 cannot form a triangle
(10, 3, 4)
Enter the 3 sides of the triangle :3,4,5
perimeter=  12
```

We executed the program 3 times with sides not fulfilling the triangle inequality rule and so we got the message that the given sides cannot form a triangle. It also printed the 3 sides given by us. We were also prompted every time to enter new values of the sides. When sides meeting the rule was given in the fourth time, we got the perimeter and the program terminated. In this manner, we can get more information about the exception.

Two more interesting case studies on exception handling are given in *Chapter 14, Data Structures and Algorithms using Python.*

Conclusion

In this chapter we understood why exceptions should be handled. The objective of handling unforeseen errors, that is, exceptions, are to enable programs to deal with exceptions gracefully and facilitate the program to continue its operations. We also covered the classes in the Python library to design exception handling. We must make it a practice to anticipate exceptions that may arise in every program we write and provide a mechanism to handle such exceptions. We understood the syntax of exception handling including the use of the keyword finally. We also built custom exception classes as derived classes of the standard exception classes. Two case studies on exception handling were given in this chapter.

In the next chapter we will study the gems, unique and special features of Python 3 added to enable the programming to be more interesting and add value.

Points to remember

- Exceptions are nothing but runtime errors after clean interpretation, during actual execution of the program. An exception occurs due to unforeseen errors occurring during program execution. We have to plan and provide remedial action so that the program does not stop abruptly. This is known as exception handling. To do this, we must anticipate exceptions in the program that we are writing and handle them gracefully.

- Python provides several standardized built-in exception classes, which can be called in the programs we write. A list of some of the standard exception classes is given in *Table 12.1*. The root of the standardized exception classes is **BaseException** class.

- Python has allocated the following 4 keywords for exception handling:

  o try

  o except

  o finally

  o raise

- The syntax of exception handling is given below:

  ```
  try:
  <body>
      except < Exception type>:
      <handler>
  ```

- One of the exceptions in reading a file is that the file does not exist.

- The **try** block can have an optional block **finally**. This block is generally used to release external resources.

- The salient points to be noted about exception handling are as follows:

  o If we suspect a code that is likely to cause an exception, place the code in the **try** block.

o Each **try** block is followed by one or more except blocks to catch the exceptions.

o If an exception is not raised, control goes to the first line just after the **except** blocks.

o In case of multiple **except** blocks, one for each type, the exception handler that matches the exception is invoked.

o If the actual exception does not match any of the programmed exceptions, default exception handler Python catches the exception and print stack trace, and aborts the program.

o It is wise to program a default **except** block, rather than allowing run time system aborting the program.

o Use of else in exception handling programs is optional.

o We can use raise to throw exceptions.

- A case study of building a user-defined custom exception class for bank operation was studied.

- A case study of building custom exception class if the sides of a triangle violate inequality rule was studied. In this case, the cause of the exception was displayed.

Questions

Choose the most appropriate answer:

1. **Purpose of exception handling is:**

    a. to handle the exception

    b. continue with the rest of the program

    c. not halting abruptly

    d. All of the above

    e. None of the above

2. **Exceptions occur:**

    a. after clean interpretation

    b. due to syntax errors

    c. due to semantic errors

    d. None of the above

3. **Superclass of standard exceptions is:**

   a. RuntimeError

   b. Exception

   c. BaseException

   d. None of the above

4. **ZeroDivisionError Exception occurs when:**

   a. The denominator is 0

   b. Numerator is zero

   c. Both are 0

   d. None of the above

5. **The code that is run at the end is:**

   a. except

   b. try

   c. finally

   d. All of the above

   e. None of the above

6. **1/xyz (x, y and z are alphabets with no assignments before) will throw:**

   a. ValueError

   b. ZeroDivisionError

   c. Unknown Error

   d. All of the above

   e. None of the above

7. **10/5 will throw:**

   a. ValueError

   b. ZeroDivisionError

   c. Unknown Error

   d. All of the above

   e. None of the above.

8. **Every exception handler must have**

   a. else

   b. finally

   c. try

   d. None of the above

9. **Catch all exception handler is:**

   a. except:

   b. stack trace

   c. None of the above

10. **Custom exception is:**

    a. customizing error

    b. customizing built-in exception class

    c. None of the above

- Write short notes on the following:

  o finally

  o multiple except

  o standard exception classes

  o Value Error

  o Custom exception

  o The syntax for exception handling

  o ZeroDivisionError

  o Built-in exception classes

  o Advantages of Exception handling

  o Use of else in exception handling

- Match the following:

A	B
except:	1. contains runtime error susceptible code
raise	2. derived from the standard exception class
try	3. catch all exceptions
BaseException	4. needs an except
Custom exception	5. root of exception classes

- Write programs for the following:

    o   Modify program for bank withdrawal to print the name, account, and balance along with exception information.

    o   To handle custom exception if a negative number or invalid entry is made in a program to calculate the area of a square.

    o   Modify custom exception for Triangle to include invalid entry instead of numbers.

    o   To raise an exception when the list of items to be sorted using bubble sort is empty.

    o   To raise exceptions when numbers are already sorted in a sorting program.

    o   [Hint: Refer to *Chapter 14* for both the above questions]

    o   To raise exception If all numbers in a list are prime numbers.

    o   To raise exception If all numbers in a Tuple are even numbers.

    o   To calculate the perimeter and area of a circle with exception handling.

    o   To raise an exception if one or more value is missing in a dictionary.

    o   To raise an exception in a file copy program if the source file doesn't exist.

Join our book's Discord space

Join the book's Discord Workspace for Latest updates, Offers, Tech happenings around the world, New Release and Sessions with the Authors:

https://discord.bpbonline.com

## CHAPTER 13

Gems of Python

Introduction

Python has many desirable features of a programming language, which we call gems. Lambda functions, the anonymous functions, are one of them. The modules and decorators are the other gems of Python. Python also helps in implementing first class functions and facilitates functional programming. Decorators is an innovative concept of programming, which is another interesting feature of Python. Namespaces and packages eliminate the clash of identifiers in programs developed by multiple programmers in the same location or different work spots. This chapter will discuss these features.

Structure

The chapter covers the following topics:

- Lambda functions
- Modules
- Date and time
- Functional programming
- First class functions
- Decorators

- Case study: Comparing methods by execution times
- Namespace
- Packages

Objectives

In this chapter we will learn some advanced, interesting, and useful features of Python such as lambda functions, modules, first class functions, function objects, decorators, namespaces and packages. These features give an edge to Python over competing programming languages.

Lambda functions

Functions are one of the important building blocks of all programming languages. Python has two ways of defining functions: using the keywords **def** and **lambda**. Till now, we have been defining functions using only **def**. In this chapter, we will study functions defined with **lambda**. The **lambda** functions were first introduced by American Mathematician *Alonzo Church* in the 1930s. Lambdas are also known as anonymous functions. They are small functions that do not need a name (that is, an identifier) unlike the conventional functions defined with **def**. Lambda is a tool for building function objects.

We will now focus our attention on the lambdas.

Constituents of lambda functions

In Python, lambda expressions (or lambda forms) are utilized to construct anonymous functions. To do so, we will use the **lambda** keyword just as we have been using **def** to define normal functions and methods in classes. Every lambda function we define in Python will have 3 essential parts:

- The **lambda**, one of the keywords of Python
- The parameters (or bound variables)
- The function body

A lambda function can have any number of parameters, but the function body will contain only one expression. Moreover, a **lambda** is written in a single line of code and can also be invoked immediately.

Syntax and examples

The syntax to write a lambda function is as given below:

```
lambda p1, p2: expression
```

Here, p1 and p2 are the parameters which are passed to the **lambda** function. There is no restriction on the number of parameters that we can pass to a **lambda** function. However, we do not give a list of the parameters in parentheses, as we do with regular functions. The expression is any valid expression that operates on the parameters we provide to the function.

Let us try a few example lambda functions with the IDLE interpreter:

Example 1:

```
>>> product=lambda a,b: a*b
>>> print (product(9,7))
63
```

The **lambda** function is simple and quick in its execution. We define a variable **product** that will store the result returned by the **lambda** function:

- The **lambda** keyword is used to define an anonymous function.

- **a** and **b** are the parameters that we pass to the **lambda** function.

- The body of the function finds the product of the 2 parameters we passed. Notice that the expression is just one statement. We cannot write more than one statement in the body of a **lambda** function.

- We call the function and print the returned value.

Example 2:

```
>>> str1='printing a string'
>>> (lambda str1 : print(str1))(str1)
printing a string
```

Here, we are defining a lambda and calling it immediately by passing the string as an argument. Note that we give **str1** again at the lambda function's end. This is called an **Immediately Invoked Function Expression (IIFE)**, and we will learn more about it in the subsequent sections.

Using lambdas with Python built-ins

Lambda functions provide an elegant and powerful way to perform operations using built-in methods in Python.

Python lambdas are small anonymous functions defined using the **lambda** keyword. They are commonly used when you need a simple function for a short period of time, especially when you want to pass a function as an argument to higher-order functions (functions that take other functions as arguments). Lambdas are useful for writing quick throwaway functions without the need to define a formal function using the **def** keyword. It is possible because lambdas can be invoked immediately and passed as an argument to these functions.

Immediately invoked function expression in lambda

IIFE means that a lambda function is callable as soon as it is defined. Let us understand this with an example:

```
>>> (lambda x: x**4)(3)
81
```

In the lambda function, we find x to the power 4. The value of x is given as 3. It immediately prints the output. This function is an example of IIFE.

We had a brief overview of lambda functions and appreciated their compactness and clearly defined rules.

Modules

Module refers to a file containing Python statements and definitions. All the Python programs we have written thus far and are yet to write are called modules. We use modules to break down large programs into small, manageable files. Furthermore, modules provide reusability of code. We can define our most used functions in a module and import them instead of copying their definitions into different programs.

Module sum.py

For instance, let us write a program for finding the sum of 3 numbers. It is given below:

```
# sum.py
def add(var1, var2, var3):
    var4=var1+var2+var3
    return var4
```

Let us save it as **sum.py**. We can import the above file and write another program **add.py** to find the sum of 3 numbers and print it. It is given below:

```
# add.py
import sum
print(sum.add(7,8, 15))
```

When we import the module **sum**, we omit the **.py** extension otherwise it will not work. In the program, we call the **add** function in the **sum** module. The result of the above program is given below:

```
===================== RESTART: E:\Py programs\add.py =====================
30
>>>
```

Since it is a small program, we can carry out the above operation in the Python interpreter in IDLE as given below:

```
>>> import sum
>>> print(sum.add(23, 67, 10))
100
```

We can repeat the above whenever we need. Note that sum is the module here.

Module swap_case

Let us write another module for swapping lower- to upper-case English alphabets. The program is familiar to you. It is given below. It is saved as a module with the name **swap_case**. It converts a lower-case English alphabet to uppercase and vice versa and returns the changed case:

```
'''swap_case.py'''
# to change case
def swap(alpha):
    if alpha >='a' and alpha<='z' :
        y=ord(alpha)
        return(chr(y-32))
    elif alpha >='A' and alpha<='Z' :
        y=ord(alpha)
        return(chr(y+32))
```

We will write another program called **swap.py**. We import the module **swap_case** and print the toggled case of the alphabet, as shown:

```
# swap
import swap_case
print(swap_case.swap('k'))
```

The result of the program is given below:

```
==================== RESTART: E:/Py programs/swap.py ====================
K
```

Instead of writing a program, we can carry the swapping of cases of alphabets in the Interpreter as shown below:

```
>>> import swap_case
>>> swap_case.swap('p')
'P'
```

Another example is shown here:

```
>>> import swap_case
>>> swap_case.swap('A')
'a'
```

In all the above examples, the lowercase alphabet is converted to the uppercase alphabet and vice versa. Note that when we use the **print** statement, we get the alphabet without a single quote surrounding it. When we directly call, it returns the string enclosed with a single quote. There is nothing wrong with it either.

Module tup_max.py

Let us write a **moduletup_max.py** for finding the maximum of two numbers. It is given below:

```
# tup_max.py
def maxm (num1, num2):
    if num1>num2:
        return (num1)
    else:
        return num2
```

The result of the program is given below:

```
=================== RESTART: E:/Py programs/tup_max.py ===================
>>> import tup_max
>>> maxm(45, 8)
45
```

Module prod.py

As we have seen, module is a single file that can be imported. We have seen a couple of examples. We will write one more example. Let us write the following program, save it as prod.py and run it:

```
# prod.py
def mult(var1, var2, var3):
    var4=var1*var2*var3
    return var4
```

After the above, the following lines were typed in Python interpreter:

```
===================== RESTART: E:/Py programs/prod.py =====================
>>> import prod
```

```
>>> print(prod.mult(5, 4, 10))
200
```

We imported **prod** and then called **mult** with three numbers and we got the product of the three numbers. The **prod** is a module.

Short names for modules

We can import a module and assign it with a short name:

```
>>> import random as ran
>>> print(ran.randint(100, 490))
419
```

Import a function from a module

It is also possible to import a function from a module. For instance:

```
>>> from math import cos
>>> print (cos(0.5))
0.8775825618903728
```

The main module

In some of the Python programs, we had defined the **main** function. In some programs, we did not define the **main** function. All Python programs have a **main** function, either specified in the program or not. Let us add a line **print(__name__)** to the **add** module:

```
# add.py
import sum
print(sum.add(7,8, 15))
print(__name__)
```

The last line will print the name of the module. Look at the result of the program given below:

```
===================== RESTART: E:\Py programs\add.py =======================
30
__main__
>>>
```

Although we had not defined the **main** function in this module, Python has identified this module as **__main__** module.

Let us check this in a module where we have defined the **main** function. In the following program, we added a new line **print(__name__)** at the end of the program:

```
'''Program 13x1.py'''
# called function
def sum(num1, num2): # function header
    total=num1+num2
    return total
# calling function
def main():
    a=eval(input('enter an integer: '))
    b=eval(input('enter an integer: '))
    print('sum of the numbers=', sum(a,b))
    print(__name__)
main() # main function call
```

The result of the program is given below. The program prints the name of the module as **__main__**:

```
==================== RESTART: E:\Py programs\E13x1.py =====================
enter an integer: 23
enter an integer: 45
sum of the numbers= 68
__main__
```

The foregoing discussions confirm that all programs we wrote are called modules, and the names of the modules are **__main__**, whether we explicitly define a **main** function in the program or not.

Importing multiple modules

We can import more than one module in a module. Look at the program below. We are importing the following 2 modules in the program:

- sum

- random

Then we generate three random numbers in the given range. We also print to know the numbers generated. Then we call **add** function in the **sum** module and pass the three random numbers. It adds them and prints the sum. Thus, we have imported two modules in the program. The program is given below:

```
# program addnew.py
# use of module
import sum
```

```
import random
var1=random.randint(3, 9)
print('var1=', var1)
var2=random.randint(4, 8)
print('var2=', var2)
var3=random.randint(12, 34)
print('var3=', var3)
print(sum.add(var1, var2, var3))
```

The result of the program is given below:

```
==================== RESTART: E:/Py programs/addnew.py ====================
var1= 9
var2= 6
var3= 12
27
```

Symbol table

Python creates a symbol table for all the variables we define in a program. It typechecks whenever it comes across a variable. If we inadvertently pass a dictionary instead of a list, it will flag an error. Thus, the symbol table is useful to check errors committed by the programmer.

vars() function

The **vars()** is a global function. It returns a dictionary of information we need about a module. A program is given below to illustrate the use of *vars* function:

```
# program E13x2.py
import sum
import random
var1=random.randint(3, 9)
print('var1=', var1)
var2=random.randint(4, 8)
print('var2=', var2)
var3=random.randint(12, 34)
print('var3=', var3)
print(sum.add(var1, var2, var3))
print(vars())
```

```
print(vars(sum))
print(vars(random))
```

The result of the program is given below. We have not expanded the squeezed texts corresponding to vars(sum) and vars (random). We can get a lot of information about the modules we are using when we expand them:

```
==================== RESTART: E:/Py programs/E13x2.py ====================
var1= 4
var2= 7
var3= 22
33
{'__name__': '__main__', '__doc__': None, '__package__': None, '__
loader__': <class '_frozen_importlib.BuiltinImporter'>, '__spec__': None,
'__annotations__': {}, '__builtins__': <module 'builtins' (built-in)>,
'__file__': 'E:/Py programs/addnewrev.py', 'sum': <module 'sum' from 'E:/
Py programs\\sum.py'>, 'random': <module 'random' from 'C:\\Users\\HP\\
AppData\\Local\\Programs\\Python\\Python38-32\\lib\\random.py'>, 'var1': 4,
'var2': 7, 'var3': 22}
Squeezed text (94 lines)
Squeezed text (150 lines)
```

Date and time

DateTime is a powerful module in Python that allows us to manipulate system data and time without risking any system changes. We can define a new date object and modify its representation. Arithmetic calculations can be done on the date and time objects for several purposes, such as finding the future date, formatting data into strings, creating a time management solution, etc.

Although we can use the **time** module to find out the current date and time, it lacks features such as the ability to create date objects. To remedy this, Python has a built-in datetime module. Hence, to do any object manipulation regarding date and time, we need to import datetime module.

The datetime module is used to modify date and time objects in various ways. It contains five classes to manipulate date and time as given below:

- **date**: Manipulate just date.
- **Time**: Time independent of the day (Hour, minute, second, microsecond)
- **Datetime**: Combination of time and date (Month, day, year, hour, second, microsecond)
- **Timedelta**: A duration of time used for manipulating dates.
- **Tzinfo**: An abstract class for dealing with time zones.

Date and time are critical in real-time applications. Here, we write a program to print today's date. It is given below:

```python
# program E13x3.py
# date today
from datetime import date
def main():
    print('The date today is: ', date.today())
main()
```

In the program, we import class data from the *datetime* module. In the main function, we print today's date as **date.today()**. The result of the program is given below:

```
==================== RESTART: E:/Py programs/E13x3.py ====================
The date today is:  2020-05-25
```

Date and Time now

Let us write a program to print the date and time now. It is given below:

```python
# program E13x4.py
# date and time now
from datetime import datetime
def main():
    print('current date and time now is: ', datetime.now())
main()
```

Since we want both date and time, we import **datetime** from the module **datetime**. The result of the program is given below. The date is returned in the following format:

```
yyyy-mm-dd
```

Time is returned in the following format:

```
hh:mm:ss.microseconds
```

```
==================== RESTART: E:/Py programs/E13x4.py ====================
current date and time now is:  2020-05-25 17:33:51.546180
```

These are small programs. We can run it in an interpreter also. For instance, to find the day of the week of today, we can run the following:

```python
>>> from datetime import date
>>> print(date.today())
2020-05-25
>>> day=date.today()
>>> print(day.weekday())
0
```

In Python the weekday starts from 0 for Monday, 1 for Tuesday...6 for Sunday. Since today is Monday, 0 has been printed at the last execution.

strftime function

To format the date into easily readable strings, we use **strftime()** in the **datetime** module.

The following example clarifies how to use this function and print the date/time in a styled manner:

```
>>> from datetime import datetime
>>> Today=datetime.now()
>>> print(Today.strftime("%a, %B, %d, %y"))
Mon, May, 25, 20
```

We can also print hour, minute, second, and microsecond by importing **time** from **datetime** as the following demonstrates:

```
>>> from datetime import time
>>> time=datetime.now()
>>> print(time.hour)
20
>>> print(time.minute)
6
>>> print(time.second)
20
>>> print(time.microsecond)
516387
```

When needed, the time, date, and year-related information can be used in our programs by importing the **datetime** module.

Finding elapsed time

We can find elapsed time between two events occurring in **Central Processing Unit (CPU)** in the computer system using the function **perf_counter()** in the time module.

Perf_counter function

At the beginning of the program, we measure the time in microseconds as t1 using the **perf_counter** function. Then, we ask the CPU to sleep for 16 seconds. At the end of the *sleep , we measured the time again using Perfcounter*. The difference between the measured times is the elapsed time between t1 and t2. The program is given below:

```
# Program E13x5.py
# perf_counter
from time import *
t1=perf_counter() # measure start time
sleep(16)
t2=perf_counter() # measure stop time
print('elapsed time =', t2-t1, 'seconds')
```

The result of the program is given below. There is a little error in the time measurement and hence it is slightly less than 16 seconds:

```
== RESTART: C:/Users/HP/AppData/Local/Programs/Python/Python38-32/E13x5.py ==
elapsed time = 15.999659499999998 seconds
```

process_time function

The **process_time** can also be used to find elapsed time. But it ignores sleep time. The following program demonstrates the use of the function:

```
# Program E13x6.py
# process_time
from time import *
t1=process_time() # measure start time
sleep(16)
t2=process_time() # measure stop time
print('elapsed time =', t2-t1, 'seconds')
```

The program is similar to the previous one. Since the program ignores sleep time, it prints the elapsed time as zero seconds:

```
=== RESTART: C:/Users/HP/AppData/Local/Programs/Python/Python38-32/E13x6.py ===

elapsed time = 0.0 seconds
```

Let us use the above two methods to find out execution time taken by a program. We use **perf_counter** function. We create a list of size 100000 using a for loop and measure the time:

```
# Program E13x7.py
# perf_counter to find CPU time
from time import *
t1=perf_counter() # measure start time
squares=[]
for num in range(100000):
```

```
    squares.append(num*num)
sleep(5)
t2=perf_counter() # measure stop time
print('elapsed time =', t2-t1, 'seconds')
```

The program execution time is small. Since **perf_counter** considers sleep time also, the result indicates time greater than five seconds:

```
=== RESTART: C:/Users/HP/AppData/Local/Programs/Python/Python38-32/E13x7.py ===
elapsed time = 5.0177092 seconds
```

The above program is repeated with **process_time** function. It ignores sleep time, and hence, we get only the execution time of the program:

```
# Program E13x8.py
# process_time for finding CPU time
from time import *
t1=process_time() # measure start time
squares=[]
for num in range(100000):
    squares.append(num*num)
sleep(5)
t2=process_time() # measure stop time
print('elapsed time =', t2-t1, 'seconds')
=== RESTART: C:/Users/HP/AppData/Local/Programs/Python/Python38-32/E13x8.py ===
elapsed time = 0.015625 seconds
```

The small difference in execution time may be due to other CPU activities.

Functional programming

Functional programming is a programming paradigm closely linked to mathematical foundations. While there is no strict definition of what constitutes a functional language, they are languages that use functions to transform data. Python is not a functional programming language, but it incorporates some of its concepts and other programming paradigms. Some of Python's features were influenced by Haskell, a purely functional programming language. With Python, it is easy to write code in a functional style, which may provide the best solution to the task at hand. It supports functions being passed as parameters to other higher-order functions. The higher order functions can accept other functions as parameters and can return new functions as output. One of the advantages of functional programming to data analytics is applying filters or transformations to set of records or columns more efficiently as discussed below.

Filtering elements in containers

In Python, the **filter()** function is used to filter elements from an iterable (like a tuple) based on a given function. It takes two arguments: the function that defines the filtering condition and the iterable to be filtered. Filters can be programmed using functional programming. The **filter()**, a higher order function takes another function and in this case a lambda function as an argument. It is used to select elements from any container, such as lists, sets, and tuples. Look at the results of execution in the interpreter:

```
>>> tup=10, 37, 89, 7, 45
>>> new_tup=filter(lambda x:x>10, tup)
>>> print(new_tup)
<filter object at 0x0351A310>
```

The explanation of the code is given below:

- Note that in the first statement above, we define a tuple called **tup** which contains five integers.

- In the next statement, using the lambda function we filter integers in the tuple *tup* which is greater than 10. The selected integers are assigned to **new_tup**. The **new-tup** will store the filtered values returned by the **filter()** function.

- A **lambda** function runs on each element of the tuple and returns True if it is greater than 10.

- In the last statement, we print the result returned by the filter function as a list.

However, we get a message and not the filtered numbers since we cannot print a tuple straight away. We must print the filtered tuple as a list, as the following demonstrates:

```
>>> print(list(new_tup))
[37, 89, 45]
```

Similarly, we can filter a set and print the filtered set as a list, as shown:

```
>>> set1={98, 7,67,6,5}
>>> new_set=filter(lambda x:x<10, set1)
>>> print(list(new_set))
[5, 6, 7]
```

The elements are selected by the **filter()** function based on some pre-defined constraints. It takes two parameters:

- A function that defines the filtering constraint.

- A container like lists, tuples, sets, etc.

map() function

The map function is used to transform every element in a container. It also takes the following two parameters:

- A function that defines the transformation to be performed on each the elements.

- A container.

Assume that we have a tuple named **tup**. We want to create another tuple called **tup_new**, which contains the square root of all elements in **tup**. The lambda function for square root and the tuple can be passed to a higher order function **map()**. The **map()** function iterates through the tuple and transforms each element using the lambda function, as the following listing illustrates:

```
>>> tup=4,9,25,49,121
>>> tup_new=map(lambda x:x**0.5, tup)
>>> print(list(tup_new))
[2.0, 3.0, 5.0, 7.0, 11.0]
```

The following is an explanation for the above code:

- Here, we define a tuple called **tup** which contains five numbers.

- We declare a variable called **tup_new** which will store the mapped values.

- A **lambda** function transforms each element of the tuple and returns the square root of that number.

- The **map()** function iterates through the tuple and transforms each element.

- Print the result returned by the **map** function as a **list**.

Reduce() function

The reduce is an interesting function. It is used to apply an operation to every element in a container. However, it differs from the map in its working. These are the steps followed by the **reduce()** function to compute an output:

1. Perform the defined operation on the first two elements of the container.

2. Save this result in the container.

3. Operate with the saved result and the next element in the sequence.

4. Repeat until no more elements are left.

It also takes two parameters like filter:

- A function that defines the operation to be performed.

- A container like lists, tuples, etc.

We have to import reduce from **functools**, as shown:

```
>>> from functools import reduce
>>> set={2, 3, 5, 7, 11}
>>> new_set=reduce(lambda x, y:x+y, set)
>>> print(new_set)
28
```

The explanation of the code is as follows:

- Note that we have to import **reduce** from the **functools** module.

- Then we define a set called set which contains five integers.

- We declare a variable called **new_set** which will store the reduced value.

- A lambda function in the next statement finds the sum of the first two numbers in set and puts the result in the first position in the **new_set**. Continue this operation of adding the first two numbers repeatedly till there is only one number.

- Print the result returned by the reduce function.

We discussed functional programming using lambdas briefly.

First class functions

In programming, a first-class object, also known by different names such as a first-class citizen or a first-class value, is an entity or an item in the programming language. It could be a number, a function, or a literal that can be operated or deployed in the same way as any other entity in the language. They may be stored in data structures such as lists, passed as arguments to a function, or used in control structures such as **for**. A programming language is said to support first-class functions if it treats functions as first-class objects. Python 3 supports the concept of first-class functions. Some of the characteristics of first-class functions are:

- We can store the function in a variable.

- Define functions inside other functions.

- A function is an instance of the object type.

- We can pass the function as a parameter to another function.

- We can return the function from a function.

- We can store them in data structures such as lists.

Assigning functions to variables

We will now try to prove that Python supports first-class functions by implementing some of the above-mentioned characteristics. The first characteristic is that we can assign functions to variables. We had assigned functions to variables in *Chapter 6, Functions and Recursion*. We will add one more program here. Here, we are assigning the function **hi** to variable **hi_man**. In the last line, **hi** will be substituted, and function **hi** will be called and passed the argument "Tushar". This demonstrates the assignment of functions to variables:

```
# Program E13x9.py
# Assign function to variable
def hi(first_name):
    return "hello " +first_name
hi_man=hi
print(hi_man("Tushar"))
```

The function works alright, and the result of the program is reproduced below. We assigned a function to variable in this program:

```
==================== RESTART: E:/Py programs/E13x9.py ====================
hello Tushar
```

Function passed as parameters to other functions

We will write a program to pass a function to other functions. Look at the program below. In the last line of the program, we are indirectly calling function **other** and pass a function **hi**:

```
# Program E13x10.py
# function passed as parameters to other functions
def hi(first_name):
    return "hello " +first_name
def other(fun):
    arg="Tushar"
    return fun(arg)
print(other(hi))
```

The result of the program shown below confirms that a function can indeed be passed to another function, confirming that Python supports first-class functions:

```
==================== RESTART: E:/Py programs/E13x10.py ====================
hello Tushar
```

Define functions inside other functions

A function defined in another function is called an inner function. We will write an example program to implement inner functions:

```python
# Program E13x11.py
# defining a function in another function
def hi(first_name):
    def greet():
        return "hello "
    result = greet()+first_name
    return result
print(hi("Tushar"))
```

In the above program, we have a function named **hi** receiving a variable as an argument. In the function, we have defined another function, which we call an inner function called **greet**, which does not receive any arguments. It returns the string "hello" when called.

In the last line of the program, we have a print statement, which indirectly calls the function *hi* and passes "Tushar" as an argument. In the outer function **hi**, we define a variable **result**. It is assigned the function **greet()** followed by a variable called **first_name**. The greet function returns the string 'hello', which is concatenated with the **first _name** of the function **hi**. It is the argument when the function **hi** was called, and it is string 'Tushar.' The concatenated string 'hello Tushar' is returned to the function print, which called **hi** and it is printed. The result of the program follows:

```
======================= RESTART: E:/Py programs/E13x11.py
=======================

hello Tushar
```

We have successfully implemented the inner function in the above program. In the same manner, we can verify other characteristics.

Decorators

A decorator is a function in Python. It adds functionality to another function without altering it. This is useful when we want to add functionality to a function but do not want to modify it in the process. Python Decorator will wrap around another function. This is like a gift wrapper in real life.

A simple decorator

A program demonstrating a decorator is given in the following *Figure 13.1*:

```
 *E13x12.py - E:/Py programs/E13x12.py (3.10.11)*
File  Edit  Format  Run  Options  Window  Help
 1 # program E13x12.py
 2 # Decorator Function
 3 def decor(fun):
 4     def wrap():
 5         print("====================")
 6         fun()
 7         print("////////////////////")
 8     return wrap
 9
10 def sayhi():
11         print("Hi Friend")
12 newfunc=decor(sayhi)
13 newfunc()
14
```

Figure 13.1: *Decorator function*

The result of the program is given below:

```
====================

Hi Friend

////////////////////
```

Now let us understand how the program works.

Function to be decorated

In line 10, we have defined the function **sayhi** that is to be wrapped. There is a print statement at line 11 in the function **sayhi()**, which prints "Hi Friend".

def decor(fun)

Now, we will define the decorator function, named here as decor. In line 3, we define the function decor, which receives a function **fun** as argument. The **fun** is nothing, but the function passed to the decor by the function calling it. This is the function that we want to decorate. Inside this function, we nest another function called **wrap()**.

The nested wrap function

In line 4, we define an inner nested function wrap. It is inside this function that we put the decoration and also call the function to be decorated. In the function, we have defined a wrapper with print statements in lines 5 and 7. In between the two print statements, we call the function **fun**. Finally, we make the **decor()** function return the *wrap* function at line 8.

Assigning and calling

It is interesting to see in line 12 that a variable **newfunc** is assigned the function décor with the function **sayhi** as an argument. In line 13, the **newfunc** is invoked. Thus, we assign this Python decorator to a variable and pass the function to be decorated as an argument to the decorating function.

Now decor receives the function **sayhi**. In line 6, when the **fun()** is invoked, function say hi will be executed, printing "Hi Friend." The string is wrapped by the two print statements in lines 5 and 7. This is how we have built a decorator for the function say hi without modifying it. This program utilized the following characteristics of first-class functions:

- Function passed as argument to **decor** function.

- Function wrap defined inside **decor** function.

- Function assigned to variable **newfunc**.

- Function **sayhi** is passed as argument to **decor** function.

Decorator function with arguments

The above example demonstrated a simple decorator function. We will now discuss decorator functions with parameters. A program given below implements the same. Before we look at the program, let us understand some concepts.

@decor1

Once a decorator has been defined, it can be used with more than one function in the program. We can decorate any number of functions with the same decorator. For this purpose, we can specify the decorator on top of the function concerned. Here we have defined decor1 and apply it to the functions by specifying @decor1 on top of the function.

Here, we have defined a decorator **decor1**, which receives a function as an argument. It has an inner function **wrap**, whose formal parameters are ***args** and ****kwargs**. This will facilitate the **wrap** function to receive variable length arguments from different functions to be decorated. When the second argument is zero in a divide function, we cannot divide.

Similarly, when the second argument is zero in a subtraction function, we have nothing to subtract. On such occasions, the wrap function will print a message and return it. If it is not so, the **decor** function will return the function with the arguments received, as shown:

```python
# program E13x13.py
# Decorator Function with arguments
def decor1(fun):
        def wrap(*args,**kwargs):
            if args[1]==0:
                print('second argument is zero')
                return
            return fun(*args,**kwargs)
        return wrap
@decor1
def div1(a,b):
    print(a/b)
@decor1
def subtn(a,b):
    print(a-b)
div1=decor1(div1)
subtn=decor1(subtn)
x,y=eval(input('Enter two numbers: '))
div1(x,y)
subtn(x,y)
```

The result of the program is given below. We have used the same decorator with both the functions:

```
=================== RESTART: E:\Py programs\E13x13.py =====================
Enter two numbers: 10, 0
second argument is zero
second argument is zero
>>>
=================== RESTART: E:\Py programs\13x13.py =====================
Enter two numbers: 9,3
3.0
6
```

Case study: Comparing methods by execution times

In *Chapter 6, Functions and Recursion*, we used two methods for finding square root of a given number. In the first method, we used built-in **math** function. In the second method, we found square root from the first principles using iteration. Now, we will compare which method is faster by comparing the execution time taken by each method for finding a square root. For this purpose, we will use a decorator.

We define a decorator **cpu_time**, which receives a function as the argument. It will receive the names of the two functions for finding square root, one after another. Then, we have defined an inner function **measure** which receives the keyword and non-keyword arguments. This will give a general framework for receiving any type and any number of arguments received from the calling function.

The **time.perf_counter** will return the time in seconds at the time of execution of the statement. We have imported **time** for this purpose. The time **t1** is measured before we start execution of the function. Then we call the function **fun** indirectly and the result of execution of the program is stored in **result**. Once the execution of the function is completed, we note the time of the clock as **t2** in the next statement. Now we find the difference between the two times as **exec_time** and print it in the next line. Along with the name of the function **fun.__name** (built-in function). We return the result to the called function and then exit the decorator.

Then we placed the function **E5x8.py** to find the square root using a math function. The function is decorated by @cpu_time. At the end of this function, we place function **E5x9. py** to find square root of a given number without using math function. We have also decorated this function with the same decorator:

```python
# Program E13x14.py
# Finding execution time with decorator
import time
def cpu_time(fun):
    def measure(*args, **kwargs):
        t1=time.perf_counter()
        result=fun(*args, **kwargs)
        t2=time.perf_counter()
        exec_time=t2-t1
        print('time taken by', fun.__name__, 'is ', exec_time, 'seconds')
        return result
    return measure
@cpu_time
```

```
# we had executed the program previously
# Finding square root of a number using math
def Sqrt1(x):
    import math
    return(math.sqrt(x))
@cpu_time
# we had executed the program previously
# Finding the square root of a number without using math function
def Sqrt2(x):
    last_guess= x/2.0
    while True:
        guess= (last_guess + x/last_guess)/2
        if abs(guess - last_guess) < .000001: # example threshold
            return guess
        last_guess= guess
def main():
    x=eval(input('Enter a number to find square root: '))
    print('square root of ', x, 'is', Sqrt1(x))
    print('square root of ', x, 'is', Sqrt2(x))


main()
```

In the main function we get the number to find square root. Then we call **Sqrt1** function and **Sqrt2** functions one after another. The result of the program is given below:

```
====================RESTART: E:/Pyprograms/E13x14.py========================
Enter a number to find square root: 25
time taken by Sqrt1 is  4.50000000107309e-06 seconds
square root of  25 is 5.0
time taken by Sqrt2 is  4.099999999951365e-06 seconds
square root of  25 is 5.0
>>>
==================== RESTART: E:/Py programs/E13x14.py ====================
Enter a number to find square root: 7845
time taken by Sqrt1 is  6.100000000230921e-06 seconds
square root of  7845 is 88.57200460642177
time taken by Sqrt2 is  4.899999998642102e-06 seconds
square root of  7845 is 88.57200460642177
```

We executed the program twice to find square root of numbers. On both executions, it is found method not using math function to be faster, clearly establishing that although **sqrt** using math function is easy to use, it is rather slower than the method based on first principles. Notice how the decorator and ***args** and ****kwargs** have simplified our experiment.

Built-in decorators

Python comes with several built-in decorators. Some of them are given below for information:

- @classmethod
- @staticmethod
- @property
- @abstractmethod

We used the last one in *Chapter 10, Inheritance and Polymorphism* to create an abstract class. Although decorators are quite useful in advanced programming, they are difficult to understand as we have observed.

Namespace

Name (also called identifier) is simply a name given to objects. Everything in Python is an object. The literals, modules, files and classes all have their unique name. Name is a way to access the underlying object. A namespace is a system to have a unique name for each and every object in Python. An object might be a variable or a method. Python itself maintains a namespace in the form of a Python dictionary. A namespace is a simple system to control the names in a program. It ensures that names are unique and won't lead to any conflict. As a program runs, Python keeps track of all the known namespaces and the information available in those namespaces.

All the variables, functions, objects and classes we used in Python were names in one namespace or another. Names are things like **x** or **num** or **infile** which are references to something. When our Python code says num=10, it means, *assign the value 10 to the name num"* and we can then refer to *num* in our code. The word **variable** is used interchangeably with names that refer to values, though names can refer to functions, classes, objects, literals etc. in Python.

When we first open the Python interpreter, the built-in namespace is populated with all the items built into Python. The Python built-in namespace contains the built-in functions like **print()** and **input()**.

These built-ins have no prefix and we don't need to do anything special to use them. Python makes them available to us anywhere in our code. This is the reason why the **print('Hello world!')** works in Python.

Unlike languages such as C++, we don't explicitly create namespaces in our Python code, but our code structure affects what namespaces are created and how they interact. For instance, creating a Python module automatically creates an additional namespace for that module. At its simplest, a Python module is a **.py** file that contains some code. For example, the code in sum.py is given below:

```
# sum.py
def add(var1, var2, var3):
    var4=var1+var2+var3
    return var4
```

This automatically creates an additional namespace for this module. Each module has a global namespace that code in the module can access freely. Functions, classes, and variables that aren't nested inside anything else are in the module's global namespace. A module that wants to use a variable, function, or class from another module must import it into its global namespace. Importing is a way of pulling a name from somewhere else into the desired namespace.

The hierarchy of namespaces in Python are given in *Figure 13.2*:

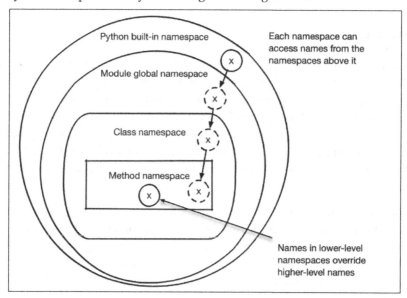

Figure 13.2: *Hierarchy of namespaces*

To refer to a variable, function, or class in Python, one of the following must be true:

- The name is in the Python built-in namespace.

- The name is the current module's global namespace.

- The name is in the current line of code's local namespace.

The precedence for conflicting names works in the opposite order; a local name overrides a global name that overrides a built-in name. This is how namespaces are organized in Python.

Packages

Suppose we have developed a large application that includes many modules. As the number of modules grows, it becomes difficult to keep track of them all if they are dumped into one location. This is particularly so if they have similar functionality. We will certainly like to group them and organize them so that managing them becomes easy.

A set of modules under a namespace or directory is called a package. Packages allow for a hierarchical structuring of the module namespace using dot notation. In the same way that modules help avoid collisions between global variable names, packages help avoid collisions between module names.

Creating a package is quite straightforward since it makes use of the operating system's inherent hierarchical file structure.

A package is made up of multiple modules, and can even include libraries written in C or C++. Instead of being a single file, it is an entire folder structure which might look like this:

pkg

__init__.py

  subt.py

fdiv.py

In the above **pkg** is a package, which contains three other files. All Python packages must contain an **__init__.py** file. When we import a package in our script (import package), the **__init__.py** script will be run, giving us access to all of the functions in the package.

Now let us test our understanding of packages. Follow the steps:

1. Create new folder in the current directory and name it as **pkg**.

2. Now create an empty file in IDLE and save it as **__init__.py** in the directory **pkg**.

3. Now create the following file in IDLE and save it as **subt.py**:

```
# subt.py
def sub(a, b):
    return (a-b)
```

4. The above program subtracts **b** from **a**. Save it as **subt.py** in the directory **pkg**.

5. Type the following file in IDLE and save it as **fdiv.py**:

```
# fdiv.py
def divn(a,b):
    return(a/b)
```

6. The above program carries out float division of **a** by **b**. Save it as fdiv.py in the directory **pkg**.

Importing files from a package

The directory **pkg** consists of the following modules:

- **__init__**
- **subt.py**
- **fdiv.py**

Now we will use IDLE interpreter to use the two modules in **pkg**. First, we import module **fdiv** from package **pkg**. Then we call method **divn()** in module **fdiv** using dot operator and pass 2 numbers. The result is displayed in the next line:

```
>>> from pkg import fdiv
>>> print(fdiv.divn(16,5))
3.2
```

Now, we import module **subt** from package **pkg**. Then we call method **sub()** in module **subt** using dot operator and pass 2 numbers. The result is displayed in the next line:

```
>>> from pkg import subt
>>> print(subt.sub(11, 5))
6
```

Let us do one more program. It is to calculate area of circle. The program is given below. Save the program as **area_circ.py**:

```
# area_circ.py
import math
def area(radius):
    return (math.pi * radius *radius)
```

Look at the program. We are importing library function **math** to use **pi**. Let us run the program in interpreter:

```
================ RESTART: E:/Py programs/pkg/area_circ.py =================
>>> import area_circ
>>> print(area_circ.area(7))
153.93804002589985
```

You may be wondering that we are not importing *pkg* in the above program. It is because we are already in the directory **pkg**.

Thus, we have created a package. We can move related files to the package and organize our work.

Conclusion

In this chapter we studied lambda functions, modules, function objects, first class functions, decorators, and packages. We also developed modules in this chapter.

In some of the Python programs, we had defined the **main** function. In some programs we did not define the **main** function. All Python programs have a **main** function either implicitly or explicitly. We learnt that the execution of **print(__name__)** will give result as **__main__**.

We discussed functional programming and lambdas that are commonly used with the following Python built-ins. The chapter also discussed the characteristics that prove that Python supports first-class functions.

We also developed decorators and wrappers. Decorators add powerful features to programming. A case study using decorator function comparing the performance of **math.sqrt()**, with user defined function for finding square root, of a given number was given.

We finally discussed how namespaces are organized in Python.

In the next chapter, we will study data structures and algorithms using Python. We will also study sorting algorithms and compare their merits.

Points to remember

- Python treats the lambdas the same way as regular functions at the interpreter level, but lambdas provide compact syntax for writing functions that return a single expression.

- We should never write complicated lambda functions. In such cases, it will be hard for coders to maintain the code.

- The lambda functions are anonymous and have no name, no signature, and no return statements.

- The primary difference between a lambda and a regular function is that the lambda function evaluates only a single expression and yields a function object.

- Every lambda function in Python has 3 essential parts:
  - o The lambda keyword
  - o The parameters (or bound variables), and
  - o The function body.

- Lambdas can have any number of parameters, but they are not enclosed in parentheses.

- A lambda can have only 1 expression in its function body, which is returned by default.

- We can import a module and assign it with a short name. For instance:

  ```
  >>>import random as ran
  ```

- It is also possible to import a function from a module: For instance:

  ```
  >>> from math import cos
  ```

- We can import more than one module in a module.

- Python creates a symbol table for all the variables we define in a program. It type checks whenever it comes across a variable. If we inadvertently pass a dictionary in place of a list, it will flag an error.

- The **vars()** is a global function. It returns a dictionary of information we need about a module.

- To format the date into easily readable strings, we use **strftime()** in the **datetime** module.

- One of the features of Python is that everything is an object, including functions. Functions in Python are first-class objects and they are called function objects.

- A module is a single file that can be imported.

- As the number of modules grows, it becomes difficult to keep track of them all if they are dumped into one location. Packages allow for a hierarchical structuring of the module namespace using dot notation. In the same way that modules help avoid collisions between global variable names, packages help avoid collisions between module names.

- All Python packages must contain an **__init__.py** file. When we import a package in our script (import package), the **__init__.py** script will be run, giving us access to all of the functions in the package.

Questions

Choose the most appropriate answer.

1. **Functions:**

   a. are modules

   b. use def

   c. use lambda

   d. All of the above

   e. None of the above

2. **lambdas consist of:**

    a. function name

    b. parameters

    c. def keyword

    d. All of the above

    e. None of the above

3. **Python functions:**

    a. have types.

    b. can be sent as arguments to another function.

    c. can be used in expression.

    d. All of the above

    e. None of the above

4. **Lambda function consists of:**

    a. *lambda*

    b. The parameters

    c. function body

    d. All of the above

    e. None of the above

5. **Execution of the following will throw:**

    ```
    >>>product=lambda a,b: a**b
    >>> print (product(2, 4))
    ```

    a. 8

    b. 16

    c. None of the above

6. **2 parameters need to be passed for operation of**

    a. map

    b. reduce

    c. filter

    d. All of the above

    e. None of the above

7. **A module:**

   a. single file

   b. promotes reusability

   c. executable

   d. All of the above

   e. None of the above

8. **The minimum number of files in a package is:**

   a. 1

   b. 2

   c. 3

   d. None of the above

9. **Date is returned by default in the following style:**

   a. yyyy-mm-dd

   b. yyyy.mm.dd

   c. dd-mm-yyyy

   d. All of the above

   e. None of the above

10. **We can import in a program:**

    a. 0 module

    b. 1 module

    c. any number of modules

    d. None of the above

- Write short notes on the following:

  o Lambdas

  o Functional programming

  o Function objects

  o First class function

  o map function

- o module

- o datetime

- o packages

- o namespace

- o finding time and date now

- Match the following:

A	B
package	1. keyword
import	2. must have __init__ module
lambda	3. module
main()	4. should not use file extension
datetime	5. present in all functions

- Write programs for the following:

  - o To create a decorator to find GCD and factorial and compare their execution times.

  - o Module to find the average of 4 given numbers.

  - o Module to find the minimum of two numbers.

  - o Lambda functions to find the sine.

  - o Lambda functions to find x**4.

  - o To access the name of the module.

  - o A package consisting of the following modules:

    - ❖ Random

    - ❖ Average

  - o A decorator with arguments for finding product and quotient.

  - o A package consisting of modules to carry out basic operations such as +, -, *, /, //, %.

Join our book's Discord space

Join the book's Discord Workspace for Latest updates, Offers, Tech happenings around the world, New Release and Sessions with the Authors:

https://discord.bpbonline.com

## CHAPTER 14

Data Structures and Algorithms using Python

Introduction

Data structures provide a way to organize and store data efficiently, enabling efficient manipulation, retrieval, and modification of information within computer programs. In essence, data structures define the way data is organized in memory, optimizing access and operations on that data. The chapter will introduce stacks and queues, uniquely defined for data insertion and deletion. A stack implements the **Last In, First Out (LIFO)** data structure, where the data inserted last is the first one to be retrieved. A queue implements a **First In, First Out (FIFO)** data structure, where the data inserted first is the one to be retrieved.

Sorting is often a required task but a time-consuming one. There are many algorithms for sorting that we will be discussing in this chapter. The analysis of algorithms helps us to estimate the time complexity of each sorting algorithm.

Structure

The chapter covers the following topics:

- Data structures
- Stack

- Queue
- Algorithm analysis

Objectives

In this chapter we will study two popular data structures -stacks and queues. We will also look at four sorting algorithms: bubble sort, selection sort, insertion sort, and merge sort. We will also understand why algorithm analysis is important. We will learn asymptotic analysis of algorithms and calculate the time complexity of the four sorting algorithms discussed.

Data structures

The study of data structures and algorithms is quite important in software development. In this chapter, we will have an introduction to data structures and algorithms using the Python container list. Data structures provide concrete ways to organize data for efficient storage and efficient manipulation. Deployment of such data structures in algorithms facilitates efficient use of resources such as the **Central Processing Unit (CPU)** and storage media such as **Random Access Memory (RAM)** and disc drive. The **Abstract Data Type (ADT)** is a logical view of the data objects together with specifications of the operations required to create and manipulate them. ADT consists of a data structure declaration and a set of operations with the data structure. Using the list, we will first study a few data structures and then 4 sorting algorithms. Now, let us look at some popular data structures.

Stack

The stack is a **Last-In-First-Out (LIFO)** data structure. A stack can be implemented using a list. Item inserted in the stack in the last is retrievable first. It resembles a stack of trays in a spring-loaded bin. A tray will be added to the bin on top of the stack every time. When we add a tray, the previous tray on top will go down by one position. We can add trays till the first tray reaches the bottom of the stack when the stack is full. Similarly, a tray can be removed only from the top of the stack. In computer science, an item is nothing but a data element or an object. Therefore, a stack is a data structure in which items are added, deleted, or examined at one end only, called the top of the stack. The top of the stack contains the item inserted last. The stack has to be imagined functioning in the manner we will be discussing.

A spring-loaded stack holder or the bin can hold 100 trays. When we add one tray, it will be stored in the first position. When we add one more item, the second tray is stored on top of the first, and the first goes down by 1 position. Since the stack is the items piled one on top of another, we can only see the item on top. Only when it is taken out, the previous one will come on top and visible. When we want to remove an item, we can only remove the item on top of the stack. Therefore, in this case, we need to remove the second item first, and only thereafter the first item can be removed. The built-in container *list* is handy for implementing a stack. We use the **append** method of the list to push data items. Initially, the *list* is implemented as an empty stack. When we push the number 10 by using the **list.append(10)**, there will be only one item in the stack on top of the stack. Then, when we append 20, it will be on top of the stack, and so on. Whenever we *pop* an element from the list, the last element will only be returned. Hence, the list is suitable for implementing a stack. The following program implements a stack. Let us look at a program:

```
# Program E14x1.py
#  simulates stack using a list


stk = []


# push using append()method of list


stk.append(10)
print('\nStack now contains:', stk)
stk.append(20)
print('\nStack now contains:', stk)
stk.append(30)
print('\nStack now contains:', stk)
stk.append(35)
print('\nStack now contains:', stk)


# pop from the stack
print('the item popped is: ', stk.pop())
print('\nStack now contains:', stk)
print('the item popped is: ', stk.pop())
print('\nStack now contains:', stk)
print('the item popped is: ', stk.pop())
print('\nStack now contains:', stk)
```

In the program, we create an empty list, **stk**, first. Then, we push one element 10 into **stk** and print the contents of the list. We repeat the two steps 3 times. Now, **stk** will have 4 elements. Then, we *pop* one element and print the contents of the stack. We repeated it twice. The result of the program is given below:

```
==================== RESTART: E:\Py programs\E14x1.py ====================
Stack now contains: [10]
Stack now contains: [10, 20]
```

```
Stack now contains: [10, 20, 30]
Stack now contains: [10, 20, 30, 35]
the item popped is:  35
Stack now contains: [10, 20, 30]
the item popped is:  30
Stack now contains: [10, 20]
the item popped is:  20
Stack now contains: [10]
```

Case study: Exception handling in a stack

We wrote one implementation of a stack in the previous paragraph. A stack is a LIFO data structure. A stack can be implemented using a list. The two operations of the stack are *push* and *pop*. The *push* operation pushes an item to a stack, and the *pop* operation retrieves an item from the stack. Since the list has a method *pop*, to avoid ambiguity, we will call the pop operation of the user-defined stack as spop and the push operation as spush.

A list expands itself without limit. However, here, for the sake of illustration, we are limiting the size of the stack to three. That is, it can hold at most three elements for the sake of illustration. The size could be any natural number, such as 100. In our example, when there are three elements already in the stack, the stack is full, and we cannot push any element thereafter. If we try to push the fourth element, an exception will be raised. It will be caught in the **except** block. The code for pushing elements (**spush**) and retrieving elements (**spop**) are put in a **try** block. Similarly, when the stack has 0 elements, the stack is empty. We also have an object **top**, which points to the top of the stack.

Look at the program in *Figure 14.1*. Assume that we have not commented on statements in lines 30, 37, and 38. All three statements exist in the program, to start with.

We define **Stk** as a class in line 3. The class **Stk** has a method **get_data** at line 4 with 4 formal parameters, including **self**. The other three are **lis**, **size**, and **top**. The parameters are initialized in the method. The actual arguments will be received when the **main** function creates **st** as an object of class **Stk** at line 25 and **st** calls **get_data** at line 26. Then at line 8, we define **spush** as another method of the class **Stk**, which receives **ele** from the calling function **main**. Now, we check if the **top** is greater than or equal to **size**. If so, the stack is full, and we *raise* exception **IndexError("Stack Full")**. If the stack is not full, append **ele** to list **lis** and increment **top**.

At line 14, we have defined the method **spop**. If the **top** is equal to zero, we cannot retrieve any element, and hence we raise the exception **IndexError("Stack Empty")**. If it is not empty, we pop an element from **lis** and decrement **top**. We return the element **ele**.

Then we have a method to display the contents of **lis**, or in other words the stack.

```
* E14x2.py - C:\Users\Subbu\Desktop\20 Bills\E14x2.py (3.10.11)

File  Edit  Format  Run  Options  Window  Help
 1 # Program E14x2.py
 2 # simulates stack using list
 3 class Stk:
 4     def get_data(self, lis, size, top):
 5         self.lis=lis
 6         self.size=size
 7         self.top=top
 8     def spush(self, ele):
 9         if self.top>=self.size:
10             raise IndexError("Stack Full")
11         else:
12             self.lis.append(ele)
13             self.top+=1
14     def spop(self):
15         if self.top==0:
16             raise IndexError("Stack Empty")
17         else:
18             ele=self.lis.pop()
19             self.top-=1
20             return ele
21     def display(self):
22         print(self.lis)

23 def main():
24     try:
25         st=Stk()
26         st.get_data([], 3, 0)
27         st.spush(10)
28         st.spush(20)
29         st.spush(30)
30         # st.spush(40)
31         ele=st.spop()
32         print(ele)
33         ele=st.spop()
34         print(ele)
35         ele=st.spop()
36         print(ele)
37         # ele=st.spop()
38         # print(ele)
39
40     except IndexError as ine:
41         print(ine.args)
42     st.display()
43
44
45 main()
```

Figure 14.1: Simulating stack using list

In the main function, in the **try** block, we create an object **st** of class **Stk** and initialize the object through the **get_data** method, with an empty list for **lis**, 3 for **size**, and 0 for the **top**. Then we **spush** 4 numbers with the *st* object. (Line 30 exists without #). This causes raising an exception in the **spush** method, which is caught in the **except** block and error message printed. Then the contents of the stack before exception are printed.

The result of the program is given below:

```
==================== RESTART: E:/Py programs/E14x2.py ====================
('Stack Full',)
[10, 20, 30]
>>>
```

Notice the usage of exception handling. Had we not handled it, all operations before the occurrence of exception would have been lost and the stack contents would have been lost. That is the essential advantage of exception handling, that is, not losing the transactions before the occurrence of an exception. It also executes the last statement after the except block and displays the contents of the stack before the exception was thrown.

Now, we comment on the statement in line 30. This means only three elements will be pushed to the stack. Following the push operations, we pop an element and print it from statements from lines 31 to 38. The first 3 pops will work fine since the top will be 3, 2, and 1 before the pop. After the third element has been popped, the top will become zero. The next pop at line 37 (it is not commented on at present) will raise an exception. The result of the program is given below:

```
==================== RESTART: E:/Py programs/E14x2.py ====================
30
20
10
('Stack Empty',)
[]
>>>
```

Note that the operations before the exception and after it (**st.display()**) have not been affected. Now, let us comment on lines 37 and 38. We have 3 push and 3 pop operations. An exception will not occur, and the result of the program is given below:

```
==================== RESTART: E:/Py programs/E14x2.py ====================
30
20
10
[]
```

Note that we print the list after the 3 pop operations. Since the list is empty, we get an empty list as the above indicates.

Queue

A queue is also a list. The stack has only one entry or gateway for pushing and popping. We can visualize a queue as a list with two gateways, left and right. We write through the right gateway which can be the rear end of the queue. We read from the left end of the queue. Reading is like popping. The element is read from the left or front and deleted after reading.

The program below implements a queue. We implement a queue by using the built-in library object **deque**. We import **deque** from collections in the Python library. In line 4, we create an empty **deque** and assign it to a variable **que**. Then we add elements to the **que** using **append** and remove elements from **que** using **popleft** method of the **deque**:

```
# Program E14x3
#   simulates queue using deque
from collections import deque

que = deque() # Empty deque

# write using append()method of the deque

que.append(10)
print('\nQueue now contains:', que)
que.append(20)
print('\nQueue now contains:', que)
que.append(30)
print('\nQueue now contains:', que)
que.append(35)
print('\nQueue now contains:', que)

# read from que
print('removed :', que.popleft())
print('\nQueue now contains:', que)
print('removed :', que.popleft())
print('\nQueue now contains:', que)
print('removed :', que.popleft())
print('\nQueue now contains:', que)
```

The result of the program is given below:

```
=================== RESTART: E:\Py programs\E14x3.py ====================
Queue now contains: deque([10])
Queue now contains: deque([10, 20])
Queue now contains: deque([10, 20, 30])
```

```
Queue now contains: deque([10, 20, 30, 35])
removed : 10
Queue now contains: deque([20, 30, 35])
removed : 20
Queue now contains: deque([30, 35])
removed : 30
Queue now contains: deque([35])
```

In the queue, the data items were added at one end and removed from the other end. It adopts the **First In First Out (FIFO)** methodology for storage and retrieval. Queues are used extensively in operating systems to keep track of users waiting for resources such as CPU, printing, etc.

Case study: Exception handling in queue

We will look at another implementation of queue with a list and with exception handling. A queue has been implemented with the list.

The two operations of queue are **writeq** and **readq**. The **writeq** operation appends an element to the queue and **readq** operation retrieves an element from the queue. Look at the program in *Figure 14.2*.

In line 3, we define a class **Queue**. In line 4, we have defined a method **get_data** with three formal parameters in addition to **self**. The parameters are **lis**, **left**, and **right**. The parameters are initialized with values when we create method **que** of class **Queue** in line 26. Here also, although the list can expand itself without limits, we restrict its size to 3 to demonstrate the concepts. In reality, the size could be any natural number, such as 100. We pass an empty list and (size-1) 2 for the left and 2 for the right to method **get_data** at line 27. Therefore, the initial values of the *left* and *right* are 2 and 2. This is one less than the size of the **que**, that is, the number of elements in it.

```
 E14x4.py - C:/Users/Subbu/Desktop/E14x4.py (3.10.11)
File Edit Format Run Options Window Help
1  # Program E14x4.py
2  # Exception handling in queue
3  class Queue:
4      def get_data(self, lis, left, right):
5          self.lis=lis
6          self.left=left
7          self.right=right
8      def writeq(self, ele):
9          if self.left<0:
10             raise IndexError("Queue Full")
11         else:
12             self.lis.append(ele)
13             self.left-=1
14     def readq(self):
15         if self.left==self.right:
16             raise IndexError("Queue Empty")
17         else:
18             ele=self.lis[self.right]
19             del(self.lis[self.right])
20             self.right-=1
21             return ele
22     def display(self):
23         print('que now contains: ', self.lis)
24 def main():
25     try:
26         que=Queue()
27         que.get_data([], 2,2)
28         que.writeq(10)
29         que.display()
30         que.writeq(20)
31         que.display()
32         que.writeq(30)
33         que.display()
34         # que.writeq(35)
35         # que.display()
36         print('removed :', que.readq())
37         que.display()
38         print('removed :', que.readq())
39         que.display()
40         print('removed :', que.readq())
41         que.display()
42         # print('removed :', que.readq())
43         # que.display()
44     except IndexError as ine:
45         print(ine.args)
46     que.display()
47 main()
48
```

Figure 14.2: Exception Handling in Queue

The program listing shows four statements in the body of the program as commented with a preceding #. Assume that no statements in the body of the program are commented on as of now. In our example, when there are three elements already in the *queue*, the queue is full, we cannot write any element thereafter. If we try to push the fourth element an exception will be raised. It will be caught in the **except** block. When the queue has 0 elements, the queue is empty. The code for writing elements (**writeq**) and retrieving elements (**readq**) are put in a **try** block from line number 25 to 43. The **readq** is called indirectly in the print statements in the block.

The **writeq** and **readq** are the methods in the class queue defined at lines 8 and 14, respectively. Initially, both the numbers *right* and *left* are assigned the value of 2 when the object **que** is created. When **writeq** is called, left is checked for its value, and if it is less than zero, an exception *Queue Full* is raised. When it is called in the main function for the first time, left will be equal to 2, and hence, the number 10 passed will be appended to the queue, that is, **lis** at line 12, and then *left* is decreased to 1 at line 13. Therefore, after three write operations, 10 will be stored in index 2, 20 at 1, and 30 at index 0, and the left will have the value -1. At line 34 in the main function, when we call write with number 35, an exception (Queue Full) will be raised at line 10 since the left is less than zero, and the program will be terminated. However, whatever we have written to the queue will not be lost. It will also go to the last line in the program and print the contents of the queue. The result of the program follows:

```
==================== RESTART: E:/Py programs/E14x4.py ====================
que now contains:  [10]
que now contains:  [10, 20]
que now contains:  [10, 20, 30]
('Queue Full',)
que now contains:  [10, 20, 30]
```

Now we exclude the statements at line 34 and 35 by adding # before them. This will allow the program when executed to go to line 36 after line 33, after writing the three numbers.

When we invoke **readq** for the first time, right is 2 and left is -1, and left is not equal to right and hence no exception will be raised at line 16. Hence element with an index equal to the right (that is, 2), which is 10 will be stored in **ele** at line 18. In line 19, the element will be deleted from the list. In line 20, the *right* is decreased. In line 21, the element will be returned to the main function. Therefore, the number 10 will be printed in the main function. The right will have the value 1, and hence, 20 will be fetched in the next read, and so on. Thus, the first number written is read first. When three numbers have been stored in the list, left would be minus 1. Similarly, when 3 characters have been read, right also will be minus 1. Initially also, both left and right were 2 and hence the queue was empty.

Now at line 42, we are trying to **readq**. (It is not commented yet.) When we try to read for the fourth time *left* is equal to *right* and hence exception (*Queue Empty*) will be raised. The program terminates. However, it goes past the **except** block and prints the contents of the queue in the last line. The result of the program is given below:

```
==================== RESTART: E:/Py programs/E14x4.py ====================
que now contains:  [10]
que now contains:  [10, 20]
que now contains:  [10, 20, 30]
removed : 30
que now contains:  [10, 20]
removed : 20
```

```
que now contains:   [10]
removed : 10
que now contains:   []
('Queue Empty',)
que now contains:   []
>>>
```

Now let us comment on lines 42 and 43. Now no exception will occur and the result of the program is given below:

```
=================== RESTART: E:/Py programs/E14x4.py =====================
que now contains:   [10]
que now contains:   [10, 20]
que now contains:   [10, 20, 30]
removed : 30
que now contains:   [10, 20]
removed : 20
que now contains:   [10]
removed : 10
que now contains:   []
que now contains:   []
```

Thus, we have seen two implementations each of the stack and queue in this chapter. The second implementations are built with exception handling and hence may be preferred over the others.

Algorithm analysis

We develop algorithms before writing a program in any language. For a given problem, there exist several algorithms. For instance, in this chapter, we will study four sorting algorithms as given below:

- Bubble sort
- Selection sort
- Insertion sort
- Merge sort

When there is a choice, we select the most efficient algorithm. Computer resources such as CPU time for execution of the program and memory space required to run the program should be estimated for each algorithm and we must select the most efficient algorithms. Some of these resources to be kept in mind are:

- **Space complexity:** It is an estimation of how much memory space is required if we implement an algorithm.

- **Time complexity:** The time it takes to run the algorithm in a computer is a measure of time complexity. With the current advancement in technology, time complexity is more important. There are three measures for finding time complexity. We will choose the most important measure to estimate the time complexity. It is big Oh notation.

- **Big O notation:** It is one of the measures of complexity. Big O notation is a way to describe how the runtime or space requirements of an algorithm grow as the size of the input grows. It is like describing how fast an algorithm gets slower or how much memory it uses as you give it more data to work with.

  Imagine you have a list of numbers, and you want to find a specific number in that list. Let us say the list is unsorted. One way to find the number is to look at each number in the list until you find the one you are looking for. If there are N numbers in the list, in the worst-case scenario, you might have to look at all N numbers.

  Now, let us say you have another list that is twice as big. With the same algorithm, you might have to look at twice as many numbers to find what you are looking for. Big O notation helps us describe this relationship. We would say that this algorithm has a time complexity of O(N), meaning that the time it takes to run grows linearly with the size of the input.

  There are other types of time complexities as well. For example, if an algorithm takes constant time regardless of the input size, we would say it has a time complexity of O(1). If the time it takes to run grows exponentially with the size of the input, we might say it has a time complexity of O(2^N).

  Big O notation helps us understand how efficient an algorithm is and how it will perform as we increase the size of the problem it is solving.

  With given functions $f(n)$ and $g(n)$, we say that $f(n)$ is $O(g(n))$ if and only if there are positive constants c and n_0 such that $f(n) \leq c\, g(n)$ for $n \geq n_0$

  Big O notation gives complexity in the worst case.

  It is a wide and interesting topic, and students will learn a lot more about algorithms in their future courses. For each of the sorting algorithms, the complexity in terms of big O will be stated. The reader can verify them at leisure. The measure of complexity will aid the comparison of the efficiency of the algorithms.

Case study: Bubble sort

Searching and sorting are important problems in computer science. There are several sorting algorithms for sorting a list. One of the earliest and most well-known algorithms for sorting is the bubble sort. In this algorithm, the elements traverse like a bubble from one location to the other during sorting and hence the name. It can be called brute force methodology. The algorithm for sorting the elements of a list in ascending order is given below:

```
1: Read list of numbers to be sorted. (Assume the list contains 5
   elements)

2. bubble(array):
        for i in range(4):
                for j in range(i+1, 5):
                        if(array[i] > array[j]):
                                temp=array[i]
                                array[i]=array[j]
                                array[j]=temp
        return array

3. End
```

It is a simple algorithm. Let us take an example to understand the algorithm:

```
arr=[89, 12, 75, 34, 2]
```

1. When we begin i=0 and j=(i+1) =1.

2. We check if array[0] is greater than array [1]. It is so and hence we exchange. New list will be:

3. [12, 89, 75, 34, 2]

4. Now i remains 0 since the inner loop has not been exhausted, j will be now 2. We compare array[0], that is, 12 with array[2] which is 75. Hence, there is no exchange.

5. This process continues, and before j is exhausted, the number 2 will reach the 0th location of the array.

6. Now we step up i and repeat to get 12 in the 1st location of the *array.*

7. In this manner, the bubble sort algorithm sorts the numbers.

The algorithm is implemented in the program **E14x5.py** below.

```
#  Program E14x5.py
# Bubble sort
def bubble(array):
    print("list to be sorted is: ", array)
    for i in range(4):
            for j in range(i+1, 5):
                if(array[i] > array[j]):
```

```
                    temp=array[i]
                    array[i]=array[j]
                    array[j]=temp
            print("after pass", i+1, ":",  array)
    return array
def main():
    arr=[89, 12, 75, 34, 2]
    arr1=bubble(arr)
    print('sorted list is:', arr1)
main()
```

The result of the program is given below.

```
=================== RESTART: E:\Py programs\E14x5.py ====================
list to be sorted is:  [89, 12, 75, 34, 2]
after pass 1 : [2, 89, 75, 34, 12]
after pass 2 : [2, 12, 89, 75, 34]
after pass 3 : [2, 12, 34, 89, 75]
after pass 4 : [2, 12, 34, 75, 89]
sorted list is: [2, 12, 34, 75, 89]
```

Time complexity of bubble sort

The big O notation gives the worst-case complexity or the upper bound. It is $O(n^2)$ for bubble sort, where n is the size of the array to be sorted.

Case study: Selection sort

Selection sort virtually partitions the list to be sorted into two segments in the list. The sorted part is on the left of the list and unsorted is on the right of the list. The sorted partition is empty to start with. The unsorted part initially contains the list with all the elements to be sorted.

Let us try to understand the algorithm Selection sort with an example. For instance, let the list of unsorted elements be: [7, 3,2, 5, 11].

We begin with the unsorted list:

7, 3,2, 5, 11

1. In the first pass, the unsorted segment has all the elements. We look through each item and determine that 2 is the smallest element. So, we swap 2 with 7. The element 2 is in the correct position now as illustrated below:

   2, 3,7, 5, 11

2. Of the remaining unsorted elements, [3, 7, 5, 11], 3 is the lowest number. Since 3 is at the right place, we do not swap.

3. Of the remaining unsorted elements, [7, 5, 11], 5 is the lowest number. So, we swap 5 with 7 and we get the sorted list as given below:

2, 3, 5, 7, 11

4. The array is already sorted. Let us write an algorithm for selection sort. It is given below:

```
def selection_sort(arr):
print('unsorted list:', arr)
for i in range(len(arr)): # the loop will iterate up to i=len(arr)-1
                min_index = i # iʰ element
                for j in range(i+1, len(arr)):
# Update the min_index if the element at j is lower than it
                if arr[j] < arr[min_index]:
                            min_index = j
        # After finding the lowest item of the unsorted regions, swap
with the first unsorted item
                endif
            end for
arr[i], arr[min_index] = arr[min_index], arr[i]
print('after pass=', i+1, arr)
        end for
        return(arr)
    End
```

Let us see how we implement this as a Python program:

```
*E14x6.py - C:/Users/Subbu/Desktop/E14x6.py (3.10.11)*

File  Edit  Format  Run  Options  Window  Help
 1 # Program E14x6.py
 2 # Selection sort
 3
 4 def selection_sort(arr):
 5     print('unsorted list:', arr)
 6     # i indicates number of items to be sorted
 7     for i in range(len(arr)):
 8 '''To find the minimum value of the unsorted segment.
 9         We first assume that the first element is the lowest'''
10         min_index = i
11 # We then use j to loop through the remaining elements
12         for j in range(i+1, len(arr)):
13 # Update the min_index if the element at j is lower than it
14             if arr[j] < arr[min_index]:
15                 min_index = j
16 # After finding the lowest, swap with the first unsorted item
17         arr[i], arr[min_index] = arr[min_index], arr[i]
18         print('after pass=', i+1, arr)
19     return(arr)
20
21 def main():
22     list1=[33, 42, 5,3, 6, 22, 1]
23     list2=selection_sort(list1)
24     print('sorted list is: ', list2)
25
26
27 main()
28
```

Figure 14.3: Selection sort

The trick to implementing this algorithm is keeping track of the minimum value and swapping two elements of the list. The result of the program is given below:

```
==================== RESTART: E:\Py programs\E14x6.py ====================
unsorted list: [33, 42, 5, 3, 6, 22, 1]
after pass= 1 [1, 42, 5, 3, 6, 22, 33]
after pass= 2 [1, 3, 5, 42, 6, 22, 33]
after pass= 3 [1, 3, 5, 42, 6, 22, 33]
after pass= 4 [1, 3, 5, 6, 42, 22, 33]
after pass= 5 [1, 3, 5, 6, 22, 42, 33]
after pass= 6 [1, 3, 5, 6, 22, 33, 42]
after pass= 7 [1, 3, 5, 6, 22, 33, 42]
sorted list is:  [1, 3, 5, 6, 22, 33, 42]
```

In the first pass, we swap the smallest element to the first position and the element in the first position to where the smallest element was originally. In the next pass the next smallest element is swapped to the second position and so on.

Time complexity of selection sort

The big O notation gives the worst-case complexity or the upper bound. It is $O(n^2)$ for Selection sort where n is the size of the array to be sorted.

Case study: Insertion sort

Here again, there are two segments, sorted and unsorted. Let us understand the method with an example. For instance, let the list that we will be sorting be as follows:

```
[5 66 45 9 1]
```

1. In the first pass, the first element 5 is sorted by itself since it is only one element.

2. In the second iteration, the second element 66 is compared with the already sorted element on the left. Since 66 is greater than 5 no changes are required.

3. In the third iteration, the third element 45 is compared with 66 and 5. Since it is more than 5 and less than 66, it moves to the second position. The list now is:

   ```
   [5 45 66 9 1]
   ```

4. In the fourth iteration, the fourth element 9 is compared with elements on the left. Its appropriate position is second. Therefore, 3 moves are made as given below:

   a. 9 moved to the second position.

   b. 45 moved to the third position.

   c. 66 moved to the fourth position.

   The list now will be:

   ```
   [5 9 45 66  1]
   ```

5. In the fifth iteration number 1 is compared with all other elements on the left. It is moved to the first position all other numbers move by one position. It involves 5 moves.

   The list now will be:

   ```
   [1 5 9 45 66 ]
   ```

Sorting is completed.

The algorithm for insertion sort is given below:

```
Insertion_sort(arr)
Step 1: print('list to be sorted=', arr)
        for i in range (1,len(arr)):
              Set temp=arr[i]
```

```
        Set j=i-1
        while (temp<arr[j] and j>=0)
                set arr[j+1]= arr[j]
                set j=j-1
        End while
        Set arr[j+1] =temp
        Print list after ith pass
        Set i=i+1
    End for
Step 2: End
```

The algorithm is implemented in Python. The program is given below:

```
E14x7.py - C:/Users/Subbu/Desktop/E14x7.py (3.10.10)
File  Edit  Format  Run  Options  Window  Help
1  # Program E14x7.py
2  # Insertion sort
3
4  def insertion_sort(arr):
5      print('list to be sorted=', arr)
6      for i in range (1,len(arr)):
7          temp=arr[i]
8          j=i-1
9          while (temp<arr[j] and j>=0):
10             arr[j+1]= arr[j]
11             j=j-1
12         arr[j+1] =temp
13         print('list after', i, ' pass', arr)
14
15     return(arr)
16
17
18 def main():
19     list1=[33, 42, 5,3, 6, 22, 1]
20     list2=insertion_sort(list1)
21     print('sorted list is: ', list2)
22
23
24 main()
25
```

Figure 14.4: Insertion sort

The result of the program is given below. The status of the list at every pass is also captured for further observation by the readers:

```
==================== RESTART: E:\Py programs\E14x7.py ====================
list to be sorted= [33, 42, 5, 3, 6, 22, 1]
list after 1  pass [33, 42, 5, 3, 6, 22, 1]
list after 2  pass [5, 33, 42, 3, 6, 22, 1]
list after 3  pass [3, 5, 33, 42, 6, 22, 1]
```

```
list after 4  pass [3, 5, 6, 33, 42, 22, 1]
list after 5  pass [3, 5, 6, 22, 33, 42, 1]
list after 6  pass [1, 3, 5, 6, 22, 33, 42]
sorted list is:  [1, 3, 5, 6, 22, 33, 42]
```

Time complexity of insertion sort

The big O notation gives the worst-case complexity or the upper bound. It is $O(n^2)$ for Insertion sort, where n is the size of the array to be sorted.

Case study: Merge sort

The merge sort algorithm uses the divide and conquer principle to sort a given list of numbers. Let us consider a list of **n** number of elements. The algorithm processes the elements in 3 steps:

1. If the list contains 0 or 1 elements then it is already sorted, otherwise, divide the list into two lists of an equal number of elements.

2. Sort the two lists recursively using the merge sort.

3. Combine the two lists to form a single list of sorted.

An example will make it clear. Let the list be as follows:

[21 12 43 85 73 57 51 34]

1. We divide the list two halves as given below:

    [21 12 43 85]   [73 57 51 34]

2. We will sort the left-hand list first. After dividing it into two parts we get four lists as given below:

    [21 12]   [43 85]

3. The two lists are again divided into lists containing one element:

    [21] [12] [43] [85]

4. Since there is one element in each list, they are already sorted. Now, merge 21 and 12 to produce a sorted list containing two elements. Similarly, merge 43 and 85 to produce a list containing two elements as given below:

    [12 21] [43 85]

5. Now merge the above two lists to give one sorted list as given below:

    [12 21 43 85]

6. By following similar steps, the list in the right side in *Step 1* can be sorted as follows:

    [34 51 57 73]

7. In the same way, finally, both the lists can be merged to get a final sorted list as follows:

[12 21 34 43 51 57 73 85]

The algorithm for merge sort is given below:

```
def merge_sort(arr, low, high):
    if(low<high):
        mid=(low+high)//2
        merge_sort(arr, low, mid) # invoking merge_sort recursively for
left sub-list
        merge_sort(arr, mid+1, high) # invoking merge_sort recursively for
right  sub-list
        c=merge_list(arr, low, mid, mid+1, high) # calling merging of both
above and assigning to c
        return c  # return to main function
def merge_list(arr, ll, lr, ul, ur):
''' ll is the  start index of left sub-list
    ul is the start index of right sub-list
    lr is the  end index of left sub-list
    ur is the end index of right sub-list'''
# merge_list create a sorted list called merged from the two sub-lists
    i=ll
    j=ul
    k=ll
    merged=[0,0,0,0,0,0,0,0] # initialize the list merged to zero for all
elements - 8 here
    while(i<=lr and j<=ur):
        if arr[i]<=arr[j]:
            merged[k]=arr[i]
            i=i+1
        else:
            merged[k]=arr[j]
            j=j+1
            k=k+1
    if(i<=lr):
        while(i<=lr):
            merged[k]=arr[i]
```

```
                    i=i+1
                    k=k+1
        if(j<=ur):
            while(j<=ur):
                merged[k]=arr[j]
                j=j+1
                k=k+1
        for k in range(ll, ur+1): # range will iterate till ur
            arr[k]=merged[k]
        return(arr)  # returns array to called function merge_sort
```

The program implementing the above algorithm is given below:

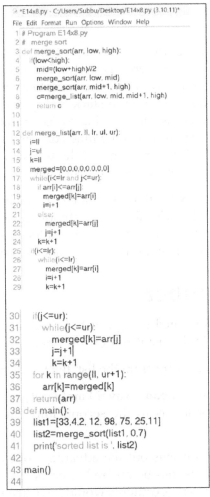

Figure 14.5: Merge sort

The result of the program is given below:

```
==================== RESTART: E:\Py programs\E14x8.py ====================
sorted list is  [2, 4, 11, 12, 25, 33, 75, 98]
```

The program worked correctly. Merge sort is one of the fastest algorithms for sorting. Type the program carefully.

Time complexity of merge sort

The big O notation gives the worst-case complexity or the upper bound. It is $O(n \log n)$ for merge sort, where n is the size of the array to be sorted. So, the worst-case complexity of merge sort is the best of all the sorting algorithms we studied. Estimate the savings in CPU time if the size of the list is 1 million.

Conclusion

Data structures provide concrete ways to organize data for efficient storage and efficient manipulation. In this chapter, we covered two prominent data structures, that is, stacks and queues. We also discussed how to handle exceptions in these abstract data types and saw examples of exception handling in stack and queue. It was followed by a brief introduction to algorithm analysis and the big O asymptotic notation to express the worst-case scenario. Sorting data is one of the time-consuming tasks in computer science. We studied the algorithms and the programs of the following sorting methods. We also deduced the worst-case time complexities of the four algorithms.

It is important to carry out visualization of data before analysis. In the next chapter, we will discuss how to carry out data visualization techniques using Python libraries. We will understand how to plot charts such as line chart, scatter diagram, histogram, bar chart using the three Python libraries: pandas, matplotlib and Seaborn.

Points to remember

- A stack can be implemented using a list. A stack is a LIFO data structure. Item inserted in the stack in the last is retrievable first.

- Whenever we *pop* an element from the list, the last element will only be returned.

- Since the list has a method **pop**, to avoid ambiguity we will call the pop operation of the user-defined stack as in the second implementation as **spop** and push operation as **spush**.

- The example program brings out the advantage of exception handling. Had we not handled it, all operations before and after the occurrence of exception would have been lost and the stack contents would have been lost.

- A queue can be implemented using a list. The stack has only one entry or gateway for pushing and popping. We can visualize queue as a list with two gateways, left and right. We write through the right gateway which can be the rear end of the queue and read through the left gateway.

- We first implemented a queue by using the built-in library object **deque**. We import **deque** from collections in the Python library.

- We looked at another implementation of queue with list and with exception handling.

- The two operations of the queue are **writeq** and **readq**. The **writeq** operation appends an element to the **queue** and **readq** operation retrieves an element from the queue.

- We develop algorithms before writing a program in any given language. When there is a choice, we select the most efficient algorithm.

- There are three measures for time complexity. We will choose the most important measure to estimate the time complexity. It is big O notation. It is an asymptotic notation and abstracts the complexity.

- The big O notation gives the worst-case complexity or the upper bound. It is $O(n^2)$ for bubble sort where n is the size of the array to be sorted.

- One of the well-known algorithms for sorting is bubble sorting. In this algorithm the elements traverse like a bubble from one location to the other during sorting and hence the name.

- The big O is $O(n^2)$ for bubble sort where n is the size of the array to be sorted.

- Selection sort virtually partitions the list to be sorted into two segments in the list. The sorted part is on the left of the list and unsorted is on the right of the list. The sorted partition is empty to start with. The unsorted part initially contains the list of all elements to be sorted.

- The big O is $O(n^2)$ for selection sort where n is the size of the array to be sorted.

- In the case of Insertion sort again, there are two segments, sorted and unsorted. The big O is $O(n^2)$ for insertion sort where n is the size of the array to be sorted.

- The merge sort algorithm uses the divide and conquer principle to sort a given list of numbers. The big O is $O(n\,logn)$ for merge sort where n is the size of the array to be sorted. So, the worst-case complexity of merge sort is the best of all sorting algorithms we studied.

Questions

Choose the most appropriate answer.

1. **Time complexity is O (nlog n) for:**

    a. Bubble sort

    b. Insertion sort

    c. Merge sort

    d. All of the above

    e. None of the above.

2. **Time complexity is O (n^2) for:**

    a. Bubble sort

    b. Insertion sort

    c. Selection sort

    d. All of the above

    e. None of the above.

3. **Computer resources include:**

    a. CPU

    b. RAM

    c. Secondary storage

    d. All of the above

    e. None of the above

4. **list.append() adds item at:**

    a. the beginning

    b. the end

    c. All of the above

    d. None of the above

5. **list.pop() deletes item at:**

    a. the beginning

    b. the end

    c. All of the above

    d. None of the above

6. **que.popleft() deletes item at:**

    a. the beginning

    b. the end

    c. All the above

    d. None of the above

7. **que.append() adds item at:**

    a. the beginning

    b. the end

    c. All of the above

    d. None of the above

8. **readq() reads from:**

    a. the left

    b. right

    c. All of the above

    d. None of the above

9. **writeq() writes from:**

    a. the beginning

    b. the end

    c. All the above

    d. None of the above

10. **Exchange elements of the list take place in:**

    a. Bubble sort

    b. Insertion sort

    c. Selection sort

    d. All of the above

    e. None of the above

- Write short notes on the following:
  - o Stack full
  - o Stack empty
  - o Queue full
  - o Queue empty
  - o Time complexity
  - o Big O notation
  - o Compare bubble sort with insertion sort.
  - o Compare selection sort with insertion sort.
  - o Compare selection sort with merge sort.
  - o Stack vs. queue
- Match the following:

A	B
LIFO	1. li[]
FIFO	2. deleting
Empty list	3. stack
Adding	4. queue
Pop	5. append()

- Write programs for the following:
  - o Rewrite the program implementing stack with exception to have a flexible size of the stack.
  - o Rewrite the program for a queue with exception to have flexible size.
  - o To find the transpose of a 4x3 matrix.
  - o Modify the Bubble sort program to capture the status of the list of numbers to be sorted for each unique value of i.
  - o To sort lower case letters using bubble sort.
  - o To sort upper case letters using selection sort.
  - o To sort strings using Insertion sort.
  - o To sort strings using Merge sort.
  - o To implement a queue for lower case letters.
  - o To implement a stack for upper case letters.

CHAPTER 15

Data Visualization

Introduction

Data visualization is like telling a story with pictures made of data. Instead of using words or numbers alone, we create graphs, charts, maps, or diagrams to represent information visually. It helps people understand complex data more easily because our brains are good at processing visual information. So, data visualization makes it simpler to spot patterns, trends, and relationships in the data, allowing us to make better decisions and share insights with others. For instance, if we have a bunch of sales numbers, we can turn them into a colorful bar graph to see which products sell the most or least. We will learn data visualization using Python libraries in this chapter.

Structure

The chapter covers the following topics:

- Importance of data
- Python libraries for data visualization
- Dataset
- DataFrame
- pandas

- Matplotlib

- Scatter diagram

- Line chart

- Histogram

- Second dataset

- Bar chart

- Seaborn

Objectives

Python is widely used in applications such as machine learning and big data analytics. To be successful in modeling in such applications, it is important to study and clean the data and carry out visualization beforehand. In this chapter, we will learn to use pandas, matplotlib, and seaborn to carry out visualization of real-life data. We will plot graphs, diagrams, and charts using the above libraries.

Importance of data

In the current millennium, data is pervasive, and humanity cannot survive without data. A large amount of data is generated every microsecond. Data is also used extensively in vital sectors such as banks, stock exchanges, government departments, healthcare, education, and industry. Data analysis leads to making appropriate decisions in the corporate world. The sentiment analysis predicts who will be the next President of the United States. Social media is one of the major contributors to data explosion. It is important to visualize the data before carrying out analysis. Such visualization gives a clear picture of the trend. In this chapter, an introduction is given to data visualization using Python.

Data is the engine for the growth of enterprises and nations globally. The key to the success of an enterprise or a nation lies in its ability to analyse past data and use it for leveraging its growth in the future. The goal of data visualization is to present past data in an easily understandable manner for the benefit of a wide audience. The audience could include all the five stakeholders of an enterprise, that is, the employees, customers, suppliers, owners, and society. The conventional form of business intelligence and data analysis seeks to provide a summary view of facts and figures in an understandable form to either inform or prepare data for further analysis.

A common example of data visualization is company reports that provide a historic review of an organization's operations, sales, financials, customers, and stakeholders. Some common data in data visualization are observations, case studies, and surveys. Data visualization rarely attempts to investigate cause-and-effect relationships. Thus, the collection and interpretation of a large amount of data may be involved in this type of visualization. It is relevant to note that in Big Data analytics, the information provided by data visualization becomes inputs for more advanced predictive or prescriptive analytics that deliver insights for business decision-making.

Data visualization is the presentation of historical data to better understand changes that have taken place in a business. Data visualization uses a range of historic data to draw comparisons. The most reported financial metrics are a product of data visualization. For instance, year-over-year pricing changes, month-over-month sales growth, growth of the number of customers, or the total revenue per subscriber. These measures all describe what has occurred in a business during a given period.

Data visualization takes raw data and plots graphs to draw conclusions that are useful and understandable by managers, investors, and other stakeholders. A report showing sales of $1 million may sound impressive, but it lacks context. If that figure represents a 20% month-over-month decline, it is a concern. If it is a 40% year-over-year increase, then it suggests something is going right with the strategy of the organization. Data visualization uses a full range of data to give an accurate picture of what has happened in a business and how that differs from other comparable periods. These performance metrics can be used to flag areas of strengths and weaknesses to inform management to determine the right strategies.

Python libraries for data visualization

Data visualization, in simple terms, is a technique or tool to understand the characteristics of the data at hand. This is achieved by plotting them as a graph so that patterns, trends, and correlations can be detected even by the naked eye. Python offers several libraries for creating various graphs. In this chapter, we will be using the following built-in libraries of Python:

- **Matplotlib**: Low-level library, and it provides flexibility.

- **pandas**: Easy to use interface, built on Matplotlib.

- **Seaborn**: A high-level interface that provides many styles.

Dataset

We will be using publicly available datasets to explain the concepts. We will be using two datasets. To get the first dataset for our experiments, type the link given below and download the file named **50_Startups**:

https://gist.github.com/kitmonisit/900affc23e780ac853c439b30fce5cd0

This dataset was data collected from New York, California, and Florida States in the USA from 50 business startups. There are 5 columns in the dataset as given below.

R&D Spend	Administration	Marketing Spend	State	Profit

File formats

The Excel file format can be of multiple types, as given below:

- Stored with **.xlsx** extension.

- **Comma-separated Values (CSV)** files stored with **.csv** extension.

We discussed the CSV files in *Chapter 11, File Handling*. Recall that the Excel file can be saved as a CSV file by choosing the type of file as CSV (comma delimited). We will be using two CSV files for our discussions in this chapter.

DataFrame

We will discuss DataFrame now. **Structured Query Language (SQL)** tables are in wide use in data analytics. They present data in the form of rows and columns. A similar structure of rows and columns is presented through DataFrames in machine learning. Language R uses DataFrames extensively. We create DataFrames in Python using the **pandas** library. DataFrames contain rows and columns and have a flat-file structure. We can use pandas to view and carry out various manipulations in the dataset.

pandas

In computer programming, pandas is a software library written for the Python programming language for data manipulation and analysis. It offers data structures and operations for manipulating numerical tables and time series. It is free software. The pandas is a high-level data manipulation tool developed by *Wes McKinney*. It is built on the Numpy package, and its key data structure is called the DataFrame. DataFrames allow us to store and manipulate tabular data in rows of observations and columns of variables.

Installing pandas

We have to first install the pandas library on our computer. For this purpose, go to the command prompt, type the following, and then click *Enter*:

```
C:\Users\HP>pip install pandas
```

Wait for pandas to install.

Reading head() of csv file

The **head()** in Python means the first five rows in the DataFrame. The **tail()** refers to the last five rows in the DataFrame. We will now write a program to print the head, the first five rows in the **50_Startups** dataset. It is given below:

```
# Program E15x1.py
```

```
# Reading first 5 rows
import pandas as pd
data= pd.read_csv('50_Startups.csv')
print(data.head())
```

In the above program, we are importing pandas and giving it a short name **pd**. Then, in the next statement, we declare a DataFrame called **data**. We read '**50_Startups.csv**' file in the current directory using pandas and assign it to the DataFrame **data**. In the next line, we are printing the head, that is, the first five rows in the CSV file.

The result of the program is given below:

```
==================== RESTART: E:/Py programs/E15x1.py ====================
   R&D Spend  Administration  Marketing Spend       State     Profit
0  165349.20       136897.80        471784.10    New York  192261.83
1  162597.70       151377.59        443898.53  California  191792.06
2  153441.51       101145.55        407934.54     Florida  191050.39
3  144372.41       118671.85        383199.62    New York  182901.99
4  142107.34        91391.77        366168.42     Florida  166187.94
```

Read the result carefully. The first row contains the column headers. The program has also assigned row numbers starting from 0 to 4. These row numbers are not present in the CSV file.

Note that we must give the full path of the file if it is not in the current directory. There is no harm in giving the full path even when the file is in the current directory. An example is shown below:

```
data= pd.read_csv('C:/Users/Subbu/Desktop/50_Startups.csv')
```

Reading tail() of csv file

Let us now write a program to read the last five rows of the '**50_Startups.csv**' file. The last five rows are known collectively as the **tail()**. Here, the DataFrame is called **df**. The program is given below:

```
# Program E15x2.py
# Reading last 5 rows of data
import pandas as pd
df= pd.read_csv('50_Startups.csv')
print(df.tail())
```

In the above program, we print the tail of **df** which represents the file. The result of the program is given below. It has printed the last five columns, indicating additionally the row numbers. Note that the column headers have also been printed:

```
================== RESTART: E:/Py programs/E15x2.py ====================
       R&D Spend   Administration   Marketing Spend      State     Profit
45      1000.23        124153.04            1903.93   New York   64926.08
46      1315.46        115816.21          297114.46    Florida   49490.75
47         0.00        135426.92               0.00 California   42559.73
48       542.05         51743.15               0.00   New York   35673.41
49         0.00        116983.80           45173.06 California   14681.40
```

Matplotlib

Matplotlib is one of the Python packages used for data visualization. It is a cross-platform library for making 2D plots from data in arrays. Matplotlib is written in Python and makes use of NumPy, the numerical mathematics extension of Python.

We need to install it in the command prompt as given below:

`C:\Users\HP>pip install Matplotlib`

When we download matplotlib, NumPy is also downloaded automatically. After it is installed successfully, we can create various useful plots for the chosen data.

The **matplotlib.pyplot** is a plotting library used for 2D graphics in Python programming language. It can be used in Python scripts, shells, web application servers, and other graphical user interface toolkits. We have to import **matplotlib.pyplot** to create plots.

Scatter diagram

A scatter diagram helps in studying the relationship between two variables. For instance, the relationship between the price of an item and demand can be plotted in a scatter diagram. In the x-axis, we plot the variable, and in the y-axis, the effect of the variable. In the case discussed above, we plot the price in the x-axis and demand on the y-axis. It may result in a straight-line relationship. The advantage of establishing such a relationship is that once an exercise is carried out in this manner, it is easy to extrapolate the results mathematically for any given situation. For instance, if an equation has been found for the demand for biscuits based on price, then the demand at any given price can be extrapolated. There may be some relationships that may not fall into any equation or any definite relationship. In such cases, no definite relationships can be established. At least, we can conclude that there is no relationship between the two entities considered.

When we wish to find out whether there exists any relationship between two entities such as age and productivity or quality of a product and price, we draw the scatter plot. Such a scatter plot may bring out the relationships between the items, which can be seen with the naked eye. There may be three types of relationships, as given below:

- Directly proportional

- Inversely proportional

- No relationship

Let us now create a few scatter plots.

Relationship between R&D spend and profit

Let us now try to visualize whether there is any relationship between R&D spend and profit in the 50_Startups data using the scatter diagram. The scatter plot is a 2-dimensional plot. We will choose the x-axis to represent R&D spend and the y-axis to represent profit.

To draw a scatter plot, we need to import **matplotlib.pyplot** as **plt**. The **plt** is the short name for **matplotlib.pyplot**. We need to import **pyplot** for drawing a scatter plot. We need to import pandas and open the file and assign it to the DataFrame. We call **subplots()** with **plt** and assign them to *figure (fig) and axis (ax)*. We then pass all the values of *R&D Spend* of the DataFrame to the x-axis and all the values of *Profit* of the DataFrame (the file **50_Startups.csv**) to the y-axis and call the scatter plot **ax.scatter**. We also wish to assign labels to the x-axis and y-axis and also a title to the plot. These are carried out in the three lines before the last line of the program is given below. In the last line, we direct the program to show the plot. *Figure 15.1* shows the scatter plot of R&D Spend and Profit using matplotlib. We use pandas in the program to read the csv file and assign it to dataframe with name **df**.

```
# Program E15x3.py
# Scatter plot
import matplotlib.pyplot as plt
import pandas as pd
df= pd.read_csv('50_Startups.csv')
# create a figure and axis
fig, ax = plt.subplots()
# scatter the R&D Spend and Profit
ax.scatter(df['R&D Spend'], df['Profit'])
# set a title and labels
ax.set_title('50_Startups')
ax.set_xlabel('R&D Spend')
ax.set_ylabel('Profit')
plt.show()
```

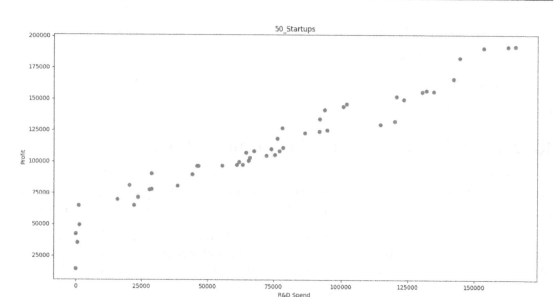

Figure 15.1: *Scatter Plot – R&D Spend and Profit using matplotlib*

The result of the program is the scatter plot shown in *Figure 15.1*. It gives the following information:

- As R&D Spend increases, the Profit increases.

- There is almost a linear relationship between R&D Spend and Profit

pandas for visualization

The pandas is an open-source high-performance, easy-to-use library providing data structures, such as data frames, and data analysis tools like the visualization tools. The pandas visualization makes it easy to create plots out of a pandas data frame. It also has a higher-level API than Matplotlib and therefore we need less code for similar plots. The pandas data visualization capabilities are also based on the Matplotlib library. However, with Pandas, we can directly plot different types of visualizations from the pandas DataFrame. Let us repeat the above exercise using pandas visualization for comparison. The program for scatter plot – R&D Spend and Profit is given below:

```
# Program E15x4.py
# Scatter plot using pandas
import matplotlib.pyplot as plt
import pandas as pd
df= pd.read_csv('50_Startups.csv')
df.plot.scatter(x='R&D Spend', y='Profit', title='50_Startups')
plt.show()
```

Note that in this program, we use **pandas** in conjunction with **matplotlib**. They are complementary. When we use the pandas library the code is shorter. When we execute the program, we get the scatter plot as shown in *Figure 15.2*:

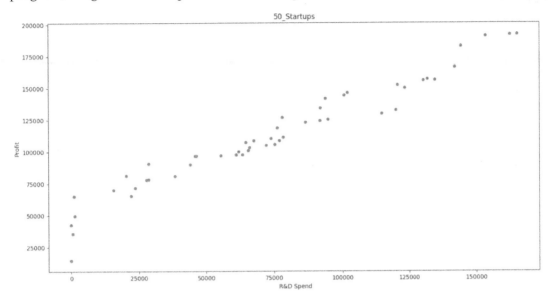

Figure 15.2: *Scatter Plot – R&D Spend and Profit using pandas*

Relationship between marketing spend and profit

Now let us try to find out the relationship between Marketing Spend and Profit. In the program **E15x5. py** we have replaced R&D Spend with Marketing Spend. The revised program is given below:

```
# Program E15x5.py
# Scatter plot
# scatter plot of Marketing Spend and Profit
import matplotlib.pyplot as plt
import pandas as pd
df= pd.read_csv('50_Startups.csv')
# create a figure and axis
fig, ax = plt.subplots()
# scatter the Marketing Spend and Profit
ax.scatter(df['Marketing Spend'], df['Profit'])
# set a title and labels
ax.set_title('50_Startups')
```

```
ax.set_xlabel('Marketing Spend')
ax.set_ylabel('Profit')
plt.show()
```

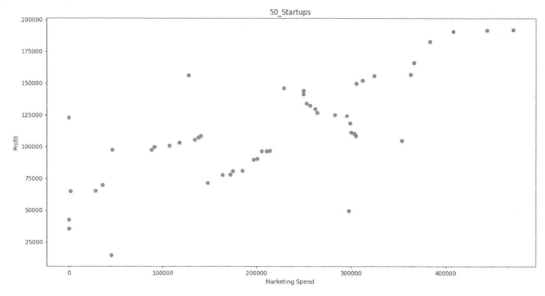

Figure 15.3: Scatter Plot – Marketing Spend and Profit using matplotlib

The result of the program is the scatter plot shown in *Figure 15.3*. The following observations can be made from the above plot:

- As Marketing Spend increases, the Profit generally increases. However, there are many outliers which do not follow the rule and so the relationship is not clear.

- If the outliers can be ignored a linear relationship between Marketing Spend and Profit can be assumed. Ignoring the outliers may lead to errors.

Relationship between administration and profit

To get the relationship between Administration and Profit 50_Startups data, let us substitute Marketing Spend with Administration in the above program. The revised program is given below:

```
# Program E15x6.py
# Scatter plot
# scatter plot of Administration Spend and Profit
import matplotlib.pyplot as plt
import pandas as pd
df= pd.read_csv('50_Startups.csv')
```

```
# create a figure and axis
fig, ax = plt.subplots()
# scatter the R&D Spend and Profit
ax.scatter(df['Administration'], df['Profit'])
# set a title and labels
ax.set_title('50_Startups')
ax.set_xlabel('Administration')
ax.set_ylabel('Profit')
plt.show()
```

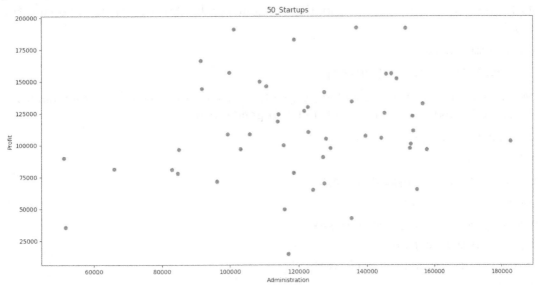

Figure 15.4: Scatter Plot – Administration Spend and Profit using matplotlib

The result of executing the program **E15x6.py** is the scatter plot given in *Figure 15.4*. The following observations can be made from the plot:

- As per the data, there is no relationship between the expenditure incurred on Administration and Profit.

- The management of the startups can thus get a strategy to control expenditure and increase Profits.

Line chart

Line charts help in visualizing trends more clearly. We have taken up the 50_Startups data. We can get a holistic picture of the start-ups by plotting a line chart. In the x-axis, we plot the serial number of the start-ups, and in the y-axis, we plot all four indicators as given below:

- R&D Spend

- Marketing Spend

- Administration

- Profit

A program is given below. Since we do not want the name of the state we write:

```
columns = df.columns.drop(['State'])
```

Here **df** refers to the 50_Startups data set. We drop the '**State**' from the plot since it is not useful. We will plot with the other columns. In the x-axis, we plot the serial number of the start-ups starting from zero. We plot the 4 columns of the start-ups by the following **for** loop:

```
for column in columns:
    ax.plot(x_data, df[column])
```

We add a legend by the statement **ax.legend()**. We have to specify the column names as in the header and pass as arguments to the **legend** function:

```
# Program E15x7.py
# Line chart
import matplotlib.pyplot as plt
import pandas as pd
df= pd.read_csv('50_Startups.csv')
# get columns to plot
columns = df.columns.drop(['State'])
# create x data
x_data = range(0, df.shape[0])
# create figure and axis
fig, ax = plt.subplots()
# plot each column
for column in columns:
    ax.plot(x_data, df[column])
# set title and legend
ax.set_title('50_Startups')
ax.legend(['R&D Spend', 'Administration',  'Marketing Spend', 'Profit'])
plt.show()
```

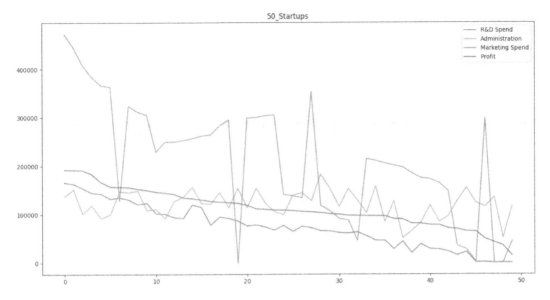

Figure 15.5: *Line chart with legends using matplotlib*

The result of executing the program is the line chart in *Figure 15.5*. The x-axis gives the serial number of the start-ups as in the 50_Startups data. A look at the figure indicates the following:

- Wide variations in the Marketing Spend from company to company.

- The Profit appears to be dependent on R&D Spend.

The program for plotting line charts can also be simplified using pandas features. The program for the above exercise using pandas is given below:

```
# Program E15x8.py
# line chart using pandas
import pandas as pd
import matplotlib.pyplot as plt
df= pd.read_csv('50_Startups.csv')
df.drop(['State'], axis=1).plot.line(title='50_Startups')
plt.show()
```

The result of the program is given below in *Figure 15.6*:

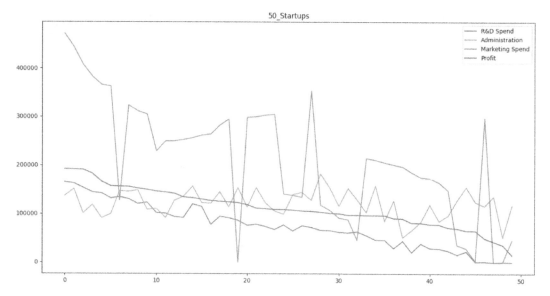

Figure 15.6: *Line chart with legends using pandas*

To summarize, the code is slightly larger when we use matplotlib. We can draw the plot either using pandas or matplotlib as convenient.

Histogram

Histograms are powerful tools for the analysis of data that contain variations. Statistics is concerned with information about phenomena that vary. No two items will be identical. Machined parts, whatever may be the superiority of the machinery, operator, materials, etc. will have variations. There will always be variations. In a resistor manufacturing company, 9 samples of 100 ohms resistors were picked up at random from the assembly line, and the measured values in ohms are listed below:

`100.0, 100.1, 99.9, 100.0, 99.8, 99.9, 100.1, 100.0, 100.2`

The result can be represented in the form of a histogram. Histogram was developed by *AM Gurrey*, a French statistician in the year 1833. The histogram is nothing but a bar graph. In the bar graph, the range of resistance values measured has to be plotted on the X-axis, and the frequency of occurrence of the range of values on the Y-axis. The frequency of occurrence is the number of times the values falling in the range were measured. We have to divide the range of values in the X-axis into several equal sub-ranges, called class intervals.

One criterion is to divide the range into several class intervals equal to the square root of the number of readings, data, or measurement results. Since nine data points are available, the square root of 9, that is, 3 groups, may even be sufficient. Each group is a class interval. We may keep the class interval as a convenient number. In the above example, the lowest point is 99.75 (just below the lowest value), and the highest point is 100.25 (just above the highest value). In the above case, we can divide the data into 5 groups. When we divide the range by five, we get a class interval for each group or class as 0.1. Thus, the lowest class interval is from 99.75 to 99.85. The highest-class interval is 100.15 to 100.25. The number of cells or class intervals is to be decided by the user. Note that the width of all cells should be equal.

A frequency table for the resistance value measured above is indicated in *Table 15.1* below:

Class interval	Frequency
	(Number of occurrence)
99.75 – 99.85	1
99.85 – 99.95	2
99.95 – 100.05	3
100.05 – 100.15	2
100.15 – 100.25	1

Table 15.1: *Frequency of Resistor values*

With this table, a histogram is constructed and shown in *Figure 15.7*:

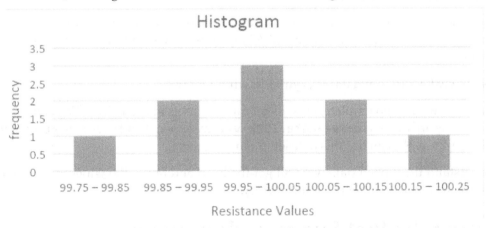

Figure 15.7: *Histogram of resistance values*

A histogram exhibits the number of data points that fall within a given cell or bar or class interval.

Let us recapitulate the steps involved in formulating histograms:

1. Measure and record data of a process.

2. Arrange values in ascending order.

3. Note the range, that is, the maximum and minimum of the values.

4. Divide the range into several sub-ranges with equal intervals called class intervals.

5. Now divide the X-axis as per class intervals.

6. Choose a proper scale for Y-axis. In our case, the maximum frequency is three.

7. Count the number of occurrences of the data in each class interval. This is called the frequency of occurrence in each interval.

8. Plot the frequency or count of the number of occurrences corresponding to each interval in the form of bars. It is essentially a column graph.

9. Give a suitable title for the histogram. Here we call *Resistance Value of 100 Ohms Resistors*.

Since histograms are drawn to depict the frequency of occurrence distribution, it is also called a frequency distribution diagram.

We constructed a histogram for a dataset containing 9 elements. It would be a lot of work if the size of the dataset is 100000 records.

Second dataset

We will download a large dataset for further experiments. We will now use publicly available wine review data containing 129970 records. Download the database by visiting the following:

https://www.kaggle.com/datasets/zynicide/wine-reviews

When the download is complete, we will get three datasets in the archive. Select the second dataset in the archive - **winemag-data-130k-v2.csv**- open it and save it as **winesreview** in your desktop. We can use this dataset in our programs.

To understand the type of data, we will get the head and tail of the wines review dataset stored by me as *wines* in my current directory.

Getting the first five records of wines

The head refers to the top 5 rows in a dataset. The program for getting the head in the wines data is given below:

```
# Program E15x9.py
# Reading the top 5 rows in the dataset
import pandas as pd
data= pd.read_csv('C:/Users/Subbu/Desktop/winesreview.csv')
print(data.head())
```

The details of the top five records were obtained by executing the above program and shown below:

```
==================== RESTART: E:\Py programs\E15x9.py ====================
    Unnamed: 0    country   ...         variety              winery
0            0      Italy   ...     White Blend             Nicosia
1            1   Portugal   ... Portuguese Red  Quinta dos Avidagos
2            2         US   ...      Pinot Gris           Rainstorm
3            3         US   ...        Riesling           St. Julian
4            4         US   ...      Pinot Noir         Sweet Cheeks
[5 rows x 14 columns]
```

Getting the last five records of the dataset

The program for finding the tail of the dataset is given below:

```
# Program E15x10.py
# Getting the tail of wines data
import pandas as pd
data= pd.read_csv('C:/Users/Subbu/Desktop/winesreview.csv')
print(data.tail())
==================== RESTART: E:/Py programs/E15x10.py ====================
           Unnamed: 0  ...                               winery
129966         129966  ...  Dr. H. Thanisch (Erben Müller-Burggraef)
129967         129967  ...                              Citation
129968         129968  ...                        Domaine Gresser
129969         129969  ...                   Domaine Marcel Deiss
129970         129970  ...                        Domaine Schoffit
[5 rows x 14 columns]
```

The above indicates the total number of rows as 129970 with 14 columns. Since there are 14 columns with specified widths, we are unable to fit them in the monitor. That is the reason many columns could not be seen in the above. But there is a way out to list all 14 columns as shown in the following paragraph.

Getting column headers

Let us write a program to understand the column headers. It is given below:

```
# Program E15x11.py
import pandas as pd
```

```
data= pd.read_csv('C:/Users/Subbu/Desktop/winesreview.csv')
print(data.columns)
```

The columns as listed by the program is given below.

```
Index(['Unnamed: 0', 'country', 'description', 'designation', 'points',
'price', 'province', 'region_1', 'region_2', 'taster_name',  'taster_
twitter_handle', 'title', 'variety', 'winery'], dtype='object')
```

Histogram for wines review

The column *points* give the score given by the wine taster. We are plotting a histogram of points given by the wine tasters to get an overall view of the likings of the tasters. The program is given below. The pandas library makes it simple.

```
# Program E15x12.py
# histogram using pandas
import pandas as pd
import matplotlib.pyplot as plt
df= pd.read_csv('C:/Users/Subbu/Desktop/winesreview.csv')
df['points'].plot.hist(title='Wines evaluation')
plt.show()
```

You may notice that although we use **pandas** for a shorter code, we also use **matplotlib. pyplot**. The result of the program, the histogram, is given in *Figure 15.8*. A look at the histogram reveals many points about the quality of the wines as evaluated by the tasters. For instance, nearly 50 % of the tasters have given a rating of about 90%.

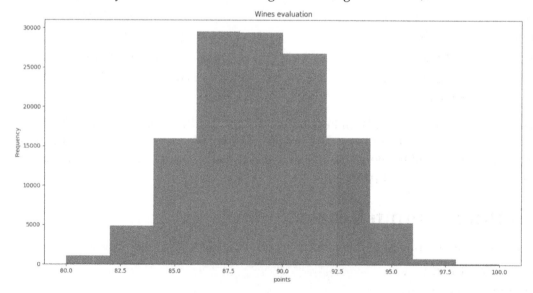

Figure 15.8: Histogram of Wines Review

Bar chart

The bar chart gives another view of the plot. We can also use a bar plot for the **winesreview** dataset using pandas visualization. The program is given below:

```
# Program E15x13.py
# bar chart using pandas
import pandas as pd
import matplotlib.pyplot as plt
df= pd.read_csv('C:/Users/Subbu/Desktop/winesreview.csv')
df['points'].value_counts().sort_index().plot.bar(title='wines Review')
plt.xlabel('points')
plt.ylabel('frequency')
plt.show()
```

The bar chart gives the frequency of occurrence of each point. Each point gives the points of satisfaction given by the tasters. When we use pandas for a bar chart, we count the frequency, that is, the number of times the score appears in the *points*. Then we sort the index. The bar charts for wine review are given in *Figure 15.9*. It gives a clear indication of the likes of the tasters:

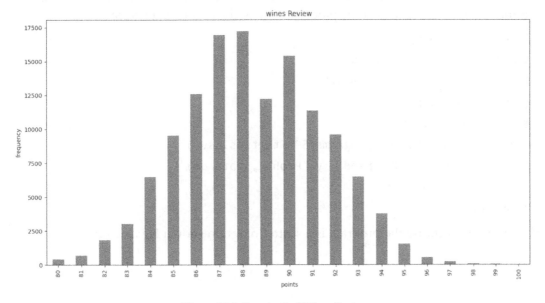

Figure 15.9: *Bar chart of Wines Review*

Seaborn

Like pandas visualization, seaborn is also a Python visualization library based on matplotlib. Both pandas visualization and Seaborn are built over matplotlib. It provides a high-level interface for creating stylish graphs. We can create graphs in one line that would take many lines in matplotlib. Its standard patterns are attractive, and it also has an interface for working with pandas DataFrames.

Installing seaborn

We have to first install the seaborn library on our computer. For this purpose, go to the command prompt, type the following, and then press *Enter*:

```
C:\Users\HP>pip install seaborn
```

Wait for seaborn to install.

Scatter diagram using seaborn

Now, we can write a program to plot a scatter diagram using the Seaborn library. We have to import seaborn as sns. We read the file '**50_Startups**' and assigned it to the DataFrame **df** as usual. Then, in one line, we give the command for drawing a scatter plot, assigning columns to the x and y-axis of the plot. The title of the plot is given separately:

```
# Program E15x14.py
# Scatter plot using pandas
import matplotlib.pyplot as plt
import pandas as pd
import seaborn as sns
df= pd.read_csv ("E:/Py programs/50_Startups.csv")
sns.scatterplot(x='R&D Spend', y='Profit', data=df)
plt.title('50_Startups')
plt.show()
```

The result of executing the program is a scatter diagram shown *Figure 15.10*:

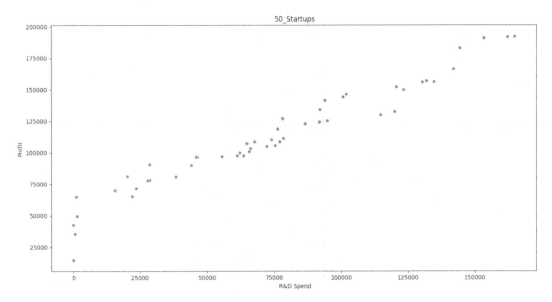

Figure 15.10: *Scatter Diagram using seaborn*

Histogram using seaborn

To create a histogram using seaborn, we use the **sns.histplot** method. One of the parameters is the name of the column we want to plot, and it will calculate the frequencies itself. We can also determine the number of class intervals which determines the number of ranges in the x-axis and pass the number as bins. If we wish to plot a simple histogram and do not want to plot a Gaussian **Kernel Density Estimate (KDE)** inside the graph, then we have to say **kde=False**. We will now plot the histogram for the wines review data we imported earlier. The program is given below:

```
# Program E15x15.py
# histogram using seaborn
import pandas as pd
import matplotlib.pyplot as plt
import seaborn as sns
df= pd.read_csv('C:/Users/Subbu/Desktop/winesreview.csv')
sns.histplot(df['points'], bins=10, kde=False)
plt.xlabel('points')
plt.ylabel('frequency')
plt.title ('Wines Review')
plt.show()
```

The result of the program- Histogram using seaborn -is shown in *Figure 15.11*.

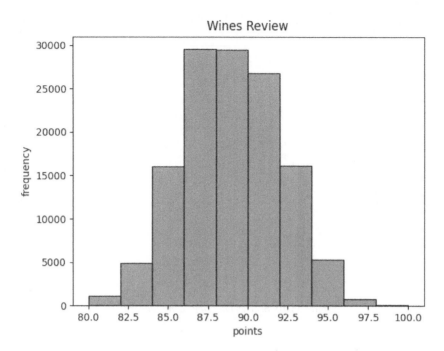

Figure 15.11: *Histogram using seaborn*

Gaussian KDE inside the plot

In Statistics, KDE is a non-parametric way to estimate the probability density function of a random variable. Kernel density estimation is a fundamental data smoothing problem where inferences about the population are made, based on a finite data sample. We plotted the points as a histogram using the sample data. To estimate the population data of points, we have to estimate KDE. We can plot the Gaussian KDE inside the Plot by stating that **kde=True** in the above program. The program is given below:

```python
# Program E15x16.py
# histogram - Gaussian Kernel Density Plot using seaborn
import pandas as pd
import matplotlib.pyplot as plt
import seaborn as sns
df= pd.read_csv('C:/Users/Subbu/Desktop/winesreview.csv')
sns.histplot(df['points'], bins=10, kde=True)
plt.xlabel('points')
plt.ylabel('frequency')
plt.title ('Wines Review')
plt.show()
```

The result of the program is shown in *Figure 15.12*. The KDE is shown inside the plot:

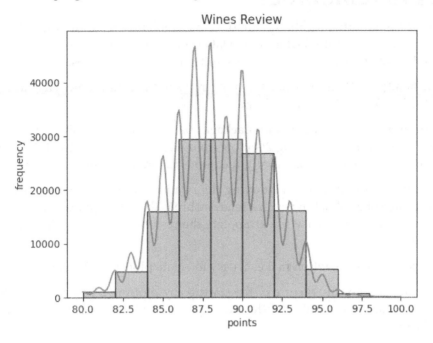

Figure 15.12: *Histogram with KDE using seaborn*

Notice that the data of the frequency is used to estimate the population estimates of the *points*.

Conclusion

Data visualization is the presentation of historical data to better understand changes that have taken place in a business. A common example of data visualization is company reports that provide a historical review of an organization's operations, sales, financials, customers, and stakeholders and their satisfaction. These measures all describe what has happened in a business during a given period. Data visualization takes raw data and plots graphs to draw conclusions that are useful and understandable by managers, investors, and other stakeholders. The three libraries matplotlib, pandas for visualization, and seaborn provide easy-to-use facilities for data visualization that is a stepping stone for data analytics.

Python finds wide use in diverse applications. Python has many standard libraries to support these applications, which enable the programmers to write concise and error free programs. An overview of Python applications and appropriate libraries will be discussed in the next chapter as a ready reckoner.

Points to remember

- pandas is a software library for data manipulation and analysis. Its key data structure is called the DataFrame. DataFrames allow us to store and manipulate tabular data in rows of observations and columns of variables.

- The **head()** in Python means the first 5 rows in the DataFrame. The **tail()** refers to the last 5 rows in the DataFrame.

- Matplotlib is one of the Python packages used for data visualization. It is a cross-platform library for making 2D plots from data in arrays. Matplotlib is written in Python and makes use of NumPy, the numerical mathematics extension of Python.

- A scatter diagram helps in studying the relationship between two variables. The advantage of establishing such a relationship is that once an exercise is carried out in this manner, it is easy to extrapolate the results mathematically for any given situation.

- The pandas visualization makes it easy to create plots out of a pandas DataFrame.

- We can get a holistic picture of the startups by plotting a line chart. In the x-axis, we plot the serial number of the start-ups, and in the y-axis, we plot all the four indicators.

- A histogram exhibits the number of data points that fall within a given cell or bar or class interval.

- Since histograms are drawn to depict the distribution of frequency of occurrence, it is also called a frequency distribution diagram.

- To understand the type of data we will get the head and tail of wines review dataset.

- The column *points* gives the score given by the wine tasters. We plotted a histogram to get an overall view of the likings of the tasters.

Questions

Choose the most appropriate answer:

1. **Data visualization means:**

   a. reading the data

   b. plotting the data

   c. writing the data

   d. All of the above

   e. None of the above

2. **Data analysis:**

   a. is unimportant.

   b. precedes visualization.

   c. follows visualization.

   d. All of the above

   e. None of the above

3. **legend() function:**

   a. receives no parameters

   b. receives the title as a parameter

   c. receives column headers as parameters

   d. None of the above

4. **Plotting histogram using pandas needs:**

   a. sort_index

   b. value_counts

   c. file name

   d. All of the above

   e. None of the above

5. **Plotting bar chart using pandas needs:**

   a. sort_index

   b. value_counts

   c. data frame name

   d. All of the above

   e. None of the above

6. **Plot of frequency vs. variable is called:**

   a. histogram

   b. line chart

   c. scatter diagram

   d. All of the above

   e. None of the above

7. **plt.show() displays:**

    a. Scatter diagram

    b. Line Chart

    c. Histogram

    d. All of the above

    e. None of the above

8. **In the 50_Startups dataset, the relationship between R&D Spend and Profit is:**

    a. Linear

    b. Not clear

    c. Non-linear

    d. All of the above

    e. None of the above

9. **In the 50_Startups dataset, the relationship between Marketing Spend and Profit is:**

    a. linear

    b. Not clear

    c. Non-linear

    d. All of the above

    e. None of the above

10. **In the 50_Startups dataset, the relationship between Administration and Profit is:**

    a. Linerar

    b. None

    c. Non-linear

    d. All of the above

    e. None of the above

- Write short notes on the following:

    o   Importance of data

    o   Importance of data visualization

    o   matplotlib.pyplot

- o pandas

- o Scatter diagram

- o Line chart

- o Seaborn

- o Bar chart

- o Histogram

- o Comparison of panda code, seaborn code, and matplotlib code for scatter diagram

- Match the following:

A	B
pandas	1. Useful for show
matplotlib.pyplot	2. Dataframe
Histogram	3. Draws continuous lines
Bar chart	4. Class intervals
Line chart	5. Frequency is plotted

- Write programs for the following:

- o To draw a scatter diagram using pandas for Marketing Spend vs. Profit for the 50_Startups data.

- o To draw a scatter diagram using pandas for Administration vs. Profit for the 50_Startups data.

- o To draw a histogram for wine's review dataset using matplotlib.

- o To draw a bar chart for wine's review dataset using matplotlib.

- o To draw the line chart for the first 20 rows of wines review dataset using matplotlib keeping only the *points* column.

- o To draw the line chart for the last 20 rows of wine's review dataset using pandas keeping only the *points* column.

- o To draw the line chart for the first 10 rows of the 50_Startups dataset using matplotlib, keeping only the *points* column.

- o To draw the line chart for the last 10 rows of the 50_Startups dataset using pandas, keeping only the *points* column.

- o Use seaborn and draw line chart 50_Starups data.

- o Use seaborn and draw a histogram for the column 'price' in the wines review dataset.

Join our book's Discord space

Join the book's Discord Workspace for Latest updates, Offers, Tech happenings around the world, New Release and Sessions with the Authors:

https://discord.bpbonline.com

CHAPTER 16

Python Applications and Libraries

Introduction

Python has gained wide popularity over the years. One of the contributors to the success of Python 3 in the marketplace is Python's *Batteries Included* philosophy of making already tested libraries for use by programmers. Python is used for programming in diverse and demanding fields of computer science, such as those given below.

- Data structures and algorithms
- Building web applications
- **Artificial intelligence (AI)**
- **Machine learning**
- Big data analytics
- **Graphical User Interface (GUI)** development

Structure

In this chapter, we will discuss the following topics:

- Overview of applications of Python

- Libraries used in data structures and algorithms

- Tasks in web development

- Machine learning

- Graphical User Interface programming

Objectives

After studying the chapter, the reader will understand the applications of Python 3 in diverse fields and know the Python standard libraries used in these applications. This will provide a ready reckoner to know the applications vis-à-vis Python standard libraries.

Overview of applications of Python

Python 3 is a versatile programming language with a wide range of applications across various domains. Here is a listing of some of its key application areas:

- Web development

- Data science and machine learning

- **Natural Language Processing (NLP)**

- Desktop GUI applications

- Game development

- Scripting and automation

- Web scraping

- Database applications

- **Internet of Things (IoT)**

- Education

These are just a few examples of the diverse applications of Python 3. Its extensive standard library and a vast ecosystem of third-party packages contribute to its popularity and widespread use across industries, institutions and organizations. The **Python Package Index (PyPI)** lists thousands of third-party modules for Python. PyPI is a repository of software for the Python programming language. PyPI helps you find and install software developed and shared by the Python community. Package authors use PyPI to distribute their software.

Now let us look closer at some of the Python applications and libraries used in critical applications.

Libraries used in data structures and algorithms

Python offers several libraries and modules that are commonly used in data structures and algorithms. These libraries provide efficient and optimized implementations of data structures and algorithms. Some of the key Python libraries used in data structures and algorithms are listed below:

- **NumPy:** NumPy is a fundamental library for numerical computing in Python. This library is used in several applications. It provides support for multi-dimensional arrays and matrices, along with a wide range of mathematical functions. NumPy is commonly used for tasks like vectorized operations, linear algebra, and handling large datasets efficiently. It is particularly valuable in scientific computing and machine learning.

- **SciPy:** SciPy is built on top of NumPy and provides additional functionality for scientific and technical computing. It includes a wide range of optimization, linear algebra, integration, interpolation, and other numerical algorithms.

- **pandas:** It is a popular library for data manipulation and analysis, which also finds uses in many applications, including machine learning and data science. It provides data structures like DataFrames, which are powerful tools for working with structured data. The pandas simplifies data loading, cleaning, and transformation, making it a staple in data preprocessing and analysis.

- **Scikit-learn**: A simple and efficient tool for data mining and data analysis, including various machine learning algorithms.

- **TensorFlow** and **PyTorch**: Popular libraries for building and training deep learning models.

- **collections:** The collections module in the Python standard library offers various specialized data structures, such as OrderedDict, defaultdict, Counter, and deque. These data structures can be valuable in specific algorithmic scenarios, such as counting elements in a list or implementing a queue.

- **heapq:** The heapq module provides a heap queue (priority queue) implementation in Python. Heaps are essential for tasks like finding the k smallest or largest elements in a collection efficiently, implementing algorithms like Dijkstra's shortest path algorithm, and more.

- **queue:** The queue module in the standard library offers thread-safe, **First-In-First-Out (FIFO)**, and **Last-In-First-Out (LIFO)** queue implementations. It is commonly used for implementing various algorithms and data structures related to multithreading and multiprocessing.

- **bintrees:** The bintrees library provides fast binary tree data structures in Python, including sorted dictionaries and sets. These data structures can be helpful in various algorithmic scenarios where data needs to be maintained in sorted order.

- **NetworkX:** NetworkX is a Python library for working with complex networks and graphs. It offers an extensive set of data structures and algorithms for graph analysis, making it useful in a wide range of applications, including social network analysis, transportation networks, and more.

- **SortedContainers:** SortedContainers is a library that offers sorted container data structures like SortedList and SortedDict, which combine the advantages of lists and dictionaries with sorted order. They can be efficient alternatives to built-in data structures when maintaining sorted data.

- **itertools:** The itertools module is part of the Python standard library and provides a collection of fast, memory-efficient tools for working with iterators and generators. It's often used in conjunction with loops and functional programming constructs for algorithmic tasks.

These libraries enhance the capabilities of Python when it comes to working with data structures and algorithms. Depending on the specific problem domain and requirements, one may choose one or more of these libraries to efficiently implement and optimize algorithms and data structures.

Tasks in web development

Before we look at Python libraries used in web development, let us look at an overview of web development tasks. Web development encompasses a wide range of tasks and activities involved in creating and maintaining websites and web applications. These tasks can vary depending on the complexity of the project, the technologies used, and the development methodology followed. Here is an overview of some common web development tasks:

- **Planning and analysis:**
  - **Requirement gathering:** Understanding the project's objectives, features, and user needs.
  - **Market research:** Analysing competitors and target audience.
  - **Project planning:** Creating a roadmap, defining timelines, and setting goals.
- **Front-end development:**
  - **HTML/CSS:** Creating the structure and styling of web pages.
  - **JavaScript:** Adding interactivity and dynamic behavior to web pages.

- o Responsive design

- o **User Interface (UI)** design

- **Back-end development:**

  - o **Server-side programming**: Writing server-side code to handle requests and responses.

  - o **Database integration**: Designing and implementing databases to store and retrieve data.

  - o **Application Programming Interfaces (API) development**: Creating APIs for data exchange.

  - o **Authentication and authorization**: Implementing user authentication and role-based access control.

- **Web frameworks and libraries:** Selecting and configuring the appropriate web framework or libraries such as Django, Flask, React, and Angular for the project.

- **Content management:** Adding and managing website content, including text, images, videos, and other multimedia elements.

- **Testing and quality assurance:**

  - o Performing various types of testing, such as unit testing, integration testing, and user acceptance testing.

  - o Identifying and fixing bugs and issues.

  - o Ensuring cross-browser compatibility and responsive design.

- **Security:**

  - o Implementing security measures to protect against common web vulnerabilities (for example, SQL injection, cross-site scripting).

  - o Regularly updating and patching software components.

  - o Configuring firewalls and other security tools.

- **Performance optimization:**

  - o Optimizing website and application performance for faster loading times.

  - o Minimizing HTTP requests, optimizing images, and utilizing caching mechanisms.

- **Deployment:**

  - o Setting up hosting environments (for example, cloud servers, shared hosting).

o Deploying code and databases to production servers.

o Configuring domain names and DNS settings.

- **Monitoring and maintenance:**

o Monitoring server performance and uptime.

o Regularly updating and maintaining software components, libraries, and plugins.

o Backing up data and having disaster recovery plans.

- **Scalability and growth:**

o Planning for future scalability and growth by optimizing code and infrastructure.

o Monitoring user traffic and making necessary adjustments.

- **Documentation:** Creating documentation for code, APIs, and configurations to facilitate future development and maintenance.

- **User training and support:**

o Providing training and support to end-users and administrators.

o Addressing user feedback and feature requests.

- **Search Engine Optimization (SEO):**

o Optimizing content and metadata to improve search engine rankings.

o Implementing SEO best practices.

- **Analytics and reporting:**

o Setting up analytics tools to track user behavior and website performance.

o Generating reports and using data to make informed decisions.

Web development is a dynamic field, and the specific tasks involved can vary significantly depending on the project's scope and objectives. Collaboration, continuous learning, and keeping up with the latest technologies and trends are essential to successful web development.

Python libraries for web development

Python offers a wide range of libraries and frameworks for web development, making it a preferred choice for building web applications. Here is an overview of some popular Python libraries and frameworks for web development:

- **Django:** Django is excellent for building robust, secure, and scalable web applications.

- **Flask:**

  o Flask is a micro-framework that is lightweight and flexible, allowing developers to choose and integrate the components they need.

  o It does not come with built-in features like Django but offers extensions for common functionalities, such as database integration, authentication, and more.

  o Flask is often favored for small to medium-sized applications and APIs.

- **FastAPI:**

  o It uses Python type hints to automatically generate documentation and perform data validation, making it a great choice for API development.

  o FastAPI is known for its speed and ease of use.

- **Tornado:**

  o Tornado is a scalable and non-blocking web server and web application framework.

  o It is well-suited for building real-time applications, such as chat applications and WebSockets.

  o Tornado's asynchronous nature can handle multiple simultaneous connections efficiently.

- **Bottle:**

  o Bottle is a micro-framework like Flask but even smaller in size.

  o It is designed for simplicity and is suitable for small web applications and prototyping.

  o Bottle is a single-file framework with minimal dependencies.

- **Pyramid:**

  o Pyramid is a flexible and modular web framework that allows developers to choose the components they need for their applications.

  o It is well-suited for both small and large projects, with a focus on the extensibility and reusability of code.

- **CherryPy:** It is lightweight and easy to get started with, making it suitable for small to medium-sized applications.

- **Web2py:**

  o Web2py is a full-stack web framework with an **Integrated Development Environment (IDE)** that simplifies web application development.

  o It comes with a built-in ticketing system for error handling and provides features for database abstraction, authentication, and more.

- **Sanic:**

  o Sanic is an asynchronous web framework built on Python's async/await features, making it suitable for high-performance web applications.

  o It is designed to handle concurrent requests efficiently and is often used for building APIs.

Machine learning

Machine learning is programming computers to optimize a performance criterion using data from experience. It involves learning from the past and predicting the future. There is no need to *learn* to calculate payroll. Learning is used when:

- Human expertise does not exist (navigating on Mars)

- Humans are unable to explain their expertise (speech recognition)

- Solution changes in time (routing on a computer network)

- Solution needs to be adapted to cases (Retail business)

- Cross-check human decisions (while the aircraft landing)

Machine learning focuses on the development of algorithms and statistical models that enable computer systems to improve their performance on a specific task through learning from past data without being explicitly programmed. The objective of machine learning is to predict the future with past data. For instance, metrologists predict whether it will rain after 30 minutes, based on experience. It is a rapidly evolving field that has applications in various domains and industries. Let us now give a brief overview of machine learning:

- **Fundamental concept:** At its core, ML revolves around the idea of learning from data. Instead of manually instructing a computer on how to perform a task, you provide it with data and algorithms that can learn patterns and relationships within that data.

- **Data:** Data is the foundation of machine learning. ML algorithms require a substantial amount of data to learn from, and this data is typically divided into two sets: training data (used to teach the model) and testing data (used to evaluate the model's performance).

Types of machine learning

The types of ML are as follows:

- **Supervised learning:** In this paradigm, the model is trained on labeled data, meaning that it learns from input-output pairs. It is used for tasks like classification and regression.

- **Unsupervised learning:** Here, the model is trained on unlabeled data, and its goal is to find hidden patterns or structures within the data. Common techniques include clustering and dimensionality reduction.

- **Reinforcement learning:** In this setup, the model learns by interacting with an environment and receiving feedback in the form of rewards or penalties. It is used in applications like robotics and game playing.

Machine learning algorithms

There are several machine learning algorithms tailored for different tasks and data types. Some popular ones include decision trees, support vector machines, k-nearest neighbors, neural networks, and, more recently, deep learning techniques like **Convolutional Neural Networks (CNNs)** and **Recurrent Neural Networks (RNNs)**.

Model evaluation

Once a model is trained, it needs to be evaluated to assess its performance. Common evaluation metrics include accuracy, precision, recall, F1-score, and mean squared error, depending on the type of task.

Hyperparameter tuning

Fine-tuning the parameters of machine learning models is often required to optimize their performance. This process involves adjusting hyperparameters like learning rate, batch size, and model architecture:

- **Overfitting and underfitting:** One of the challenges in machine learning is finding the right balance between a model that performs well on the training data but poorly on new, unseen data (overfitting) and a model that is too simplistic to capture the underlying patterns in the data (underfitting).

Machine learning applications

Machine learning is applied in a wide range of fields, including:

- **Natural Language Processing (NLP):** For tasks like language translation, sentiment analysis, and chatbots.

- **Computer vision:** In image and video analysis, object detection, facial recognition, and more.

- **Healthcare:** In disease diagnosis, drug discovery, and patient outcome prediction.

- **Finance:** For fraud detection, stock market prediction, and algorithmic trading.

- **Autonomous vehicles:** In self-driving cars for perception and decision-making.

- **Recommendation systems:** For personalized content recommendations in streaming services and e-commerce.

- **Ethical considerations:** As machine learning becomes more pervasive, there are increasing concerns about bias in algorithms, privacy issues, and the potential for automation to displace jobs.

Machine learning advances rapidly, with new techniques and applications emerging regularly. It plays a crucial role in the development of AI systems and has the potential to revolutionize many aspects of our lives and industries.

Python libraries for machine learning

The libraries discussed in this section are not exclusive to machine learning and may find use in more than one application.

pandas

pandas provides data structures and functions that make it easier to work with structured data, such as tabular data (like tables in a database or spreadsheet). It is a popular library for data analysis and is widely used in the field of data science and data engineering.

NumPy

NumPy is a general-purpose array-processing package. It provides high-performance multidimensional array objects and tools to work with the arrays. NumPy is an efficient container of generic multi-dimensional data.

NumPy's main object is the homogeneous multidimensional array. It is a table of elements or numbers of the same datatype, indexed by a tuple of positive integers. In NumPy, dimensions are called axes, and the number of axes is called rank. NumPy's array class is called ndarray aka array.

We can do the following with NumPy.

- **Basic array operations**: Add, multiply, slice, flatten, reshape, index arrays.

- **Advanced array operations**: Stack arrays, split into sections, broadcast arrays.

- Work with DateTime or Linear Algebra

- Basic slicing and advanced indexing in NumPy Python

NumPy, like pandas, is a general-purpose library and is used in a variety of applications.

SciPy

The SciPy library is one of the core packages that make up the SciPy stack. Now, there is a difference between SciPy Stack and SciPy, the library. SciPy builds on the NumPy array object and is part of the stack, which includes tools like Matplotlib, pandas, and SymPy with additional tools.

SciPy library contains modules for efficient mathematical routines.

SciPy uses arrays as its basic data structure. It has various modules to perform common scientific programming tasks such as linear algebra.

Matplotlib

Data visualized with Matplotlib can be used to create stories. Matplotlib is another library from the SciPy Stack that plots 2D figures.

With a bit of effort and tint of visualization capabilities, with Matplotlib, you can create just any visualizations, which are useful before embarking upon statistical learning and big data analytics.

Seaborn

Seaborn is based on Matplotlib, which provides a high-level interface for drawing attractive and informative statistical graphics.

You can do the following with Seaborn:

- Determine relationships between multiple variables (correlation)

- Observe categorical variables for aggregate statistics.

- Analyze univariate or bi-variate distributions and compare them between different data subsets.

- Plot linear regression models for dependent variables.

- Provide high-level abstractions and multi-plot grids.

Scikit Learn

Scikit Learn is a robust machine-learning library of Python. It features algorithms such as **Support Vector Machines (SVM)**, random forests, k-means clustering, spectral clustering, mean shift, cross-validation, and more. Even NumPy, SciPy, and related scientific operations are supported by Scikit Learn, with Scikit Learn being a part of the SciPy Stack.

Scikit-learn provides a range of supervised and unsupervised learning algorithms via a consistent interface in Python. Supervised learning models like Naive Bayes to group unlabeled data, such as KMeans and Scikit learn, would be your go-to.

Scikit Learn focuses on modeling data, not manipulating data. We have NumPy and pandas for summarizing and manipulation. Scikit Learn is useful in most machine learning models, such as regression, classification, and clustering.

TensorFlow

TensorFlow is an AI library that helps developers create large-scale neural networks with many layers using data flow graphs. TensorFlow also facilitates the building of deep learning models, pushes the state-of-the-art in ML/AI, and allows easy deployment of ML-powered applications.

TensorFlow is one of the most developed websites among all libraries. Here is what you can do with TensorFlow:

- **Voice/sound recognition**: IoT, Automotive, Security, UX/UI, Telecom

- **Sentiment analysis**: Mostly for CRM or CX

- **Text-based apps**: Threat Detection, Google Translate, Gmail smart reply

- **Face recognition**: Facebook's Deep Face, Photo tagging, Smart Unlock

- **Time series**: Recommendations from Amazon, Google, and Netflix

- **Video detection**: Motion Detection, Real-Time Threat Detection in Gaming, Security, Airports

Keras

Keras is TensorFlow's high-level API for building and training deep neural network code. It is an open-source neural network library in Python. With Keras, statistical modeling, working with images and text is a lot easier with simplified coding for deep learning.

What is the difference between Keras and TensorFlow?

Keras is a neural network Python library, while TensorFlow is an open-source library for various machine learning tasks. TensorFlow provides both high-level and low-level APIs, while Keras provides only high-level APIs. Keras is built for Python, which makes it way more user-friendly and modular than TensorFlow.

Statsmodels

Statsmodels is the ultimate Python package that provides easy computations for descriptive statistics and estimation and inference for statistical models.

You can do the following with Statsmodels:

- Linear regression

- Correlation

- **Ordinary Least Squares (OLS)** for the economist in you

- Survival analysis

- Generalized linear models and Bayesian models.

- Univariate and bi-variate analysis, hypothesis testing (basically, what R can do)

Plotly

Plotly is an excellent plotting library for Python. Users can import, copy, paste, or stream data that is to be analyzed and visualized.

You can use Plotly if you want to create and display figures, update figures, and hover over text for details. Plotly also has an additional feature of sending data to cloud servers.

The Plotly graph library has a wide range of graphs that you can plot:

- **Basic charts:** Line, Pie, Scatter, Bubble, Dot, Gantt, Sunburst, Treemap, Sankey, Filled Area Charts

- **Statistical and Seaborn styles:** Error, Box, Histograms, Facet and Trellis Plots, Tree plots, Violin Plots, Trend Lines

- **Scientific charts:** Contour, Ternary, Log, Quiver, Carpet, Radar, Heat maps, Windrose and Polar Plots

- Financial charts

- Maps

- Subplots

SpaCy

SpaCy is an open-source library used for advanced NLP for Python and Cython (A Python programming language to give a C-like feel and performance with Python code, with a C-inspired syntax).

Bokeh

Bokeh is a Python library for interactive data visualization. With tools like Tableau, QlikView, or PowerBI, why would we need Bokeh? This is because Bokeh allows building complex statistical plots with simple commands quickly. It supports HTML, notebook, or server output. Second, it is possible to integrate Bokeh visualization into Flask and Django apps or visualizations written in other libraries like matplotlib, seaborn, and ggplot.

Gensim

Gensim is so different from what we have seen so far. It automatically extracts semantic topics from documents with high efficiency and effortlessly. The Gensim algorithms are unsupervised, which hints that no human input is necessary —just plain text documents and the extraction is then performed.

Natural Language Processing

The **Natural Language Toolkit (NLTK)** is a comprehensive library in Python designed to support research and development in **Natural Language Processing (NLP)**. It provides a wide array of tools and resources for tasks such as tokenization, stemming, tagging, parsing, and semantic reasoning. Here is a breakdown of its key features and functionalities:

- **Corpora:** NLTK includes a vast collection of corpora, which are large bodies of text used for linguistic analysis and research. These corpora cover a wide range of languages and domains, including the well-known Brown Corpus, WordNet, and Treebank.

- **Tokenization:** NLTK provides functions for breaking down text into smaller units called tokens. Tokenization is a fundamental step in many NLP tasks, as it allows for further analysis at the word or sentence level.

- **Stemming and lemmatization:** NLTK supports stemming, which involves reducing words to their root or base form by removing suffixes. It also supports lemmatization, which is a similar process but considers the word's lemma or dictionary form.

- **Part-of-speech tagging:** NLTK allows for the automatic tagging of words in a text with their respective parts of speech, such as nouns, verbs, adjectives, etc. This information is crucial for many NLP tasks, including syntactic analysis and information extraction.

- **Parsing:** NLTK provides parsers for analyzing the grammatical structure of sentences. These parsers can generate parse trees representing the syntactic structure of sentences, which can be used for tasks like semantic analysis and question answering.

- **Named Entity Recognition (NER):** NLTK includes tools for identifying and classifying named entities in text, such as people, organizations, locations, and dates. NER is essential for tasks like information extraction and document summarization.

- **Sentiment analysis**: While not as comprehensive as some specialized libraries, NLTK offers tools and resources for sentiment analysis, allowing users to classify the sentiment of texts as positive, negative, or neutral.

- **WordNet integration:** NLTK provides access to WordNet, a lexical database of English words organized into synonym sets (synsets) and linked by semantic relations. WordNet integration in NLTK facilitates tasks like synonym detection, semantic similarity calculation, and word sense disambiguation.

- **Machine learning integration:** NLTK seamlessly integrates with machine learning libraries such as scikit-learn, allowing users to build and train custom models for various NLP tasks using NLTK's preprocessing and feature extraction capabilities.

Overall, NLTK is a powerful and versatile library that serves as a valuable resource for both beginners and experts in NLP, providing a rich set of tools and resources for text analysis and language understanding in Python.

Theano

Theano is used for defining, evaluating, and optimizing mathematical expressions, which also efficiently involves multi-dimensional arrays. It is achieved by optimizing the utilization of the CPU and **Graphics Processing Unit (GPU)**. As machine learning is all about mathematics and statistics, Theano makes it easy for users to perform mathematical operations. Theano is a powerful library that can be used on a large-scale, computationally intensive scientific project.

PyTorch

PyTorch is also an open-source Python library for machine learning based on Torch, which is implemented in C language and used for machine learning. It has numerous tools and libraries supported on the computer version and many other machine learning programs. This library also allows users to perform computational tasks on Tensorflow with GPU acceleration.

Python libraries for data science

Most of the Python libraries discussed above are also used in data science. Some additional libraries are discussed below.

The Python libraries for data mining are as follows:

- Scrapy

- BeautifulSoup

The Python libraries for data processing and modelling are as follows:

- NumPy

- SciPy

- pandas

- Keras

- SciKit-Learn

- PyTorch

- TensorFlow

- XGBoost

The Python libraries for data visualization are:

- Matplotlib

- Pandas

- Seaborn

- Bokeh

- Plotly

- pydot

Graphical User Interface programming

Graphical User Interface (GUI) programming is a branch of software development that focuses on creating visual interfaces for computer applications. GUIs provide users with a more intuitive and user-friendly way to interact with software compared to text-based command-line interfaces. GUI programming involves designing, creating, and managing graphical elements like windows, buttons, menus, and dialog boxes to enable users to interact with the application through visual components.

Here are some key concepts and components of GUI programming:

- **Widgets/Controls:** GUIs are constructed using various graphical elements called widgets or controls. These include buttons, text boxes, checkboxes, radio buttons, sliders, and more. Each widget serves a specific purpose and allows users to input data or trigger actions.

- **Event handling:** GUI programming involves responding to user actions, such as clicking a button or entering text. Event handling is the process of defining how the application should respond to these events. Programmers use event handlers or callbacks to specify what actions should be taken when a user interacts with a widget.

- **Layout management:** Proper arrangement and positioning of widgets on a GUI screen are crucial for usability. Layout management involves techniques to organize widgets within windows or frames so that the GUI looks clean and organized. Common layout managers include grids, boxes, and absolute positioning.

- **Graphics and multimedia:** GUIs often incorporate graphics, images, and multimedia elements to enhance the user experience. This can include displaying images, playing videos, or drawing custom graphics.

- **Menus and toolbars:** Menus and toolbars provide users with a way to access various application features and functions. These typically include options like File, Edit, View, and Help menus, as well as toolbars with icons for common actions.

- **Window management:** GUI applications can have multiple windows or dialog boxes. Proper window management involves handling the opening, closing, and arrangement of these windows, including modal and non-modal dialog boxes.

- **User feedback:** Providing feedback to users is crucial in GUI design. This includes displaying messages, progress bars, tooltips, and status indicators to keep users informed about the application's current state.

- **Accessibility:** Accessibility is an important consideration in GUI programming, ensuring that the interface is usable by people with disabilities. This may involve features like screen readers, keyboard navigation, and text-to-speech capabilities.

- **Cross-platform development:** GUI programming often involves making applications that run on different operating systems (for example, Windows, macOS, Linux). Frameworks and libraries are available to facilitate cross-platform development.

- **Testing and debugging:** GUI applications require thorough testing to ensure that they function correctly and provide a good user experience. Debugging graphical interfaces can be more complex than debugging command-line programs.

Languages and frameworks for GUI programming

Popular programming languages and frameworks for GUI programming include:

- **Java Swing and JavaFX:** Used for creating cross-platform Java applications with GUIs.

- **C# and Windows Presentation Foundation (WPF):** Widely used for Windows-based applications.

- **Python with Tkinter, PyQt, or Kivy:** Python offers various libraries for GUI development.

- **JavaScript with HTML/CSS:** Used for web-based applications with interactive interfaces.

- **C++ with Qt:** A popular cross-platform framework for C++ developers.

GUI programming plays a vital role in modern software development, as it enables developers to create user-friendly applications that cater to a wide range of users, from novice to expert, across various devices and platforms.

Python libraries for GUI programming

Python provides several libraries and frameworks for developing GUIs. Here are some of the most commonly used ones:

- **Tkinter:** Tkinter is the standard GUI library that comes bundled with Python. It provides a simple way to create windows, dialogs, buttons, menus, and various other GUI elements. While Tkinter's functionality may be considered basic compared to some other GUI libraries, it is easy to learn and is a good choice for simple desktop applications.

- **PyQt:** PyQt is a set of Python bindings for the Qt application framework, which is a powerful and widely used C++ framework for GUI development. PyQt allows you to create cross-platform applications with a native look and feel. PyQt5 and PyQt6 are commonly used versions of Python 3.

- **wxPython:** wxPython is a set of Python bindings for the wxWidgets C++ library. It provides native-looking GUI applications for various platforms. It is known for its ease of use and extensive widget set.

- **Kivy:** Kivy is an open-source Python library for developing multi-touch applications. It is particularly well-suited for creating touch-based user interfaces and is often used for mobile and tablet applications. Kivy also supports desktop platforms.

- **PyGTK:** PyGTK is a set of Python bindings for the GTK+ toolkit, which is used for creating graphical user interfaces. It is mainly associated with the GNOME desktop environment and is a good choice for Linux-based applications.

- **PyQtGraph:** PyQtGraph is a pure Python library for creating interactive and fast 2D and 3D graphics and plots. It is particularly useful for data visualization and scientific applications.

- **Dear PyGui:** Dear PyGui is a fast, simple-to-use Python GUI framework developed primarily for use in scientific and engineering applications. It aims to provide a modern, GPU-accelerated GUI experience.

- **PySimpleGUI:** PySimpleGUI is a lightweight and easy-to-learn GUI framework designed to make GUI development straightforward for beginners and experienced developers alike. It is a good choice for quickly creating simple GUI applications.

- **Eel:** Eel is a Python library for creating simple Electron-like desktop apps with HTML, CSS, and JavaScript. It is a unique approach to GUI development that leverages web technologies.

- **Toga:** Toga is a Python-native, cross-platform widget toolkit. It aims to provide a consistent API for creating GUI applications across various platforms, including Windows, macOS, and Linux.

The choice of which GUI library to use depends on your specific needs, platform requirements, and personal preferences. Each of these libraries has its own strengths and weaknesses, so you should evaluate them based on your project's requirements and your familiarity with the library's API.

Game development

The following libraries are useful in game development:

- **Pygame**: A set of Python modules designed for writing video games.
- **Unity with Python**: Unity game engine allows scripting with Python using libraries like Python.NET or IronPython.

Scripting and automation

Python is widely used for scripting and automation tasks due to its simplicity and readability. It is commonly used for tasks like file manipulation, system administration, and workflow automation.

Web scraping

Libraries like Beautiful Soup and Scrapy make it easy to extract data from websites.

Database applications

The following Python libraries are useful in database applications:

- **SQLAlchemy:** A SQL toolkit and **Object-Relational Mapping (ORM)** library for Python.

- **SQLite3:** A lightweight, serverless database engine that is included in Python's standard library.

Internet of Things

Python is increasingly used in **Internet of Things (IoT)** applications due to its ease of use and availability of libraries like MicroPython and CircuitPython.

Education

Python offers several libraries and tools specifically tailored for educational purposes, making it an excellent choice for teaching programming and computer science concepts in colleges and schools. Here are some notable Python libraries for education:

- **Turtle graphics:**

  o **turtle:** A module in Python's standard library that allows users to create simple drawings and graphics using a turtle metaphor. It's particularly useful for teaching basic programming concepts like loops and conditionals in a visual and interactive manner.

- **Pygame Zero:** A beginner-friendly wrapper around the Pygame library, designed for teaching programming through game development. It simplifies the process of creating games and interactive simulations, making it accessible to learners with minimal programming experience.

- **Jupyter:** An open-source web application that allows users to create and share documents containing live code, equations, visualizations, and narrative text. Jupyter Notebooks are widely used in educational settings for teaching and learning programming, data science, and other computational topics in an interactive environment.

- **CircuitPython:** A variant of Python specifically designed for programming microcontrollers, such as those used in educational robotics kits like Adafruit Circuit Playground and BBC micro:bit. It offers a beginner-friendly environment for learning physical computing and electronics concepts.

- **PythonTurtle:** An educational environment that extends Python's built-in turtle module with additional features and enhancements. It provides an interactive programming interface for creating drawings, animations, and simple games.

- **Mu:** A simple Python editor designed for beginner programmers. It provides a user-friendly interface and features like syntax highlighting, code completion, and integrated documentation. Mu is often recommended for teaching programming to children and beginners.

- **Skulpt:** A Python-to-JavaScript compiler that enables running Python code in web browsers. It's commonly used in educational websites and online coding platforms to provide an interactive coding environment for learning Python programming concepts.

- **EduBlocks**: A visual programming tool that introduces students to Python programming concepts using a block-based interface similar to Scratch. It helps beginners transition from visual block-based programming to text-based coding gradually.

These libraries and tools cater to a wide range of educational needs, from teaching fundamental programming concepts to exploring advanced topics in areas like game development, data science, and physical computing. They make Python an accessible and effective language for educators and learners alike.

Conclusion

The day is close when Python becomes a de facto standard for programming languages. In this chapter, we discussed a few well-known applications of Python and the Python libraries used in them. The reader should have a preliminary idea about the libraries used to quickly select them for their projects. For more details, they can visit the Python home page.

In this book, we discussed the following Python has libraries for developing applications:

- Data structures and algorithms
- Building web applications
- Statistical learning
- Deep learning
- Big data analytics
- Data visualization
- Graphical User Interface (GUI) development
- Game development

Multiple choice questions

1. **Internet protocols supported by Python standard library includes:**

    a. JSON

    b. XML

    c. HTML

    d. All of the above

    e. None of the above

2. **Kivy is used for:**

   a. Developing multi-touch applications

   b. Big data analytics

   c. Data visualization

   d. All of the above

   e. None of the above

3. **Programming languages and frameworks used for GUI Programming include:**

   a. Javascript

   b. Python

   c. C sharp

   d. All of the above

   e. None of the above

4. **Data visualization library includes:**

   a. XGboost

   b. Plotly

   c. Sklearn

   d. All of the above

   e. None of the above

5. **The library suitable for inference for statistical models include:**

   a. Svm

   b. Matplotlib

   c. Statsmodels

   d. All of the above

   e. None of the above

6. **The heapq module:**

   a. Provides priority queue implementation in Python

   b. Is essential for finding the k smallest or largest elements in a collection efficiently

    c. Required for implementing algorithms like Dijkstra's shortest path algorithm

    d. All of the above

    e. None of the above

7. **The itertools module:**

    a. Provides tools for working with iterators

    b. Provides tools for generators

    c. Used in conjunction with loops

    d. All of the above

    e. None of the above

8. **Web development involves:**

    a. Back-end development

    b. Front-end development

    c. performance optimization

    d. All of the above

    e. None of the above

9. **Plotly can be used to draw:**

    a. Scientific charts

    b. Financial charts

    c. Maps

    d. All of the above

    e. None of the above

10. **Libraries used in machine learning include:**

    a. pandas

    b. numpy

    c. Scikitlearn

    d. All of the above

    e. None of the above

Questions

1. List the Python libraries used in GUI development.

2. List the Python libraries used in machine learning.

3. List the Python libraries used in data visualization.

4. List the Python libraries in Natural Language Tool kit.

5. List the Python libraries used in web development.

6. List the Python libraries used in data structures and algorithms.

7. List the Python libraries in teaching applications.

Join our book's Discord space

Join the book's Discord Workspace for Latest updates, Offers, Tech happenings around the world, New Release and Sessions with the Authors:

https://discord.bpbonline.com

Appendix 1
Python Projects

Python has been used in several applications successfully. In this section, we will look at a few student projects implemented using Python 3.

Project 1: Text-to-speech conversion using Python library Google Text To Speech

Converting a text to speech is the aim of this project. We will initially give the text as part of the program as a string. Then, we will extend the program to convert the text into a file. We can use the techniques for speech conversion in several languages with minor modifications. We will test the program with text in English and later in the Tamil language.

There are a few **Application Programming Interfaces (APIs)** available in Python to convert text to speech. One such API is Google **Text To Speech (TTS)**. It converts the text entered in English or other supported languages into a voice that can be saved as an mp3 file. The recording can also be viewed later.

Requirement: Internet connection during the execution of the program.

Google Text To Speech

Google Text-to-Speech (gTTS) is a Python library and **Command Line Interface (CLI)** tool to interface with Google Translate's text-to-speech API. It writes spoken mp3 data to a file, a file-like object (byte string) for further audio manipulation. It features flexible pre-processing and tokenizing, as well as automatic retrieval of gTTS supported languages. The gTTS API supports many languages such as English, Hindi, Tamil, French, and German.

Installation of gTTS

To install gTTS follow the steps given below:

1. Check whether the paths have been set correctly on your computer. Type the following in the command line:

   ```
   C:\Users\HP>python --version

   Python 3.8.5
   ```

   If the environmental variables have been set properly, you will get the result as above. If not, your system will not recognize Python. Set this right before going to the next step.

2. Check whether *pip* is already installed by typing the following in your command line:

   ```
   C:\Users\HP>pip help
   ```

   If **pip** is already installed, then you will get a listing. If it is not already installed, install pip.

3. Now type the following in the command line:

   ```
   C:\Users\HP>pip install gTTS
   ```

   After the successful installation of gTTS, we are ready to write the program.

Languages supported

We can find out the languages supported by gTTS by typing the following in the command prompt:

```
C:\Users\HP>gtts-cli --all
```

Here is the result:

- af: Afrikaans

- ar: Arabic

- bn: Bengali

- bs: Bosnian

- ca: Catalan

- cs: Czech

- cy: Welsh

- da: Danish

- de: German

- el: Greek

- en-au: English (Australia)

- en-ca: English (Canada)

- en-gb: English (UK)

- en-gh: English (Ghana)

- en-ie: English (Ireland)

- en-in: English (India)

- en-ng: English (Nigeria)

- en-nz: English (New Zealand)

- en-ph: English (Philippines)

- en-tz: English (Tanzania)

- en-uk: English (UK)

- en-us: English (US)

- en-za: English (South Africa)

- en: English

- eo: Esperanto

- es-es: Spanish (Spain)

- es-us: Spanish (United States)

- es: Spanish

- et: Estonian

- fi: Finnish

- fr-ca: French (Canada)

- fr-fr: French (France)

- fr: French
- gu: Gujarati
- hi: Hindi
- hr: Croatian
- hu: Hungarian
- hy: Armenian
- id: Indonesian
- is: Icelandic
- it: Italian
- ja: Japanese
- jw: Javanese
- km: Khmer
- kn: Kannada
- ko: Korean
- la: Latin
- lv: Latvian
- mk: Macedonian
- ml: Malayalam
- mr: Marathi
- my: Myanmar (Burmese)
- ne: Nepali
- nl: Dutch
- no: Norwegian
- pl: Polish
- pt-br: Portuguese (Brazil)
- pt-pt: Portuguese (Portugal)
- pt: Portuguese
- ro: Romanian

- ru: Russian

- si: Sinhala

- sk: Slovak

- sq: Albanian

- sr: Serbian

- su: Sundanese

- sv: Swedish

- sw: Swahili

- ta: Tamil

- te: Telugu

- th: Thai

- tl: Filipino

- tr: Turkish

- uk: Ukrainian

- ur: Urdu

- vi: Vietnamese

- zh-cn: Chinese (Mandarin/China)

- zh-tw: Chinese (Mandarin/Taiwan)

- zh: Chinese (Mandarin)

Program steps to convert text to speech

Ensure that your system is connected to the Internet and follow the given steps:

1. Import the required module for text to speech conversion:

   ```
   from gtts import gTTS
   ```

   This module is imported so that we can play the converted audio.

2. Import os

3. Specify the text that you want to convert to voice as a string:

   ```
   str1 = 'Python is an interesting language'
   ```

4. Specify the language in which the text is written. For instance, if it is in English:

```
language = 'en'
```

5. Passing the text and language to the engine: here we have marked slow=False which directs the module that the converted audio should be played at normal speed, but not slow. The default is slow:

```
obj1 = gTTS (text=str1, lang=language, slow=False)
```

6. Saving the converted audio in an mp3 file named **output1**:

```
obj1.save("output1.mp3")
```

7. Playing the converted file:

```
os.system(output1.mp3)
```

The output of the program:

The output of the above program should be a voice saying, ' Python is an interesting language.'

Text to speech conversion of string in English

The program listing for text to speech conversion of the text in English is given below:

```
# program text to voice 1.py
from gtts import gTTS
import os
str1='Python is an interesting language'
obj1=gTTS(text=str1, lang='en', slow=False)
obj1.save('output1.mp3')
os.system('output1.mp3')
```

Execute the program and you will get the voice as the output. Now let us carry out a project to convert text in Tamil language to voice.

Text to speech conversion of string in Tamil

We would like to convert the text in another language, say Tamil. It is given below. Note the change of lang='ta' and the string in Tamil:

```
# Program text to voice 2.py
from gtts import gTTS
import os
str2=('தம்பிக்கை உடையைஓானே! சித்தி வினாயகனே!')
obj2=gTTS(text=str2, lang='ta', slow=False)
```

```
obj2.save('output2.mp3')
os.system('output2.mp3')
```

Execute the program and you will get the Tamil Voice as the output.

Text to speech conversion of words in a text file in English

We can convert the words in a text file to speech. The program for it is given below:

```
# program English text file to voice 3.py
from gtts import gTTS
import os
with open('str3.txt', 'r') as infile:
    str1=infile.read().replace("\n", " ")
obj1=gTTS(text=str1, lang='en', slow=False)
obj1.save('output3.mp3')
os.system('output3.mp3')
```

In this program after opening a text file, we are reading it and converting it to speech. Execute the program and you will get the file read out to you.

Text to speech conversion of words in a text file in Tamil language

When we wish to convert text to speech in other languages, we have to specify the encoding as given below:

```
# program  text file to voice 4.py
from gtts import gTTS
import os
with open('str4.txt', 'r', encoding='utf-8') as infile:
    str1=infile.read()
obj1=gTTS(text=str1, lang='ta', slow=False)
obj1.save('output3.mp3')
os.system('output3.mp3')
```

Note the changes in the program. When we wish to read the text in other languages from a file, we have to specify the encoding format as given in the program.

Execute the program and the contents of a file containing Tamil text will be read out to you.

The advantages of this library are:

- It is quite simple, and we use Google API.

The disadvantages of this library are:

- It is an online conversion and Internet connection is a must.

- There is only one voice.

Project 2: Offline text to speech conversion using Python library pyttsx3

We can convert text to speech offline. For this purpose, we use Python API pysttx3. Speech synthesis is the computer-generated simulation of human speech. It converts text into human-like speech.

The steps involved in speech synthesis are given below:

1. Import pyttsx3.

2. Then we have to initialize the Text To Speech engine:

```
# initialize Text-to-speech engine
engine = pyttsx3.init()
```

3. Now to convert some text, we need to use **say()** and **runAndWait()** methods as given below:

```
# convert this text to speech
str1 = "Python is an interesting language"
engine.say(str1)
# play the speech
engine.runAndWait()
```

The **say()** method adds a string to speak to the event queue, while **runAndWait()** method runs the actual event loop until all commands queued up. So you can call multiple times the **say()** method and run a single **runAndWait()** method in the end, to hear the synthesis.

4. Another useful property is voices, which allow us to get details of all voices available on our machine. To get details of all voices available, execute the following:

```
voices = engine.getProperty("voices")
print(voices)
```

A program to display voices available in our machine is given below. The program also plays out the given string in all the available voices in our system:

```python
# text to voice 5.py
# to find out voice indices available in our system
import pyttsx3
engine= pyttsx3.init() # initialize the engine
voices=engine.getProperty('voices')
for voice in voices:
    print(voice.id)
    engine.setProperty('voice', voice.id)
    engine.say("Python is an interesting language")
    # play out the string in the chosen voice.id
engine.runAndWait()
```

The execution of the program in IDLE gives the ID of two voices in our system:

```
================ RESTART: E:/Py programs/text to voice 5.py ================
HKEY_LOCAL_MACHINE\SOFTWARE\Microsoft\Speech\Voices\Tokens\TTS_MS_EN-US_
DAVID_11.0
HKEY_LOCAL_MACHINE\SOFTWARE\Microsoft\Speech\Voices\Tokens\TTS_MS_EN-US_
ZIRA_11.0
```

It also plays out the string, one in a male voice and another a female voice.

Setting properties of the speech

This library facilitates adjusting properties based on our needs. For instance, we can get details of the speaking rate:

```python
# get details of speaking rate
rate = engine.getProperty("rate")
print(rate)
```

The output will be as shown:

```
200
```

We can change this to 300 (make the speaking rate much faster):

```python
# setting new voice rate (faster)
engine.setProperty("rate", 300)
engine.say(text)
engine.runAndWait()
```

We can also reduce the speaking rate:

```
# slower
engine.setProperty("rate", 100)
engine.say(text)
engine.runAndWait()
```

We can also reduce the volume to 90% as given below:

```
engine.setProperty('volume', 0.9)
```

A program is given below, where we have chosen one of the two voices supported by our system. We have also altered the speaking rate and volume:

```
# text to voice 6.py
# to find out voice index
import pyttsx3
engine= pyttsx3.init()
voices=engine.getProperty('voices')
engine.setProperty('voice', 'HKEY_LOCAL_MACHINE\SOFTWARE\Microsoft\Speech\
Voices\Tokens\TTS_MS_EN-US_ZIRA_11.0')
engine.setProperty('rate', 120)
engine.setProperty('volume', 0.9)
engine.say("Python is an interesting language")
aengine.runAndWait()
```

When the program is executed, we get the synthesized voice in the rate and volume set by us.

Playing from a text file

A program is given below that synthesizes text in a file under the Windows platform. Before executing the program, type a few lines of English text in Notepad. Save the file as **str3.txt** in the current directory:

```
# text to voice 7.py
# to find out voice index
import pyttsx3
engine= pyttsx3.init()
voices=engine.getProperty('voices')
engine.setProperty('voice', 'HKEY_LOCAL_MACHINE\SOFTWARE\Microsoft\Speech\
Voices\Tokens\TTS_MS_EN-US_ZIRA_11.0')
engine.setProperty('rate', 120)
```

```
engine.setProperty('volume', 0.9)
with open('str3.txt', 'r') as infile:
    text=infile.read()
engine.say(text)
engine.runAndWait()
```

Here a file **str3.text** is opened, and the text is converted to voice.

A brief introduction to text to speech conversion was given here. The reader may further improve the techniques using open-source information.

Join our book's Discord space

Join the book's Discord Workspace for Latest updates, Offers, Tech happenings around the world, New Release and Sessions with the Authors:

https://discord.bpbonline.com

APPENDIX 2

List of Built-in Functions in Python

Python has several built-in functions. Their functionalities are pre-defined in Python. Some of these functions used often are listed below with their syntax and purpose. Examples as command line interpreter output are also given for some built-in functions. The list may not be complete.

S.No.	Syntax	Purpose

1	`abs(num)`
	`>>> abs(4+3j)`
	`5.0`
		Returns the absolute value of num. The argument can be an integer or a floating-point number. If the argument is a complex number, then, abs() returns its magnitude

2	`all(object)`
	`>>> k=[1, 2, 6]`
	`>>>print (all(k))`
	True
	`>>> k=[1, 0]`
	`>>> print(all(k))`
	False
	`>>> k=[]`
	`>>> print(all(k))`
	True
		Accepts an iterable object (such as list, dictionary, etc.). It returns true if all items in passed iterable are true. Otherwise, it returns False. If the iterable object is empty, the all() function returns True.

S.No.	Syntax	Purpose

3	`any()`
	`>>> k=[0, False, -5]`
	`>>> print(any(k))`
	`True`
	`>>> m=[0, False]`
	`>>> print(any(m))`
	`False`
		Returns true if any item in an iterable is true. Otherwise, it returns False. Number 0 is considered False. Other integers, both positive and negative, are True. This function checks if at least one item is True.

4	`bin(x)`
	`>>>bin(27)`
	`'0b11011'`
		Returns the binary representation of a specified integer x with the prefix 0b.

5	`bool(x)`
	`>>> bool(0)`
	`False`
	`>>> bool(9)`
	`True`
		Converts a value x to boolean(True or False) using the standard truth testing procedure.

6	`bytearray(string, 'utf-8')`
	`>>> str1='supreme'`
	`>>> p=bytearray(str1, 'utf-8')`
	`>>> print(p)`
	`bytearray(b'supreme')`
		Returns a bytearray object and can convert objects into bytearray objects, or create an empty bytearray object of the specified size.

7	`bytes(string, 'utf-8')`
	`>>> bytes('hello', 'utf-8')`
	`b'hello`
		Used for returning a bytes object of a given string.

8	`chr()`
	`>>> print(chr(100))`
	`D`
		Returns a character from the specified Unicode code.

9	`complex()`
	`>>> print(complex(5))`
	`(5+0j)`
	`>>> print(complex(5,7))`
	`(5+7j)`
		Used to convert numbers or string into a complex number.

S.No.	Syntax	Purpose

10	**dict()**
	>>> k= dict(x='ten',
	y=10)
	>>> print(k)
	{'x': 'ten', 'y': 10}
		Function is a constructor which creates a dictionary.

11	**divmod()** >>> print(divmod(25, 3)) (8, 1)	To get the quotient and remainder of two numbers as a tuple.

12	**exec()**
	>>> x=12
	>>> exec('print(x+8)')
	20
		Used for the dynamic execution of Python programs which can either be a string or object code. It accepts large blocks of code, unlike the eval() function, which only accepts a single expression

13	**eval()** >>>eval('9+4') 13	Evaluates and executes an expression.

14	**float()**
	>>> float(10)
	10.0
	>>> float(-123.7)
	-123.7
		Returns a floating-point number from a number or string.

15	**format()**
	>>> print(format(17, 'b'))
	10001
	>>> print(format(123.45, '6.2f'))
	123.45
		Returns a formatted representation of the given value.

16	**getattr()**
	>>> class Person:
	    name = "John"
	>>> x=getattr(Person, 'name')
	>>> print(x)
	John
		Returns the value of the specified attribute (property or method).

17	**hex()** >>> hex(1024) '0x400'	Returns the hexadecimal value of the given number.

S.No.	Syntax	Purpose

18	`sum()`
	`>>> sum([1, 2, 6, 7])`
	`16`
	`>>> sum((1, 2, 7))`
	`10`
		Used to get the sum of numbers of an iterable like a list or tuple.

Table 1: Syntax and purpose of built-in Python functions

A list of built-in functions, including the above, are given below for reference:

Function	Description
`abs()`	Returns the absolute value of a number
`all()`	Returns True if all items in an iterable object are true
`any()`	Returns True if any item in an iterable object is true
`ascii()`	Returns a readable version of an object. Replaces non-ascii characters with escape character
`bin()`	Returns the binary version of a number
`bool()`	Returns the boolean value of the specified object
`bytearray()`	Returns an array of bytes
`bytes()`	Returns a bytes object
`callable()`	Returns True if the specified object is callable, otherwise False
`chr()`	Returns a character from the specified Unicode code.
`classmethod()`	Converts a method into a class method
`compile()`	Returns the specified source as an object, ready to be executed
`complex()`	Returns a complex number
`delattr()`	Deletes the specified attribute (property or method) from the specified object
`dict()`	Returns a dictionary (Array)
`dir()`	Returns a list of the specified object's properties and methods
`divmod()`	Returns the quotient and the remainder when argument1 is divided by argument2
`enumerate()`	Takes a collection (for example, a tuple) and returns it as an enumerate object
`eval()`	Evaluates and executes an expression
`exec()`	Executes the specified code (or object)
`filter()`	Use a filter function to exclude items in an iterable object

Function	Description
float()	Returns a floating point number
format()	Formats a specified value
frozenset()	Returns a frozenset object
getattr()	Returns the value of the specified attribute (property or method)
globals()	Returns the current global symbol table as a dictionary
hasattr()	Returns True if the specified object has the specified attribute (property/method)
hash()	Returns the hash value of a specified object
help()	Executes the built-in help system
hex()	Converts a number into a hexadecimal value
id()	Returns the id of an object
input()	Allowing user input
int()	Returns an integer number
isinstance()	Returns True if a specified object is an instance of a specified object
issubclass()	Returns True if a specified class is a subclass of a specified object
iter()	Returns an iterator object
len()	Returns the length of an object
list()	Returns a list
locals()	Returns an updated dictionary of the current local symbol table
map()	Returns the specified iterator with the specified function applied to each item
max()	Returns the largest item in an iterable
memoryview()	Returns a memory view object
min()	Returns the smallest item in an iterable
next()	Returns the next item in an iterable
object()	Returns a new object
oct()	Converts a number into an octal
open()	Opens a file and returns a file object
ord()	Convert an integer representing the Unicode of the specified character
pow()	Returns the value of x to the power of y
print()	Prints to the standard output device

Function	Description
`range()`	Returns a sequence of numbers, starting from 0 and increments by 1 (by default)
`repr()`	Returns a readable version of an object
`reversed()`	Returns a reversed iterator
`round()`	Rounds a numbers
`set()`	Returns a new set object
`setattr()`	Sets an attribute (property/method) of an object
`slice()`	Returns a slice object
`sorted()`	Returns a sorted list
`@staticmethod()`	Converts a method into a static method
`str()`	Returns a string object
`sum()`	Sums the items of an iterator
`super()`	Returns an object that represents the parent class
`tuple()`	Returns a tuple
`type()`	Returns the type of an object
`vars()`	Returns the __dict__ property of an object
`zip()`	Returns an iterator, from two or more iterators

Table 2: Complete list of built-in functions

Note: The list is not complete since more and more functions are being added with each revision to Python.

For getting the complete list as per the latest version of Python, that is, 3.12.2., visit:

https://docs.python.org/3.12/library/functions.html#round

Join our book's Discord space

Join the book's Discord Workspace for Latest updates, Offers, Tech happenings around the world, New Release and Sessions with the Authors:

https://discord.bpbonline.com

APPENDIX 3

Answers to Review Questions

Chapter 1		
Multiple choice questions		Match the following
S.no.	Answer	Answer
1	d.	2
2	c.	3
3	b.	5
4	d.	1
5	d.	4
6	d.	
7	a.	
8	b.	
9	c.	
10	a.	

Chapter 2		
Multiple choice questions		Match the following
S.no.	Answer	Answer
1	a.	2
2	b.	3
3	c.	5
4	d.	1
5	d.	4
6	c.	
7	b.	
8	a.	
9	a.	
10	b.	

Chapter 3		
Multiple choice questions		Match the following
S.no.	Answer	Answer
1.	d.	5
2.	c.	2
3.	d.	4
4.	a.	1
5.	b.	3
6.	a.	
7.	a.	
8.	c.	
9.	d.	
10.	a.	

Chapter 4		
Multiple choice questions		Match the following
S.no.	Answer	Answer
1	d.	4
2	b.	3
3	d.	5
4	d.	1

5	a.	2
6	b.	
7	a.	
8	a.	
9	a.	
10	b.	

Chapter 5		
Multiple choice questions		Match the following
S.no.	Answer	Answer
1	d.	2
2	c.	4
3	b.	5
4	a.	3
5	b.	1
6	c.	
7	a.	
8	b.	
9	b.	
10	a.	

Chapter 6		
Multiple choice questions		Match the following
S.no.	Answer	Answer
1	a.	4
2	d.	5
3	c.	2
4	d.	3
5	c.	1
6	b.	
7	c.	
8	d.	
9	c.	
10	a.	

Chapter 7		
Multiple choice questions		Match the following
S.no.	Answer	Answer
1	d.	4
2	c.	1
3	a.	2
4	b.	5
5	b.	3
6	a.	
7	b.	
8	c.	
9	a.	
10	e.	
Chapter 8		
Multiple choice questions		Match the following
S.no.	Answer	Answer
1	b.	3
2	c.	5
3	b.	1
4	b.	2
5	c.	4
6	c.	
7	a.	
8	c.	
9	d.	
10	a.	
Chapter 9		
Multiple choice questions		Match the following
S.no.	Answer	Answer
1	b.	3
2	b.	5
3	a.	4
4	b.	2

S.no.	Answer	Answer
5	d.	1
6	b.	
7	c.	
8	d.	
9	a.	
10	b.	

Chapter 10		

Multiple choice questions		Match the following
S.no.	Answer	Answer
1	c.	4
2	b.	5
3	d.	3
4	b.	1
5	c.	2
6	a.	
7	a.	
8	a.	
9	b.	
10	c.	

Chapter 11		

Multiple choice questions		Match the following
S.no.	Answer	Answer
1	b.	5
2	d.	4
3	d.	1
4	d.	2
5	d.	3
6	d.	
7	d.	
8	b.	
9	a.	
10	c.	

Chapter 12		
Multiple choice questions		**Match the following**
S.no.	**Answer**	**Answer**
1	d.	3
2	a.	4
3	c.	1
4	a.	5
5	c.	2
6	a.	
7	e.	
8	c.	
9	a.	
10	b.	

Chapter 13		
Multiple choice questions		**Match the following**
S.no.	**Answer**	**Answer**
1	d.	2
2	b.	4
3	d.	1
4	d.	5
5	b.	3
6	a.	
7	d.	
8	b.	
9	a.	
10	c.	

Chapter 14		
Multiple choice questions		**Match the following**
S.no.	**Answer**	**Answer**
1	c.	3
2	d.	4
3	d.	1
4	b.	5

S.no.	Answer	
5	b.	2
6	a.	
7	b.	
8	a.	
9	b.	
10	a.	

Chapter 15

Multiple choice questions		Match the following
S.no.	Answer	Answer
1	b.	2
2	c.	1
3	c.	4
4	e.	5
5	d.	3
6	a.	
7	d.	
8	a.	
9	b.	
10	b.	

Chapter 16

Multiple choice questions		
S.no.	Answer	
1	d.	
2	a.	
3	d.	
4	b.	
5	c.	
6	a.	
7	d.	
8	d.	
9	d.	
10	d.	

Index

Made in United States
North Haven, CT
24 November 2024

60903740R00311